PARADISE LOST

and the Rise of the American Republic

PARADISE LOST

and the Rise of the American Republic

LYDIA DITTLER SCHULMAN

NORTHEASTERN UNIVERSITY PRESS · BOSTON

Northeastern University Press
Copyright 1992 by Lydia Dittler Schulman

Library of Congress Cataloging-in-Publication Data

Schulman, Lydia Dittler.
  Paradise lost and the rise of the American republic / Lydia Dittler
Schulman.
    p. cm.
  Includes bibliographical references and index.
  ISBN 1-55553-125-3
  1. Milton, John, 1608–1674. Paradise lost. 2. Milton, John, 1608–
1674—Political and social views. 3. Milton, John, 1608–1674—Appre-
ciation—United States. 4. United States—History—Revolution, 1776–
1783—Literature and the revolution. 5. Politics and literature—United
States—History—18th century. 6. Revolutionary poetry, English—
History and criticism. 7. United States—Civilization—English influences. 8. Republicanism in literature. I. Title.
PR3562.S326   1992   91-35876
821'.4—dc20

Designed by Christine Leonard Raquepaw

This book was composed in Caslon 540 by Coghill Composition Company in Richmond, Virginia. It was printed and bound by Princeton University Press in Lawrenceville, New Jersey. The paper is Writers Offset, an acid-free sheet.

Manufactured in the United States of America
96 95 94 93 92   5 4 3 2 1

For my Mother and Father

Contents

Preface   ix

Introduction: *Paradise Lost* Revisited   3

1   The Fall as a Republican Theme   17

2   The Rise of Commercial Republicanism in England   33

3   *Paradise Lost* and the Fall of the English Republic   51

4   The Commonwealth Tradition   97

5   Commonwealth Ideas and the Prelude to Revolution   117

6   *Paradise Lost* and the Language of the Revolution   141

7   Milton Defends the Republic   181

Epilogue: Milton, the Most American of Poets   215

Endnotes   221

Bibliography   257

Index   265

Preface

The political activism of the late
1960s focused the attention of scholars on Milton's politics and, in
particular, on how the man who postponed his poetic vocation for twenty
years to serve the English Commonwealth contributed to political reform
in his own and later times. Christopher Hill was the first to study Milton's
dialogue with the "radical underground," the "third culture," of the mid-
seventeenth-century English Revolution. Andrew Milner, Christopher
Kendrick, and others sought to delineate his relation to seventeenth-
century English revolutionary thought and culture in general. Jackie
DiSalvo pursued Blake's radical critique of Milton's theology and sexual
politics, while other scholars investigated Milton's relation to the incipient
feminism of the seventeenth century and the response to his works by
early feminist and African-American writers.[1]

The present study explores the connection between Milton and still
another tradition of political reform: the line of Anglo-American republican thought that culminated in the American Revolution. My chief literary
inspiration was George Sensabaugh's *Milton in Early America* (1964).[2] This
ground-breaking work establishes, through copious citations, Milton's
central place in American letters and political life during the nation's
formative years. As Sensabaugh shows, it was not just Milton the author
of *Areopagitica* and other republican prose tracts, but also Milton the
Christian poet who was widely read and invoked by diverse American
political factions, from the eve of the Revolution through the first crises
of the new Republic. Milton's language and imagery—his wily Satan, the
conclave of devils in Pandemonium, Death's all-devouring maw—figured
in debates on such key issues as whether the colonies should separate

from Britain and how the Constitution might best be designed to safe-guard liberties while guarding against human fallibility.

While Sensabaugh records the diverse allusions to Milton's poetry and prose works in early America, he does not seek to explain their popularity, as I attempt to do in the present study. I seek to account for the special kinship between English Commonwealth poet and American founding fathers and, in particular, to show just why it was that *Paradise Lost*, with its traditional religious parable of the Fall of man and the promise of redemption, proved so compelling to American readers engaged in a secular, modernizing revolution. To explain these matters I draw on the wealth of recent historical scholarship on the roots of the American Revolution. The American Republic's enormous debt to the seventeenth-century English Commonwealth, Milton included, and to the school of thought known as classical republicanism is now generally acknowledged, thanks to the work of Caroline Robbins, Bernard Bailyn, Gordon Wood, and others.[3]

Other historians and Americanists, among them Alan Heimert, Sacvan Bercovitch, Cushing Strout, Nathan Hatch, and Patricia Bonomi, argue in different ways that, in preparing the ground for 1776, a central role must be accorded to religious doctrines and institutions and to the interplay of religion and politics.[4] These scholars reject the view that religion underwent a broad decline in the colonies during the decades before the Revolution. They argue, instead, that the political movement for independence was nourished and reinforced not only by eighteenth-century sectarian struggles against church authority (as in the Great Awakening) but also by the continuing hold of an older religious sensibility.

I have borrowed from both schools of thought in an effort to reconstruct the background of shared political ideas and religious sensibility that connected Milton with his late eighteenth-century American readers, to whom both *Paradise Lost* and *Areopagitica* were so congenial. Indeed, the inclination of Americans of that time to see their struggle against a corrupt Britain apotheosized in Milton's depiction of the cosmic battle between God and Satan is an excellent example of the "convergence of millennial and republican thought" that Hatch describes in *The Sacred Cause of Liberty*. It is an example, moreover, that illustrates key points of intersection of the English libertarian and Puritan traditions, such as their shared emphasis on individual liberty and their concern over its degeneration into satanic license.

Of course, my focus differs in an obvious way from that of the historical literature on Anglo-American republicanism: I study responses to poetic language and narrative rather than to formal political discourse as indicators of political beliefs and cultural values. Today the distinction between literary texts and historical documents has begun to break down as students of literature and history broaden their notions of which texts deserve their attention; the "historicity of texts" and "textuality of history" are widely assumed in both disciplines. In line with this trend, scholars in various fields have begun to explore the important role that certain narratives have played in the way cultures perceive and evaluate their experiences. The story of the Fall as retold by Milton is, I propose, one such "experience-shaping" tale, a story framework through which Americans reflected on and assimilated their fears and hopes during the struggle for independence and the crises of the early Republic.[5]

Because this is a literary rather than a historical study, my principal objective is to show how an understanding of the eighteenth-century American response to *Paradise Lost* illuminates the epic's social and political subtext—how the insights of those American readers can be read back into Milton's text, clarifying and highlighting its political undertones. Thus, the American reception of *Paradise Lost* provides a vantage point for re-viewing Milton's epic in its seventeenth-century English context and drawing broad conclusions about the significance of Milton's theme—temptation under conditions of liberty—for the emergent commercial republics of the seventeenth and eighteenth centuries. Where one present-day critic argues that Milton settled on the biblical Fall story because of its neutrality, its distinct lack of political affect, I regard Milton's choice and handling of the biblical story as central to his political intentions.[6] The notion of true liberty as obedience to God and reason, the belief that God insists on freedom in obedience (consent of the governed), the fear of passionate self-interest—these and other themes of Milton's rendering of the Fall story have clear parallels in principles of republican political theory that were fighting issues during the English and American revolutions.

The picture of Milton that emerges through this eighteenth-century American lens is quite distinct from that presented in a number of other recent studies of Milton's political legacy. Under the banners of feminism, the New Historicism, and other new theoretical schools, critics have examined Milton's views on egalitarianism and women's rights, his relation to the emergence of new concepts of the author and the individual, and his effect on later female and African-American writers. "English literature's paradigmatic patriarch" (Mary Nyquist), "an ideologist and poet of emergent capitalism" (Christopher Kendrick), "the supreme literary emblem of the cultural power of whites" (Carolivia Heron)—these are but a few of the epithets that have been used recently to describe the seventeenth-century poet-statesman.

Among authors sympathetic to the Left, Milton is commonly lauded for proto-democratic sentiments but castigated for residual elitism and sexism. He is eyed suspiciously as a progenitor of bourgeois possessive individualism and as an oppressive symbol of the myth of Western (white male) cultural superiority.[7] The Marxist-feminist critic Catherine Belsey, who correctly regards Milton as a central figure in the Anglo-American bourgeois revolutionary tradition, states this position bluntly. She declares his notion of liberty to be unjust (applying only to white, property-holding males) and his notion of truth, authoritarian (single, denying difference).[8]

Indeed, some of Milton's views on political enfranchisement, relations between the sexes, and other current concerns may not meet late twentieth-century standards. But can we really ask that of a seventeenth-century author? Milton's neo-Marxist critics would be the first to acknowledge that the problems writers address are conditioned by the times in which they live; yet Milton is routinely criticized for failing to solve the problems of democratic republicanism, feminism, and socialism. In answering the recent feminist assault on Milton's "misogyny," Joan Webber points out that, as a seventeenth-century writer, Milton was necessarily patriarchal to a degree; it is more fruitful, therefore, to show how he transcended his time, how in fighting for the rights of common humanity—male and female—he anticipated subsequent feminist concerns. (It is of special interest for my study that Webber enlists in support of her view the nineteenth-century American writer Margaret Fuller, for whom, in Webber's words, "Milton was one of the fathers of her own age, a true understander of liberty, justice, marriage, and education, a father whose achievement still outdistances that of America, his child.")[9] Webber's observation about the importance of proper historical perspective is broadly true. The imposition of current political agenda on classic authors often leads to predictable conclusions: all such authors are discovered to have been complicit to a greater or lesser degree in the hegemonic bourgeois ideology of their times, and in the process, their unique contributions to posterity are overlooked.[10]

Looking back at Milton from the vantage point of revolutionary America enables us to study the fruitful impact of his writings on future generations of republicans and to appreciate, again, the uniqueness of his legacy. Through both his prose tracts and his poetry he passed down an understanding of the moral and cultural requirements of enduring republics and of the essential roles of individual liberty and reason in "exercising" and strengthening public virtue. It is ironic that today, while the revolutionary ferment in the East bloc reasserts these values and confirms his contemporary relevance, Milton's politically correct critics in the advanced sector continue to focus on the ways in which his views were bounded by his sex, class, and race, and by the times in which he lived.

I have endeavored to relate my study to current work on both Milton's politics and early American political culture and to indicate how I have borrowed from that work. My debts, of course, are of a more immediate and personal sort as well. Foremost, I would like to thank Andrew Delbanco and Edward Tayler of Columbia University, co-sponsors of the dissertation on which the present book is based, for responding to my ideas and pointing me in the direction of pertinent debates in their respective fields. Their encouragement and insights were especially important inasmuch as my research and writing were conducted extramurus as an independent scholar. The other members of my dissertation committee raised important questions for me to consider further: Eric McKitrick, about the persistent role of religion in early American culture; Robert Amdur, about the founding fathers' understanding and use of English republican thought and the issue of influence in general; and Carl Hovde, about the perennial fascination with Milton's Satan.

I am grateful to Deborah Kops of Northeastern University Press and my three anonymous reviewers for their suggestions on revising my manuscript and sharpening its arguments. Emily McKeigue and Martha Yager performed their functions as production editor and copy editor, respectively, with painstaking care. My friend Richard Katz applied his journalist's penchant for clarity and concreteness in reading my manuscript and offering suggestions on editing it. My father, Edgar Dittler, was a source not only of financial support but of encouragement for this and all my intellectual endeavors; I hope I have improved upon the image of *Paradise Lost* as a removed and rather forbidding work that he had from reading in his youth the illustrated edition by Gustave Doré. The completion of this book was truly inconceivable without the support of Richard Schulman, my husband. His interest in the American Revolution, especially the underestimated role of John Adams, was one of the initial sparks for my study, and thereafter he played multiple roles as intellectual respondent, psychological counselor, editor, and, not the least important, computer consultant. I would like to thank these individuals and the many others who expressed interest in and encouraged my work while, of course, absolving them from responsibility for its errors and shortcomings.

PARADISE LOST

and the Rise of the American Republic

Introduction: *Paradise Lost* Revisited

Thanks to deep conviction and an accident of geography—the Puritan belief in the godliness of all believers and the vast ocean separating colonies and mother country—the New England colonists enjoyed institutions of republican self-government from the early years of the seventeenth-century settlement. Thus, Britain's attempt, beginning in the 1760s, to overthrow "ancient liberties" ignited in the colonies reactions similar to those provoked in England in the 1630s by the Stuart monarchy's policy of "Thorough."[1] Americans of various persuasions eagerly seized on century-old tracts defending the English Commonwealth, many of them written by Milton.

In recent decades, historians have noted the colonists' debt to the "Commonwealthmen" and their eighteenth-century English successors. Where Locke was once regarded as the chief inspiration of the founding fathers, it is now commonly agreed that the intellectual roots of the American Revolution reach back to mid-seventeenth-century English republicans such as James Harrington, Algernon Sidney, and Milton, who were themselves indebted to the Florentine and classical republican traditions.[2] From Harrington, Sidney, and other systematic political thinkers, the colonists gathered arguments on the natural rights of Englishmen and the need for governmental safeguards against arbitrary power. When constructing their own state and federal governments, the former colonists borrowed from seventeenth-century republican blueprints for mixed and balanced constitutions.

What attracted Americans to Milton, however, was not his institutional proposals but his defense of republican liberty, qualified by his insistence that true liberty requires an educated, virtuous citizenry ("for what obeys

/ Reason," Adam tells Eve, "is free").[3] Americans encountered this qualified notion of liberty in Milton's prose tracts, where it is prominent and explicit. They also found it centrally embedded in *Paradise Lost*, his epic statement of the problem of individual temptation under conditions of liberty. The poem addressed the urgent moral concerns of citizens struggling to establish a stable republic and facing the dangers of tyranny and corruption at every turn. For this reason it occupied a central place in American popular consciousness.

In one respect what follows is a "reception study": an examination of how one group of readers responded to Milton's texts. What makes this a special case is that the readers used those texts in a major political crisis. We shall hear colonial ministers invoking Milton's arguments on the right and duty of Christians to resist tyranny, Whig leaders bemoaning in Miltonic language the diabolical wiles of the Tories, and patriot satirists ridiculing Britain's generals in imagery drawn directly from Milton's war in Heaven. Taken together, such allusions suggest a coherent reading of *Paradise Lost*, and they reveal a "republican Milton" quite distinct from the radical, bourgeois, feminist, and misogynist Miltons, to name a few, who have appeared in recent scholarship.

In endeavoring to explain the affinity eighteenth-century Americans felt with Milton, I argue that they were a privileged audience, one whose political assumptions and religious sensibility closely resembled Milton's. Thus, against the grain of current reader-response theory, I claim that reading Milton from the perspective of the American Revolution brings us closer to understanding a "true," historically determinate Milton. I argue that the clear moral and political meaning that *Paradise Lost* held for eighteenth-century Americans reflects the political resonances of Milton's epic, because that meaning carries traces of the work's seventeenth-century context. A study of the American colonists' response to Milton suggests why the republican pamphleteer of twenty years was attracted to the Fall story and why his Dutch contemporaries Grotius and Vondel, living in a similar historical context (that of a new republic in rapid commercial development, threatened by tyranny and corruption), also wrote dramas on the Fall.[4]

Each of these contexts in which the Fall theme proved compelling—seventeenth-century England and Holland and eighteenth-century America—featured a national agenda of independence, republicanism, and commercial expansion, whose success required the curbing of market society's propensity to corruption. As Milton recognized, commercial republics were more agreeable than traditional societies to religious and civil liberty, but they also placed greater political responsibilities on individual citizens. They offered greater opportunities for "advancements of every person according to his merit" but created more temptations to succumb to ambition, greed, and other passions.[5] And because such republics extended political participation beyond the few, their virtue was closely tied to the virtue of the many. Both individuals and society were freer to achieve but also to fall—like Adam and Eve in *Paradise Lost*.

The Fall story, as elaborated by Milton and his Dutch contemporaries, proved peculiarly conducive to reflection on the paradoxes of early commercial republic. On the one hand, the story encapsulates the problem of corruptibility, suggesting (through the figures of Satan and, to a lesser degree, postlapsarian humanity) the new forms of tyranny that threaten individuals and society when a popular majority throws off old forms of bondage only to submit to the bondage of private interests and passions. On the other hand, the story revolves around free choice in the matter of the apple, an issue equally resonant for modern republican revolutions and independence movements. Milton's God creates man and woman in His own image, endowing them with right reason and free will; whether they stand or fall is entirely a matter of their unconstrained choice.[6] Thus, in adapting the biblical material of *Paradise Lost*, Milton insists upon both the fallibility of human beings and their capacity to make rational choices. The latter, in fact, is for Milton the essence of human nature; it is what distinguishes humankind from the brutes and constitutes its likeness to God, who is not bound by necessity or chance but acts according to free will.[7]

In his earlier *Tenure of Kings and Magistrates*, Milton argued that the people may, "as oft as they shall judge it for the best, either choose" their king or magistrate "or reject him, retain him or depose him . . . merely by the liberty and right of freeborn men to be governed as seems to them best."[8] He declared that the principle of free choice in forms of government, which arises from the conception of human nature as free and rational, is set forth in Scripture, which confirms "that the right of choosing, yea of changing their own government, is by the grant of God himself in the people."[9] Thus, for Milton, what applies in the theological sphere of *Paradise Lost* also applies in the political sphere.[10]

This view of the human soul as fallible but potentially rational, free to choose and if in error choose again, was central to both the English and American revolutions. It underlay the defense of inalienable natural rights against all forms of despotism and gave rise to the revolutionary notion that governments must reflect human nature as free and self-determining while at the same time taking precautions against human fallibility through checks on the temptations of power.

Interestingly, it is precisely the notion of human autonomy articulated by Milton that has come under attack recently by the New Historicism.[11]

5

Milton's celebration of the individual's essential capacity to choose freely on the basis of right reason is to Stephen Greenblatt "the illusion that I am the principal maker of my own identity."[12] For Catherine Belsey, "the subject is a subjected being, an effect of the meanings it seems to possess."[13] New Historicists have challenged both the "illusion" of a rational, self-determining subject and (borrowing from the work of the cultural anthropologist Clifford Geertz and others outside the field of literature) the very notion of a transhistorical human essence independent of cultural determination. Jonathan Dollimore, for example, maintains that the essentialist view mystifies the actual conditions in which human identity at a given moment in history is rooted. Drawing on the "anti-humanism" of Michel Foucault, he contends further that "it is those discourses centred around 'man' and human nature which, historically, have regulated and repressed *actual* diversity and *actual* human difference"; have proved a barrier to social change; and have provided the intellectual justification for ethnocentrism and even racism:

> The crucial point is surely this: essentialism, rooted as it is in the concept of centred structure and determining origin, constitutes a residual metaphysic within secularist thought which, though it has not entailed has certainly made possible the classic ideological effect: a specific cultural identity is universalised or naturalised; more specifically, in reaction to social change this residual metaphysic is activated in defence of one cultural formation, one conception of what it is to be truly human, to the corresponding exclusion of others.[14]

Belsey, in her Marxist-feminist study of late Renaissance tragedy, lays responsibility for this illusory, reactionary view of the self at the doorstep of Milton, among other theorists of England's seventeenth-century bourgeois revolutions. She cites Milton's description of the grounds for divorce—"that indisposition, unfitness, or contrariety of mind, arising from a cause in nature unchangeable, hindring and ever likely to hinder the main benefits of conjugal society, which are solace and peace"—as early evidence of the emergence of a new view of the human subject: unified, stable, and unchanging, seeking to project itself as universal human nature and therefore excluding all other notions of self.[15] Where Milton argues that the power of kings and magistrates derives from the people, who are endowed with the right and ability to approve their form of government, Belsey sees a cooptive justification for establishing "new but equally ruthless mechanisms of power."[16] In her view, Milton's penetrating observation on the voluntary nature of both political and private covenants (e.g., the state and marriage) is also bourgeois ideology, mystification of the real relations of power in society and, hence, a means of naturalizing the status quo.[17]

However, Milton's writings themselves represent a formidable challenge to the New Historicism's critique of essentialism. For Milton, the certainty of a transhistorical human identity—with its corollary, inalienable natural rights—is not a barrier to political reform and social change but the very rationale for attacking historically specific forms of tyranny. The New Historicists would likely reply that the seventeenth-century bourgeois state merely replaced one form of despotism with another, that its notion of freedom was restricted to men and to certain property-holding men at that.[18] C. B. Macpherson's 1962 study of "possessive individualism" is often enlisted by New Historicists arguing that the autonomous self of the liberal humanist tradition is really the rapacious, determined subject constituted by seventeenth-century market society.[19] However, it should be noted that Milton, the accused spokesman for patriarchy and property (the "phallocracy"), himself offers a trenchant critique of possessive individualism in his rendering of Satan—not free, as the faithful Abdiel points out, but enslaved to his passions. Moreover, Milton articulates an alternative notion of individual freedom understood as obedience to a higher law—subordination of selfish private interests to the common weal or to divine direction.[20] This second notion of individualism, it will be argued here, was also conditioned by seventeenth-century market society.

Granted that inequalities persist in Western democratic society, the question becomes, what political-economic system is the alternative? On this point the New Historicists offer nothing more explicit than Belsey's observation that "the future implications of change, its direction and the interests it serves are questions for us to resolve. The pressure to do so is increasingly urgent."[21] Instead of improving upon imperfect bourgeois liberty, they would throw out the entire idea. Their approach is a historical descendent, via nineteenth-century Marxism, of the theories of the French *philosophes*, who regarded human nature as the creation of environment and of the state and believed that it was possible to erase by fiat all barriers to perfect equality. The republican political tradition to which Milton belonged recognized that the degree of freedom in any given society is dependent upon that society's level of material and intellectual development and that the task of political reformers, therefore, is to advance political freedom in tandem with social improvements. John Adams, for one, expressed incredulity at the French Jacobins' bold confidence in the immediate perfectibility of man, while insisting that the state and society be reformed to foster human improvement.

Although I counterpose Milton's arguments on free choice and natural rights to recent critiques of the essentialist self, it will be clear from the remainder of this introduction that I share many of the concerns of the New Historicism. The very nature of my project is historicist. In examining the way in which Milton's epic both reflects and intervenes in the conflicts of the early commercial republic, this study assumes a dialectical relationship between literature and history, refusing to view literature either as a privileged realm removed from the vagaries of history or as a passive reflector of "the real world." I seek to resituate *Paradise Lost* in the political discourse of Milton's times, aided by the insights of eighteenth-century American readers, whose assumptions were shaped significantly by Milton and other thinkers of the English Commonwealth and who may, therefore, be considered the epic's "fit audience." Further, this study recognizes that the habit of reading through the lens of the present distorts the full difference of texts of the past—another chief concern of the New Historicists.

In fact, the history of responses to *Paradise Lost* through the ages offers an especially fertile case study for pursuing this last point and for demonstrating the political determination of diverse readings of a classic text. The period under consideration here, the late eighteenth century, witnessed the articulation of several interpretations of *Paradise Lost* along political lines: the Jacobin and Tory readings, each interpreting the epic as a manifesto of its own cause, and the republican reading will be explored here. Few scholars today would defend or replicate the Tory reading; Jacobinism, however, is apparently alive and well. The last twenty years have seen renewed interest in "the revolutionary Milton," motivated in part by the broader effort in literary studies to reassert the connection between literature and history. However, many of these efforts to recover the political dimensions of *Paradise Lost* take as their starting point the Romantic interpretation of the epic that regards Satan as its hero and as the embodiment of Milton's true identity as a revolutionary. In recent variants of this view, Milton is seen as anticipating the radical democratic ideology of the nineteenth century or as falling short of it by clinging to an elitist and patriarchal worldview.[22]

American republicans, by contrast, viewed Satan as the archetype of the corrupted politician or citizen who subordinates the public good to private interests and seeks to corrupt others by awakening their selfish passions. This early American understanding of Satan, I argue, coincides with Milton's and therefore can serve as a corrective to anachronistic interpretations of both the radical and elitist varieties. It is ironic that the contemporary critics who perpetuate the Romantic interpretation of Milton's politics seek, by re-establishing the relation between art and politics, to vindicate Shelley's (and Milton's) notion of the poet as *vates*. In his effect on late eighteenth-century Americans, Milton was precisely the sort of unacknowledged legislator Shelley had in mind in his *Defence of Poetry*. Indeed, the influence of *Paradise Lost* during the founding of the American Republic is a compelling—perhaps unparalleled—case of a poem's conditioning a major historical event through its impact on key leaders and on society at large.

The notion that eighteenth-century American readers, because of their sensitivity to Milton's political propensities and concerns, are exemplary readers of his epic will doubtless be controversial on both theoretical and empirical grounds. The question of who Milton's fit readers are, always a thorny one, is especially so today, when reader-response and other subjectivist theories have cast doubt on the usefulness of attempting to discover an author's original meaning or even of pursuing an objective text produced under recoverable historical circumstances. Hanford observed many decades ago that the diverse interpretations of *Paradise Lost* often have revealed more about the moral and intellectual biases of successive generations of readers than about the poem written by Milton.[23] Subjectivist critics infer from such diversity that the text has no objective meaning, only different, individualistic interpretations. By contrast, this study assumes that there are more and less valid ways of reading texts and that the more we can learn about an author's life and times and their relationship to his work, the closer we can come to understanding a given text.

All of this is not to espouse an "original intent" position, dismissing subsequent readings of *Paradise Lost* or of any literary work as mere distortions with no relevance to the work's significance and lasting value.[24] The history of the critical reception of *Paradise Lost* is among the best known examples in literary history of the way subsequent interpretations adhere to a text and influence later readings. What informed reader can think about *Paradise Lost* without recalling Blake's views and in some way incorporating them into his or her own response? A text is not an autonomous thing-in-itself, as some members of the New Critical and other formalist schools once supposed, but a cultural artifact that accretes to itself the historical perspectives and interpretations of successive readers. Nevertheless, later readings must be kept conceptually distinct from the inferred context and intentions of the original author. The experience of *Paradise Lost* or any literary work is clearly impoverished when either radical subjectivism or radical objectivism is practiced. Rather, the full experience of a work arises in the interplay of the work's meanings for its author and for its contemporary and later readers, up to

9

the present. However, this complexity is quite different from the indeterminacy of meaning asserted by deconstructionist critics.

The "later readers" I summon to enrich the present discussion were members of a continuous Anglo-American republican current extending from the English Commonwealth to the American Revolution, with roots in the Aristotelian and Machiavellian traditions of political thought.[25] Their "republican Milton" differs from the two presently dominant presentations: Milton the radical, who shared the egalitarianism and anti-Trinitarian theology of the English Revolution's left-wing sectaries, and Milton the "thoroughgoing elitist," who was completely unsympathetic to democratic government.[26] These irreconcilable views say more about contemporary England's continuing battle of Left versus Right, Labour party versus Tory, than about Milton. In truth, Milton is best viewed as belonging to a third, republican tendency, neither egalitarian nor elitist, which was distinguished by its complex understanding of humanity as corruptible yet ameliorable through education, religious and political reform, and economic improvement. To "repair the ruins" of the Fall and restore society to a condition of right reason: the republican program as well as outlook was the product both of classical political theory and of the Christian precepts.[27]

This English republican outlook persisted in eighteenth-century colonial America, above all in New England. Citing Milton, James Harrington, Algernon Sidney, and other seventeenth-century Commonwealthmen, John Adams defined republicanism in 1776 as government of laws, not men. Adams and his republican predecessors sustained a deep-seated hatred for capriciousness in government, and they sought to design forms of government that would guarantee the public good and the rights of the individual against the encroachments of selfish private interests ("passions"), whether of kings, aristocrats, or commoners.

A century earlier, on the eve of the Stuart Restoration, Milton's *Ready and Easy Way to Establish a Free Commonwealth* celebrated the free commonwealth as the form of government commended by Christ and Scripture because it was most agreeable to religious and civil liberty and "proportioned equality." In the pamphlet he argued that, unlike absolutist states, where the people necessarily were kept in a servile and abject condition, republics fostered and rested on the virtue and free obedience of an educated citizenry. Herein lay the superiority of republics but also, Milton recognized, their vulnerability. While republican government unleashed the potential in individuals, giving them greater scope to realize their talents than was possible in traditional societies, it also exposed them to more temptations to put private interests ahead of the public good. They were freer to achieve but also to fall. Thus, the

English Republic, like its historical predecessors, was fragile and subject to decay.

Throughout the Commonwealth and Protectorate periods, Milton pointed to the problem of venal legislators ("every man more attentive to his private interest than to that of the state")[28] and malleable commoners (who in 1660 clamored for the return of the king, believing that only monarchy could restore commerce and their livelihoods). Milton responded to the erosion of public virtue by prescribing a program of education, religious liberty, and other improvements in the life of the "misguided and abused multitude." He hoped in this way to inoculate men and women against the sway of destructive, satanic passions and to strengthen their capacity for godlike reason. When the Restoration arrived, Milton continued this project by other means. He wrote *Paradise Lost* in an attempt to bring good out of evil, projecting on a cosmic scale the kind of selfish, intemperate passions that had led to the fall of the English Republic.[29]

Clearly, there is nothing novel about proposing that there are connections between Milton's late prose tracts and his poetry: between his sentiments toward the fall of the English Republic, which he served as pamphleteer and Latin Secretary for nearly twenty years, and his representation of the archetypal Fall. Milton's concern as a political theorist with the fragility of republics is widely recognized. To my knowledge, however, no one has shown to what extent his political theory runs parallel to the moral and theological themes of *Paradise Lost*. Written in the aftermath of the fall of the Republic, the epic embodies Milton's reflections on the difficulties of creating and sustaining republics—governments that ultimately rest upon the virtue and self-discipline of their citizens. *Paradise Lost* is characteristically republican as well in its depiction of humanity as at once corruptible and ameliorable: subject to satanic passions but, when "Improv'd by tract of time," capable of regaining and even improving upon the state of free obedience that prevailed in Eden before the Fall.[30]

Milton's American readers, steeped in the same republican culture and undergoing a political crisis of their own, were sensitive to the moral and political dimensions of *Paradise Lost*. They often invoked Milton's Satan as a symbol for the private passions that contended with the "Rights of Society" (John Adams's phrase) and threatened first the movement for independence and later the stability of the new Republic. In the 1770s, a "diabolical" feature of British policy was the deliberate creation, through corruption, of a loyal faction of colonists who could be counted on to side with Britain in any conflict. Colonists were offered lucrative posts as revenue collectors, socially distinguished positions as members of local

11

oligarchies, even cheap tea—the last as a bait to elicit consent to the principle of extraconstitutional taxation. In this atmosphere Milton's epic of the cosmic battle between corruption and virtuous forbearance was enlisted to inspire citizens to put aside private interests and support the common good. On the eve of 1776, John Adams and other revolutionary leaders depicted the Tory oligarchs as satanic tempters and tormenters: having succumbed to the temptation to gratify selfish interests, they sought, like Milton's Devil, to corrupt others through the snare of preferments and pensions.

After the Revolution, many of its initiators feared that in the absence of a strong federal government and a constitution with appropriate checks and balances, and without the rapid extension of education, the nation's newfound liberty might degenerate into license. Again, Milton's imagery spoke to the immediate crisis: his Satan, the embodiment of license, was seized upon to demonstrate that the excessive indulgence in liberty—as manifested in popular protests against taxation and governmental authority in general—was not true liberty but anarchy. In the 1790s his scene in Pandemonium, in which the devils "democratically" debate their future course of action, became a favorite satirical device for moderates in both the Federalist and Republican parties for warning of the pitfalls of pure democracy, with its manipulative demagogues and factious aristocratic cliques seeking to control the machinery of government from behind the scenes. Thus, *Paradise Lost* continued to mirror the foremost concerns of many Americans.

In positing a dynamic interaction between history and literature, I do not propose that *Paradise Lost* or any great poem be read as a species of political allegory, with one-to-one correspondences between characters and events in the poem and in life. Robert Fallon trenchantly analyzes the fallacies inherent in such a mechanistic approach to *Paradise Lost*, while making a compelling case for what he terms "experiential criticism": criticism that views the lives and times of writers as holding important keys to the interpretation of their work.[31] Fallon credits Christopher Hill with reaffirming the relevance of historical context to Milton's epic but points to absurdities that arise when Hill and others assert one-to-one analogies between art and life. Like Fallon, I see the historical context as impinging on *Paradise Lost* in a much more general and, in the end, more pervasive manner. The historical and political background is evident in Milton's choice of theme, in his rejection of an earlier plan to write an epic on King Arthur, and in his shaping of his biblical material.[32] The artistic decision to make Satan an eloquent and at times persuasive orator (whose deceptive rhetoric continues, to this day, to beguile the susceptible reader) was motivated, one suspects, by Milton's direct experience of corrupt politicians and gullible followers during his twenty years of public service.

In *Surprised by Sin*, a work that still raises hackles, Stanley Fish argues that the attractiveness of Satan was part of Milton's conscious strategy to confront readers with their own fallen nature, not a symptom of the poet's unconscious identification with Satan and enmity toward God, as Blake, Empson, Waldock, and others in the Romantic tradition would have it. (Fish notes that rhetoric, upon which Milton's devils rely heavily, was regarded with disfavor by seventeenth-century Puritans, in contrast to the "right reason" of dialectic.)[33] In line with this reading, and against mechanistic political interpretations linking Satan with specific historical figures (Cromwell, the parliamentary generals, egocentric radicals, and Charles I all have been candidates at one time or another) I wish to assert that the Satan of *Paradise Lost* represents a universal human condition: thralldom to narrow self-interest.

This approach to the "Satan problem" coheres with seventeenth-century classical republican theory, according to which each element of society—monarchy, aristocracy, and democracy—if unchecked by the others, might degenerate into its passionate, tyrannical counterpart: despotism, oligarchy, or ochlocracy (tyranny of the one, the few, or the many). Thus, the fact that Satan is alternatively imaged as oriental despot and democratic orator (even within a single episode, viz., the council in Hell in Book II) need not dismay the reader: it reflects the view (which in classical republican theory is a commonplace) that unchecked self-interest arises in all unbalanced forms of government. Milton's portrait of Satan is historically specific not in the sense that Satan stands for any particular contemporary figure but in the sense that the problems of corruptibility and demagogic manipulation, summed up in Satan's career, were central for Milton's time and for more than a century thereafter.

If a poet's personal experiences and historical context shape his art, it is no less true that art shapes historical individuals and, through them, politics and history. The influence of *Paradise Lost* in late eighteenth-century America is a striking example of the active role poetry can play in shaping political culture.[34] The effect of this kind of art on life is more subtle, but also more profound, than that of topical satire, occasional political poems, and other works visibly written out of a desire to influence the immediate course of events. Milton did not avoid the topical or the occasional. His sonnets to Fairfax, Cromwell, and Vane, for example, while eulogizing those leaders for eternity, also gave England's generals clear marching orders regarding church disestablishment and other pressing policy issues facing the Republic. However, *Paradise Lost*, like most of Milton's poetry, is political not in any topical sense but on the subtler and deeper level at which great art shapes the values of generations of readers.[35]

Milton himself understood poetry, especially epic poetry, to have precisely such a long-term, value-forming effect. In *The Reason of Church-Government Urg'd against Prelaty* he declared his intention to write a poem that would be "doctrinal and exemplary to a Nation" and called his poetic vocation "the inspired guift of God . . . of power beside the office of a pulpit, to imbreed and cherish in a great people the seeds of vertu, and publick civility."[36] *Paradise Lost,* composed for the most part after the failure of England's republican experiment and published in the evil days of the restored monarchy, could have only a limited immediate impact on the English nation he had hoped to celebrate and inspire. The project was fulfilled in helping to educate and inspire future readers, some of whom successfully established a republic a century later on another continent.[37]

While Milton's prose tracts supplied Americans with arguments on natural law, freedom of the press, liberty of conscience, and the like, his poetry instilled an appreciation for the complexity and lawfulness of human society and of the physical universe—all guided by God's overarching providence—and a hatred for capricious, passionate, self-aggrandizing behavior. His poetry reinforced the colonists' respect for constitutional government and fueled their resistance to despotic, unconstitutional measures. Ultimately, it is in terms of this shaping of moral and political values that the influence of Milton's epic in revolutionary America must be understood.

Early in this study I suggested that Milton's readers in late eighteenth-century America might be considered his fit audience. A qualification is now in order. When we turn to the American material we discover not one but diverse and opposing uses of *Paradise Lost.* During the Revolutionary War, Whigs and Tories alike ransacked Milton's epic for appropriately satanic epithets in order to portray their antagonists as ambitious, law-defying devils. After the Revolution, in the wake of popular insurrections such as Shay's Rebellion in western Massachusetts and the Jacobin Terror in France, Federalist writers and francophile Republicans both freely "Satan-baited" their opponents. For Federalists defending the government against pro-Jacobin agitation, Milton's Satan was the demagogue who woos the uneducated masses by appealing to their immediate passions; for francophile Republicans, the Federalists were fallen Lucifers who had betrayed the revolutionary cause. Meanwhile, Thomas Jefferson anticipated the Romantic reading of the epic in his admiration for Satan's defiant speeches, which he copied into his youthful commonplace book.

While such ubiquity of citation underlines Milton's centrality to eighteenth-century political culture, the diversity of readings should not be construed to mean that there is no objective text, no true Milton, and that all readings of *Paradise Lost* in that or any period are equally valid. Blake's theory of Milton's unconscious intentions notwithstanding, some eighteenth-century adaptations of the epic are clearly in contradiction with the poet's stated political views. The question of who read Milton right in eighteenth-century America will be taken up later. For the moment, suffice it to say that, although various American factions endeavored to attach the epithet "satanic" to their political opponents, all implicitly agreed that Milton's Satan was the embodiment of the evil of selfish private interests (although Jefferson's fascination with Satan's individualistic declarations looks ahead to a later, Romantic view).

It is one of the ironies of history that the republican theory and program generated during the English Revolution were only fully realized a century later in America. The reforms of the English Interregnum were notoriously incomplete and short-lived, and the Glorious Revolution of 1688 departed from the republican model. Thus, the present study of the American reception of Milton may be a case in which historical hindsight is clarifying rather than distorting. The real victory of the English Commonwealth was the American Revolution, which gave flesh to republican principles through a constitution with checks and balances to harmonize particular interests with the national good. The American Revolution brought a bill of rights to safeguard individual liberties; the separation of church and state to protect religious freedom; the banning of primogeniture, entail, and other feudal relics; and a commitment to universal public education and national economic development to eliminate the disparities of wealth and opportunity that underlay the volatile class stratification of the Old World.

Those thinkers and political reformers who carried on the Commonwealth tradition within England itself remained a tiny minority; their major significance, as Caroline Robbins and others have shown, was in keeping the legacy alive and transmitting it to the American colonies. Andrew Milner goes further, arguing that Milton criticism in the twentieth century has been more fertile in the United States than in Britain because of a living republican tradition among Americans, who better understand Milton's outlook. British Milton criticism has been relatively impoverished, Milner maintains, because British critics are out of touch with the outlook that flourished in England under the Commonwealth and for which Milton was a principal spokesman. Following Engels, Milner argues that in England the republican-rationalist ideal was supplanted by the political strategy of gradualism and the philosophic outlook of empiricism after the defeat of the English Commonwealth and the

15

subsequent compromise between the emerging commercial class and the landed aristocracy in the Glorious Revolution of 1688.[38]

All this provides a motivation for revisiting Milton in his seventeenth-century context and then voyaging ahead to his eighteenth-century New World realization. The purpose is to gain an appreciation of his distinctive insight, contrary to Plato, that humanity must be free to fall, for without freedom there can be no ameliorability, no convergence with the angels.[39] Accordingly, the first part of the text that follows (chapters 1 through 3) reexamines Milton and his seventeenth-century context from the standpoint just adumbrated. The second part discusses the transmission of the Commonwealth's political tradition to the American colonies (chapter 4), the importance of Milton's writings to the colonies' "natural leaders" in the prerevolutionary period (chapter 5), the adaptation of his writings to the struggle for independence (chapter 6), and their adaptation, during the 1790s, to the raging debate between the Federalists and the Jeffersonian Republicans (chapter 7).

1

The Fall as a Republican Theme

Eighteenth-century Americans felt a deep affinity with the theme of *Paradise Lost*, steeped as they were in a political and religious culture similar to Milton's. However, readers since the early nineteenth century have been perplexed by Milton's choice of the biblical Fall story as the raw material for his epic. The Romantic view that Milton's theme betrays his attachment to the retrograde dogmas of his age continues to attract adherents, who now attribute those retrograde attitudes to his class and sex.[1]

The political consciousness of Blake, Shelley, and other Romantics of their period was shaped by the ideals and events of the French Revolution and the post-1815 reaction. These writers admired Milton as an inspired poet and as a spokesman for human liberty, and they could square their admiration for him with what appeared to be a reactionary story only by discovering unacknowledged or hidden sympathy in the poet for his Devil. Shelley, in his famous pronouncement on the matter, claimed that "Milton's poem contains within itself a philosophical refutation of that system of which, by a strange and natural antithesis, it has been a chief popular support": in giving us a perseverant, magnificent Devil and a vengeful, tyrannical God, Milton had "violated the popular creed" and proved his poetic genius.[2]

The Romantic approach, inverting Milton's worldview and reconceiving his "anti-authoritarian" Devil as the epic's moral touchstone, is enjoying a revival today. Where Blake once proclaimed that Milton was "of the Devil's party without knowing it," Jackie DiSalvo, in her study of Blake's revision of Milton, maintains that Satan is indeed the true, republican hero of the poem, free of the patriarchalism that finally

17

subdued Milton's revolutionary spirit. The epic's "contradictions" and 'incongruities"—the "magnetism" of Milton's Satan and "repulsiveness" of his God—arise, according to DiSalvo, from a dilemma within the poet: Milton's ambivalence toward the egalitarian impulses of the English Revolution.[3]

Another recent critic suggests alternatively, that Milton was drawn to the Fall theme not because of any political overtones, conscious or unconscious, but because of its neutrality, its distinct lack of political affect. Christopher Kendrick argues that Milton selected the "neutral" Fall story in order to "seal off" his poetry from his politics, specifically from his response to the failure of the English Commonwealth. But since "the poem wants to be about the revolution," this "repressed political intent or libido . . . takes up residence on the poem's borders, and projects the revolution as would-be referent."[4]

The broad seventeenth- and eighteenth-century interest in the theme of *Paradise Lost* militates against such a view and suggests, on the contrary, that the theme held a special appeal for early modern republics. I have already noted the evidence for this in the contemporaneous Dutch writings of Grotius and Vondel and in the popularity of Milton's epic in the early United States.[5]

Later in this chapter I will review the case that Milton's choice of the Fall story paralleled his growing republicanism. Admittedly, the intensity of theological controversy in the seventeenth century made the Fall a vital theme for poets and dramatists—more vital, doubtless, than the life of Arthur, the theme Milton ultimately rejected. The United Provinces were sundered by religious warfare during the lifetimes of Grotius and Vondel, and the conflict between Arminians and Gomarists over the issue of free will versus predestination led in 1619 to Grotius's exile from his native country, to Johan Oldenbarnevelt's execution, and to the suppression of the republican faction within Holland. The Thirty Years' War pitted Protestant and Catholic countries against each other across Europe. The English Civil War was fought, in significant part, over the issues of religious toleration and church disestablishment. Eighteenth-century American republicans, although their goals were secular, often envisioned their political struggle against Britain in millennial imagery inherited from their Puritan forbears, perceiving their revolution, like the original settlement of the country, as a milestone in the unfolding of redemptive history. Thus, given the centrality of religious issues and habits of thought in the period, it was natural that leading poets and intellectuals should express themselves through biblical themes.

However, the Fall story and its attendant theological issues—original sin, God's foreknowledge of the Fall, humanity's role in its own salvation—were also laden with political implications, just as a century earlier the Reformation, in emphasizing the individual believer's unmediated relation to God and Scripture, carried with it a new consciousness of the value of the individual and new demands for political equality. As elaborated by Milton, Grotius, and Vondel, the story of Satan's rebellion and his successful temptation of mankind encapsulates a problematic aspect of this individualism: the rampant growth of private economic interests. Although the conflict between private interests and the public good is present in all societies, it was heightened in the emergent commercial republics of the seventeenth and eighteenth centuries because the dominant form of accumulated wealth in such states, private capital, gave rise to the problem of selfish individualism at the very moment when the demise of royal monopolies, feudal land tenure, and other economic restrictions of precapitalist society promised to be a great boon to society as a whole. Furthermore, the form of political organization in seventeenth-century England and Holland and in the early United States, with their relatively representative institutions, allowed for the expansion of a politically responsible citizenry and for upward mobility based on merit; but it, too, had its attendant dangers: the problems of backward, manipulable masses and clever demagogues.

Therefore, a major concern for Milton and other republicans was to strengthen, through education, religious reform, and other means, the population's ability to resist such blandishments and corrupting influences. This was possible because, from the republican point of view, humanity conforms neither to the pessimistic vision of Hobbes nor to the optimistic vision of some of the radical sectaries of Milton's day: human nature does not consist wholly of self-interested passions or wholly of divine reason. The principle at the heart of all republican constitutions was, and is, that they should allow scope for human improvement while guarding against human corruptibility.

In the hands of Milton and his Dutch contemporaries, the biblical stories of Satan's rebellion and man's fall reverberate with these issues. Unlike the Romantics of a later time, the republican reformers of the seventeenth and eighteenth centuries saw in Satan's passionate ambitions a warning against individualism gone awry. In raising the rebellion in Heaven, Satan appeals to the selfish desires of others and, archetypal demagogue that he is, conceals his subversive designs behind republican-sounding rhetoric; slyly, he urges the rebel angels to refuse the "Knee-tribute" and "prostration vile" owed to the "King annointed."[6] Satan's fall is repeated in humanity's, but with a major difference: human beings are susceptible to redemption. They learn that true freedom consists not in license but in the fusion of individual desire and providential or social ends. The Fall story thus retold encapsulates the complex republican view of man's corruptibility and ameliorability. That the Romantics failed to appreciate political resonances in *Paradise Lost* that were available to earlier generations of reformers is a reflection on their age, not Milton's. Indeed, the Romantics' view was one symptom of the attenuation of the republican tendency by the early nineteenth century in a Europe increasingly polarized between conservatives and radical democrats.

The Dutch Antecedents of *Paradise Lost*

An examination of the Dutch antecedents of *Paradise Lost* casts light on the political significance of the Fall theme for the seventeenth century. *Adamus Exul* (1601) by the Dutch statesman Hugo de Groot (Grotius) and Joost van den Vondel's two complementary dramas on Satan's rebellion and man's Fall, *Lucifer* (1654) and *Adam in Ballingschap* (1664), stand together with *Paradise Lost* at the end of a rich exegetical and literary tradition. This tradition—the Genesis or Celestial Cycle tradition, whose object was to trace events from the war in Heaven through the Fall to the Redemption—is the primary context of these works.[7] However, in elaborating Satan's personality, his rebellion in Heaven, and his successful temptation of the first couple—aspects of the story merely suggested in Scripture—Grotius and Vondel were responding to an immediate historical context as well.

Milton almost certainly knew *Adamus Exul*. When he returned from his continental tour of 1638–39, one of whose highlights was a meeting in Paris with the exiled Grotius, Milton began work on a series of drafts for a dramatic poem on the Fall theme. As J. M. Evans reports, Milton's third draft, with its allegorical figures Justice, Mercy, and Wisdom, owes much to medieval treatments of the story. The fourth draft, however, bears unmistakable resemblances to Grotius's five-act classical drama.[8] The draft opens with lines that Milton later used in Book IV of *Paradise Lost* ("O Thou that with surpassing Glory Crown'd! / Look'st from thy Sole Dominion, like the God / Of this New World").[9] *Adamus Exul* begins in a similar manner with Satan alone on stage, delivering an introspective soliloquy. Milton's draft then follows the same narrative sequence as Grotius's drama. Even Milton's projected title, *Adam unparadiz'd*, seems to be an imitation or echo of *Adamus Exul*. Every modification that Milton adopted in the fourth draft, Evans argues, could have been inspired by Grotius.[10]

The strong similarities in conception and the direct verbal echoes between Grotius's classical drama and Milton's plan for *Paradise Lost* have been extensively analyzed by Evans and others. (During Milton's lifetime, some detractors even accused him of plagiarism.) What I wish to suggest here is that *Adamus Exul* and Milton's mature epic also shared a polemical intent: both writers gravitated toward the Fall story in part because of its implicit republican themes.

When the youthful Grotius completed his drama in 1601, the United Provinces had won their independence from Spain but for nearly a century would be torn by intermittent factional strife between the stadholderate (the quasi-monarchical military office held by the House of Orange) and the civilian leaders of Holland, the most economically advanced province. Demagoguery, corruption, and oligarchical manipulation for factional advantage threatened the newly independent merchant republic. In 1619 the rivalry exploded into armed conflict between the Gomarists, staunch Calvinists who sought to institute their denomination as state church, and the more tolerant Arminians. Maurice of Orange allied with the Gomarists; Johan Oldenbarnevelt, political leader of Holland, and his ally Grotius joined with the Arminians. Oldenbarnevelt and Grotius had tried unsuccessfully to defuse the conflict but were finally maneuvered into siding with the Arminians, whose opposition to the doctrine of predestination and whose support for religious toleration were more consonant with the cosmopolitan character of bourgeois Holland. When the dust settled, Oldenbarnevelt, who had led his province for several decades, was tried for treason and executed by the Orangists. Grotius was sentenced to life imprisonment but soon escaped in a spectacular fashion and spent the rest of his life in exile.

The problems that led to the disaster of 1619 (notably the demagogic manipulation of the gullible populace by the aristocratic Orange faction) were already alive in 1601 and are reflected in Grotius's drama. Grotius's imaginative representation of these problems culminates in the successful temptation of Eve, in a scene that anticipates Satan's manipulative behavior in *Paradise Lost*. Satan has previously approached Adam undisguised, proposing an alliance between the adjacent realms of Hell and Earth against the unjust Thunderer. His open diplomacy rejected, Satan now turns to his traditional method: guile. He enters the serpent and mimics republican arguments, which he rightly suspects will disarm Eve. He begins by praising Adam and Eve's benevolent lordship over the beasts in Paradise:

> All we beasts indeed
> Whom earth and sea and air possess within their bounds
> Rejoice in our good fortune. 'Tis a privilege,
> For those born to obey, not to endure wild tyrants

But to receive the clemency of human sway.
When reason rules the rulers, servitude is free. (p. 159)

Having insinuated himself through flattery into Eve's good graces, Satan proceeds to the matter of the tree of knowledge. God must be a tyrant, Satan argues, because of His prohibition against eating "yonder fruits" (p. 159): the Deity is preventing Adam and Eve from attaining knowledge so as to keep them in servitude. Grotius frames Satan's argument in a manner seemingly calculated to create ambivalence in his post-Renaissance audience, for whom an inquiring spirit was the characteristic that distinguished humankind from mere beasts. Satan's rhetoric must have been especially appealing to seventeenth-century audiences because his argument mimicked the contemporary republican theory that broadly diffused knowledge was a prerequisite for self rule in a nation whereas popular ignorance invited tyranny.

Satan proceeds by playing on Eve's vulnerability to the gamut of irrational feelings. Before long, he has kindled in her feelings of envy and a desire for the "secret power" contained in the golden apples; he has awakened the "guileful fascination of the senses" (pp. 167, 169). Eve can no longer hear the voice of reason that once guided her actions. Follow your "nature" instead, Satan tells her:

> Let not thyself be cozen'd by fond superstitions,
> Neither against thy nature foolishly rebel!
> If anything has brought sweet pleasure to thy mind,
> Consider it permitted; where thy senses lead,
> Follow straightway, nor join in war against thyself.
> Nature, thy guardian and parent, has assign'd
> Senses to living things as teachers. (p. 169)

If Eve is easily beguiled by Satan's appeal to the law of nature and by his seemingly rational arguments, perhaps fear of God's anger will dictate greater caution. But Satan has already convinced Eve that eating the apple can have no consequence, for God has predetermined her fate:

> How can those perish whom to everlasting life
> God hath predestined? For the Fates control all things.
> We merely do that which has been ordain'd, and suffer
> That which comes down from heav'n. Writ by the Hand divine,
> Decrees endure forever. (p. 161)

This Satan is a Calvinist! Grotius seems to be suggesting the baneful political consequences of the doctrine of predestination and of the

22

complementary view of man as a determined being, a creature of the senses. Strict Calvinism, he seems to say, to the extent that it denies free will and de-emphasizes individual responsibility for the consequences of actions, may render its adherents susceptible to manipulation by evil-intentioned Satans. The appeal by Grotius's Satan to Eve's sensual desires and his insistence on the inconsequentiality of her actions in the larger framework of the universe is suggestive of the way a demagogue might manipulate a crowd, playing on its sense of political impotence and unjust treatment, while promising to gratify its immediate desires.

Satan's rhetorical skills are an even more prominent feature of *Lucifer*, Vondel's drama of the rebellion in Heaven. Lucifer at first conceals his own rebellious intentions while drawing out the festering resentments of the more egoistical members of the angelic population. When the incited mob finally demands that he lead them in rebellion against the tyrant God, Lucifer showers them with false-republican speeches. (Milton's Satan later uses the same tactics.)

Vondel, in his foreword to the drama, cites Grotius as an authority on his subject (along with Scripture, patristic commentaries, Du Bartas, and the treatise on fallen angels of the English Protestant Richard Baker). Vondel was, moreover, a friend and political ally of Grotius, and he continued to defend Grotius after the latter's exile from Holland in 1619. The question of whether Milton knew Vondel's works (in particular, *Lucifer* and its sequel, *Adam in Ballingschap*, and *Samson*) has been the subject of much speculation. Milton knew Dutch and, as the English Commonwealth's Secretary for Foreign Tongues, was well versed in Dutch politics; it is likely that he would at least have heard of *Lucifer* after the storm of controversy that greeted its stage premiere in 1654.[11]

The play was denounced by the Amsterdam Consistory as being full of "unholy, unchaste, idolatrous, false, and utterly depraved things" and was banned after two performances. This denunciation, however, served only to advertise the play, and the first edition of one thousand sold out in a week.[12] The Calvinist establishment may have interdicted the play for political reasons as well as for the alleged immorality of its anthropomorphic depiction of the angels. The United Provinces had recently entered into a truce with the English Commonwealth following the first Anglo-Dutch War. The head of state, the republican leader Johan de Witt, sought to reduce the war debt and the crushing levels of taxation on the population and to effect constitutional reform. However, the political situation was highly unstable. Although the stadholderate had fallen into abeyance with no heir of age, the Dutch parliament was still controlled by the militaristic Orange faction, which disliked the truce and de Witt's reform program and hoped to unseat him. Vondel was an ally of de Witt.

One of his last poems was an elegy for the republican statesman, who was lynched in 1672 by a frenzied mob during a period of intense political turmoil.

Vondel's Lucifer, identified in the *dramatis personae* as the Stadholder, is a familiar type: a self-serving political leader who camouflages his egoistic aims behind altruistic rhetoric.[13] His flaws are the traditional satanic ones: pride, envy, ambition, jealousy. He stirs up the rebellion in Heaven with "cunning hatch'd from subtlety" (p. 379) and through his demagogic arts turns the angelic population into an instrument of his own vengeance and self-advancement. Vondel's fallen angels have been compared to "the dissatisfied people, brought to the verge of frenzy by the wily arts of the demagogue; the howling mob, wanting only the kindling spark to flash into the flame of revolt; the maddened rabble, waiting for the master-spirit to spur them into open revolution."[14] The Calvinist establishment may have recognized its own political wiles mirrored covertly in Vondel's biblical drama.

But if Vondel portrays Lucifer's rebellion as egoism parading under the pretext of selfless public service and respect for law (Lucifer's chief grievance against God is that He has violated His own celestial hierarchy in creating and elevating man), Vondel's God is not a "conservative," nor is the universe He designed a static hierarchy. Through its dramatic structure, Vondel's tragedy immediately confronts the audience with the ironical truth about Lucifer's revolt: Lucifer rebels not because he wants change, but because he wants to preserve his original place in the celestial hierarchy, which God Himself is changing and perfecting.

Lucifer opens with an extraordinarily bold conceit. Apollyon has been dispatched by the archfiend to survey the newly created universe and has returned to Heaven. He describes Eden for his comrades Beelzebub and Belial:

> What I have seen
> With mine own eyes forsooth deceives me not.
> Earth's fields and their delight now beggar us,
> And Eden quite outdoes our Paradise. (p. 363)

The Earth is more beautiful and more perfect than Heaven, a testimony to the Deity's infinite powers of creativity. God's supreme creations on Earth are Adam and Eve:

> No heavenly creature has so pleased my eyes
> As these two on the earth. Who can so twine

With subtlety a body and a soul,
Creating double angels out of clay?
The body, beautiful of shape, bears witness
To the Creator's art, whose glory glows
Most in the face, the mirror of the mind.
Upon the face is stamped the soul's bright image,
That lights the countenance, and makes life fair
With godlike glances out of human eyes,
The rational soul set in a human face. (p. 365)

The as-yet-unfallen angels appear to be captivated by God's handiwork, particularly by the unusual fusion of body and soul, the transformation of mere clay into a luminous spiritual essence.[15] But soon their attitude changes: the angels are seized by envy. Most hateful to them is humanity's "twofold" sex and the prospect that, through marriage, human beings will soon outnumber the angels, "For no angel / Has power, from out his loins, to sow his seed / In myriad hosts of countless progeny" (p. 366). Adam and Eve are distinguished from the angels by their Godlike souls and their capacity for infinite creativity. The angels' disquiet at the prospect of being upstaged explodes into rage when Gabriel, God's messenger, announces that henceforth the angels' role will be to assist human beings in their ascent above Heaven toward the divine radiance of God.

Lucifer enters at this point and protests to Gabriel that God is violating the angels' rights of primogeniture and the fixed, unchangeable hierarchy of the universe ("Our birthright goes to him, the favorite son, / Who violates our primogeniture" [p. 372]). Lucifer continues with a self-righteous diatribe that betrays his utter incomprehension of God's ways:

Why does His Grace degrade us thus so early?
What Angel has been tardy in His service?
How, too, can Deity be mix'd with man?
How could He pass His chosen Angels by
And pour His Essence in a human body,
How knit the finite with the Infinite,
The Highest with the lowest thing of all,
The great Creator with the creature made? (pp. 374–75)

Thus, Vondel portrays Lucifer and his followers as rebelling explicitly against the process of continuous creation—the process whereby the finite becomes infinite—in favor of a static, immoveable order. As Fred J. Nichols writes,

Lucifer would limit the complexity of God's cosmos to what
he can understand. God works in time, for one thing, and
Lucifer cannot understand this. He stands for a simplistic,
rationally ordered view of a static universe that never changes.
Opposed to this is a universe perhaps most effectively expressed as a symbolic dance, such as that . . . at the heart of
Adam in Ballingschap.[16]

God's creation, to the dismay of Lucifer and his followers, perfects itself
through time and change. In answering Lucifer's complaint that God has
violated his rights as firstborn, Gabriel explains that God can change His
laws when necessary to enhance His creation.

Lucifer, the "Stadholder," clings to the old order even if it means war,
while God unfolds His infinitely complex, changing, and self-perfecting
universe. It can hardly be an accident that these two figures mirrored the
social conflict in contemporary Dutch society between the Orange faction,
whose power was based on hereditary landed wealth and military might,
and the emergent class of entrepreneurs and improving farmers, who had
transformed seventeenth-century Holland into a leading center of capitalist development—a conflict whose theological expression centered on the
debate over the Calvinist doctrine of predestination. Although Vondel is
often portrayed as a traditionalist, it seems clear that his sympathies lay
not with the old *jonkheer* order but with God's latest creation: the new
class composed of diverse elements all contributing harmoniously to an
expanding market economy. The new order, characterized by increasing
complexity and power over nature and offering greater opportunities for
individual self-realization, is represented in *Adam in Ballingschap* by the
angelic dance that celebrates the nuptials of Adam and Eve. With its
multitude of individual voices and dancers weaving in and out and
resolving into an orderly, harmonious circle—mirroring the dance of the
starry heavens above—it contains diversity within harmony, order within
change. The fusion of body and spirit in newly created humankind may
also be regarded as symbolic of the dynamic conditions of early capitalist
development, in which ideas, mediated through technology, rapidly
transform both nature and human social relations, thus preparing the
ground for new ideas and technological innovations: a continuous interpenetration of spirit and matter.

After the war in Heaven, Lucifer vows revenge. Gabriel sadly tells
Michael of Lucifer's determination

to ruin Adam and his seed,
And, through transgression of God's primal law,

26

To lay on them such stain past remedy
That, poison'd with their sad posterity,
They never shall inherit that high throne
From which we have been cast. (p. 417)

Lucifer closes with Gabriel's account of the successful temptation and the despair of Adam and Eve. (In Vondel's version of the story, it is Belial who enters the serpent and does the tempting.) A final Chorus offers the hope that the Redeemer will bruise the head of the serpent and ransom fallen humanity and that the progeny of Adam and Eve will one day "ascend / The holy throne from which the Angels fell" (p. 421).

From Arthurian Legend to the One True History

In 1654, when *Lucifer* was first produced and banned, Milton was still immersed in the political life of his nation, if no longer in the day-to-day affairs of state. By the end of the decade he would begin work on his epic of the Fall, drawing on the same literary tradition as Vondel and Grotius, and like them, he would be influenced in his choice of material by the course of events in his native country.

By the late 1640s, Milton had abandoned his youthful plan to write a poem on a subject from early British history, notably the legendary King Arthur, and many commentators interpret his eventual adoption of the Fall theme as a sign of political as well as aesthetic development. The character of this political development is a matter of some debate. What I would like to suggest here is that Milton's decision not to write an "Arthuriad" was related to his realization, by the end of the 1640s, that much-needed political, economic, and religious reforms could not take place as long as the great Presbyterian nobles continued to dominate England's Parliament. Milton concluded that only a republican settlement, stripping the monarchy and aristocracy of their hereditary and prerogative power, could resolve the nation's political crisis.[17]

Milton's earlier plan to write an epic on Arthur had political implications of another sort. In writing such an epic, Milton would have been continuing Spenser's unfinished project in *The Faerie Queene* to fashion a virtuous, noble character with all of Arthur's legendary virtues. In early manhood Milton was strongly influenced by Spenser (his Elizabethan "original"), sharing his taste for chivalric literature and his esteem for England's constitutional monarchy. However, by the time Milton was ready to write his epic, much had changed, both in England's political landscape and in the associations of the Arthurian legend. Once the

27

property of the Tudors and their allies in the gentry and newer nobility—including the nationalistic, reform-minded Protestants of the Ralegh-Sidney-Spenser circle—the legend had been rehabilitated and reforged by the Stuarts to justify *their* claims to the throne. By the eve of the Civil War, it was firmly associated with royalist absolutism and the execrated alliance between priest and king.[18]

Meanwhile, Milton's research into ancient British history, undertaken in the late 1640s in preparation for writing *The History of Britain*, had convinced him that Arthur was "more renown'd in Songs and Romances, then in true stories"[19] and that the ancient Britons of history were quite different from the romanticized knights of Arthurian legend. Among their shortcomings as noted by Milton: the Britons had fallen into a state of anarchy after the departure of the Roman legions; they had begged their departed conquerors for military aid, vowing "perpetual subjection to *Rome* if the *Northern* foe were but repuls't";[20] they had later invited the barbarous Saxons to defend them against the Scots and Picts. In his *History of Britain* (in the unpublished introduction to Book III, the so-called Digression), Milton drew an extended parallel between the pusillanimous Britons of Arthur's time and Milton's own contemporaries in "the late civil broils" who were squandering their newly acquired liberty. Contemporary England, like ancient Britain, proved "fruitful enough of men stout and couragious in warr" but "naturallie not over fertil of men able to govern justlie & prudently in peace."[21]

In her study of Arthurian legend in the seventeenth century, Roberta Brinkley cites Milton's disillusionment with both the ancient Britons and his own people to explain why he ultimately abandoned the Arthur story and adopted his biblical theme:

> With the failure of the Commonwealth the likeness of his own age to the biblical story which he had studied for its dramatic qualities became so striking that it seemed as though the account of the fall of man embodied the joy, the despair, and the consoling hope of contemporary times. . . . When finally Milton turned to his ideal work, it was with the realization that *Paradise Lost*, not the legend of Arthur, was the true expression of his age and that it revealed the justification of "the ways of God to man" in the course of history as well as in the life of the individual.[22]

What I would like to emphasize here is that Milton's chief animus in the Digression, probably written in late 1647 or early 1648, was directed against the Long Parliament and the Westminster Assembly; the unflattering parallel with the ancient Britons was aimed specifically at the dominant Presbyterian faction of parliamentarians and their clerical allies, who at that moment were engaged in secret negotiations to bring back the king, establish their own form of state church, and abort the reform process under way.[23] Thus, the Digression reflected Milton's decisive break with Presbyterianism (religious and political) several years earlier. He now favored the outlook of Independency, which stressed the necessity of freeing the individual from both external and internal restraints—from privilege and tradition and from the passions.[24]

Milton accused the politicians and divines of pursuing private interests at the expense of the public good: of continuing unjust taxes and impositions, tolerating monopolies (some original members of the Long Parliament were beneficiaries), and attempting to impose their Presbyterian church on the whole nation through the power of the magistrate. Given Milton's views on the Presbyterian Parliament and the ancient Britons and his discovery of the lack of historicity of the Arthurian legend, we may infer that he was disillusioned with the political ideal that the legend had symbolized for reform-oriented Elizabethans: the ideal of benevolent rule by an enlightened monarchy and aristocracy. Thus it is not difficult to understand why Milton came to reject Arthurian legend as epic material. Masson sensed in the Digression Milton's growing conviction that a republican settlement was the only viable solution to the "civil broils" engulfing the nation;[25] that same conviction seems to have decided Milton against a chivalric theme with royalist and aristocratic overtones, a theme that would have been an anachronism in the new political situation. In the meantime, moreover, he had arrived at his radical redefinition of aristocracy (only adumbrated by Spenser) as consisting in merit and virtue, not in noble birth. Once ambitious to emulate "those lofty Fables and Romances" of the Middle Ages,[26] Milton now rejected the unchaste, adulterous love characteristic of feudal aristocratic society, in which marriage was largely a matter of property transfer, and the equally false ideal of the Christian knight-errant. The former he held inferior to the bourgeois wedded love celebrated in his divorce tracts (love as a union of congenial spirits), the latter, to the ideal of the selfless, warfaring Christian of *Areopagitica*.[27]

Whereas Milton's rejection of Arthurian legend as epic material reflected his break with the Presbyterians and his emerging republicanism, his choice of the Fall theme, as Brinkley suggests, suited both his growing awareness of the difficulties of creating and sustaining republican government and his hope that this could be accomplished. The period of Presbyterian reaction after the first Civil War gave Milton his first bitter taste of the problem of corruptibility in his nation's leaders and people, and he recorded his disillusionment not only in the Digression but in the sonnets of the period. Instead of repealing bad laws and constituting just ones, the parliamentary majority had voted for "new impositions, taxes, excises . . . not to reck'n the offices, gifts, and preferments bestow'd and shar'd among themselves." They had ruined the public credit by squandering and pocketing borrowed funds and had sequestered church wealth and "secretly contriv'd and fomented . . . troubles and combustions in the land" to justify their own authority.[28] Although some members of Parliament were "affected to the public good, & some indeed men of wisdome and integritie," the majority, Milton charged, had attained their positions of public trust through "wealth and ample possessions or bold and active ambition rather then merit"; and when their superficial ardor was spent, "straite every one betooke himself, setting the commonwealth behind and his private ends before, to doe as his owne profit or ambition led him."[29] Those of the mercantile class who had been called to serve their nation soon "fell to hucster the common-wealth."[30]

Milton's most vituperative language in the Digression was reserved for the Presbyterian divines—"godlie men, but executing thir places more like childern of the devil"—who, after decrying the "avarice & pluralities of bishops and prelates," were not ashamed to appropriate plural livings and lucrative university posts for themselves.[31] Milton attacked the divines for enlisting the power of the magistrate to compel conscience and, having established a spiritual tyranny through secular power, attempting to advance their own authority above the magistrate's. These charges are similar to others Milton made shortly thereafter in *The Tenure of Kings and Magistrates*, in his two defenses of the English Republic, and in his sonnet "On the New Forcers of Conscience under the Long Parliament." The last derided the hypocritical divines who had thrown off the prelates and renounced their offensive high church liturgy only to seize for themselves "the widow'd whore Plurality."[32]

Shepherds who feed their own bellies, flocks who are led astray, corruptors and the corruptible—these ubiquitous motifs in Milton's prose and poetry were also central to his republican political philosophy, which was based on his consciousness of the ever-present conflict in society between reason and passion, public good and private interests. The Interregnum years in England afforded unprecedented opportunities for advancing the cause of liberty, but as Milton recorded the observation in the Digression, "libertie hath a sharp and double edge fitt onelie to be handl'd by just and vertuous men, to bad and dissolute it becomes a mischief unwieldie in thir own hands."[33] The cases of the Roman Republic, ancient Britain, and now England illustrated the ease with which liberty could degenerate into license and bring about a new kind of slavery, bondage to selfish passions: "ffor stories teach us that libertie sought out of season in a corrupt and degenerate age brought Rome it self into further slaverie."[34] The tragedy of Adam and Eve, created free to stand or fall, is the same story writ large: Milton was already anticipating in the late 1640s the epic he would begin to write a decade later.

As social critic and poet, Milton, like his Dutch contemporaries, was responding to a cultural milieu shaped by early capitalist development, its positive and negative features. However, the English capitalism of Milton's time was on a grander scale than the Dutch. England began by emulating Dutch financial methods and agricultural techniques but soon surpassed its Dutch prototype. Whereas seventeenth-century Dutch capitalism revolved largely around the Amsterdam market (a financial center and entrepot for the sale and resale of produced goods) and was dominated by competing financial houses with little allegiance to the relatively weak Dutch state, English capitalism developed on a national scale, permeating not just trade but production as well. The next chapter explores the rise of early capitalism in England and the paradoxical nature of the individualism it engendered, considered as the setting of Milton's late prose works and his epic.

2

The Rise of Commercial Republicanism in England

> In the times of *Papistry* all in this *Island* were either *Souldiers* or
> *Scholars*. . . . And in those times *Gentlemen* thought it an honour
> to be carelesse, and to have *houses, furniture, diet, exercise,*
> *apparell*, &c. yea all things at home and abroad, *Souldier-like*:
> *Musick, Pictures, Perfumes, Sawces*, (unless good stomacks) were
> counted, perhaps unjustly, too effeminate. In *Queen Elizabeth's*
> dayes *Ingenuities, Curiosities* and *Good Husbandry* began to take
> place, and then *Salt Marshes* began to be fenced from the seas
> . . . very great therefore is the improvement [of] draining of
> lands, and our own negligence very great that they have been
> wast so long . . . for the improving of a Kingdome is better
> than the conquering of a new one.[1]

Thus, Sir Richard Weston, writing in
1645, summed up the remarkable transformation of England's economic
and social order during the century or so before 1640. In that year
Parliament presented the king with a list of grievances, the chief among
them directed at state-issued monopolies and other barriers to economic
growth. Weston, one of Samuel Hartlib's circle of agricultural improvers
and inventors, painted a vivid picture not only of the economic basis of
England's shift to a market-oriented, capitalist economy but of the
simultaneous social transformation: the rise of the gentry and its adoption
of the bourgeois values of ingenuity and enterprise. The new enthusiasm
for music, art, and luxuries that Weston noted was, to be sure, a sign of
new affluence and leisure; but it was also an outward manifestation of the

emergence of a new sense of individualism integral to an economic system that placed a premium on human initiative. This new valuation of the individual was evident in a broader cultivation of personal tastes, in an increased interest in and patronage of the arts, and in the fashion for realistic portrait painting.[2]

The most famous contemporary account of the rise of the entrepreneurial gentry in sixteenth-century England and its political consequences in the seventeenth century appears in James Harrington's *Oceana*, an idealized history of England and of the changing power relations therein among kings, nobility, and commons. Harrington documents the shift in the balance, or distribution, of landed property from the feudal aristocracy to the commons that began under Henry VII and continued at a faster pace under his successor. In stripping the nobility of its military retainers and confirming the property holdings of a large part of the yeomanry, Henry VII began the process of transforming dependent vassals into independent and prosperous landowners.[3] The dissolution of the monasteries by Henry VIII transferred an estimated one quarter of English real property to the Crown, which soon placed much of it up for sale, laying the basis for what one modern historian has called the "central fact about English social history between 1540 and 1640, and in consequence of English political history, . . . the growth in numbers and wealth of the landed classes and the professions."[4]

The economic consequences of this shift in the balance of property were enormous. The newly landed gentry, or at least its more successful members, responded to unprecedented price inflation and unprecedented opportunities for profit (the latter created by the expansion of the London and foreign markets) by reorienting themselves toward capitalist farming. Lesser landowners and yeomen farmers seem to have been the first to develop the qualities of industriousness and thrift necessary to succeed as capitalist farmers, but greater landowners soon followed suit.[5] As their leases came due, enterprising gentry and peers often took over the tilling of farms themselves or leased them out again on a short-term basis to anyone willing to pay the exorbitant rack rents. The 120 years before 1640 witnessed a doubling of the English population, and landowners responded by vastly expanding the area of land under cultivation: royal forests were opened up, commons and wastelands were enclosed and cultivated, and the Fens and other marsh lands were drained and planted. New capital-intensive agricultural techniques were harnessed, including better fertilization, scientific breeding, and innovative drainage and reclamation methods. Root crops were introduced. Meanwhile, the expansion of foreign trade between 1540 and 1640 and the growth of a domestic market for food and goods acted as spurs to the cloth trade, especially the lighter, New Draperies woolens, and to new extractive industries such as Newcastle coal mining. (Coal was becoming important not just for household fuel but for use in the iron, steel, and copper industries, among others.)

Early English capitalist development indirectly benefited from the political turmoil on the continent in the first half of the seventeenth century, as England became a haven for well-educated, utopian-minded refugees from the Thirty Years' War. Samuel Hartlib, Prussian by birth, was the most famous and influential of these émigrés. He settled in England in 1628 with vast schemes for educational reform, national economic planning, and state patronage of scientific research and development; he spent the next thirty years as an indefatigable promoter of "the best experiments of Industrie practised in Husbandrie and Manufactures; and other Inventions and Accomodations tending to the good of this Nation."[6] Called "the Great Intelligencer of Europe" (by John Winthrop, Jr., first governor of Connecticut), Hartlib maintained a network of scientific and political contacts that extended from Transylvania to the New England colonies. He regarded himself in rather more homespun terms as "a conduit-pipe . . . towards the Publick" for the mechanical inventions and improvement schemes of others.[7] Among those whose ideas he publicized were émigrés from Moravia, Poland, and the Palatinate who arrived in England in the 1620s and 1630s bringing advanced expertise in fen drainage and mining, novel ideas for the harnessing of steam power, and a millennial faith that the new Heaven and Earth were at hand. The principal lay patrons of Hartlib and his associates were the capitalist landowners who later became famous for their leadership of the parliamentary opposition to King Charles, among them John Pym, Oliver St. John, and members of the Rich and Greville families. During the 1650s, Lord Protector Cromwell himself was one of the most enthusiastic supporters of Hartlibean schemes for economic and social reform.[8]

As this coincidence between advanced economic ideas and opposition to the established political order suggests, the rapid transformation of England's economic and social system that began under the Tudors led to profound political consequences by the time of the Stuarts. Harrington believed that the prerequisite for stability in any state was agreement between the balance of property and the distribution of political power, and that the two must change in tandem to avoid major political upheavals. He attributed the seventeenth-century English Revolution to the Crown's failure to adjust political power to the marked shift in social and economic power of the preceding century, a theory that has been reformulated by generations of historians.[9]

The centuries since Weston and Harrington have seen a proliferation of theories to explain the English Revolution. Engels attempted to fit the events to the Marxist model of class struggle, transforming the Henrician nobility and gentry into "bourgeois landlords" and the Revolution into a "bourgeois upheaval" against a feudal monarchy, a decisive stage in the transfer of power from one social class to another. R. H. Tawney provided quantitative support for the thesis that a rising, economically progressive gentry formed the backbone of opposition to a Crown whose chief supporters were old-fashioned and feudal. However, Trevor-Roper subsequently pointed out that not all landowners had the enterprising sense to orient themselves toward market production. Some "declining gentry" ruined themselves by attempting to maintain sumptuous life-styles in a period of rapid inflation without raising rents, increasing agricultural profits, or obtaining lucrative court offices. Declining as well as rising gentry could be found on both sides of the Civil War. Finally, it has been argued that the Parliament of 1640 was composed largely of conservatives and reformers, men who hoped to restore England's immemorial mixed constitution but were pushed into revolution by the intransigence of the Crown; its members were "revolutionaries" only in the seventeenth-century sense that they wished to re-establish the traditional balance between king and Parliament, which was threatened by Charles's innovatory divine-right monarchy on the continental model.[10]

Despite such disputes, historians today are in general agreement about the importance of economic factors in the English Revolution, particularly the great shift in landed wealth and the growth of the capitalist market in the late sixteenth and early seventeenth centuries. As Lawrence Stone notes, "It can hardly be an accident that the first of the 'Great Revolutions' in the history of the West should have occurred in one of the two societies [the other being the United Provinces] in which proto-capitalism was most highly developed."[11] Thus, a nuanced appreciation of material factors, viewed as acting in conjunction with other causes, has superseded the theory of the Puritan Revolution (S. R. Gardiner), in which religious motivation was key; it has also superseded the Whig interpretation (Macaulay), which stressed Parliament's efforts to limit royal power through constitutional reform, and the orthodox Marxist interpretation in terms of class struggle.[12]

In fact, the threat to private property by arbitrary royal government was a leading factor in the unbridgeable antagonism that arose between Court and Country parties in 1640. In April of that year, the Short Parliament named "the propriety in our goods" as one of its three principal grievances, listing for discussion under that heading monopolies and other restraints on trade, Ship Money, restrictions on land use by royal forest commissions, and revived military dues.[13] Monopolies were a burden and source of frustration to producers and consumers alike. Ship Money, an occasional port-town tax that had been extended to inland towns in 1635 without parliamentary approval, was hated for its unconstitutional expansion as well as for the economic burden it imposed. The government's reassertion of royal forest rights, so that it could fine those who encroached, was a direct challenge to private landowners' efforts to consolidate large holdings for capital-intensive farming for both food and cloth production.

Whereas the seventeenth-century edifice of economic and social controls might have been justified initially to protect nascent industries, to smooth out market fluctuations, and to prevent hardships arising from enclosure and other economic dislocations, it hardly served such aims as an instrument of Stuart policy. The above-mentioned and other provocative features of state policy, such as forced loans, new import duties, and wardship and purveyance, were merely desperate attempts by the Crown to increase revenues. Monopolies were especially hated because their purchase required court influence: the Crown played favorites with rival economic interests, favoring entrenched monopolists such as the East India Company over "interlopers" in established markets and pioneers in new ones. Among those slighted were the companies involved in North American trade and colonization, many of which became thoroughly alienated from the Crown and joined the parliamentary opposition.[14]

In speaking for independent yeoman farmers, the aspiring squirarchy, and the segment of the peerage involved in North American ventures, the majority in Parliament in 1640 sought to bring the state and its economic policies into conformity with the realities of seventeenth-century capitalist development. This meant eliminating the disincentives to individual ingenuity and initiative in trade and industry (monopolies, favoritism in the award of patents, guild regulation) and the barriers to the private accumulation of wealth necessary for large-scale capitalist enterprise (burdensome taxes, feudal dues, restrictions on land use). In the political sphere, it meant establishing a republic. Francis Bacon had observed that whereas trading companies, which strictly regulated the conduct of traders, were appropriate to monarchy, free trade was appropriate to a republic. This sentiment was enshrined in the Act of 1649 declaring England a commonwealth and citing the economic and political benefits that the Dutch had won through the establishment of their republic at the end of the previous century.[15] Samuel Hartlib, in his dedication of a tract on husbandry to the Council of State in 1650, noted that the establishment of a commonwealth in England had given "to all men a more open door then ever heretofore, to enter upon a concurrence to serv the Publick, that thereby they might both preserv and encreas their own welfare."[16] Milton expressed the same commonplace at the close of *The Ready and Easy Way*. Countering those who clamored for a return of the Stuarts on the grounds that only monarchy could restore trade and economic prosperity, he pointed out that "trade flourishes nowhere more than in the free commonwealths of Italy, Germany, and the Low Countries."[17]

Commonwealths promoted trade because, as Milton observed earlier in the same pamphlet, they were the form of government most agreeable to "the civil rights and advancements of every person according to his merit."[18] Republican government promised civil and religious liberties, protection against capricious personal rule by a hereditary monarch, and greater representation of the interests of all citizens (though during the Interregnum different factions disagreed over which sections of society would be represented). Taken together, these were the political rights necessary to foster ingenuity and enterprise in individual citizens and, as Samuel Hartlib observed, to mobilize those talents for the public good.

Seventeenth-Century Individualism

Beginning with Engels and Weber, generations of sociologists have speculated on the connection between the rise of capitalism in England and the belief that all individuals possess equal moral value, a view commonly held to originate from such Protestant (and especially Puritan) concepts as the believer's direct relationship with God, the validity of independent Bible study, and the individual spiritual balance sheet. Today, New Historicist critics seek to re-evaluate seventeenth-century individualism and its relation to England's developing market economy. Jonathan Dollimore challenges the entire notion that individualism, in the modern sense of the word, emerged in the early seventeenth century. While granting that greater social and geographical mobility gave rise to heightened consciousness of the self and its possibilities, Dollimore dismisses arguments that attribute to the period the idea of the individual as an indivisible spiritual essence. That form of individualism, he holds, was a product of post-Enlightenment thought.

Building on the work of C. B. Macpherson, Dollimore sees Hobbes as a precursor of the materialist notion of the individual insofar as Hobbes rejected the notion of a rational human essence, replacing it with instincts or passions. Hobbes, in Dollimore's view, implicitly understood the individual as a socially determined being and recognized the autonomous, self-determining individual of the seventeenth century as a construct of emergent market society.[19] Dollimore admires Hobbes for substituting "the much more malleable notion of instinct or passion" for essence.[20] Yet it is precisely instincts that are fixed, while the concept of a rational soul allows for free choice and the alteration of behavior. As Milton put it, God trusts man "with the gift of reason to be his own chooser."[21]

In insisting on the complete social determination of human identity and denying the autonomy and natural rights of the individual, Dollimore and other New Historicists fail to appreciate the appearance in the seventeenth century of a sophisticated understanding of the dialectical relationship between individual and society. Here, the individual is understood not as being in conflict with society but as realizing his or her individuality through contributions to the social good. This positive, religiously derived form of individualism was further promoted by the market economy of early capitalist society, in which the greater division of labor encouraged the development of specialized individual talents, and the need for innovation was filled by contributions of unique individuals.

This new appreciation of the value of the individual is evident in the praise for enterprising farmers and inventors that one finds in the improvement tracts of the middle of the century. The highest praise is reserved for inventors, who are represented as embodying the most exalted of human qualities. In a pamphlet promoting a new "engine of motion" for raising agricultural productivity, one engineer-improver of the Hartlib circle identifies the capacity for invention as what is divine within man and places human inventiveness on a par with the work of the Creator. The pamphlet opens with a translation of a passage from Bacon's *Novum Organon*:

> The introduction of Noble Inventions seemeth to be the very chief of all humane actions, which former Ages sufficiently witnessed; in as much as they attributed Divine Honours to such Inventors, whereas they alotted only the Honour or Title of Heroes to the well-deserving in civil Affaires. . . . For the benefits of new Inventions may extend to all mankind universally; but the good of civil achievements can respect but some particular Cantons of men; these latter do not endure above a few ages, the former forever. . . . new Inventions are as it were new Creations and Imitations of Gods own works.[22]

Bacon then goes on to name printing, gunpowder, and the mariner's needle as inventions that "have changed the face and state of things throughout the whole world" and concludes, "no Empire, no Sect; nor no Constellation seemeth to have had a greater influence upon humane affairs then these Mechanical Inventions have had." The emphasis on the public and universal, and not merely private, benefits of invention is typical of such improvement tracts. The inventor is viewed as realizing his individual talents in the service of mankind: self-enhancement and the public good are complementary.

This is not to deny the rise in the same period of what C. B. Macpherson calls "possessive individualism," the view that individuals are the owners of their own capacities and therefore are "free" of all social connections and obligations. Macpherson, unlike his recent followers, acknowledges a continuum of "individualisms" that have characterized capitalist market society since its beginnings; he speaks, for example, of the "desirable values of individualism" in the Puritan and Lockean theories. He refrains from reducing seventeenth-century concepts of freedom, rights, obligation, and justice to the concept of possession that is characteristic of market society, while arguing that "they were powerfully shaped by it."[23]

The central difficulty of seventeenth-century individualism, as Macpherson sees it, was its *possessive* quality. This was

> found in its conception of the individual as essentially the proprietor of his own person or capacities, owing nothing to society for them. The individual was seen neither as a moral whole, nor as part of a larger social whole, but as an owner of himself. . . . The individual, it was thought, is free inasmuch as he is proprietor of his person and capacities. The human essence is freedom from dependence on the wills of others, and freedom is a function of possession. Society becomes a lot of free individuals related to each other as proprietors of their own capacities and of what they have acquired by their exercise. Society consists of relations of exchange between proprietors. Political society becomes a calculated device for the protection of this property and for the maintenance of an orderly relation of exchange.[24]

As the vocabulary of this passage suggests ("proprietor," "possession," "relations of exchange," "property"), Macpherson regards possessive individualism as a reflection of the development of market society in seventeenth-century England. In fact, he holds that the concept could have evolved only in a society based on alienable property and alienable labor, as distinct from a customary, or status, society, in which each class, person, or rank is confined to a traditional way of working, and in which neither property nor labor is the unconditional possession of any individual. Possessive individualism, in Macpherson's view, arises in market society with a Marxian inevitability as autonomous market forces drive the individual entrepreneur to maximize private gain and disregard any overarching communal or societal concerns. In this view, Hobbes's vision of self-created, atomistic, warring selves—his state of nature—is not really the *natural* condition of humanity but is a universalized projection of the competitive nature of the capitalist marketplace; it is a vision of the way human beings whose nature has been molded by civilized—that is, market—society would behave if all governmental constraints were removed.

For Macpherson, the chief danger in the possessive character of seventeenth-century individualism was the extent to which it divorced the individual from a sense of his debts and obligations to society. The problem of self-interest—that is, of selfish disregard for communal interests—is evident in the abuses of early capitalists eager to extract profits at any social price (by the privatization of commons and marsh lands, for example, with no provision for the people dependent on them) and in the failure of successive Interregnum parliaments to rectify these and other long-standing economic and social abuses. The problem of self-interest filled the pamphlet literature of the Revolution and preoccupied reformers such as Milton and members of the Hartlib circle.

Market society swept away traditional social and economic restraints and mobilized individual energies in political and economic life in a way not possible in customary society. But the process of liberalization widened the scope for corruption, affording self-serving mercantile interests and other factions more latitude to run roughshod over the general welfare. Thus, the central antithesis of classical political thought from Plato and Aristotle through Machiavelli—the conflict between private interests and the public good—took on redoubled meaning. Sir Thomas More's *Utopia*, written at the threshold of early English capitalist development, exposed, among other abuses of the emerging economic order, the impoverishment caused by the enclosure of common lands for sheep farming. Protesting the pervasive greed and economic injustice of the times, More declared that the sheep were eating up the men.

Harrington, writing more than a century later, had a greater appreciation for the beneficial aspects of England's capitalist revolution and for the positive notion of individualism that it promoted. Macpherson argues that Harrington had more insight into the new political economy than is recognized by those who represent him as a classical republican, analyzing society principally in terms of the traditional socioeconomic orders. Indeed, Harrington defended private accumulation, bourgeois industriousness, moneylending at interest, and even the racking of rents (when not excessive, as an incentive to productivity by the yeomanry). He favored income derived from trade, manufacture, and husbandry, where the incentive for intelligent effort is the desire for accumulation, over income derived from the ownership of land, where "the rents and profits of a man's land . . . com in naturally and easily"; and he pointed out that "the revenue of industry in a nation, at least in this, is three or fourfold greater than that of the mere rent."[25]

More important for the present discussion, Harrington presented a positive portrait of the enterprising bourgeois individual whose industry benefits society as a whole. Harrington's description of the reciprocal growth of cities and countryside in early capitalist England is a telling example of the contemporary consciousness of shared benefits in dynamic growth, benefits arising from the mutually enhancing efforts of individual producers linked together by the capitalist marketplace:

> [T]he more mouths there be in a city, the more meat of necessity must be vented by the country, and so there will be more corn, more cattel, and better markets; which breeding more laborers, more husbandmen, and richer farmers, bring the country so far from a commonwealth of cottagers, that . . . the husbandman, . . . his trade thus uninterrupted, in that his markets are certain, gos on with increase of children, of servants, of corn, and of cattel. . . . The country then growing more populous, and better stock'd with cattel, which also increases manure for the land, must proportionably increase in fruitfulness.[26]

Thanks to the interdependence resulting from the greater division of labor in a market economy, "fruitfulness" engenders "fruitfulness": the industriousness and profits of individuals in one part of the economy call forth the same in others, and erstwhile "cottagers" see the effects of their talents and industry vastly multiplied as they become integrated into the larger market.

This theme of the complementarity of private and public profits, or "fruits," was a commonplace in the improvement pamphlets of the Interregnum. One tract encouraging the English farmer to adopt Brabantine husbandry techniques in cultivating barren heath lands assures the farmer that, in doing so, his labor "redounds not only to his own particular profit, but also to the Publique benefit."[27] Another pamphlet recommending similar techniques argues as follows:

Besides the excessive profit you will reap by Sowing these
Commodities [flax, turnips, oats, and clover grass in rotation],
imagine what a pleasure it will bee to your Eies and Sent, to
see the Russet heath turn'd into greenest Gras . . . and what
Prais and Reputation you will gain by your Examples, first
introducing that into your Countrie, which being followed by
others, must needs redound to the general benefit of the
whole Common-wealth.[28]

Thus, side by side with possessive individualism arose a positive individualism, based on the potential in a market economy for enhanced relations between the individual and society.

One of the paradoxes of seventeenth-century market society was its liberation of the individual as both a socially beneficent and a selfish, antisocial force. For Milton and his Puritan contemporaries, the unique capacity of each individual to serve God ("that one Talent that it is death to hide") epitomized the positive form of individualism, which was clearly distinguished from the perverted form, the egoism of Milton's Devil. The goal of Milton and other seventeenth-century reformers was to create a society in which the scope for selfish satanic behavior would be restricted and individual talent and ingenuity, the divine sparks in man, would flourish. They seized the opportunity of the English Revolution to advance their program.

Founding Antilia in England

Throughout the Interregnum, Parliament was flooded by pamphlets advocating all varieties of economic and social reforms: proposals for improving husbandry, encouraging invention, training artisans, educating the poor, reforming pedagogy, fostering trade, even educating the Indians of New England. These proposals were justified not only as means of increasing public and private revenues but also as prerequisites for general moral reformation. For the reformers recognized that "whilst People are not free but straitened in Accommodations for Life, their Spirits will be dejected and servile":[29] they will think only about their immediate needs and will lack the economic independence necessary to become responsible, politically independent citizens of a free commonwealth.

A central figure in this reform activity was Milton's acquaintance Samuel Hartlib, a prolific writer on husbandry and education who also served as patron and publicist of others.[30] Hartlib had a keen political sense, and as the second session of the Long Parliament opened in

October 1641, he published the first of many proposals directed at the improving of farmers and entrepreneurs in the Commons: *A Description of the Famous Kingdom of Macaria* by the inventor Gabriel Plattes. The proposal took the form of a dialogue modeled on More's *Utopia* and Bacon's *New Atlantis*, advocating rational economic planning and state-sponsored scientific research.

While Milton's prose tracts were principally polemical and theoretical (concerned with discrediting the Commonwealth's detractors, arguing for the legitimacy of political revolutions, showing the benefits of church disestablishment, and so forth), the pamphlets of the Hartlib circle were practical how-to manuals. For both, however, the primary motivation was the same: the spiritual and moral reformation of England's population. And in one area in particular—education—their concerns and immediate agendas overlapped. To students of seventeenth-century literature, Hartlib is best known as the individual to whom Milton dedicated his 1644 tractate *Of Education*: "a person sent hither by some good providence from a far country to be the occasion and the incitement of great good to this island."[31]

Before his arrival in England, Hartlib was associated with various semi-underground learned societies of eastern Europe, including Antilia (after the Antilles), a little-known society whose members were diffused throughout the German-speaking areas of Europe. "Antilia" was the "*tessera* [watchword] of that society, used only by the members thereof," Hartlib wrote in a letter in 1659. The society "was interrupted and destroyed by the following Bohemian and German wars."[32] It is believed that Antilia was formed around 1625, lasting for about twenty years, and that the works of Johann Valentin Andreae, who drew on Tommaso Campanella's *Civitas Solis*, were its philosophical basis. The Antilians hoped to establish a colony secure from the Thirty Years' War where they could put into practice the principles of the rational state. Many of the members envisioned settling in some area bordering the Baltic under Swedish (and Protestant) domination; Hartlib apparently favored Virginia. Hartlib never reached Virginia but remained in England until his death shortly after the Restoration, hoping to establish "Antilia" there and use a reformed England as a base for disseminating advanced scientific and technological knowledge throughout Europe and the American colonies. When the Restoration arrived and Hartlib received no reply to his appeal to Parliament to resume payment of his state pension (granted during the Interregnum for his educational projects), his thoughts turned once again to Antilia: "Of the Antilian Society the smoke is over, but the fire is not altogether extinct," he wrote to a correspondent. "It may be it will flame in due time, though not in Europe."[33] Perhaps Hartlib was thinking again of establishing his ideal state in the American colonies. He became especially active in circulating his utopian proposals there in the waning years of the English Republic and after 1660. As things turned out, it was in New England that some of the proposals of the Hartlib circle found their best reception.[34]

The key to the new society that Hartlib and his associates envisioned was the creation of rational human beings through educational reform. In 1629, when he had barely arrived in England, Hartlib set up a short-lived academy in Chichester for the education of the sons of the local gentry. He subsequently introduced the works of Comenius to England and encouraged the Bohemian educational reformer to visit in person to present his radical pedagogical ideas (which Comenius did in 1641, at the invitation of Parliament). During the Interregnum Hartlib introduced before Parliament various proposals for the advancement of learning. An excerpt from *Some Proposals towards the Advancement of Learning* (an unpublished manuscript later found among Hartlib's papers) indicates the general drift of his criticisms of the existing educational system:

> Children are not taught to pronounce and write accurately
> their own language before learning other languages; are not
> taught to draw pictures while being taught to write; are not
> taught the rudiments of arithmetic at the same time as writ-
> ing; are not taught Holy Scripture. Youths are not exercised in
> reasoning about the truths of Natural and Moral Philosophy;
> so that they know not the grounds of natural justice and
> equity and the duties of morality in the law of nature, know
> nothing of the constitution and government of their own coun-
> try, are not taught the common forms of transaction between
> man and man, and do not learn the history of the world or of
> their own country; and spiritual truths are not taught at all.[35]

This criticism of the dry scholasticism of the prevailing system, with its emphasis on rote memorization at the expense of practical, moral, and humanistic studies, is reminiscent of Milton's *Of Education*. G. H. Turn-bull believes that this and other documents among Hartlib's papers were connected to a resolution of Parliament in 1641 to employ all the lands taken from the Deans and Chapters of Cathedrals to promote learning and piety throughout the nation. (Parliament's interest in educational reform was cut short by the Civil War, however, and it was not until 1653 that a committee from the House of Commons was appointed by the Barebones Parliament to consider plans for the advancement of learn-ing.)[36] Other documents among Hartlib's papers take up the subject of university education; one letter to Hartlib tells of its writer's petition urging Parliament to set aside a proportion of the revenue of all church lands for maintaining grammar school and university education, as the original donors of the lands intended.[37]

In 1646, with the Independents in the ascendancy in Parliament, Hartlib advanced a proposal to establish an Office of Address, which would coordinate international scientific correspondence and centralize information related to trade, manufacture, and employment. It was also to function as a labor exchange and promote technological innovation, thus incorporating the program for rational economic planning advanced in *Macaria*. The following year, a parliamentary committee dominated by Independents recommended that Hartlib be made Agent for Universal Learning and receive a state pension. However, because of the second Civil War and the unceasing conflicts that followed, the hope for greater parliamentary support of education faded steadily, and soon even Hartlib's pension fell into arrears.

The relation between Milton's ideas on education and Hartlib's Comenian reform movement is a matter of controversy. Ernest Sirluck maintains that, at least in 1644, Milton was antagonistic to the theories of Comenius and his English followers.[38] Both Milton and the Comenians emphasized the importance of religious and moral training. Both complained that prevailing curricula and modes of instruction, particularly in the languages, made studies overly prolix and difficult. However, as Sirluck points out, the methods of language teaching they proposed were completely different. The Comenians, out of a pragmatic bent, minimized the importance of literature. They recommended that students learn Latin by repeating simple synthetic sentences without first learning grammatical rules; excerpts from classical authors would be introduced later merely to reinforce learning. Milton, on the other hand, held that the fundamental rationale of teaching languages (as described in his *Of Education*) was to make available to students as quickly as possible the great literature of previous cultures. He proposed to dispense with the years of rote memorization of grammatical forms and postpone composition to a stage when students would have ideas worth expressing. His young scholars would study the rudiments of grammar and then promptly be immersed in short books by the best authors, so that "they might then forthwith proceed to learn the substance of good things, and arts in due order, which would bring the whole language quickly into their power."[39]

Sirluck is correct to stress Milton's disagreement with the Comenian view that the predominant aim of education is to impart "real" knowledge, "to prepare a Scholar to bee abel to do and execute the duties of a vocation and trade of living."[40] He is also correct in claiming that Milton hoped to revive the humanist curriculum of St. Paul's School in the days of John Colet and Erasmus: language and literature studies shorn of the Ciceronianism that stultified education in contemporary grammar schools. However, in making these points, Sirluck misses an important innovation in Milton's proposal.[41] He writes, for example, that while Milton's proposed readings in agriculture could have led to the improvement of tillage, Milton would have regarded such a result as a mere happy by-product of studies whose chief function was to provide a liberal education. But Milton simply spent too much time discussing scientific and engineering studies to support the view that he regarded them as mere adjuncts to a gentlemanly liberal education. He recommended readings in agriculture, physiology, arithmetic, geometry, astronomy, geography, trigonometry, fortification, architecture, engineering, and navigation, among other technical subjects. Furthermore, he proposed that young scholars learn about these subjects firsthand from architects, engineers, gardeners, anatomists, and other lecturers active in their fields. After several years of study, the students would be ready to ride out

> to all the quarters of the land: learning and observing all
> places of strength, all commodities of building and of soil, for
> towns and tillage, harbors and ports of trade. Sometimes
> taking sea as far as to our navy, to learn there also what they
> can in the practical knowledge of sailing and of sea fight.[42]

Milton's proposal, with its dual emphasis on classical literature and science, looked forward rather than back. It anticipated the dissenting academies of northern England that helped prepare the ground for the Industrial Revolution; the academy movement in the American colonies that put dual stress on classical and modern (scientific) knowledge; and the French polytechnical institutes established by Lazare Carnot and his associates in the late eighteenth century, which improved the economy, science, and general standard of living of France.

Admittedly, Milton is concerned in *Of Education* with the education of the leaders of society (he describes a private academy for the sons of the gentry). Yet in focusing on the education of leaders, he is addressing the broader issue of the virtue and health of the commonwealth as a whole. The reason for starting students with the classics—Socratic discourses, Plutarch, Greek epic poetry—is "to season them and win them early to the love of virtue and true labor, ere any flattering seducement or vain principle seize them wandering."[43] (Here, again, is the familiar Miltonic theme of reason versus passion.) Once the students have assimilated the classical examples of virtue and heroism, once they have developed a sense of moral purpose, they are ready to absorb, and put to good use, the most advanced ideas in history, science, and the arts.

If Milton's conception of the methods and aims of education was more classical and less pragmatic than that of the Comenian reformers, he nevertheless engaged in an ongoing dialogue with the Hartlib circle and evidently was influenced by their proposals for more widespread education. As early as the 1640s, he recommended that the sequestered lands and livings of the bishops be used for schools, libraries, and colleges for the training of artisans, a proposal advanced by Hartlib and his associates on many occasions.[44] In 1654, disillusioned with backsliding legislators, London "hucsters," and disaffected rural mobs, Milton wrote *A Second Defence of the English People,* urging Cromwell to make the education of the young "at public expense" a state priority, though he continued to believe that education was the right of a meritorious elite.[45]

Events of the next five years seem to have convinced Milton that more extensive educational and social reforms, reaching greater numbers of people and localities, were necessary. In *Considerations Touching the Likeliest Means to Remove Hirelings out of the Church* (1659), Milton expressed his immediate concern with the reform of the corrupt clergy and the training of future ministers. This focus on ministers, the shepherds and teachers of the populace, reflected his continuing preoccupation with the education and virtue of all of society. In fact, some commentators believe that the schools outlined in *The Likeliest Means* were intended not only for ministers of religion but for the broader population, and the ambiguity of the proposal may be symptomatic of Milton's evolving ideas on religion, education, and society. Milton's hope in 1659, on the eve of the Restoration, appears to have been for a society in which religious and theological training—and Christian virtue—would be widely diffused, with every educated person receiving ministerial training and becoming, in effect, a part-time minister.

In the same pamphlet, Milton turned his attention to the economic burden of tithes. This reflected the influence of economic and social reformers such as Moses Wall, together with Milton's own awareness of the danger posed to the republic by the abject economic condition of most of the population.[46] Later that year, in *Proposalls of Certaine Expedients,* Milton repeated his earlier plea for church disestablishment and the elimination of tithes. He also called for the reform of national laws to make possible the erection of "schooles where all arts & sciences may be taught in every citty & great towne, . . . whereby the land would become much more civilized"; and he briefly referred to the necessity to effect "the just division of wast Commons, whereby the nation would become much more industrious, rich & populous."[47] In *The Ready and Easy Way*, Milton envisioned an expanded network of lay schools and academies communicating knowledge to the most neglected areas of England, making "the whole nation more industrious, more ingenuous at home, more potent, more honorable abroad."[48]

It is also in *The Ready and Easy Way* that Milton presented his most explicit arguments on the relationship between education and republican government. He explained that broad-based education is possible only in a commonwealth—the form of government that "aims most to make the people flourishing, virtuous, noble, and high-spirited"[49]—and is essential there if people are to be fit to elect their governors and if governors are to be fit to rule. (This sentiment appeared later, with equal urgency, in the writings of John Adams and other American republicans.) Toward the end of the tract Milton wrote:

> To make the people fittest to choose, and the chosen fittest to govern, will be to mend our corrupt and faulty education, to teach the people faith, not without virtue, temperance, modesty, sobriety, parsimony, justice; not to admire wealth or honor; to hate turbulence and ambition; to place every one his private welfare and happiness in the public peace, liberty, and safety.[50]

A number of Milton's central themes are condensed here. The people's corruptibility is due to their inadequate or faulty education, and the right sort of education will "repair the ruins" of their former innocence. The overriding goal of education is to strengthen reason in the individual and minimize selfish passions, because the happiness of individuals and society depends on the subordination of private interests to the public good. Furthermore, the passage intimates, there is no conflict between private interests and the public good: private welfare and happiness are best realized when society as a whole flourishes. Finally, the success of republican government, in which the people freely choose their leaders and those leaders advance through merit, hinges on the virtue, the public spiritedness, of all concerned.

In emphasizing the key *political* role that education must play in safeguarding a republic, Milton anticipated those eighteenth- and nineteenth-century reformers who recognized that increasing popular participation in government made it imperative to extend to everyone the education that had previously been reserved for society's elite. If Milton's proposals for educational reform fell short of calling for universal public education of the sort that only came into being in nineteenth-century

America, they nevertheless represented an important step in that direction. In calling for state-supported education and for an extended, nationwide system of schools equipped to teach "all liberal arts and exercises,"[51] Milton's proposals were rivaled in their day only by the 1647 mandate of the Massachusetts General Court requiring all towns of a certain size to provide publicly funded education to the children of all citizens.

3

Paradise Lost and the
Fall of the English Republic

The world of *Paradise Lost* seems far
removed from the problems of early capitalist development in England
and from the political events of 1640–60. Yet from the days of its first
publication, astute readers of *Paradise Lost* have suspected that in writing
an epic based on the biblical Fall story, Milton did not abandon his
political vocation. Christopher Hill has called attention to the surmise of
one of Milton's contemporaries that "This very wily politician concealed
under this disguise exactly the sort of lament that his friends had
originally expected." In his own reading of the poem, Hill explores the
traces of Milton's lament for the fall of the republic he had served for two
decades.[1]

More recently, neo-Marxist and deconstructionist critics have plumbed
the text of *Paradise Lost* for contradictions, seeking evidence of simultaneous resistance to and complicity in the emergent capitalist order of
seventeenth-century England. It has been proposed, for example, that
the "poem's tortuous form"—the clash of classical device, religious
belief, and bourgeois realism—is really "an historically determined clash
of semiotic codes"; and that Milton's sonorous, sensuous language,
criticized by realist readers such as Leavis, is "a last-ditch resistance to
[bourgeois empiricism's] shackling of the sign."[2] At the same time,
Milton is accused of participating in a dubious bourgeois enterprise: the
claim of self-origination and self-authorship.

While new and provocative points have been raised in the effort to put
politics and history back into Milton's epic, there have been attendant

51

dangers. Those readers (such as Hill) who have looked for resemblances between personages and events in the epic and in history have flirted with reductionism and, occasionally, have succumbed to it; in pressing analogies too far they have over-particularized Milton's vision and lost sight of its transcendent significance.[3] On the other hand, the feminists, Marxists, and New Historicists who have searched Milton's corpus for historical and ideological discontinuities often have been motivated by political agenda of their own and have measured Milton against absolute standards, losing sight of the particular and the unique in his work.

Aided by Milton's republican prose tracts and the insights of his American political descendants, I propose to revisit the "politics of *Paradise Lost*" and to offer an alternative political reading of certain aspects of the epic. By attending to both the historically specific and the transcendent, I hope to cast light on inconsistencies and contradictions that have bedeviled recent political readings and to avoid the distortions that arise from judging Milton's project against anachronistic standards.

As other commentators have assumed, an important key to the epic's political subtext is to be found in the concerns of Milton's prose pamphlets, especially those written during the second decade of the revolution.[4] When Milton began to compose *Paradise Lost* in the closing years of the Protectorate, he was preoccupied with the moral flaws that had undermined England's experiment in republican government.[5] "Every man more attentive to his private interest than to that of the state," Milton had written of England's parliamentary leaders in 1654; later he applied the same condemnation to the "misguided and abused multitude," which in 1660 called for the return of the Stuart monarchy on the "groundless apprehension that nothing but kingship can restore trade." Similarly, he had accused Charles I of self-interest in 1649 and, on that basis, had justified the tyrant's overthrow.[6]

Contrary to the view of many commentators, who hold that England's failure at republican government left Milton disillusioned and inward-turning, he continued to turn out his highly polemical political tracts up to and following the return of Charles II.[7] At the same time, he picked up the outline of the major poem he had projected two decades earlier and sought to treat the recurring social problem of selfish private interests on a general level suitable to an immortal epic. Milton had admonished the English people at the close of *A Second Defence* that if their efforts to create and sustain new republican institutions were to fail, they would have no second chance at liberty, though other, "better men" might succeed thereafter. When failure seemed imminent in the early months of 1660, he had addressed himself to the virtuous remnant and to future generations, those "whom God may raise of these stones to become children of reviving liberty."[8] Now he embarked on what he had once described as the second function of a serious national poet: "to deplore the general relapses of Kingdoms and States from justice and Gods true worship."[9]

In writing *Paradise Lost,* Milton the epic poet may have sought to create something positive out of the wreckage of the fallen English Republic by inoculating subsequent generations against the errors of his contemporaries. If that was his intention, Milton's *"Paradise Lost* project" was eminently successful, for it helped American republicans rise above special interests and jointly dedicate themselves to higher tasks, succeeding where England's republicans had failed.

Milton's Devil and the Problem of Passion

No aspect of *Paradise Lost* has excited more controversy about its political significance than Milton's depiction of the Devil. To the Romantics, Satan was the archetypal rebel, the Promethean antagonist of all authoritarian political and social institutions, whose heroism the orthodox Milton could not consciously acknowledge. This view has been perpetuated most recently by Milton's interpreters on the Left. Jackie DiSalvo, for example, sees Satan as the quintessential republican hero and maintains that Milton "has poured into him the most passionate of his own sentiments in defense of that 'diabolical' party which for twenty years had been turning English society upside down."[10] In *Chariot of Wrath: The Message of John Milton to Democracy at War* (1942), G. Wilson Knight likewise treated Satan as the embodiment of antimonarchical rebellion. But Knight saw the epic as a whole as the expression of Milton's latent but unambiguous royalism and enlisted *Paradise Lost* to defend the British monarchy during World War II.[11]

The pursuit of the epic's political ramifications has inevitably inspired efforts to match Satan and other characters in the poem with historical personages. Satan's ranging up and down the fighting line during the war in Heaven, fortifying and encouraging his troops to attack, reminded Sir Walter Raleigh of accounts of Cromwell's selfless bravery and military prowess. More recent commentary has linked Cromwell with God, the New Model Army with Christ's Army of Saints, and Charles I with Satan. "The advantage of this point of view," writes Stevie Davies, "is that it allows coherency between the message of Milton's prose works and that of his poetry. His political writings may be brought to bear upon analysis of the poetry."[12]

The positing of a "counterrevolutionary Satan," however, shuts out other clear resonances of Milton's depiction of the Devil. Northrop Frye finds that the portrait of Satan is imbued with Milton's revulsion against the egocentrism of the revolutionaries of his day and their deceptive, romantic rhetoric.[13] Christopher Hill, though he follows the Romantics in viewing Satan as the locus of Milton's true radicalism, concurs that Milton embodied in his Devil some of the worst characteristics of the revolutionaries, for example, the avarice and ambition of the parliamentary generals and the license of the Ranters.[14] The view that Milton criticized the revolutionaries through Satan is consistent with the message of his republican prose tracts, where not only the Stuart monarchy but also the "inconsiderate multitude" and the supporters of the "good old Cause" (such as the Rump Parliament that Cromwell dissolved in 1653) come in for stinging criticism reminiscent of Milton's earlier attacks on Charles I and the Presbyterian timeservers.

Milton's Satan probably echoes all of the proposed "sources"—the tyrannical Stuart king, the vainglorious generals, the corrupt and deceitful parliamentarians, the licentious sectaries, and more. All typified for Milton the problem of private interests, which if unchecked might lead to tyranny, and in that respect there is nothing contradictory in the diverse political resonances that have been perceived in Satan. As a student of classical political theory, Milton recognized that tyranny existed in many forms and could afflict monarchy, aristocracy, or democracy: government by the one, the few, or the many.[15] Milton's understanding of tyranny's protean nature, which he so brilliantly embodied in his portrayal of Satan—imaged now as an oriental despot, now as a popular demagogue—is an important reason for the poem's congeniality to Americans of the late eighteenth century. These Americans shared Milton's classical republican outlook and, like Milton and his contemporaries, were engaged in a political struggle to replace government of men with government of laws, whose built-in checks and balances would guard against the overweening passions of individuals and social groups.

Having noted this historical-political context, we can better appreciate the significance of Satan's "magnificent" speeches in the early books of the epic. Are they really the distillation of Milton's revolutionary ardor unconsciously embodied in his Devil, as so many commentators have posited? At the first mention of Satan's revolt ("what time his Pride / Had cast him out from Heav'n"), we learn that his motives were envy, revenge, and ambition: the desire to set himself above his peers and put himself on equal footing with God (I, 36 ff.). However, Satan is no political innocent, and he attempts to disguise his self-serving motives in addressing his public. In his opening speech, addressed to Beelzebub as the two lie sprawled, temporarily stunned, on the burning lake, Satan insists that it was a "sense of injur'd merit" (I, 98) that led him to contend with the Mightiest and that motivated other rebellious spirits to join him.

Satan is revealed in this speech to be an abuser of rhetoric, a perverter of the Miltonic ideal of the orator-statesman who awakens right reason in his audience. Furthermore, Satan's complaint that his true merit has been overlooked by the reigning power in Heaven introduces the reader to what will be his rhetorical strategy throughout the early books: the conscious mimicking of republican principles. The concept of advancement according to merit was fundamental to the seventeenth-century idea of a commonwealth and to the social and political reform program of Milton and others. Within a few lines Satan sounds like the consummate republican orator:

> What though the field be lost?
> All is not lost; the unconquerable Will,
> And study of revenge, immortal hate,
> And courage never to submit or yield:
> And what is else not to be overcome?
> That Glory never shall his wrath or might
> Extort from me. To bow and sue for grace
> With suppliant knee, and deify his power
> Who from the terror of this Arm so late
> Doubted his Empire, that were low indeed,
> That were an ignominy and shame beneath
> This downfall. (I, 105 ff.)

Many readers of the epic (among them Thomas Jefferson) have admired these lines as an expression of the Devil's undaunted, heroic defiance. Indeed, Satan's repudiation of the bowing and suing required of the angels might easily have appeared in *The Ready and Easy Way*, where Milton deplores the servility of subjects in a monarchy—"the perpetual bowings and cringings of an abject people, on either side deifying and adoring him [the monarch] for nothing done that can deserve it."[16] Satan acts the part of the outraged republican in winning a faction of the angels over to his side in Heaven and, later, in establishing his hegemony over his generals during the council in Pandemonium. If he cuts an attractive figure here or elsewhere in the early books of the epic, it is due to the reflected glory of the republican—Miltonic—arguments that he mimics. Milton's political savvy and the epic's historical specificity are evident in Satan's stratagems; Milton recognized that, in an age of increasing democratization, tyranny would have to cloak its aims in a demagogic appeal to the overlooked merit and interests of the people.

55

Satan is a master at manipulating others, but he is not in control of himself; from the early moments of the poem he betrays his endless capacity for self-delusion. This raises another issue that would benefit from historical clarification: Satan's alleged freedom. Hill argues that the bourgeois in Milton was ambivalent toward Satan because "Satan has freedom without self-discipline, dynamic energy and driving individualism with no recognition of limits." Milton's view, Hill says, was that "Satan's kind of liberty, like the Ranters' kind, became license—and so ceased to be truly free."[17] But Milton's Satan is never free in the seventeenth-century sense of the term, despite his boasts to the contrary. His revolt spurred by envy and revenge, he is revealed to be more and more a slave of his own passions. After raising himself off the burning lake, Satan consoles himself in the manner of a stoical classical hero, claiming to be

> One who brings
> A mind not to be chang'd by Place or Time.
> The mind is its own place, and in itself
> Can make a Heav'n of Hell, a Hell of Heav'n.
> What matter where, if I be still the same,
> And what I should be, all but less than hee
> Whom Thunder hath made greater? Here at least
> We shall be free;
> . . . .
> Here we may reign secure, and in my choice
> To reign is worth ambition though in Hell:
> Better to reign in Hell, than serve in Heav'n. (I, 252 ff.)

The Romantic tradition regards these lines as the quintessential expression of individual freedom, the victory of interiority over external constraints. But Thomas Newton, the eighteenth-century editor of *Paradise Lost*, annotated "Better to reign in Hell" thus: "It was a memorable saying of Julius Caesar that he had rather be the first man in a country-village than the second at Rome."[18] Newton recognized Satan's boast as a sign of imperial pride and desire for glory—corrupting passions, from the classical republican point of view, capable of transforming a free commonwealth into a tyranny in which subjects were enslaved to the whims of their rulers, the rulers to their own passions.[19] It was the power of such passions—which had been the downfall of all previous empires—that the American founding fathers hoped to constrain when they drafted a federal constitution.

Milton's reader has to wait for Abdiel's rebuttal to Satan in Book VI—

"thyself not free"—to grasp fully the falsity of Satan's claims about heavenly servitude and his newfound freedom. However, Satan's boast here that he is self-created, independent, and free already rings false. For one thing, Satan's recent declaration of his intentions to Beelzebub shows him to be consumed by the desire for revenge: "To do aught good never will be our task, / But ever to do ill our sole delight, / As being the contrary to his high will / Whom we resist" (I, 159 ff.). Henceforth he and his rebellious crew will do whatever is contrary to God's will: "Evil be thou my Good," Satan declares, inverting the moral categories of Heaven (IV, 110). The rebels will not act autonomously; they will react and pervert. Their sole motivation will be revenge, the most reactive of passions.[20] To borrow the language of John Winthrop (Milton's contemporary and the first governor of Massachusetts), Satan's kind of liberty is the "liberty to do what he lists" the pursuit of which "makes men grow more evil, and in time worse than brute beasts."[21]

Satan's brief awareness that his independence of mind is an illusion comes, appropriately, during his first approach to Eden, a realm in which freedom does exist, not yet subverted by Satan, because Adam and Eve give free obedience to the higher law of Heaven. (True liberty, John Winthrop asserted, "is maintained and exercised in a way of subjection to authority; it is of the same kind of liberty wherewith Christ hath made us free.")[22] One of the recurrent themes of *Paradise Lost* (and a favorite of American patriots in the 1770s) is the maxim that it is the nature of evil to redound upon itself. Milton first uses the image of the cannon, the "devilish Engine" that recoils upon itself, to describe the mental torment and self-doubt of Satan as he approaches Eden in order to subvert God's new creation. Satan is no longer boasting as he

> Begins his dire attempt, which nigh the birth
> Now rolling, boils in his tumultuous breast,
> And like a devilish Engine back recoils
> Upon himself; horror and doubt distract
> His troubl'd thoughts, and from the bottom stir
> The Hell within him, for within him Hell
> He brings, and round about him, nor from Hell
> One step no more than from himself can fly
> By change of place. (IV, 15 ff.)

Satan's earlier philosophic reflection that "The mind is its own place" has come to pass with a vengeance, for only now does he understand the true meaning of his earlier statement: the hellish torment he experiences arises when the individual lives within the narrow compass of his own desires, cut off from the Good; he cannot escape Hell because he is himself Hell.[23] After a moment of doubt and self-pity, Satan emerges confirmed in his evil attempt: "So farewell Hope, and with Hope farewell Fear, / Farewell Remorse: all Good to me is lost; / Evil be thou my Good" (IV, 108 ff.). Henceforth, Satan is more and more consumed by the desire for revenge. He is the image not of freedom but of bondage.

It is clear from Milton's prose tracts that he regarded the condition of thralldom to self, summed up in his portrait of Satan, as a crucial political issue for the English Revolution and for republics throughout history. In *The History of Britain* Milton warned his contemporaries to avoid the errors of the ancient Romans and Britons, who through their licentiousness had fallen into a new kind of slavery. In *The Tenure of Kings and Magistrates* he followed Plato in attacking the subordination of reason to the "blind affections within," the slavery "within doors" that opens the way for tyranny in the state; and he followed Aristotle in declaring that "none can love freedom heartily but good men; the rest love not freedom but license, which never hath more scope or more indulgence than under tyrants."[24] When citizens are dominated by pride and base desires at home, Milton wrote in *A Second Defence*, "They can perhaps change their servitude; they cannot cast it off. This often happened even to the ancient Romans, once they had been corrupted and dissipated by luxury."[25]

The single-minded pursuit of self-interest is an insidious form of slavery, Milton argued, for when individuals allow their reason to become subservient to internal passions, such as political ambition and the desire for wealth and luxury, it is only a short path to their being subjected to the passions of others. The result is tyranny in the state. Milton adhered to classical political theory in believing that the invariant characteristic of tyranny was unchecked self-interest, that is, passion, and that this invariant afflicted both tyrants and their abject subjects. In the opening of *Tenure* he echoed Aristotle's insight that "neither do bad men hate tyrants," for the licentiousness of each, oppressor and oppressed, is complementary. All of these insights about political processes inform Milton's portrait of the Devil, whose condition suggests at once the passion-dominated subjects in a tyranny and their passionate overlords.

For Satan, despite his republican pretenses, is an archetypal tyrant, as Milton's imagery repeatedly makes clear. Enslaved to himself, Satan seeks to project his internal condition onto the whole of Creation. A number of different patterns of imagery accomplish this unmasking, the most conspicuous of which is the comparison of Satan to an oriental despot.[26] The first such comparison occurs in Book I as Satan and his leading general, Beelzebub, rally their armies for a new assault on Heaven

(I, 315 ff.). Lifting himself off the burning lake, Satan rouses his dazed, defeated troops, employing exactly the right mix of flattery ("Flow'r of Heav'n") and humiliation ("abject posture") to reawaken their fighting spirits. He plays on their shame at having been defeated by the tyrant of Heaven but at the same time gives them hope of ultimate success. Satan's performance is magnificent and has the desired effect: up they rise like the locusts responding to Moses' potent rod. (Once they have reassembled into formation, Satan continues his flattery, predicting that "these puissant Legions" shall reascend to Heaven "Self-rais'd, and repossess thir native seat" [I, 632 ff.].)

The imperial aspirations behind the studied rhetoric of Satan's address to his fallen legions, embellished with flattery and appeals to shared heroic principles, become clear when Satan is unmasked unambiguously as "thir great Sultan," their emperor. He waves his spear and all his fallen armies swoop down, filling the plain of Hell:

> A multitude, like which the populous North
> Pour'd never from her frozen loins, to pass
> *Rhene* or the *Danaw*, when her barbarous Sons
> Came like a Deluge on the South, and spread
> Beneath *Gibraltar* to the *Libian* sands. (I, 351 ff.)

This image of the Vandals and Goths that overran the Roman Empire is a fine one for conveying the vastness of the infernal armies, their irresistible force and barbaric nature, but it suggests something else as well. The fall of Rome—first to internal tyrants, then to foreign barbarians—appears throughout Milton's prose tracts as an example or "type" of the consequences of a people's corruption. The political lesson directed at Milton's English contemporaries was clear: the Romans fell to external lords because they had first fallen to luxury and corruption. Similarly, in Milton's account of cosmic history, the devils (who according to patristic tradition were later worshipped as the pagan gods) gain a foothold in the world only because men first forfeit their powers of reason and enslave themselves to base passions.

In fact, as the infernal powers are named and described in the catalogue of devils that follows, they are revealed to be, first of all, *corruptors*: "By falsities and lies the greatest part / Of Mankind they corrupted to forsake / God thir Creator" (I, 367 ff.). (Their chief, Satan, is "The Tempter ere th'Accuser of man-kind" [IV, 10]—an insight into devilry that John Adams borrowed from Milton to describe the modus operandi of the British satans of the 1770s.) King Solomon, because he erected a temple to

Mammon beside the temple of God, appears here as an example of the good man and leader who has been corrupted by sensuality and beguiled by fraud: he is "that uxorious King, whose heart though large / Beguil'd by fair Idolatresses, fell / To Idols foul" (I, 444 ff.). Milton shows that evil operates—and can only operate—by corrupting the moral condition of its victims.

In speaking to his legions, Satan consistently refers to God as a monarch or as a tyrant. This is good demagogic strategy. It also is a kind of unconscious projection, for Satan understands external reality only in terms of the categories of his own perverted consciousness (to himself enthralled, he is an embodiment of the doctrine of radical psychologism). The obedience that God asks must, Satan assumes, be the servility that he himself wishes to impose on others—the utter self-abnegation demanded by an Eastern potentate. In her study of the various patterns of kingship imagery in *Paradise Lost*, Stevie Davies notes that the image of the oriental despot is "the most chilling, corrupt, sensual and worldly that Milton could have invoked."[27] Throughout the Renaissance the Turkish sultans were regarded as the embodiment of cruelty, barbarity, and arbitrary rule—the scourge of Christendom. It was believed that God allowed the constant military threat they posed as punishment for Christian backsliding. As Secretary for Foreign Tongues during the Interregnum, Milton composed letters of state that indirectly involved him in Turkish affairs, and on one occasion he congratulated the Grand Duke of Russia for his war efforts against the Turkish sultan: it was acceptable policy, upheld by biblical precedent, to scourge the scourgers of Christendom.[28]

Also quite revealing is the way Milton's contemporary James Harrington treated "monarchy of the Turkish type" in *Oceana* and other works. For Harrington, the Turkish monarchy was the consummate type of "overbalanced," absolute monarchy—in contrast to the English monarchy, whose power was said to be limited, from time immemorial, by the power of the nobility and the Commons. Harrington describes the Turkish monarchy as the perfect model of "a monarchy of arms," in which the monarch "overbalances" the people in wealth acquired through military power. Thus, in describing Satan as a sultan, Milton has chosen the most suggestive contemporary referent for conveying the idea of absolute, forceful rule. Furthermore, according to Harrington, the Turkish form of monarchy had an inherent weakness: "that the *Janizarys* [the militia] have frequent interest and perpetual power to raise sedition, and to tear the magistrat, even the prince himself, in pieces"; hence it was "no perfect government."[29] Continual vigilance—and manipulation—were required of the prince to maintain his supremacy. As Book II of *Paradise Lost* reveals, Satan's overbalanced monarchy has the same weakness, and he, too, will employ forms of manipulation to keep his generals in line.

All of these images suggestive of the tyrannical state—the sultan, the emperor, the locusts that "o'er the Realm of impious *Pharaoh* hung" (I, 342), the multitude greater than the barbarian hordes that overran Rome, the corrupted Solomon—lead to the revelation of Satan as the great tyrant of the East at the opening of Book II:

> High on a Throne of Royal State, which far
> Outshone the wealth of *Ormus* and of *Ind*,
> Or where the gorgeous East with richest hand
> Show'rs on her Kings *Barbaric* Pearl and Gold,
> Satan exalted sat, by merit rais'd
> To that bad eminence. (II, 1 ff.)

This image was seized on and adapted by the American colonists in the 1770s to depict the succession of Western satraps who were sent to enforce Britain's imperial aspirations. An extraordinary feature of Milton's portrait of Satan sitting on his despotic throne is the clash between the trappings of despotism—the overbalance of riches and luxury, pearls and gold, the untold wealth of the East—and Satan's republican language, compressed in the uneasy coexistence of "exalted" and "by merit rais'd" in the same line. Davies points to a "striking congruity between the presentation of Satan and the rise of the early Caesars as recorded by Tacitus, Plutarch, Suetonius, and Herodian (authorities to whom Milton sarcastically refers his scholarly opponent, Salmasius, in *A Defence of the People of England*)." Satan resembles the Caesars in his opulence and military status; his snatching of power while pretending merely to receive it; his hiding of the illegality of his revolt under the cloak of *iustitia*; and his use of sham egalitarian rhetoric to mask his imperial aspirations, which in turn become a mask for his aspirations to divinity.[30] In his speech to the council, Satan claims his rule is based on justice, "ancient rights," and merit-based advancement:

> Mee though just right and the fixt Laws of Heav'n
> Did first create your Leader, next, free choice,
> With what besides, in Counsel or in Fight,
> Hath been achiev'd of merit. (II, 18 ff.)

An interesting kind of parody operates here; for Satan, now visible to all as the absolute tyrant that he is, describes himself in language that Milton might have used to praise the meritorious rule of a republican leader (or virtuous constitutional monarch). But before further examining the council scene and Satan's "republican" arguments therein, let us consider exactly what it is that is parodied here through Milton's Satan.

The Republic of Heaven

Readers who have expected to find Milton's republican politics mirrored in a literal fashion in *Paradise Lost* have been perplexed by the indisputable fact that Milton represents Heaven as a monarchy.[31] And the Heaven of *Paradise Lost* is not even a limited monarchy, like England's traditionally mixed state, in which the sovereign's will was checked by laws and other centers of power. The "Almighty Father" of Heaven sits "High Thron'd above all highth," surrounded by the angelic hierarchies upon whom His sight bestows "Beatitude past utterance" (III, 56ff.). The paternal imagery is like that used by Milton's royalist opponents, Claudius Salmasius and Peter DuMoulin, to deify the Stuart monarch and defend the principle of royal prerogative.

To a certain extent the representation of Heaven as an absolute though benevolent monarchy is a matter of literary decorum—of finding the most suitable imagery for conveying the ineffable, as Raphael must do in relating the war in Heaven and other heavenly matters to Adam and Eve, "By lik'ning spiritual to corporal forms, / As may express them best" (V, 573 f.). The undivided, unlimited sovereignty lodged in an absolute but virtuous monarch is the most appropriate, decorous referent for conveying to mortal sense the perfection and infinity of the One. Furthermore, Milton followed the prophets and apostles in regarding God as the one true king, condemning with Samuel the idolatry of the Israelites who wished to worship a human monarch and grant him honors fit only for God.[32] Milton opposed the continental style of absolute monarchy in the state precisely because of its divine pretensions, its aspirations to equal the one true king of Heaven. Thus, from this point of view as well, there is nothing inconsistent in Milton's representation of Heaven as an absolute monarchy.

All of this argues for the appropriateness of Milton's choice of image for conveying God's omnipotence. At the same time, a closer look at the matter reveals striking ways in which the government of Heaven, though formally an absolute monarchy, resembles nothing so much as a free commonwealth of precisely the sort that Milton praised in his prose tracts. The notion that the monarchy of Heaven is republican in character seems a contradiction in terms unless one recognizes that Milton and other seventeenth- and eighteenth-century republicans, who advocated the classical theory of mixed and balanced government, saw no inconsistency in a republic whose executive, or "monarchical," function was lodged in a king. John Adams, for example, looked admiringly to England's traditional ideal of government as a republic in which the king was the chief executive; to Adams, a republic meant government of laws not men, and there was nothing in theory to prevent a limited, or constitutional, monarchy from conforming to this model.

Milton adhered to the same view of the immemorial English Constitution in his antiepiscopal tracts, in which he argued that the secular ambitions of the clergy were upsetting the traditional balance in the commonwealth among king, nobles, and commons—the one, the few, and the many.[33] (After 1649 it would have been impossible, for tactical reasons, for Milton to uphold the executive role of the king in the commonwealth, but his continuing habit of distinguishing between limited monarchy and tyranny suggests that he continued to believe in the viability of a mixed state in which a king held a share of the power.) Thus, for seventeenth- and eighteenth-century readers of Milton's epic, the terms "monarchy" and "republic" were by no means mutually exclusive, as they have tended to be for subsequent audiences. For the former it would have been entirely conceivable for Milton's heavenly monarchy to be republican in spirit—and so it is.

The first thing to notice about the government of Heaven is that, although it is hierarchical, with the Almighty Father sitting at the highest pinnacle atop a well-defined order of angelic ranks, its hierarchy is based on merit: God and the Son represent unmatched virtue, and they rule, as in a republic, as the representatives of the rest.[34] Milton followed Augustine in believing that government originally came into being after the Fall because human beings were no longer fit to govern themselves.[35] However, he maintained that through education and the reform of institutions, mankind could be restored to the condition of right reason and self-government. A republic was, to Milton, a state in which citizens who have demonstrated the capacity for self-government rule as the people's representatives—Cromwell as Milton eulogized him in *A Second Defence* was such a citizen—while the rest of the population is raised to that pattern; and Milton extolled republican government as the form of government most agreeable to human improvement and advancement according to merit.

In Milton's Heaven, the Son demonstrates his unmatched virtue—and his right to his place atop the celestial hierarchy—by offering to atone "death for death," for man's sins: he alone demonstrates such selfless concern for futurity. The passage in which God expresses His joy at the

Son's willingness to sacrifice himself to save mankind is thoroughly imbued with the principle of merit:

> Because thou hast, though Thron'd in highest bliss
> Equal to God, and equally enjoying
> God-like fruition, quitted all to save
> A world from utter loss, and hast been found
> By Merit more than Birthright Son of God,
> Found worthiest to be so by being Good,
> Far more than Great or High; because in thee
> Love hath abounded more than Glory abounds,
> Therefore thy Humiliation shall exalt
> With thee thy Manhood also to this Throne;
> Here shalt thou sit incarnate, here shalt Reign
> Both God and Man, Son both of God and Man,
> Anointed universal King. (III, 305 ff.)

The Son's worth is due more to his individual merit than to his birthright and is proven through acts. Similarly, citizens in a Christian commonwealth must prove themselves by virtuous deeds (theologically speaking, both works and faith are required). Furthermore, the Son's worth is measured by his goodness and love, not by the greatness or glory of his deeds. The latter values are associated with the older heroic ethos that Milton eschews for his "higher Argument"; they are the values of the Homeric heroes and the chivalric knights of medieval and Renaissance epics, and of the absolutist state with its aristocratic ideology.[36] Goodness and love, on the other hand, are the qualities appropriate to both the Christian hero, who exemplifies charity, and the republican citizen, who acts for the public good: both hold universal law (in God's Creation or the commonwealth) above personal glory and advancement. Finally, the Son reigns as God and Man, spirit and flesh, just as in a republic the leader is one with the rest of the population but is also raised by merit above the people. The republican leader serves impartially the interests of society as a whole and is, in a Christian Commonwealth, an instrument of divine providence. (In keeping with such views, which were widespread in seventeenth- and eighteenth-century America, John Winthrop was regarded by many as a type of Nehemiah, the prophet of the return, as well as Jacob, Moses, Job, and other Old Testament prefigurations of Christ; and even in the 1770s John Adams was hailed as the Lycurgus-Moses-Nehemiah of New England.)

God proclaims that the Son's power and his place above all the other angels derives from his proven worth:

> all Power
> I give thee, reign for ever, and assume
> Thy Merits; under thee as Head Supreme
> Thrones, Princedoms, Powers, Dominions I reduce:
> All knees to thee shall bow, of them that bide
> In Heaven, or Earth, or under Earth in hell. (III, 317 ff.)

The honor and obedience shown to Christ by the other angels, the bowing and kneeling, is not like that exacted by force in a tyranny (or by Satan when he emerges in all his autocratic splendor). It flows from the sense of respect and awe with which the angels regard their meritorious king; it is freely given.

This voluntary service is the other central "republican" feature of the government of Heaven. God explains to the Son that He created all the ethereal powers and spirits free to stand or fall, for "Not free, what proof could they have giv'n sincere / Of true allegiance, constant Faith or Love . . . ?" (III, 103 ff.). Human beings, of course, He created in the same way—"Sufficient to have stood, though free to fall" (III, 99)—and for the same reason: that necessitated obedience is not genuine obedience. The voluntary nature of the covenant between God and humanity thus glorifies God; however, it also works to human advantage. As Milton explains in *Areopagitica*,

> Many there be that complain of divine providence for suf-
> fering Adam to transgress. Foolish tongues! when God gave
> him reason, he gave him freedom to choose, for reason is but
> choosing; he had been else a mere artificial Adam, such an
> Adam as he is in the motions.[37]

Without freedom Adam cannot stand on his own; he cannot exercise his reason—which exercise, for Milton, is identical with choosing, making discriminations, distinguishing good from evil. Consequently, without freedom, Adam cannot be truly virtuous.[38] Milton applies the same reasoning in his polemic against book licensing, concluding, not without irony, that the temptation of bad books offers citizens an opportunity to demonstrate their powers of discrimination and to choose freely the path of virtue; for to be able to "apprehend and consider vice with all her baits and seeming pleasures, and yet abstain, and yet distinguish, and yet prefer that which is truly better" is far preferable to "a fugitive and cloistered virtue."[39]

For Milton, the form of government that best promotes reason and intelligent choice is a free commonwealth, which "of all governments . . .

aims most to make the people flourishing, virtuous, noble, and high-spirited"; absolute monarchy, by contrast, demands "the perpetual bowings and cringings of an abject people."[40] The freedom afforded the citizen in a republic is not license to pursue selfish private interests, however; this the individual does only at the expense of the higher good embodied in the commonwealth. To prosper, the commonwealth requires a synergistic balance between freedom and necessity, between individual development and the overarching communal order. This balance is analogous to the unity of freedom and obedience that characterizes God's government in Heaven and on Earth. As Abdiel explains to Satan, the angels are exalted, not demeaned, by their freely given service to the One.[41]

In Book V of the epic, the angel Raphael descends to Eden to warn the first couple of the danger that Satan, now approaching their blissful bower, poses to their continued happiness. The hospitable pair offer some of their savory fruits to the visitor; Adam inquires whether earthly food agrees with Raphael's spiritual nature; and a discussion follows, comparing Heaven and Earth, "pure / Intelligential substances" and "Rational" (one of many memorable examples in the epic of theology made palatable). Raphael assures his human host that both angels and men contain spiritual and corporeal essences, though in differing degrees. Angels, too, are equipped with the lower faculties of sense, "whereby they hear, see, smell, touch, taste, / Tasting concoct, digest, assimilate, / And corporeal to incorporeal turn" (V, 411 ff.).

The whole of Creation is similarly composed of both gross and pure elements; all are in a continuous state of flux, whereby the grosser, corporeal elements are sublimed into purer, spiritual ones. The universe is monistic because all things proceed from God—"one first matter all"—and are part of a self-perfecting continuum "more refin'd, more spirituous, and pure, / As nearer to him plac't or nearer tending / Each in thir several active Spheres assign'd, / Till body up to spirit work, in bounds / Proportion'd to each kind" (V, 472 ff.). Raphael, seeking to relate spiritual realities to mortal sense, conveys to Adam the monistic character of Creation through the celebrated simile of the flowering plant:

> So from the root
> Springs lighter the green stalk, from thence the leaves
> More aery, last the bright consummate flow'r
> Spirits odorous breathes. (V, 479 ff.)

This description of the universe calls to mind Vondel's dynamic picture of the created world—a world that is beyond the comprehension of his aristocratic, Calvinist Satan, whose own character is unchanging and who regards nature and society as predetermined and forever fixed. It seems reasonable to assume that the monistic visions of Vondel and Milton reflected the conditions of their societies, in which, over the course of a lifetime, an individual might witness both rapid economic evolution—as spirit (human ingenuity) interacted with gross matter (unimproved nature)—and rapid social transformation, as customary society gave way to early market society.

Raphael's disquisition on God's unceasing creativity and on the voluntary nature of obedience in Heaven leads to a discussion of those angels who disobeyed and thence to an account of the war in Heaven, which in one respect is the clash between change and stasis. The angel recounts the events of the day when God "begot" His Son and appointed him head of the hierarchies of Heaven, uniting all "as one individual Soul / For ever happy" (V, 610 f.). Thus, the Son's exaltation, which Satan egocentrically interprets as demeaning to his own stature, is an expression of God's infinite creativity through change. Pertinent here is an observation by Joseph Summers about Milton's celebration of change and his rejection of Spenser's dream of a time when change will cease:

> Lacking Spenser's nostalgic attachment to a former world of supposedly fixed classes and cosmology . . . the Milton of *Paradise Lost* became the celebrator of change, of that movement which is eternal so long as God's creations continue to exist.[42]

Milton's non-Spenserian picture of the universe as illimitable and continuously changing is appropriate to his contrasting moral-political outlook: his rejection of hereditarily fixed classes and his faith in the possibility of individual and social improvement. The angels spend the rest of the day in song and dance around the holy hill, in "Mystical dance, which yonder starry Sphere / Of Planets and of fixt in all her Wheels / Resembles nearest, mazes intricate, / Eccentric, intervolv'd, yet regular / Then most, when most irregular they seem" (V, 620 ff.). Milton's rejection of stasis and limitation, as Summers points out, is evident in the unceasing motion and variety of the angelic dance that greets the exaltation of the Son. With its intricate mazes and harmonic motions, the dance also seems the perfect image for the republican government of Heaven, in which each angelic citizen freely serves the higher good in an individual manner.

But all are not pleased and all do not participate in the angelic dance. Satan, until that day "of the first, / If not the first Arch-Angel" in Heaven, is seized with envy against the Son for he "thought himself impair'd" (V, 659 ff.). He fails to understand that in appointing the Son the angels' head, God has united and raised them all. Satan puts into practice his deceptive arts: with "Ambiguous words and jealousies" and "lies," he lures the third part of Heaven's angelic host to his "Royal seat" in the north, dazzling from the false glow of diamonds and gold, where he affects equality with God (V, 703 ff.). Here, Milton demonstrates his understanding of politics, showing us that Satan's method in seducing others is to play upon their egocentric impulses: Satan incites the revolt in Heaven by stirring up the angels' resentment of Christ. Like Vondel's Devil, Satan maintains the pretense that he is God's loyal subject and that he has called this council to determine how best to receive and honor the Son. His rhetoric, however, is carefully calculated to awaken the angels' envy, so that they will instigate the revolt. To that end, Satan's speeches to the angels are couched in republican language:

> Another now hath to himself ingross't
> All Power, and us eclipst under the name
> Of King anointed, for whom all this haste
> Of midnight march, and hurried meeting here,
> This only to consult how we may best
> With what may be devis'd of honors new
> Receive him coming to receive from us
> Knee-tribute yet unpaid, prostration vile,
> Too much to one, but double how endur'd,
> To one and to his image now proclaim'd?
> But what if better counsels might erect
> Our minds and teach us to cast off this Yoke?
> Will ye submit your necks, and choose to bend
> The supple knee? (V, 775 ff.)

Such has always been the ruse of demagogues. Until now, Satan maintains, all angels were equally free in Heaven, despite the existence of orders and degrees; they were neither bound by any laws nor in need of them. However, God has overthrown their freedom and equality, imposing a "Monarchy over such as live by right / His equals, if in power and splendor less, / In freedom equal" (V, 795 ff.).

Satan's rhetoric has the intended effect; all seem to concur—except one. Abdiel, the sole faithful angel, steps forward to unmask Satan's sham republicanism and to explain God's intention "to exalt / Our happy state under one Head more near / United" (V, 829 ff.). Abdiel exposes Satan's hypocrisy and ingratitude in forgetting that he himself owes his being and his place in the celestial hierarchy to God's providence:

> All things, ev'n thee, and all the Spirits of Heav'n
> By him created in thir bright degrees,
> Crown'd them with Glory, and to thir Glory nam'd
> Thrones, Dominations, Princedoms, Virtues, Powers,
> Essential Powers, nor by his Reign obscur'd,
> But more illustrious made, since he the Head
> One of our number thus reduc't becomes,
> His Laws our Laws, all honor to him done
> Returns our own. (V, 837 ff.)

Or, to put the thought in the terms of Milton's republican prose tracts, virtuous leadership does not demean; it elevates. The republican leader instills in the people a sense of purpose higher than immediate self-interest and thereby raises them up and makes them truly human.

Satan, however, is deaf to such reasoning and replies that the angels owe nothing to God: "We know no time when we were not as now; / Knowing none before us, self-begot, self-rais'd / By our own quick'ning power" (V, 859 ff.). This is the crux of the matter. Satan's illusion that he is "self-begot" and "self-rais'd" is also his bondage, for his subjection to pride and other selfish passions cuts him off from the higher law of God's providence. Implicit in the conflict between Abdiel and Satan, then, are the competing notions of freedom and individualism characteristic of seventeenth-century political culture. Satan's illusion that he is self-created and therefore "free" to act as he pleases calls to mind Macpherson's "possessive individualism," the earlier-mentioned view that the individual is "essentially the proprietor of his own person or capacities, owing nothing to society for them."[43] To the possessive individualist, freedom is freedom *from* debts and obligations to society. Macpherson argues that the form of accumulation of wealth in market society inevitably drives individuals to this kind of antisocial view: it propels them in Hobbesian fashion to maximize their self-interest and disregard overarching societal concerns.

The brilliance of Milton's portrait of possessive individualism lies in its demonstration that the "free," self-consuming pursuit of private interest is in fact the strictest bondage. On the evidence of his depiction of Satan and his treatment elsewhere of the problem of self-interest, Milton seems to have understood how the social and economic forces of his day shaped individual behavior and concepts of freedom. Unlike recent adherents of historical determinism, however, he did not therefore deny the reality of human freedom but defined it in contradistinction to the illusory freedom of the possessive individualist. Speaking through Abdiel, Milton proposes a freedom that is realized through obedience to higher laws and an individualism realized through participation in a greater whole. On this view, all members of society have unique and complementary roles to play in a complex, differentiated, self-perfecting whole, as in the angelic dance in Heaven celebrating God's elevation of the Son.

The two conflicting notions of individual freedom enunciated by Abdiel and Satan had political correlates in another critical issue for seventeenth-century republican theory: the difference between lawful revolution and self-serving rebellion. In his political tracts Milton clearly distinguished between "the lawfulness of raising war against a tyrant in defense of religion or civil liberty" and "the lawlessness of rebellion" to achieve personal ends.[44] In *Paradise Lost* the former is suggested by God's infinite creativity, through which reality is continually transformed and perfected; the latter, by Satan's revolt, which is, in fact, a form of bondage.

The apostate angels, their reasoning powers stymied by blind passions, do not recognize the truth that Abdiel speaks. They ridicule him and he returns to the faithful legions, who welcome him with joyful acclamation. He is loved all the more because he stood when others fell. As God observes,

> Servant of God, well done, well hast thou fought
> The better fight, who single hast maintain'd
> Against revolted multitudes the Cause
> Of Truth, in word mightier than they in Arms;
> And for the testimony of Truth hast borne
> Universal reproach, far worse to bear
> Than violence: for this was all thy care
> To stand approv'd in sight of God, though Worlds
> Judg'd thee perverse. (VI, 29 ff.)

Beyond its central narrative and thematic importance, the Abdiel episode has rich political and historical resonances. A closer examination of the passage quoted above is suggestive of the way such resonances work here and throughout the epic. The passage reveals, first of all, Milton's keen insight into political processes. Abdiel has fought and won the better and harder fight in standing up to the pressure of his peers. The difficulty of choosing between principled behavior and conformity to majority opinion clearly exists in all times and places and applies to many domains of life; however, it was an especially pertinent issue for the representative republics of the seventeenth and eighteenth centuries because of their expanded opportunities for political participation. (During the eleven years of Charles I's personal rule, by contrast, the problem of peer pressure was hardly an issue for England's legislators and electorate.) Thus, the angel

Abdiel reflects, on the most general level, one of the key political problems of Milton's age.

One suspects that Milton's understanding of the centrality of this issue
for emerging republics arose from his own experience as a participant and
observer in a major period of political transformation. The whole Abdiel
episode, particularly God's speech praising Abdiel's kind of bravery,
abounds with autobiographical resonances and is an instructive example
of the transmutation of a poet's experience into art. Abdiel is mightier in
words than the rebel angels are in arms. Similarly, in the autobiographical
passages of the prose tracts, Milton distinguishes between the two kinds
of weapons, arms and reason, insisting that proficiency in the latter, which
is his special skill, is not to be belittled. In *A Second Defence*, for example,
he writes:

> I exchanged the toils of war, in which any stout trooper might
> outdo me, for those labors which I better understood, that
> with such wisdom as I owned I might add as much weight as
> possible to the counsels of my country and to this excellent
> cause, using not my lower but my higher and stronger powers.
> And so I concluded that if God wished those men to achieve
> such noble deeds, He also wished that there be other men by
> whom these deeds, once done, might be worthily praised and
> extolled, and that truth defended by arms be also defended
> by reason—the only defence truly appropriate to man.[45]

Milton is also a genuine combatant, as important to the cause of liberty
as the "stout trooper," and his weapon is the only truly human one:
reason. Hill remarks that "the Abdiel incident gets us close to the political
theme, and to Milton's own personal feelings. . . . What the poet has to
say about Abdiel could have been said of Milton's own courage in
publishing the second edition of *The Ready and Easy Way* just before the
return of Charles II."[46] It could also be said of many points in Milton's
career. Milton informs us again and again of his feeling that he is
defending truth against the incomprehending and faithless multitudes
and (like Abdiel) earning only reproach and scorn. This was his situation
in defending the English Republic against its formidable royalist opponent Salmasius: "When he with insults was attacking us and our battle
array, and our leaders looked first of all to me, I met him in single combat
and plunged into his reviling throat this pen, the weapon of his own
choice."[47]

The Abdiel episode is also especially pertinent to Milton's situation in
the late 1640s, when he was pronounced a libertine ("Judg'd . . .

perverse") by the Presbyterians for the views expressed in his divorce tracts. But although the episode brings us close to Milton's own feelings and individual situation, Abdiel's lonely defense of truth against the pressure to conform also suggests the condition of every citizen in a republic. Indeed, it suggests the battle for truth in any time and place. The Abdiel episode, like the entirety of the epic, operates on all of these levels at once, each possible resonance enriching the others.

The War in Heaven: Backsliders and the Army of Saints

Milton's representation of the war in Heaven is similarly rich in autobiographical and historical resonances, as Robert Fallon shows in his detailed reading of that episode. Most pertinent here is Fallon's observation that, if the war in Heaven resembles anything in Milton's experience, it is "the cross fire of debate over grievances, provocations, and political theory that precedes the action" of the civil wars. That Satan's justification for his rebellion sounds a great deal like Milton's vindication of the English Republic is not as puzzling as it seems, Fallon explains: it is the politician's art to present himself in the best light, as Satan does in representing himself as the foe of slavery and oppression.[48]

Another possible inspiration for the "Intestine War in Heav'n," I would like to suggest, was the struggle between Presbyterians and Independents surrounding the second Civil War—a turning point in the revolution to which Milton returns continually in his prose tracts and in the topical poems of the late 1640s. During the first day of the battle, Abdiel is afforded the opportunity to meet Satan in combat, to put might behind his courageous words. Abdiel no longer stands alone, and he takes great pleasure in vindicating himself and his cause before Satan:

> but thou seest
> All are not of thy Train; there be who Faith
> Prefer, and Piety to God, though then
> To thee not visible, when I alone
> Seem'd in thy World erroneous to dissent
> From all: my Sect thou seest, now learn too late
> How few sometimes may know, when thousands err. (VI, 142 ff.)

This is the voice of the righteous, who on Judgment Day will be rewarded for maintaining their faith in a world polluted by sin. We know from personal testimonials, sermons, and other contemporary documents that the English republicans were often sustained by the same kind of conviction that they, a minority, were fighting God's cause against the ministers of Satan.

In these lines we also may detect Milton's personal voice, expressing the isolation he felt in the late 1640s, "blind among enemies" and a target of Presbyterian rebuke. We may sense as well his feeling of vindication in the military and parliamentary victories of the Independents, which led in 1649 to the establishment of a free commonwealth. In two sonnets attributed to 1646, "A book was writ of late" and "I did prompt the age," Milton replied to the vituperative attack on his recently published divorce tracts.[49] This rebuttal was double-edged in that it was directed against both his conservative Presbyterian opponents, who rejected the bold defense of individual liberty implied in his arguments for divorce on the grounds of incompatibility, and the radical sectaries, who had become his unsolicited allies in the mistaken belief that he advocated divorce at pleasure.

Milton's personal experience in this period was not unique, of course. It was shared by all those republicans who discovered that the conclusion of the first Civil War in late 1646 was just the beginning of a protracted political struggle to solidify and extend the gains of the revolution. In that year a split emerged in the forces opposing the king. Since the abolition of the episcopacy in 1643, the Westminster Assembly of Divines had been deliberating on matters of church government and liturgy, with the Presbyterian majority favoring the establishment of a new tithe-supported state church based on Presbyterian principles. Milton denounced the Presbyterian ministers—"*New Presbyter* is but *Old Priest* writ Large"—for proving to be as covetous as the bishops they had secretly envied, and for attempting to seize the bishops' pluralities for themselves and ride the English "with a classic Hierarchy."[50] (The proposed new state church would have established the kind of unnatural hierarchy that Milton could not abide.)

In early 1647, after the king was handed over to Parliament by his Scottish captors, the Presbyterian faction in Parliament proposed to disband the politically radicalized Army and enter into conciliatory negotiations with Charles I. An emerging Independent party, whose assorted membership ranged from Puritan generals and gentlemen such as Cromwell to Levellers and religious radicals, opposed the Presbyterians. The Independents advocated broad toleration, church disestablishment, and—when the king's escape later that year precipitated the second Civil War—an aggressive war-winning strategy against Charles and his supporters. Ultimately the Independents prevailed: Parliament was purged by the Army of its recalcitrant Presbyterians, the king was tried and executed, and the House of Lords was abolished. By the end of February

1649, England was, in outward form at least, ready to become the free commonwealth Milton and others had hoped for. Thus, whereas Milton may have appeared to his antagonists in 1646 to be one of a small minority, by early 1649 this sect of the righteous had been vindicated against royalists and Presbyterian backsliders alike and was holding the reins of government.

Milton returned repeatedly to this juncture in the revolution in his prose tracts, reserving some of his most biting polemics for the Presbyterian party, which had, in his view, betrayed the revolution—God's cause—for personal glory and gain. "[T]here is no abyss so deep that it cannot be filled more quickly than the avarice of the clergy," Milton wrote concerning the ministers' hopes of inheriting the livings of the bishops. "Sheep, rather than shepherds, should they be called; they are fed more than they feed. With them, virtually everything is fat, not excepting their wits, for they are stuffed with tithes, a custom rejected by all other churches."[51] In their shameless greed, the Presbyterian ministers exemplified for Milton the root of all evil: rampant private interests, lack of faith in God, and because they pretended to be God's ministers, perversion of the good. Milton complained that the Presbyterians had vociferously defended the war against the king and bishops while it was in their interest to do so, but that once the revolutionary tide turned against them, they protested the king's execution and incited riots from their pulpits against the new government. By contrast, those citizens who remained faithful to the revolution

> with pre-eminent virtue and a nobility and steadfastness surpassing all the glory of their ancestors, invoked the Lord, followed his manifest guidance, and after accomplishing the most heroic and exemplary achievements since the foundation of the world, freed the state from grievous tyranny and the church from unworthy servitude.[52]

In this passage, Milton anticipated his later poetic rendering of Christ's Army of Saints.

Now, if we attend carefully to Milton's war in Heaven, we can hear distinct echoes of the struggle between the Presbyterian timeservers—the Westminster Synod and their parliamentary allies—and the committed republicans of the Commonwealth. Challenged by Abdiel, Satan alleges the constitutional legality of the behavior of the rebels, who have

> in Synod met
> Thir Deities to assert, who while they feel

Vigor Divine within them, can allow
Omnipotence to none. (VI, 156 ff.)

In truth, Satan and his followers are hypocrites and rationalizers: they
have deserted the true cause out of envy and faction but, like the covetous
Presbyterian ministers, attempt to disguise their motives by professing to
uphold the ancient constitution of Heaven. Satan's rationalization—"At
first I thought that Liberty and Heav'n / To heav'nly Souls had been all
one; but now / I see that most through sloth had rather serve" (VI, 164
ff.)—is reminiscent of the hypocritical protestations of the Presbyterians
and royalists who claimed in 1649 that the new republic was an extraconstitutional tyranny demanding a new form of servitude. Abdiel's final
words to Satan, before he lets loose the powerful stroke that begins the
battle, bring to completion the thematic motif of servitude that has been
unfolding throughout the first half of the epic:

Unjustly thou deprav'st it with the name
Of *Servitude* to serve whom God ordains,
Or Nature; God and Nature bid the same,
When he who rules is worthiest, and excels
Them whom he governs. This is servitude,
To serve th' unwise, or him who hath rebell'd
Against his worthier, as thine now serve thee,
Thyself not free, but to thyself enthrall'd;
Yet lewdly dar'st our minist'ring upbraid. (VI, 174 ff.)

Satan's rebellion is revealed as a form of bondage to the passions, whereas
obedience to the Deity, to the principle of universal law, is the highest
form of freedom; it liberates the individual from the fixed laws of his
nature and unites him with the Infinite. The Gospel's "and the truth
shall make you free" has a political parallel in the notion of leadership in
a representative republic: leadership by the virtuous, those who have
demonstrated the capacity for self-government and are truly the "worthiest," frees all citizens to fulfill their human potential by releasing them
from thralldom to selfish interests.

This was clearly Milton's hope when the English Commonwealth was
established in 1649, after the second Civil War and the political defeat of
the Presbyterians. However, the next decade would witness the repeated
re-enactment, in different forms and with different actors, of the struggle
between corruption and virtue, private interests and public good. Milton
illustrated this continuing struggle in his depiction of the opposing armies
that meet on the battlefield of Heaven. The rebel angels come into battle

proud and disdainful, aspiring to personal glory like the classical heroes of old. The faithful, not seeking personal fame, fight in "Cubic Phalanx," a military formation that enables them to band together and maneuver in a highly coordinated way to achieve their shared goal. The very strategy and posture of Christ's Army of Saints reflect the fusion of individual identity with higher purpose that distinguishes the saints from Satan's glory-seeking devils.

The Council in Pandemonium

Following their defeat on the third day of the battle, the rebel angels, hurled out of Heaven by the Almighty, fall nine days to the burning lake. There, in the farthest reaches of Chaos, the place that will become known as Hell, the devils erect their capital, Pandemonium. The infernal oligarchy convenes in council to debate "democratically" the question put before them by Satan, their *primus inter pares*: whether to employ open force or guile in resuming their war on Heaven. American republicans in the 1770s and again in the 1790s drew on this scene to portray the infernal art of political demagoguery as practiced by populists and oligarchs alike. Milton was familiar with the problem of demagoguery—of the streets and of the council chamber—both from his study of classical political theory and from experience. As a defender of the republic he decried the popular mobs instigated by royalists and Presbyterians and denounced the timeservers in Parliament who won allies by professing concern for the public welfare.[53] The council scene of Book II, which stimulated American polemicists to imitation, clearly owes its depth of insight to Milton's firsthand political experience during the Interregnum.

Various critics have likened the infernal council to a representative assembly and have pointed to possible contemporary sources for the scene. In 1900 Walter Raleigh speculated that Milton's memories of the Long Parliament provide him with "examples of the types he has embodied under the names of Belial, Mammon, Moloch, and Beelzebub." As Raleigh pointed out, the philosophers of Hell, who retire to a hill and reason "Of Providence, Foreknowledge, Will, and Fate" (II, 559), are engaged in the precise employments of the Westminster Assembly of Divines.[54] F. R. Leavis believed that the devils' speeches embodied "a kind of ideal parliamentary oratory," a type of rhetorical argument and exposition in which Milton was particularly skilled.[55] Milton's drawing of the council scene was undoubtedly guided by his firsthand knowledge of parliamentary oratory and its abuse. As each devil rises self-assuredly to present his viewpoint on the best course for the future, one thinks of the

76

Presbyterian divines and corrupt legislators of the Long and Rump parliaments and successive assemblies, whom Milton denounced repeatedly in his prose tracts for invoking the public good while assiduously pursuing private interests.

Joseph Summers offers a further and important observation on the political dynamics of the council scene:

> Book II begins with the enthronement of Satan. Although the populace is under control [the military rank and file have popularly acclaimed him], Satan must make sure of the nobility (from which challenges to sovereignty so often come), and he must give the appearance of consulting them in Council.[56]

Satan, it will be remembered, has just been enthroned in the manner of an Eastern tyrant, the brilliance of his royal seat outshining all the wealth of Persia and India; we are reminded of Harrington's observation about the inherent flaw in Turkish-style monarchy (and, by extension, in all oriental-style despotisms): the continual threat of sedition by the generals of the Janizaries, the sultan's militia. This is precisely the danger that the Prince of Hell now anticipates; as Summers suggests, Satan's overriding concern in this scene is to secure control over his fellow oligarchs. To do so he uses the tried-and-tested method of the demagogue, pretending to give all an equal say in the decision at hand. He professes concern for the welfare of all while manipulating public opinion along the lines he desires. Maintaining that he is their king by "just right," by the "free choice" of his followers, and by his superior "merit" in debate and war, Satan invokes republican arguments as well as "the fixt Laws of Heav'n" as he opens the great Consultation (II, 18 ff.).

Clearly, I am using the term "demagogue" here in an extended sense. This is a council of aristocrats, not of the people; however, the appeal to emotion, above all to the sense of injured merit, based on alleged egalitarian principles, is a demagogic technique. Employing that technique, Satan solidifies his position by the close of the scene, when the debating egalitarians are suddenly revealed as a council of "grand infernal Peers," aristocratic lords, who have been reduced to a state of utter subservience to "Hell's dread Emperor." Satan's pseudodemocratic climb is complete, and the situation of the council is parallel to that of the Roman Senate after the rise of the Caesars: it has become a powerless shell of its former self.[57]

A close examination of the "democratic" debate that consolidates Satan's power reveals his skill in manipulating the various personalities of his oligarchs. Each of the devils who rises to speak has his own idea about what course of action should be taken, determined by his idiosyncratic flaw; it is tempting to think of the council as democracy run amuck. Moloch, the furious king of the battle in Heaven, declares for open war, unmindful that the rebels will only be setting themselves up for an even greater defeat. (Addison admired the consistency with which Milton drew Moloch's character: in keeping with his description in Book I, "All his sentiments are rash, audacious, and desparate.")[58] Of all of the devils, Moloch most resembles a stoical military leader of classical times. Subjection is abhorrent to him. The only thinkable course is action: they must disturb the enemy "with perpetual inroads to Alarm," even if only to secure revenge and not victory. Moloch's sense of identity and his stature among the devils is based on his military prowess; open war, therefore, is in his self-interest. Like all of the devils—and like the Greek chieftains of the early council in the *Iliad* (clearly an inspiration for this scene)— Moloch is a skillful orator. He attempts to persuade the others of his point of view, to win them over to the course most in his self-interest, by reminding them of the ignominy of their situation: they are prisoners in a "dark opprobrious Den of shame," "Vassals" of God's anger, and so forth.

Belial, who speaks next, is a different sort of orator:

> A fairer person lost not Heav'n; he seem'd
> For dignity compos'd and high exploit:
> But all was false and hollow; though his Tongue
> Dropt Manna, and could make the worse appear
> The better reason, to perplex and dash
> Maturest Counsels. (II, 110 ff.)

Bentley annotates the phrase "and could make the worse appear / The better reason" thus: "Word for word, from the known profession of the Sophists."[59] Belial truly is a Sophist in that he abuses—perverts—rhetoric, the art of speaking effectively, to further his personal ends. All of the devils, and especially Satan in Book IX, are Sophists in this sense: they are tempters who seek to corrupt their victims, as Belial does, with "words cloth'd in reason's garb." Belial's reasoning powers and ability to manipulate others through language are more subtle than Moloch's. He points out that the course recommended by the unthinking Moloch might bring God's never-ending rage upon them; it would be wiser, therefore, to endure their fate in the hope that God might remit his anger against them (slothful and ignoble Belial!).

Here, as Newton observes, the infernal spirits "have wander'd from the point in debate, as is too common in other assemblies."[60] Indeed, the entire council has already approved Satan's declaration for continued war against the Tyrant of Heaven; the question under debate is supposed to be, should the war be open or covert? Should the devils follow the method of Achilles, Hector, and the older classical heroes, or should they emulate Odysseus? But Belial opposes any war, whether "open or conceal'd." Then, as Newton notes, "Mammon carries on the same arguments, and is for *dismissing quite all thoughts of war*. So that the question is changed in the course of the debate, whether thro' the inattention or intention of the author it is not easy to say."[61]

It is true that Mammon, like Belial, is against war, but his characterization suggests still a third parliamentary type, the one with the most contemporary ring. Mammon opposes war not out of cowardice or sloth, but because its result will be, at best, to restore the devils to "splendid vassalage." He is a pragmatist; furthermore, he has a positive alternative: "To found this nether Empire, which might rise / By policy, and long process of time, / In emulation opposite to Heav'n" (II, 296 ff.). Milton's Mammon, named after the false god of worldly riches, calls to mind the successful capitalist entrepreneur who has turned his back on the spiritual world. Presumptuously, he encourages his cohorts to "seek / Our own good from ourselves, and from our own / Live to ourselves" (II, 252 ff.). A possessive individualist, he believes that he and the other devils are self-created and self-sufficient, owing nothing to society or to God. Mammon has already surveyed Hell's resources—"This Desert soil / Wants not her hidden lustre, Gems and Gold" (II, 270 f.)—and he proposes that the devils adopt the work ethic and apply all of their industry, skills and arts in founding a new empire to rival God's:

> prosperous of adverse
> We can create, and in what place soe'er
> Thrive under evil, and work ease out of pain
> Through labor and endurance. (II, 259 ff.)

Mammon's proposal is loudly applauded. But Beelzebub, second-in-command after Satan, now intervenes in the debate, reminding the devils that Hell is in truth a dungeon and that they are there against their will. He proposes a course of subversion: the devils must seduce and undo God's latest creation, man. This, of course, is the proposal that was first advanced by Satan himself in Book I, as the two plotters conferred on the burning lake. Numerous commentators have pointed to the rigged nature of the supposedly democratic debate in Pandemonium: it was a sham from the beginning, contrived by Satan to provide the infernal oligarchs with a false sense of their equality and rights and thereby to secure his autocratic rule. Beelzebub is pivotal to this strategy. First, he challenges Mammon's proposal, to which "the popular vote / Inclines," but which is dangerous to Satan's hegemony because it suggests that the devils can control their fate if they build a new empire in Hell. Then he reminds the assembly of God's prophesied plan to create, around this time, "another World, the happy seat / Of some new Race call'd *Man*" (II, 347 ff.). He proposes that the devils either waste God's new creatures or "Seduce them to our Party" (choosing, in "party," a word that underlines the earthly and political parallel of the conflict).

In case the reader is unconscious of the crafty dynamic unfolding here, the narrator points it out: "Thus *Beëlzebub* / Pleaded his devilish Counsel, first devis'd / By *Satan*, and in part propos'd" (II, 378 ff.). Satan's strategy is to have another put forth his counsel, a trusted advisor, lest he seem too imperious. It has succeeded beautifully:

> The bold design
> Pleas'd highly those infernal States, and joy
> Sparkl'd in all thir eyes; with full assent
> They vote. (II, 386 ff.)

Their eyes sparkle, no doubt, both because they like the proposed scheme (temptation and corruption being their wonted activities) and because they feel they have exercised their aristocratic right to debate policy as equals in council. Beelzebub does not disabuse them but reinforces their illusions with mock-adulation: "Well have ye judg'd, well ended long debate, / Synod of Gods" (II, 390 f.). The self-delusion of the infernal spirits invites derision.

The proposal is popularly acclaimed. But which devil has the courage of his convictions? Who will undertake the perilous voyage through Chaos to the new-created world, risking the implacable anger of the Almighty? Having steered the proceedings to a predetermined conclusion, Beelzebub now asks these questions, providing Satan with an opportunity to demonstrate his unmatched heroism. Satan, in "transcendent glory rais'd / Above his fellows, with Monarchal pride / Conscious of highest worth" (II, 427 ff.), presently speaks, and with a false-heroic gesture offers to make the sacrifice for the public good. He instructs the devils to do what they can to make life in Hell more tolerable, "while I abroad / Through all the Coasts of dark destruction seek / Deliverance for us all" (II, 463 ff.). Then the "Monarch" rises to prevent others from speaking, "Prudent, lest from his resolution rais'd / Others among the chief might offer now / (Certain to be refus'd) what erst they fear'd" (II, 468 ff.). Satan's every word and action have been carefully calculated to secure his hegemony, and he has proved himself the arch-politician: any potential rivals have been transformed into slavish sycophants.

The scene closes with a startling apotheosis:

> Towards him they bend
> With awful reverence prone; and as a God
> Extol him equal to the highest in Heav'n:
> Nor fail'd they to express how much they prais'd,
> That for the general safety he despis'd
> His own: for neither do the Spirits damn'd
> Lose all thir virtue; lest bad men should boast
> Thir specious deeds on earth, which glory excites,
> Or close ambition varnisht o'er with zeal. (II, 477 ff.)

One imagines that Moloch, Belial, Mammon—all the high and mighty spirits—would blush to see themselves cower before their new emperor. But, thoroughly captivated by Satan's masterful rhetoric, they are awed by his apparent sacrifice for "the general safety." Satan's false-heroic gesture anticipates and parodies Christ's sacrifice for mankind, which is foretold in the next book of the epic. The triumphant show of Satan's powers of manipulation also looks ahead, forebodingly, to the temptation of Eve in Book IX. The power of this scene attests to Milton's profound insights into human psychology, political processes, and their intersection. To this day, the story of Satan's apotheosis in Hell endures as an unflattering commentary on one of the less noble moments of English parliamentary history.

The Heavenly Paradise

Perhaps the most politically charged and controversial aspect of *Paradise Lost* for late twentieth-century audiences is not any of the aforementioned heroic or cosmic events but what in earlier ages was regarded as a domestic matter: relations between the sexes. Sensabaugh reports that the passages in Book IV describing Adam and Eve in Paradise were among the most popular in early America and that these passages were frequently invoked as the very picture of wedded bliss.[62] Not so today. With few exceptions, recent feminist criticism has been unforgiving toward Milton for depicting Eve as weaker than and subordinate to Adam, a "temptress" responsible for the Fall. In a now classic manifesto on Milton's "misogyny," Sandra Gilbert describes Milton's Adam as "absolute master and guardian of the patriarchal rights of primogeniture" and maintains that "Eve is the only character in *Paradise Lost* for whom a rebellion against the hierarchical status quo is as necessary as it is for Satan." Catherine Belsey likewise applauds Eve for resisting the "patriarchal absolutism" of God, Adam, and Milton.[63] Such comments, however, betray a fundamental misapprehension of Milton's politics, sexual and otherwise. Granted that Milton's depiction of gender relations is patriarchal to a degree (not an unexpected bias in a seventeenth-century male author), to insist that the overriding political issue in *Paradise Lost* is Milton's "misogyny" overlooks the way the epic actually participated in the political debates of its day.

For the "hierarchical status quo" in Eden, as in Heaven, is founded not on birth or custom but on merit; it is not feudal and aristocratic in nature (characterized by "patriarchal rights of primogeniture" or "patriarchal absolutism"), but republican. Eve's subordination to Adam, objectionable as it may be in our age, is consistent with traditional ("phallocratic"?) beliefs in the priority of Adam's creation, his greater resemblance to God's image, and his higher degree of reason: "For contemplation hee and valor form'd, / For softness shee and sweet attractive Grace, / Hee for God only, shee for God in him" (IV, 297 ff.). The Fall comes about in large part because Adam abdicates his responsibility, as the more reasonable of the pair, to guide and educate his helpmate. Every aspect of Eden, in fact, is governed by a hierarchy based on degrees of godlike reason. This ordering principle pervades Milton's account of paradisal history: it is evident, for example, in Adam's dominion over the animals and in his plea for a helpmate who, like him (and in contrast to the instinct-determined brutes), will be a "spirit . . . free" (VIII, 344 ff., 383 ff.). The same principle informs Adam and Eve's inner life, where fancy and the passions are properly subordinated to the government of reason. Raphael, departing Eden, warns Adam not to allow passion to usurp reason's rightful dominion over the lower faculties and thereby "sway / Thy Judgment to do aught, which else free Will / Would not admit" (VIII, 635 ff.).

The hierarchy within mirrors the hierarchy without; and freedom, in every case, depends on the principle of merit-based hierarchy. This association between freedom and hierarchy, perhaps jarring to the modern sensibility, was central to the political thought of seventeenth- and eighteenth-century republicans, who believed the proper end of government was to preserve individual and public liberty by holding in check the selfish interests of classes and individuals. One is reminded of Abdiel's argument to Satan that obedience to the worthiest is not servitude: "This is servitude, / To serve th' unwise, or him who hath rebell'd / Against his worthier" (VI, 178 ff.). As Milton asserts repeatedly, servitude consists in subordinating one's will either to one's own passions or to a passionate other, and the two kinds of servitude are usually found together.

Paradise shares with Heaven the free quality of the obedience owed to God. The kind of obedience that exists in Paradise is free in the sense that it is free-ing: it releases individuals from bondage to their own unworthy passions. In this respect it resembles the freedom imparted by virtuous republican leaders. This obedience is also free in the sense that it is freely given, not necessitated by custom or force, a point that Raphael stresses in comparing Heaven and Earth; and in this respect, too, Paradise resembles a republic: government is by consent of those ruled.

The free nature of the obedience owed to God also stands, of course, at the theological center of the epic. "I made him just and right, / Sufficient to have stood, though free to fall" (III, 98 f.), God tells the Son in Book III; for otherwise man's obedience would have been merely outward conformity to law motivated by dread, neither worthy of praise nor demonstrating an inner disposition to obey:

> What pleasure I from such obedience paid,
> When Will and Reason (Reason also is choice)
> Useless and vain, of freedom both despoil'd,
> Made passive both, had serv'd necessity,
> Not mee. They therefore as to right belong'd,
> So were created, nor can justly accuse
> Thir maker, or thir making, or thir Fate;
> As if Predestination over-rul'd
> Thir will, dispos'd by absolute Decree
> Of high foreknowledge; they themselves decreed
> Thir own revolt, not I. (III, 107 ff.)

The Calvinist principle of inextricable fate or destiny, on the other hand, both detracts from the service shown to God and negates man's nature as a free, rational being, created in God's image.[64]

As the foregoing paragraphs suggest, the debate over predestination in Milton's age was thoroughly imbued with political implications. Like the Dutch republicans Vondel and Grotius, and in contrast to the Calvinist orthodoxy of the *Westminster Confession*,[65] Milton rejected the doctrine of predestination and its implication that God not only foreknew but also predestined the Fall. Milton's God has foreknowledge of the Fall because He is omnipotent and the universe is a coherent whole. However, He does not predetermine human disobedience: He makes Adam and Eve free to stand or fall, and because they are accountable for their actions, He is blameless. Thus, Milton's version of the Fall story has more than one parallel in his political thought: Adam and Eve's free choice in the matter of the apple parallels, as we have seen, Milton's republican emphasis on citizen participation in political decision making. And God's overarching providence parallels the republican principle of the public good ("truth"), which transcends private interests and guides the free choice that might otherwise be bound by these interests.

In the passage quoted above, God is speaking about both man and the angels who fell through willful disobedience. Both were created free, "and free they must remain, / Till they enthrall themselves" (III, 124 f.). However, Milton stresses the important difference between the two: "The first sort by thir own suggestion fell, / Self-tempted, self-deprav'd: Man falls deceiv'd / By th' other first" (III, 129 ff.). Adam and Eve, because they were deceived by the arch-Tempter, will be shown mercy and grace. And the freedom that God grants them, one of whose consequences is their fall, has its positive side in the cooperative role that they will play in their own regeneration. Where the *Westminster Confession* asserted the powerlessness of human beings to cooperate in their own salvation, Milton insisted on the synergistic cooperation of divine grace and human volition in the soul's regeneration.[66] Thus, he stood the doctrine of predestination on its head, arguing that it applied only to election: God elects those who are faithful and repentant to everlasting life, and He rejects only those who refuse to believe. Synergism is the overriding principle here because Milton, it should be emphasized, also disagreed with the Pelagian sects of his day. Their doctrine of radical free will, which denied original sin and left redemption entirely up to human volition, was no more acceptable to him than the Calvinist dogma of predestination. As Vondel's *Lucifer* suggests, the predestinarian position was associated with belief in a fixed social hierarchy determined by birth (unlike Milton's continuously evolving universe created by God). The Pelagian doctrine of free will, on the other hand, anticipated the notion of society as an aggregation of particular interests with no definable communal or public good. Seventeenth-century republicanism rejected both extremes. Thus, Milton's theological notion of human-divine cooperation in the matter of salvation has an important parallel in the political notion that successful republicanism results from the fruitful relationship (synergism) between individual and societal interests: between individual initiative and a society that appreciates that initiative and therefore guarantees individual liberties.[67]

Man's Fall and Restoration

The parallels between Milton's theological and political views are likewise evident in his depiction of the Fall. In that account, he stresses Adam and Eve's responsibility for the loss of Paradise ("I form'd them free, and free they must remain, / Till they enthrall themselves" [III, 124 f.]). This emphasis parallels his republican argument that the continuance of a free commonwealth rests on the virtue of its citizens. Milton's prose tracts warn the English people against the enthralling luxury and corruption that ruined the Roman Republic—a historical fall that he invokes repeatedly in his poetry, as well. The first couple, moreover, are enjoined to obey *freely*: for them, as for the citizens of a successful republic, virtuous behavior is accomplished through inner discipline, not by remaining in the "perpetual childhood of prescription" that characterizes customary society and absolutist forms of government. The governed in a republic must give their consent because, as Milton explains in *Areopagitica*, "God trusts man with the gift of reason to be his own chooser."

But the first couple prove to be deficient in the inner discipline required to withstand temptation. Eve is susceptible to Satan's blandishments because she is infected with his perverted kind of individualism, if to a lesser degree: her pride, her presumption, momentarily overcomes her reason. She allows her lesser faculties to usurp reason's rightful place in the government of the soul, violating the hierarchy within. Nor is Adam blameless, for he has abdicated his appointed role as her guide in the merit-based hierarchy of Paradise. Thus, Milton interprets the first couple's disobedience according to republican theory. But that theory holds human nature to be amenable to redemption; in both their sinfulness and their ameliorability, therefore, Milton's Adam and Eve reflect a republican worldview.

The Fall is foreshadowed when, in Book IV, Satan is discovered "Squat like a toad" at Eve's ear, tempting her with vain illusions as she sleeps. The conditions of this first temptation are significant, for as Adam explains to Eve when she awakens and recounts her troubling dream, reason retires when the body goes to sleep, leaving the lesser faculty of fancy free to reign. Satan has endeavored with his devilish art to reach "The Organs of her Fancy," forging as he wishes dreams, illusions, discontented and vain thoughts, and "inordinate desires / Blown up with high conceits ingend'ring pride" (IV, 802 ff.). As Eve recounts her dream to Adam in the next book, we learn that Satan has first appealed to her female vanity: "Heav'n wakes with all his eyes, / Whom to behold but thee, Nature's desire, / In whose sight all things joy, with ravishment / Attracted by thy beauty still to gaze" (V, 44 ff.). Thus ingratiating himself, he plucked a fruit from the tree of knowledge and invited her to follow suit, promising that she would become a goddess and ascend to Heaven, "by merit thine."

Satan's subtlety as a tempter is already evident in his claim that everything he promises, Eve already deserves by merit: by eating the fruit she will attain the godlike knowledge that is rightfully hers. Upon hearing this, Adam immediately recognizes that the evil dream was not willed by Eve ("Yet evil whence? in thee can harbor none, / Created pure" [V, 99 f.]) but that it arose from her fancy, the faculty that in waking serves reason but in sleep may temporarily usurp the government of the soul, imitating the synthetic work of reason, misjoining and misrepresenting the data of the senses.

Adam's discourse on faculty psychology is full of dramatic irony: although he expertly expounds upon the hierarchical ordering of faculties under the government of reason, and although he is subsequently warned by Raphael against subjecting his judgment to sensuality, he fails to maintain proper esteem—"grounded on just and right"—for his godlike mental faculties (VIII, 572). As dawn breaks on the fatal day, Eve proposes to Adam that they henceforth divide their labors, he gardening in one place, she in another, so that their work will not be interrupted by their wonted smiles and conversation. This prelude to the Fall is couched in language that seems calculated to tempt the reader to side with Eve: a case of the principle of the "good temptation," which Stanley Fish finds operating throughout the epic. "Good temptation" invites readers to identify with a character and feel temptation along with him or her; the readers then recognize their error and successfully resist the bait, emerging strengthened by the experience.[68]

Eve's proposal seems to make good horticultural sense, and her apparent desire for greater independence to demonstrate her unshakable, free obedience to God seems commendable. However, Adam's fear that in his absence their envious foe might harm her elicits the passionate undercurrent of her feelings: her pride in her independent capacity to withstand Satan's blandishments. She immediately takes offense at the implication that her faith and love could be shaken by Satan's guile: "His fraud is then thy fear, which plain infers / Thy equal fear that my firm Faith and Love / Can by his fraud be shak'n or seduc't" (IX, 285 ff.). Adam tries to assure her that no such slight was intended; he wants her to remain in his sight only to prevent the attempt, which alone would bring foul dishonor through insinuation. Adam observes further that Eve's presence strengthens his every virtue, so "Why shouldst not thou like sense within thee feel / When I am present, and thy trial choose / With me, best witness of thy Virtue tri'd" (IX, 315 ff.). But Eve still protests, her desire to prove

86

her incorruptibility growing by the minute. How can they be happy "thus to dwell / In narrow circuit strait'n'd by a Foe" (IX, 322 f.), in mortal fear even of being tempted? Besides, the tempter's attempt will dishonor him but doubly honor them who have withstood "his surmise prov'd false":

> And what is Faith, Love, Virtue unassay'd
> Alone, without exterior help sustain'd?
> Let us not then suspect our happy State
> Left so imperfet by the Maker wise,
> As not secure to single or combin'd.
> Frail is our happiness, if this be so,
> And *Eden* were no *Eden* thus expos'd. (IX, 335 ff.)

This argument echoes God's justification for allowing Satan's attempt: that it gave Adam and Eve the opportunity to demonstrate their inner discipline and virtue. It also echoes Milton's argument in *Areopagitica* that true virtue is that which has been tested and has withstood temptation: a cloistered virtue is not true virtue. The reader—and especially the seventeenth-century republican reader—might be tempted to agree with Eve's argument. However, as Adam points out, Satan, no ordinary tempter, is a powerful deceiver. And since it is possible for reason to be confused and to swerve, it is folly to invite such temptation. More important, Eve's arguments sound reasonable but her motives—self-vindication and pride—are wrong, and they adumbrate the presumption in aspiring to godlike knowledge that will be her downfall in the temptation scene. Eve's desire to assert her independence, certainly a positive attribute, has become an end in itself, a selfish end, because she has been warned about the fatal consequences for posterity of disobedience. Adam admonishes her not to seek temptation, for "Trial will come unsought" (IX, 366). But she persists, manifesting a kind of pride in her willful desire to demonstrate her independence and vindicate herself, unmindful of the consequences. Adam finally submits, propitiates her whim, rather than risk her continued anger. "Go; for thy stay, not free, absents thee more" (IX, 372). He errs in subordinating his judgment to immediate feelings, abdicating his rightful leadership of the pair.[69]

This "eleventh-hour" domestic conflict in Eden, as Satan enters the serpent and begins to stalk his prey, is suggestive of Milton's views on a political question of great concern to his age: that of the relative merits of representative republics and unmixed democracies. In representative republics, at least in theory, the people's voice is balanced by elected officials of superior wisdom; in unmixed democracies, undivided sovereignty is lodged in a single popular assembly, without a strong executive branch or upper chamber to check its power. This is not to suggest that the scene described above should be read as a covert presentation of Milton's views on this political matter. However, we know from the divorce tracts that Milton regarded marital relations as a microcosm of relations among citizens in the political state. The merit-based hierarchy of Paradise resembles a representative republic, if it is not a deliberate symbol of one, and Eve's rejection of the companionship and counsel of the wiser Adam and her peremptory demand for immediate independence bring to mind the weaknesses of an unbalanced democracy.

To Milton and other seventeenth- and eighteenth-century classical republicans, unbalanced democracy meant the subjection of the state to the changing passions of the people. Milton argued against this form of political organization on historical grounds: the popular assemblies of Athens and Rome, adopted as a means of protecting the people's liberty, "either little availed the people, or brought them to such a licentious and unbridled democracy as in fine ruined themselves with their own excessive power."[70] (A little more than a century later, James Madison maintained in the tenth *Federalist* that republics were superior to pure democracies because in the former, representatives of proven merit tended to regulate the public voice and make it more consonant with the public good, whereas in the latter there was no check against the "mischiefs of faction.") Pure democracy, in which the people's upstart passions were unchecked by the counsel of an upper house or strong executive, was believed to be especially prone to faction, demagoguery instability, and the tyranny of the majority. This debate over the best form of government subtly informs Milton's rendering of the Fall scene of Book IX.

The long tradition that Milton drew upon in depicting the Fall was a battlefield of competing theological positions, all with political undercurrents. As J. M. Evans has shown, Milton's depiction of the scene was most indebted to Saint Augustine's synthesis of Jewish, Pauline, and patristic ideas about the Fall.[71] For Augustine, the Fall was caused by pride:

> [F]or if a heart . . . leaves God and turns in upon itself in the desire to bear fruit of its own power . . . pride then swells up within, and pride is the beginning of every sin. And with this, the sin of the heart will bring on its own punishment, for by experience it will learn what is the difference between the good it has forsaken and the evil into which it has fallen. And this will be to that soul the tasting of the fruit of the tree of discernment of good and evil.[72]

As Evans points out, Augustine and other fathers of the church elaborated the myth of the Fall as a bulwark against the dualism of the Gnostic and Manichaean sects that flourished during the second, third, and fourth centuries after Christ. The patristic interpretation was a refutation of dualism inasmuch as it explained evil within the framework of a monistic universe: evil was simply the absence of good and lacked independent existence. This interpretation placed responsibility for the Fall on Adam and Eve's lapse from the ways of right reason, yet it also allowed them free will to seek atonement through grace.

By contrast, the Gnostics maintained that Jahew, the god who laid down the prohibition against eating the fruit, was the servant of a malicious deity who wished to keep man ignorant of the supreme God. Consequently, the tree of knowledge was good and the serpent was the first couple's best friend in offering them redemptive knowledge (gnosis). Both Gnostics and Manichaeans believed in the inherent evil of matter and the obligation of humanity to free itself from this evil by means of spiritual knowledge—a complete inversion of the traditional Pauline interpretation of the Fall story.

Evans makes the interesting observation that the modern interpretation that "inverts the traditional meaning assigned to Milton's version of the Fall and sees in it a great humanist declaration of human liberties" has many affinities with the Gnostic and Manichaean readings.[73] All falter on the same point—God's prohibition against the tree of knowledge—denying that God would deprive humanity of its distinguishing capacity for illumination. But Augustine answered the dualists by explaining that the tree of knowledge of good and evil was so called to signify the *consequence*, not any imagined benefit, of eating the fruit: the first pair would know good if they kept the prohibition and evil if they transgressed. Or as Milton explains,

> It was called the tree of knowledge of good and evil from
> the event; for since Adam tasted it, we not only know evil, but
> we know good only by means of evil. For it is by evil that
> virtue is chiefly exercised, and shines with greater bright-
> ness.[74]

Milton's rendering of the Fall suggests perversions of knowledge especially pertinent to his age: knowledge as self-aggrandizement and power. Eve desires the knowledge for self-aggrandizement. Her first thought after eating the fruit is of whether to share her godlike wisdom with Adam or use it to gain power over him: thus, the perverse notion of knowledge as power enters human history. Eve's new knowledge is also, as Adam learns, "forbidd'n knowledge" sought by "forbidd'n means." This description links it with *curiositas* and even magic,[75] calling to mind the knowledge of the black arts—necromancy and astrology—that Marlowe's Faustus seeks from Mephistophilis to be able to manipulate the world (knowledge as power). This, in turn, evokes the anti-Christian pseudoscience of Augustine's Faustus, the Manichaean bishop who figures in the *Confessions.*[76] In all of these cases, knowledge is devoid of moral purpose, serving only as a means of aggrandizing the self and manipulating others. We are reminded of Raphael's warning at the close of Adam's astronomy lesson: he advises Adam to "be lowly wise: / Think only what concerns thee and thy being" (VIII, 173 f.). The angel's warning applies not to scientific curiosity but to the intellectual pride of those, like Marlowe's Faustus and Milton's Satan, who have divorced knowledge from faith and pursue it as a means to some selfish end. When Adam remarks on the earth's smallness in proportion to the immensity of the stars that furnish it with light ("a spot, a grain, / An Atom, with the Firmament compar'd" [VIII, 17 f.]), Raphael encourages him to maintain an attitude of humility in his inquiries, lest pride overtake him: "And for the Heav'n's wide Circuit, let it speak / The Maker's high magnificence, who built / So spacious, and his Line stretcht out so far; / That Man may know he dwells not in his own" (VIII, 100 ff.). The sin of pride is hardly restricted to particular historical periods; however, to judge by the evidence of poetry and drama, the problem is one that especially afflicts ages of great achievement, which foster intellectual arrogance. Marlowe and Milton lived in such times.

Milton's contemporary audience must also have recognized, in his version of the Fall story, the aspirations to knowledge of some of England's radical, ultrademocratic sects. Eat the fruit, Satan tells Eve, "and ye shall be as Gods, / Knowing both Good and Evil as they know" (IX, 708 f.). Such language smacks of the different varieties of "immediate revelation"—instant flashes of knowledge—reported by the sectaries.[77] The Family of Love spoke of the "divine possibilities" of humanity and preached the doctrine of "personal revelation" and successive "breakings through" of the spirit through history. Gerrard Winstanley, the Digger leader, promoted an "experimental" religion based on intuition and rejecting the "imaginary" knowledge of books. George Fox, the founder of the Quakers, spoke of "openings" of the Lord to him. The Anabaptists practiced adult baptism, or "dipping," whereby the believer was born again in Christ's image. In all cases, knowledge was immediate, mystical, and highly subjective; its attainment had nothing to do with the aspirant's good works, understanding of patristic commentary, or even, for some sects, study of Scripture.

Some corollaries of this view of the attainment of truth were the belief in human perfection or perfectibility in the here and now; the notion of God as "the spirit in all men"; rejection of the doctrine of original sin; and, in the political domain, simple or pure democracy—for if every man is Christ, then the people, in their present condition, are capable of direct self-government. Thus, for many sectaries the doctrine of "divine possibilities" brought not a virtuous life lived in imitation of Christ, but an unhinged identification with Christ. This was the moment in English history when would-be messiahs like James Naylor adorned themselves with crowns of thorns and rode through the country proclaiming their divinity.[78] The form of organization of the sects, as well as the political implications of their belief that God is the spirit in all men, led the Quaker historian Rufus Jones to argue that the self-governing sects of the Interregnum were the forerunners of later radical democratic movements.[79] Milton rejected the sectaries' claims to godlike perfection through personal revelation—immediate knowledge—as he rejected all shortcuts to illumination. The ultrademocracy they preached likewise seemed folly to him; his own political republicanism was anchored in his belief in original sin and in the necessity of education to repair the ruins of the Fall. Gradual amelioration of the human condition was the prerequisite to broader political participation.

We can safely assume that Milton's views on such fundamental issues entered into his writing of the Fall story. Eve, blinded by the desire for her own aggrandizement, is unable to distinguish between truth and the pseudoknowledge offered by Satan. At first Satan hesitates in his course, momentarily disarmed by Eve's goodness and beauty. "But the hot Hell that always in him burns" quickly turns his delight to envy and torture, "the more he sees / Of pleasure not for him ordain'd" (IX, 467 ff.): he can never escape from himself, and so he renews his evil purpose. He begins with flattery, complimenting Eve on her physical beauty. When she marvels at the serpent's powers of speech, his ascent "above the rest / Of brutal kind" (IX, 564 f.), he claims that his marvelous transformation was wrought by eating the fruit of a certain tree in the garden. He leads her to the tree of prohibition but meets resistance from the still-obedient Eve. Then he musters all of his perverted, demagogic powers to overcome her:

> now more bold
> The Tempter, but with show of Zeal and Love
> To Man, and indignation at his wrong,

> New part puts on, and as to passion mov'd,
> Fluctuates disturb'd, yet comely, and in act
> Rais'd, as of some great matter to begin.
> As when of old some Orator renown'd
> In *Athens* or free *Rome*, where Eloquence
> Flourish'd, since mute, to some great cause addrest,
> Stood in himself collected, while each part,
> Motion, each act won audience ere the tongue,
> Sometimes in highth began, as no delay
> Of Preface brooking through his Zeal of Right. (IX, 664 ff.)

The comparison of Satan to the orators of ancient times is the culmination of a pattern of imagery that has been unfolding since the first book of the epic. Satan never simply speaks; he makes speeches, conscious of his effect on his audience. This is true of his colloquy with Beelzebub and of his addresses to his allies in Heaven and Hell; and it is true of his temptation of Eve. In invoking the oratory of the ancients, which he admired enough to imitate in *Areopagitica*, Milton drives home the point that a central aspect of Satan's evil is his abuse of this highest of human arts—which is a vehicle of reason and hence of knowledge—for his own perverted ends. It is his perversion of reason that entraps Eve, and his suggestion that God has forbidden the couple to eat the fruit to keep them ignorant. Eve is susceptible because she feels inferior to Adam on this score, and she succumbs to the serpent's false promise that the forbidden fruit will instantaneously confer godlike knowledge: "That ye should be as Gods, since I as Man, / Internal Man, is but proportion meet, / I of brute human, yee of human Gods" (IX, 710 ff.).

Eve eats the fruit, and all of nature groans. Immediately, she wonders whether to share her knowledge with Adam:

> But keep the odds of Knowledge in my power
> Without Copartner? so to add what wants
> In Female Sex, the more to draw his Love,
> And render me more equal, and perhaps,
> A thing not undesirable, sometime
> Superior: for inferior who is free? (IX, 820 ff.)

For the first time, Eve truly chafes under Adam's rule—until now obedience was not subjection—and she contemplates misusing the knowledge to gain power over him. The perversion of knowledge—its use as a means of manipulation—has become possible in the world, and along with it the idea of subjection, until then unknown in Paradise. Adam follows Eve in eating the fruit, drawn by "Bond of nature" to share the consequences of her sin. Nature groans for a second time. It is not long before the faculties within their souls become disordered: fancy gains free reign, and Adam and Eve imagine that they feel divinity within them. Presumptuous thoughts turn to carnal desire and soon "high Passions, Anger, Hate, / Mistrust, Suspicion, Discord" disrupt their inner peace. "For Understanding rul'd not, and the Will / Heard not her lore, both in subjection now / To sensual Appetite, who from beneath / Usurping over sovran Reason claim'd / Superior sway" (IX, 1123 ff.). The government within has been upset; will and understanding are now ruled by passion.

As the next consequence of their disobedience, the external world in which Adam and Eve dwell is transformed to mirror their inner worlds. Adam hears the voice of the Son not with love, as in the past, but with fear; his disobedience and sense of guilt have turned free obedience into dread. He learns from the Son the nature of his error:

> Was shee thy God, that her thou didst obey
> Before his voice, or was shee made thy guide,
> Superior, or but equal, that to her
> Thou didst resign thy Manhood, and the Place
> Wherein God set thee above her made of thee,
> And for thee, whose perfection far excell'd
> Hers in all real dignity: Adorn'd
> She was indeed, and lovely to attract
> Thy Love, not thy Subjection, and her Gifts
> Were such as under Government well seem'd,
> Unseemly to bear rule, which was thy part
> And person, hadst thou known thyself aright. (X, 145 ff.)

Eve is properly under Adam's government, but she has come to feel that as subjection. Therefore, her punishment will be true subjection: she will bring forth children in sorrow and submit to her husband's will. And what is true in domestic relations will also be true in the state: after Adam's forfeiture of self-government, his true subjection will begin. The republic of Paradise has been lost; henceforth men and women will be subjected to violent lords. This phase of human history—mankind's subjection to the scourge of tyrannical overlords—is foretold in the final two books of the epic, when Michael descends to Paradise to expel the first couple from their heavenly bower and to prepare them for the sojourn ahead. Satan's triumphant return to Paradise on the causeway built by Sin and Death provides a foretaste of the tyranny to come and brings to a culmination the despotic imagery of the early books. The whole of Hell's population, from "Plebian" angels to the "great consulting peers," pours out to congratulate Satan, now a Turkish sultan in full splendor.

The Fall, of course, is only half of Milton's story. In Milton's universe human beings are corruptible, but not debased; the upward movement of the epic concerns their re-education in the ways of right reason. Satan and his followers, by contrast, devolve at their moment of triumph into a swarm of hissing, supine serpents, becoming the lowly creatures they have always been. Thinking to allay their appetite with fruit, the serpents chew bitter ashes, falling into the same illusion again and again, just as they will repeatedly fall into disobedience. Not so, man, who learns from his experience and is amenable to redemption. When the archangel Michael descends from Heaven to pronounce Adam and Eve's sentence and lead them out of Paradise and into history, Adam is contrite. After this first stage of expiation, Michael leads Adam to the top of the highest hill in Eden and shows him a panorama of future history.

The prospect is disheartening. Adam sees men and women in the grip of envy, intemperance, lust, and other sins that spring from the lapse of reason and the upsetting of the government within the soul. He sees Cain's murderous jealousy and the wicked sons of Cain living in luxury and riot. Viewing scene after scene of corruption and death, the fruit of his original sin, Adam nearly succumbs to despair: "O miserable Mankind, to what fall / Degraded, to what wretched state reserv'd! / Better end here unborn" (XI, 500 ff.).

Adam is pulled back from despair, however, by the sight of the righteous few. The first is Noah, "the only Son of light / In a dark Age," the "one just Man alive" (XI, 808–9, 818). The wicked multitude, slaves to their passions, do not heed Noah's calls for repentence and his warnings of the coming destruction. But on the eve of the Flood that will depopulate the earth, Noah gathers into his ark the seeds of a new world, so that when the waters subside and the air lightens, mankind can have a second chance.[80] Noah prefigures Abraham and Moses, who in turn prefigure Jesus. In subduing the passions to reason, these exemplary figures will exercise freedom, and their example and leadership will enable future men to free themselves from self-bondage.

Michael is explicit about the connection between self-bondage and political tyranny:

> Since thy original lapse, true Liberty
> Is lost, which always with right Reason dwells
> Twinn'd, and from her hath no dividual being:
> Reason in man obscur'd, or not obey'd,
> Immediately inordinate desires

And upstart Passions catch the Government
From Reason, and to servitude reduce
Man till then free. Therefore since hee permits
Within himself unworthy Powers to reign
Over free Reason, God in Judgment just
Subjects him from without to violent Lords;
Who oft as undeservedly enthral
His outward freedom: Tyranny must be,
Though to the Tyrant thereby no excuse. (XII, 83 ff.)

This formulation condenses the analysis of political tyranny in the prose tracts, especially that in the celebrated opening of *The Tenure of Kings and Magistrates*. Both are built on Milton's Platonic understanding of the complementarity between tyranny in the state and bondage to passions in the individual:

> If men within themselves would be governed by reason and
> not generally give up their understanding to a double tyranny
> of custom from without and blind affections within, they
> would discern better what it is to favor and uphold the tyrant
> of a nation. But being slaves within doors, no wonder that
> they strive so much to have the public state conformably
> governed to the inward vicious rule by which they govern
> themselves. For, indeed, none can love freedom heartily but
> good men; the rest love not freedom but license, which never
> hath more scope or more indulgence than under tyrants.[81]

In *Paradise Lost*, Milton locates this political perception in the larger framework of the unfolding of divine providence: the supersession of pagan immorality by the law of the Old Testament, followed by Christ's new Dispensation of love and faith. From the hilltop, Adam sees the next series of scenes. After the Flood the multitudes are still prone to every depravity; in fact, the sins are even greater. The irreverent, those who willfully reject God's rule, erect the Tower of Babel, repeating Satan's sin of pride. Therefore, God leaves the sinful to their polluting ways, choosing to live among "one peculiar Nation . . . A Nation from one faithful man to spring" (XII, 111 ff.).

The one faithful man is Abraham; his people, the Hebrews. Unlike their blasphemous neighbors, the Hebrews live according to law. They are chosen by God to begin mankind's deliverance from depravity. Moses, as receiver of the Law, is a mediator between man and God. In this way he is a "type" of Christ; his role is "to introduce / One greater." Similarly, the Old Testament is a type of the New Testament, its rule of law a transition to the rule of reason and faith.

Under the old Dispensation, "natural pravity" is subdued by law. But sin still abounds, held in check only by external commandments. Adam wonders why God has chosen to dwell with a people subject to so many laws: "So many Laws argue so many sins." Michael agrees: "Law can discover sin, but not remove, . . . Some blood more precious must be paid for Man" (XII, 283, 290 ff.).

> So Law appears imperfet, and but giv'n
> With purpose to resign them in full time
> Up to a better Cov'nant, disciplin'd
> From shadowy Types to Truth, from Flesh to Spirit,
> From imposition of strict Laws, to free
> Acceptance of large Grace, from servile fear
> To filial, works of Law to works of Faith. (XII, 300 ff.)

From "shadowy Types to Truth": the rule of love supersedes that of law; inner strength replaces external restraints. The superiority of the new Dispensation consists in the notion of free obedience, which arises from inner virtue and self-discipline.[82] Man's future condition under the Gospel, the condition of adult freedom, calls to mind Milton's description in *Areopagitica* of the warfaring Christian, who freely chooses virtue over indulgence.

This distinction between the new and old Dispensations also clearly parallels that in the prose tracts between republican government and monarchy. Reading *Paradise Lost* in conjunction with the prose tracts reinforces one's sense of Milton's consciousness of the fragility of republics. In his view, the English people had failed themselves and God by inviting back the Stuart monarchy instead of forging new republican institutions. Free to stand or fall, they had repeated the errors of the Israelites, who demanded of God a king, and the mistakes of the ancient Romans and Britons who forfeited their liberty.

Milton believed, however, that regeneration was still possible for his contemporaries, as it had been for Adam and Eve, through "Faith not void of works" and education; he wished his epic to be "doctrinal and exemplary" to subsequent generations of republicans. Inspired in part by his vision, educated descendants of the Puritan settlers in America successfully established a republic a century after his death, profiting from the mistakes of their predecessors. That story is the subject of the next chapters.

4

The Commonwealth Tradition

The affinity that American colonists felt with "the divine Milton" on the eve of their Revolution was due, in significant part, to the transplanting of the republican ideas and sensibility of the English Commonwealth to the more fertile ground of the colonies in the century after 1660. John Adams acknowledged his debt to the theorists of the English Commonwealth and their heirs when he named "Sidney, Harrington, Locke, Milton, Nedham, Neville, Burnet, and Hoadley" as having convinced him "that there is no good government but what is Republican."[1] In recent decades an extensive body of literary and historical scholarship (the work of Zera Fink, Caroline Robbins, George Sensabaugh, Bernard Bailyn, Gordon Wood, J. G. A. Pocock, and others) has traced the transmission of the ideas of Milton, James Harrington, Algernon Sidney, and lesser-known seventeenth-century republicans to the American colonies. As a result, the body of English political thought generated by the Great Rebellion and the Glorious Revolution is now generally recognized as a major ideological influence on the American Revolution.[2]

The Commonwealth legacy centered on ideas of natural and inalienable rights, the contractual nature of government, the subjection of magistrates to law, the legitimacy of revolution when rulers cease to govern for the good of the people, the superiority of mixed and balanced government, and the importance of education. By means of governmental checks and balances, rotation in office, expanded secular education, and other programmatic measures, the original Commonwealth thinkers and their heirs hoped to foster the divine sparks of reason in citizens while preventing the usurpation of government—in the individual and in the state—by corrupting passions.

In late seventeenth- and early eighteenth-century England, this legacy was kept alive by the "Real Whigs," liberal publicists who disassociated themselves from the Whiggish political establishment that came to power in 1688 and who openly identified with the still-unfulfilled program of the Commonwealth.[3] Important in the preservation and transmission of Commonwealth ideas were opposition politicians such as the Tory Viscount Bolingbroke (a favorite writer of John Adams and other American patriots), who devised the term "Robinocracy" to describe England's corrupt and unbalanced cabinet government under Robert Walpole. Both Real Whigs and Tories decried the growth of a "fourth branch" of king's ministers and favorites, which was upsetting the traditional balance of England's mixed government and threatening civil liberties. Within a few decades, Whig and Tory complaints against the abuses of an overpowerful and corrupt executive were being echoed almost verbatim by American colonists. The colonists enlisted the rhetoric of the eighteenth-century Commonwealthmen in the growing conflict between their provincial assemblies and royal officials, who were believed to be conspiring to revoke the colonists' right to self-government and even their civil liberties as prescribed by the English Constitution.

In the American colonies this English and European body of theory fused with an indigenous republican tradition that Tocqueville, writing in the 1830s, traced back to the institutions of self-government and compulsory education laws of Puritan New England. To Tocqueville, early New England culture was in many respects more politically advanced than anything in the mother country. He observed in his analysis of the New England town:

> The general principles which are the groundwork of modern constitutions, principles which, in the seventeenth century, were imperfectly known in Europe, not completely triumphant even in Great Britain, were all recognized and established by the laws of New England: the intervention of the people in public affairs, the free voting of taxes, the responsibility of the agents of power, personal liberty, and trial by jury were all positively established without discussion.
>
> These fruitful principles were there applied and developed to an extent such as no nation in Europe has yet ventured to attempt.[4]

In transforming the charter of the Massachusetts Bay Company into the constitution of a commonwealth in 1630, Governor John Winthrop empowered all "freemen" of the Bay colony to elect a legislative assembly. Winthrop's definition of "freemen" included only church members, a limitation he felt was necessary to ensure responsible participation. However, as Edmund Morgan points out, this policy "extended political rights to a larger proportion of the people than enjoyed such rights in England—and to people who were better qualified to use them than the mere possessors of a forty-shilling freehold."[5] With respect to secular education as well, Massachusetts was far ahead of England: the seventeenth-century mandates of the Massachusetts General Court requiring towns to provide publicly funded education had no precedent in the Old World.

Tocqueville and later political scientists attribute the flourishing of republican principles and institutions in New England to broad land ownership, which was associated with consciousness of political rights and responsibilities. (This was an application of the theories of Machiavelli and James Harrington on the importance of freehold property in shaping the independent, civic-minded personality.) Tocqueville also observed that, in contrast to other colonies that had been established by merchant adventurers without families, those of New England had been settled by people of the "independent classes," who were well educated and motivated not by the desire to better their social or economic position but by "a purely intellectual craving."[6]

Another Puritan legacy that contributed to the distinctive cast of eighteenth-century American republicanism was the millennial habit of thought that assigned to America a special role in God's providential design. Radical Whigs later recalled New England's "errand in the wilderness" and spoke of the founding of the "New Jerusalem" through the trials of revolution. It may be the "Will of Heaven," John Adams wrote to his wife on the eve of Independence, that "Americans shall suffer Calamities still more wasting and Distresses yet more dreadfull"; but out of such suffering, he believed, would come deliverance, as it had for the children of Israel.[7] Adams's confident prediction a decade earlier that "America was designed by Providence for the Theatre, on which Man was to make his true figure, on which science, Virtue, Liberty, Happiness and Glory were to exist in Peace," exemplified the fusion that had taken place in colonial thought between the millennialism of the Puritan founders and the republican values of individual liberty and progress.[8]

Admittedly, Milton was not the most original or systematic of the Commonwealthmen. However, he was popularly and frequently cited, in the decades leading up to the Revolution, as a leading authority on republican ideas. His inimitable expression of what were, by then, commonplaces of Whig political theory—the right of resistance to tyrants like Charles I, the inalienable rights of the individual—must have in part accounted for the fact that Americans cited *his* formulations of the Whig verities. As one twentieth-century historian notes, "Milton popularized much of the language and imagery with which subsequent writers would carry on the seventeenth century radical heritage."[9]

Milton's writings incorporated both republican and millennial ideas and thus resonated with the two central impulses of prerevolutionary American culture. Beginning in the 1760s Jonathan Mayhew, minister of Boston's West Church, and other stalwarts of the "black regiments" hailed Milton as an impassioned spokesman for liberty and an enemy of all arbitrary government. But Milton also appealed to what Sacvan Bercovitch calls "the old figural outlook," which still held sway—the Puritan manner of thought and rhetoric that fused secular and sacred history in a vision of America as the New Eden prophesied for the end of time. The same cultural impulse that allowed the Congregationalist minister Abraham Keteltas to declare American republicanism "the cause of heaven against hell—of the kind Parent of the universe, against the prince of darkness"—made *Paradise Lost* a natural literary handbook of the revolutionary polemicists.[10]

This vibrant interpenetration of religious and political traditions has been explored recently by a number of historians, countering a tendency toward polarization among scholars over the relative importance of republican ideology, on the one hand, and religious doctrine, rhetoric, and institutions, on the other. Nathan Hatch points to "the paradox of a republican eschatology, of growing secularity amid heightened religious consciousness" and argues that "the [revolutionary] clergy appropriated the means of traditional religion to accomplish the ends of civic humanism."[11] Nor was this "convergence of millennial and republican thought"[12] a mere grafting of traditional religious rhetoric onto a contemporary political agenda. As Cushing Strout shows, there was a thoroughgoing coherence between the Puritan doctrine of covenant and the political principle of consent: "The Calvinist clergy, whether pietist or liberal, easily assimilated republican talk of rights, charters, and contracts because they had always been engaged in a theology that emphasized the role of consent in all of man's important relations."

Strout suggests that Calvinist theology, despite the doctrine of predestination, fostered voluntarism—an active pursuit of good works—as a means of relieving anxiety over salvation, just as republican ideology encouraged individual involvement in public life as the true expression of political freedom. He also argues, elaborating Tocqueville's famous observation about the relationship between the "spirit of religion" and the "spirit of liberty" in America, that the Puritan tradition, together with the active involvement of so many of the clergy on the patriot side, was responsible for the uniquely "sober" character of republican liberty on American shores: "No rebels have been more saturated with respect for traditional morality and civic order, yet without calling for dictatorship or terror.[13]

By the second half of the eighteenth century, the principal apocalyptic goal in the American colonies was civil and religious liberty rather than the conversion of all nations to true religion—a shift in priorities that was to have momentous political consequences. Hatch points to Mayhew as the first to articulate the new myth of the Puritan fathers as stalwarts of *civil* liberty, a theme further popularized by John Adams's "Dissertation on the Canon and the Feudal Law."[14] Patricia Bonomi shows that congregational networks, which continued to grow over the eighteenth century, were mobilized "as devices for political instruction and propaganda." The pulpit was, in effect, as important a revolutionary institution as the town meeting.[15]

All of this helps to explain why Milton's works, with their distinctive amalgam of republican principles and Puritan theology, were seized on to express the spirit of "civil millennialism" sweeping the country.[16] In contrast to the reform-minded Romantics who regarded Milton's epic subject matter as "retrograde dogma," eighteenth-century Americans were entirely at home with his fusion of politics and religion. And it was precisely this fusion of the "spirit of liberty" and the "spirit of religion" in colonial culture that enabled the American radicals to understand— much better than their European counterparts—Milton's distinctive notion of liberty as obedience to reason and to read with special acuity his epic treatment of the problem of temptation under conditions of liberty.

In this chapter I will explore the persistence of the concerns and values of Milton's writings during the century between the fall of the English Republic and the first stirrings of independence in the colonies. Examining the role of Milton's writings in the transmission of the republican sensibility casts a new light on the generally accepted view of the political tradition that comprises Milton and American republicans such as John Adams. If Milton, as a Puritan, was ever-conscious of the human propensity to sin and ever-vigilant against human seduction into error, he was also (again, as a Puritan) confident in human ameliorability and looked forward to a time when all the Lord's people might become prophets. It is true, as Robbins, Bailyn, Wood, and other historians have argued, that seventeenth- and eighteenth-century republicans opposed as unbalanced the form of democracy in which all power was lodged in a frequently returned popular assembly. However, in their concern to purify corrupt

101

constitutions and to restore or preserve harmonious social relations, the republicans were not indifferent to social and economic injustices (as these historians imply).[17]

Republicans of the Commonwealth era believed that expanded secular education and economic opportunities—"to repair the ruins" of the fall—were prerequisites for broader political participation: the people must first be elevated through education, economic improvements, and political reform. The immediate leveling of economic and social distinctions was not thought to be the proper task of the new republic, whose poorly educated population stood vulnerable to the demagoguery of scheming Satans.

On similar premises, Milton's contemporaries in Massachusetts enacted their famous 1647 law, without precedent in England, ordering all towns of fifty or more households to supply teachers of reading and writing so that all citizens could study the Bible for themselves, without the "false glosses of saint-seeming deceivers."[18] To be sure, the "Old Deluder Satan Law," as it was called, had a denominational, anti-episcopal cast; yet it also reflected the republican idea that the virtue of citizens depends on the development of their independent intellectual powers and moral understanding, as does the prosperity and durability of the republic. Of the numerous classical republican ideas that took root in America through the writings of Milton and his contemporaries, this was one of the most important in the development of the new republic.

Mixed Government and the Problem of Passion

One concern that connected the thinkers of the Commonwealth tradition with the American founding fathers and distinguished both from nineteenth-century democrats was the problem of corrupting passions. As was noted earlier, the faculty psychology popular in Milton's day and in the eighteenth century prescribed a balance of the lesser faculties under the government of reason; when unregulated, the lesser faculties became destructive "passions." That loss of liberty resulted when reason submitted to passion was a widespread idea, reaching back to the Renaissance and ultimately to Plato's *Republic*.

Thus, Milton expressed a commonplace of his age in the advice the archangel Michael offers to Adam as he prepares the first couple to go out into the world: "True Liberty," Michael tells Adam, ". . . with Right reason dwells / Twinn'd." Furthermore,

> Reason in man obscur'd, or not obey'd,
> Immediately inordinate desires

And upstart Passions catch the Government
From Reason, and to servitude reduce
Man till then free. (XII, 83 ff.)

The lines following those just quoted extend the theme into the political domain, connecting the inner disposition of the individual to the outward form of the state. The giving up of internal liberty leads to outward tyranny. Since man "permits / Within himself unworthy Powers to reign / Over free reason, God in Judgment just / Subjects him from without to violent Lords" (XII, 90 ff.).[19]

Michael offers this advice, part of his history lesson on the hill, immediately after relating to Adam the fate of Nimrod, the proud empire-builder whose presumptuous schemes would be confounded by God at Babel. Nimrod is described as having a "proud ambitious heart" (XII, 25). Not content to live among other men as an equal, he rules tyrannically and attempts to challenge Heaven's sovereignty. To secure earthly fame, he presumes "to build / A city and Tower, whose top may reach to Heav'n." Nimrod and his rebellious crew, with "whom like Ambition joins," are types of Satan and the rebel angels (XII, 43 f., 38). Like their infernal antitypes, they are enslaved to their own ambition and seek to subject others to their violent passions. They epitomize the inversion of the happy state of affairs when reason reigns over appetite.

Such beliefs on the relation between reason and passion, liberty and tyranny, dominated moral and political philosophy through the next century. John Adams reflected the continuing influence of faculty psychology in the eighteenth century when he wrote as a young man that "Passions should be bound fast and brought under the Yoke. Untamed they are lawless Bulls, they roar and bluster, defy all Controul, and some times murder their proper owner."[20] In his later years he wrote, in a similar vein, that "Men should endeavour at a *balance* of affections and appetites, under the monarchy of reason and conscience, within, as well as at a balance of power without."[21] In applying such insights about individual psychology to man-in-society, the older Adams saw the dangers of passion infinitely compounded. For him, as for his republican predecessors, the central problem of government became the problem of designing institutions that would restrain passion under the monarchy of reason.

In other words, for seventeenth- and eighteenth-century republican theorists, the proper end of government was the subordination of private interests to the public good (an ideal embodied in the very definition of *res publica* and its English equivalent, "commonwealth"). Politics was conceived of as the transcending of the competing interests of society, whether social classes or political factions, not merely as the reconciling of them. (The latter idea was articulated at the close of the eighteenth century, along with the advent of interest group politics.)[22] These premises about human fallibility and the role of government were shared by Milton, Harrington, Sidney, Needham, Neville, and other seventeenth-century political thinkers who, because they looked to Greek and Roman political models, were described by Zera Fink as "classical republicans."[23] Although there were important differences among them, seventeenth-century republicans all took for granted the classical association between liberty and virtue, and they all pointed to the degenerate condition of people living under absolutist governments: "license . . . never hath more scope or more indulgence than under tyrants," Milton declared in the opening of *The Tenure of Kings and Magistrates*.[24] The job of government, republicans believed, was to promote reason in the individual and the state and to inhibit passion.

After the Restoration, the second generation of classical republicans, including Sidney and Neville, drew on the arguments of the first generation in the controversies that arose under the reigns of Charles II and James II. In answering Sir Robert Filmer's defense of royal prerogative, Sidney echoed Milton's arguments on the compact between governor and governed, the sovereign's duty to obey the law, and the legitimacy of rebellion when a sovereign violates the law. Sidney's contentions in his celebrated *Discourses Concerning Government* "remind one of nothing so much as Milton's arguments in the *First defense*," Zera Fink observes. "It is, in fact, no exaggeration to say that Sydney in these matters answered Filmer with the very theories with which Milton had replied to Salmasius."[25] Fink also points to the striking similarities between the views of Milton and Sidney on virtue, discipline, liberty, and forms of government:

> Sydney's contentions that liberty can never be upheld except by virtue, a point on which he cites Machiavelli but might as easily have cited Milton; that it cannot be preserved if the manners of a people are corrupted; that tyrants foster corruption as a means of enslaving the people; that a people cannot be enslaved as long as they remain uncorrupted—everyone of these is Miltonic in character. So also . . . was his definition of virtue as "the dictate of reason, or the remains of divine light, by which men are made benevolent and beneficial to each other" (II, xxii, p. 229). Both men saw the grand problem in government to be so to contrive it that the evil in man would have no scope, and the good would be fostered and placed in

control. They differed on the extent to which this problem could be solved.[26]

The persistent intent to limit the scope for evil was behind all facets of the republican political program: written constitutions, limitations on royal prerogative, rotation in positions of power, and structures for mixed and balanced government. Necessitated by human fallibility, mixed and balanced government was regarded as a critical aspect of the classical republican program to restrain human passions—to prevent the brutal despotism of a tyrant, the violent factional contests of aristocratic rule, and the self-destructive instability of pure democracy. John Adams later explained in his *Defence of the Constitutions of Government of the United States* that the advantage of mixed government, in which the monarchical (or executive), aristocratic, and democratic elements of society were all constitutionally represented, lay in the balance arrived at through the ability of each element to check the ambition of the others. In a properly mixed and balanced government, Adams argued, the self-interested passions of the different orders of society would be held in check, and the universal interests of the nation would thus be served.[27]

The most influential model of mixed and balanced government, from the standpoint of later American developments, was that proposed by James Harrington, the "English Machiavelli." Harrington's *Oceana* (1656) was prompted in part by the precarious condition of Cromwell's Protectorate government and in part by Hobbes's *Leviathan* (1651), a defense of undivided power and of the de facto school of government that justified political authority entirely by its ability to curb men's destructive impulses. Granting Hobbes's view that human actions are significantly determined by passion or interest, Harrington argued that the job of political theory was to devise the institutions that would best neutralize selfish ambitions and foster the interests of the people as a whole. He believed this could be accomplished through the separation of powers and the continual rotation of the men who exercised them. Harrington insisted on a bicameral legislature—because he believed no unicameral legislature could be just—consisting of a senate, whose members were elected for their "excellent parts" and whose sole responsibility was to initiate and debate laws, and a representative council, whose role was to accept or reject them. Other devices he proposed to keep the commonwealth in balance were a magistracy (executive) separate from the legislature; an agrarian law to prevent the concentration of land in the hands of a few; a secret ballot; and a constitutionally-provided dictator to act in emergencies, in the manner of a Lycurgus or Solon.[28]

In principle, Milton agreed with Harrington on the efficacy of mixed governments as a means for reining in human passions. However, on particulars the two differed. Milton argued in *The Ready and Easy Way* for a perpetual council (an executive body appointed by Parliament) whose wisdom would increase as a function of its experience, and he admitted the principle of rotation only as a contingency to check the council's power. Harrington, on the other hand, criticized the Rump Parliament as a single-house legislature both of debating and resolving. Furthermore, he disliked all governments lacking provisions to prevent the abuse of power, such as rotation in office and a clear division between legislative and executive functions.

Zera Fink's claim that Milton was a staunch advocate of mixed and balanced government from his first prose tracts to his last seems overstated.[29] Milton did invoke the theory in his anti-episcopal tracts, as Fink demonstrates. Like other supporters of the English Parliament against the king's personal government, Milton maintained that the English government traditionally had been a mixed state in which the king, the aristocracy, and the people had their due shares of power. In *Of Reformation in England* he wrote of the traditional government that "there is no Civill *Government* that hath beene known, no not the *Spartan*, not the *Roman*, though both for this respect so much prais'd by the wise *Polybius*, more divinely and harmoniously tun'd, more equally ballanc'd as it were by the hand and scale of Justice, then is the Common-wealth of *England.*"[30] Milton believed that the episcopacy, in appropriating the temporal powers of the king and endeavoring to establish its own supremacy, had overturned the balance in government. However, as Fink points out, his views reflected the influence of the Venetian model, favoring that type of mixed state in which the worthiest men—an aristocracy of virtue— ruled through a parliament. Parliaments, Milton wrote in *The Tenure of Kings and Magistrates*, were originally established to check the power of monarchs. Later he argued that the magisterial element was in fact the creation of parliaments (which represented the people) and derived from them all of their power.[31] He seems to have seen no contradiction between the ideal of a mixed polity and the predominance in it of the aristocratic order of society.

When Salmasius declared that sovereignty resided in the monarch according to divine and natural law, Milton countered with *A Defence of The People of England*, which argued that England was traditionally a mixed state, not an absolute monarchy with indivisible sovereign power residing in the king. Milton was one of a number of advocates of mixed government who, in response to the royalist assertion that sovereignty was by nature undivided, granted that proposition but argued that indivisible sovereignty resided not in the king but in the people, who partly retained it and partly delegated it to the aristocratic and magisterial elements of the state. Thus, through the idea of the delegation of power, he harmonized the notions of mixed government and of the indivisibility of sovereignty.[32]

Although Milton continued throughout his life to adhere to the principle of mixed government—insofar as he continued to see the need to check the passions of the "one"—no satisfactory institutional embodiment of the principle appears in his writings. His last statement on the subject was the earlier-mentioned recommendation, in *The Ready and Easy Way*, of a perpetual council of wise and able men, chosen by and responsible to Parliament; such a council, he believed, would be the best embodiment of the magisterial element in a free commonwealth. He still held that the power of the executive should be limited, to which end he noted the role that local assemblies and the army could play in counteracting the possible corruption of the perpetual council. However, in an insightful analysis in his *Defence of the Constitutions*, John Adams treated Milton's proposal as an example of an improperly mixed and therefore *unbalanced* arrangement—first, because the executive council was a creation of the legislature, and second, because the system offered no effective counterweight to the council's unlimited powers.

Adams and other Americans inherited the theory of mixed and balanced government via the Real Whig publicists and opposition politicians of early eighteenth-century England, a small minority of Englishmen who borrowed the earlier republican arguments in attacking the corruption-ridden "Robinocracy." As Bailyn and other historians have shown, the Americans of the 1760s also adopted the rhetoric of their precursors. They decried the "corruption" and "venality" of the British ministers and warned that a "fourth power" of colonial governors and other crown appointees was usurping the authority of the colonial legislatures. The colonists thus echoed the alarm of mid-century English writers over the threat to English liberties by a conspiracy of cabinet ministers led by Robert Walpole. As Pocock argues, the American Revolution grew, in part, out of the "rearticulation" of the language and outlook of English opposition thought, which in turn was anchored in the Aristotelian and Machiavellian traditions.

The story of how the theory evolved in the American colonies and Republic (for example, how the balance among the traditional socioeconomic orders was reconceptualized as the separation of powers) is clearly beyond the scope of this discussion. However, a brief look at Adams's arguments for the theory in his *Defence of the Constitutions* will remind us of its original (Miltonic) rationale. Adams drew on political theory from ancient to modern times in order to combat the notion (increasingly popular in France, the United States, and elsewhere) that unmixed governments with all power concentrated into a single popular assembly were superior to the mixed and balanced state governments the former colonies (with the exception of Pennsylvania) had adopted in the wake of 1776. The principal defenders of unicameralism—including the French *philosophe* Turgot, Benjamin Franklin, Franklin's English friend Richard Price, and Thomas Paine—maintained that annually elected popular assemblies, presided over by a limited executive, would be more democratic. Adams replied that unbalanced governments would lead to tyranny of the majority, under the pretense of popular rule.

His argument for mixed and balanced government was premised on the belief in human corruptibility that he shared with Milton and other seventeenth-century classical republican thinkers. However, in accordance with their monistic theology, Adams denied that human nature was essentially evil.

> It is weakness rather than wickedness which renders men
> unfit to be trusted with unlimited power. The passions are all
> unlimited; nature has left them so: if they could be bounded,
> they would be extinct; and there is no doubt they are of
> indispensable importance in the present system. They cer-
> tainly increase too, by exercise, like the body. The love of
> gold grows faster than the heap of acquisition: the love of
> praise increases by every gratification, till it stings like an
> adder, and bites like a serpent; till the man is miserable every
> moment when he does not snuff the incense: ambition
> strengthens at every advance, and at last takes possession of
> the whole soul so absolutely, that the man sees nothing in the
> world of importance to others, or himself, but in his object.
> The subtilty of these three passions, which have been se-
> lected from all the others because they are aristocratical pas-
> sions, in subduing all others, and even the understanding
> itself, if not the conscience too, until they become absolute
> and imperious masters of the whole mind, is a curious specu-
> lation.[33]

This view of the passions as capable of overtaking the human mind was a commonplace in the classical republican tradition; the particular images call to mind Milton's depiction of Satan's condition (to himself enthralled) and his seduction of Eve by entering the serpent. Whether or not Adams thought of *Paradise Lost* in formulating this passage, it is clear that he was drawing on the tradition in which Milton was a central figure. In fact,

Adams's moral outlook and understanding of politics were informed by his early reading of Milton, as will be discussed in the next chapter.

In the above-quoted passage, Adams goes on to propose mixed and balanced government as an antidote to the reign of passions. He inveighs against the folly of simple forms of government, on the one hand, and of utopian schemes, on the other, the latter being those that rely exclusively on the reason of mankind:

> If Socrates and Plato, Cicero and Seneca, Hutchinson and
> Butler, are to be credited, reason is rightfully supreme in
> Man, and therefore it would be most suitable to the reason of
> mankind to have no civil or political government at all. The
> moral government of God, and his vice-gerent Conscience,
> ought to be sufficient to restrain men to obedience to justice
> and benevolence, at all times and in all places; we must
> therefore descend from the dignity of our nature, when we
> think of civil government at all. But the nature of mankind is
> one thing, and the reason of mankind another; and the first
> has the same relation to the last as the whole to a part: the
> passions and appetites are parts of human nature as well as
> reason and the moral sense. In the institution of government
> it must be remembered, that although reason ought always to
> govern individuals, it certainly never did since the Fall, and
> never will till the Millennium; and human nature must be
> taken as it is, as it has been, and will be.[34]

Adams's appreciation of human corruptibility since the Fall, the principal motivation for his defense of mixed and balanced government, placed him squarely in the political tradition of the English Commonwealth.

"The World Was All Before Them . . ."

If mixed and balanced government was conceived of as a means to check the evil in humanity, what was the force for good and how was it to be fostered? In Sidney's definition of virtue as "the dictate of reason, or the remains of divine light, by which men are made benevolent and beneficial to each other," Zera Fink saw a striking parallel with the thought of Milton. Indeed, both men, while recognizing that humanity was corruptible and that measures were required to limit the scope for evil, also maintained—and here was their difference with the Hobbesians—that human beings were capable of moral, intellectual, and spiritual improvement. After all, they possessed right reason, the remnant of the divine intuition with which they had been endowed before the Fall. Thus, the legacy of Milton and other seventeenth-century Commonwealthmen was characteristically two-sided. Their solicitude for the individual and their defense of civil and religious liberty against the infringements of arbitrary government differed fundamentally from the subsequent Romantic celebration of the self. The entire sweep of libertarian causes espoused by Milton and others—free press, religious toleration, divorce, the expansion of secular education—was conceived of not as permitting the individual "to do what he lists"[35] but as strengthening individual reason, virtue, and civic responsibility.

This republican notion of autonomy is poetically embodied in Milton's depiction of Adam and Eve as freely acting, morally accountable individuals. Adam and Eve are all too capable of sinning. They are nevertheless endowed with reason, and thus are not only capable of but responsible for pursuing the future course of their lives in accordance with God's providence. In making Adam and Eve free to fall and free to find their way in the world, Milton emphasizes the role of free will in faith. He also implies, here, the central republican notion of the individual's responsibility for his or her secular existence. Of course, Adam and Eve are prepared for their independence by education—the extended lesson in providential history from the archangel Michael, which, like education generally, is designed to inoculate them against future errors.

In fact, *Paradise Lost* anticipated an entire complex of ideas that permeated eighteenth-century moral and political thought and culture and found expression in the American Revolution: self-determination, moral accountability, the ameliorability of man and society, the role of education in preparing individuals and nations for independence. Milton's final glimpse of the first couple struck a resonant chord with readers in an age preoccupied with the self-determination of individuals and nations: "The World was all before them, where to choose / Thir place of rest, and Providence thir guide" (XII, 646 f.).

Over the course of the eighteenth century, this theme of "spiritual pilgrimage," as it has been called, appeared in more secular form. Jay Fliegelman points to the persistent theme in eighteenth-century fiction of the fallen hero who, after his expulsion from the "Eden" of a traditional hierarchical society, is thrown back on his inner resources to educate himself and work out his personal salvation in the sight of God. This pattern appears in the fortunes of such characters as Robinson Crusoe, Tom Jones, and Richardson's Clarissa. After a falsely accused Tom is expelled from Squire Allworthy's Paradise Hall, Fielding's narrator concludes: "The world, as Milton phrases it, lay all before him; and

Jones, no more than Adam, had any man to whom he might resort for comfort and assistance."[36] Fliegelman shows that the whole genre of novels about prodigal sons and daughters acquired heightened resonances for American audiences on the eve of the Revolution, when *Robinson Crusoe* and *Clarissa* were bestsellers. Such novels challenged traditional notions of patriarchal authority and filial obedience while positing a new paradigm of affectional relations between parent and child, based on the Lockean and Rousseauean understanding that the child would not remain a child forever and had to be educated for responsible adulthood. For American audiences, Clarissa's subjection to the whims of her tyrannical father, which made her an easy prey for the libertine Lovelace, was a classic example of the abuse of filial obedience—and one that had clear implications for the relationship between an ungrateful mother country and her colonies, whom she refused to release into national adulthood.[37]

Milton treated education as necessary to spiritual pilgrimage both in *Paradise Lost* and in his theoretical writings. Adam and Eve's education takes up half of *Paradise Lost* (including Raphael's admonishments and Michael's revelations about future history), and the theme of the importance of education appears throughout the prose tracts, from early to late. Milton clearly did not embrace the notion of complete moral self-sufficiency promoted by eighteenth-century writers. He believed individual initiative and divine grace cooperate in bringing about the soul's salvation. In the secular domain, he implied that society cannot simply loose individuals into the world and expect that they will make the right choices. Education, like grace, is necessary "to repair the ruins of our first parents" and "to make the people fittest to choose, and the chosen fittest to rule."

Where Milton's epic offered prerevolutionary America a paradigm of independent, morally responsible adulthood, his prose tracts suggested a program for its attainment: freedom of expression and religion, educational reform, and economic improvement. *Areopagitica*, for example, which appeared in numerous adaptations in post-Restoration England and was paraphrased or cited by Americans as diverse as John Peter Zenger, Jonathan Mayhew, and Thomas Paine, provided not only a stirring defense of a free press but a guide for fostering public virtue. Prepublication censorship is not only impractical, Milton argues in *Areopagitica*, but is demeaning in its treatment of readers as untrustworthy children. It is also harmful inasmuch as it curtails dialogue and debate, the exercises upon which reason thrives and by means of which true ideas are strengthened.

Milton's tractates on religious freedom and church disestablishment proceed from similar arguments for the superiority of inner, unconstrained

111

virtue and faith. Of all of his prose works, these were the most commonly cited and the most influential in the Anglo-American world of the eighteenth century. The first tract to be republished in the colonies was *The Likeliest Means to Remove Hirelings*, which appeared under the title *An Old Looking-Glass* . . . in Philadelphia in 1770 and again in New Haven in 1774, amid fears that Britain was secretly scheming to impose a tithe-supported state church that would constrain the colonies' de facto religious toleration.[38] Milton's arguments for religious toleration and disestablishment, like his case against prepublication censorship, implied the conception of the kind of individual required in a Christian republic: one whose virtue is unconstrained, arising from an inner disposition rather than outward conformity.

In their tracts on the freedom of the press and of religion, Milton and other Commonwealth thinkers defended the individual against the encroachments of arbitrary government; they encouraged dialogue and debate as necessary to enhance the virtue of citizens and the welfare of the whole of society. In agitating for the extension and reform of education, a cause that peaked during the Protectorate, they sought to institutionalize the positive means for developing morally and politically responsible individuals. For Milton, as we have seen, education was indispensable for elevating the moral and spiritual character of postlapsarian man, for winning people to a love of virtue and weaning them from corrupting passions. He was interested in both clerical and secular education, the first as an adjunct of ecclesiastical reform and as a source of worthy spiritual leadership; the second as a direct means of instilling virtue and industry.

In his study of the Puritan Revolution's contribution to subsequent educational reform, Richard Greaves praises as especially forward-looking Milton's insistence that education take into account the specific capacities of youth, so as to instill a love of learning and build moral character.[39] In *Of Education*, Milton was contemptuous of contemporary pedagogical methods that forced "the empty wits of children" to compose themes and orations that were properly "the acts of ripest judgment." He also criticized the practice of the universities—"not yet well recovered from the scholastic grossness of barbarous ages"—for starting novices with logic and metaphysics, the most abstract and difficult of subjects, rather than with more accessible ones. As a result of being "tossed and turmoiled with their unballasted wits in fathomless and unquiet deeps of controversy," the students developed a hatred and contempt for learning and departed at the earliest opportunity to become mercenary divines, avaricious lawyers, or libertines.[40] In favoring education suited to the capacities of youth, curriculum reform to include new scientific and technological knowledge, public financing of broad-based education, and vocational training for artisans, Milton and other educational reformers of the English Commonwealth anticipated many of the developments of the next two centuries.

The Transmission

The return of the Stuart monarchy, Milton feared, would mean the end of the republican program for the moral and spiritual regeneration of England. On the eve of the Restoration, in *The Ready and Easy Way*, he contrasted the iniquitous thralldom of kingship with the virtuous liberty of a commonwealth, where citizens lead sober, Christian lives and participate in government through their representatives. When the "evil days" of the restored monarchy did arrive, Milton's liberty tracts were kept alive by the opposition and put to continuous use against religious conformity, unlimited monarchical power, the divine-right theory of kingship, press licensing—all aspects of the resurgence of ecclesiastical and civil tyranny.

Immediately after the Restoration, the Nonconformists adopted Milton's arguments in favor of religious toleration. On that issue he had gone further than any Interregnum government in insisting that complete separation of church and state was necessary for true liberty of conscience.[41] Even where the Nonconformist polemicists did not directly cite him, their opponents suspected the pernicious influence of the "blind Milton": *Eikonoklastes* and *A Defence of the People of England* were suppressed as seditious books and burned by the common hangman before the end of 1660. In 1662 *The History of the Wicked Plots and Conspiracies of Our Pretended Saints* declared ominously that the Puritan party was using the arguments of Needham, Milton, and other "Billingsgate" authors to advance its cause.

In the most famous example of Milton's notoriety during this period, Andrew Marvell, his former assistant and friend, was accused in 1672 of being under the influence of Milton, the "regicide," in a public debate over conformity and liberty of conscience. Marvell's opponent, a divine-right royalist named Samuel Parker, argued that the king possessed absolute power over his subjects, even the power to regulate conscience—an argument that recalled Salmasius's defense of Charles I. Marvell replied with a witty, learned tract *(The Rehearsal Transpos'd)*, whose style and arguments were reminiscent of Milton's rebuttal to Salmasius. (The following year, in a sequel to his satire, Marvell cleared Milton of having assisted him.) As these events suggest, the issues of religious toleration and the power of kings were closely related in post-Restoration England,

and Milton was associated with both. When Roger L'Estrange, a divine-right theorist who became Surveyor of the Imprimery, included *The Tenure of Kings and Magistrates* on a list of seditious books, the reason was its claim that "The Power of the King is but Fiduciary; and the Duty of the Subjects but Conditional."[42]

In the 1680s, during the agitation to exclude the Catholic James Stuart from the throne and to establish a limited constitutional monarchy under William and Mary, Milton's pamphlets were made to serve the cause of parliamentary supremacy. His writings on the contractual nature of government were drawn on freely to counter the resurgence of divine-right theory. *A Defence* inspired Whig polemicists writing in favor of the Bills of Exclusion, which were designed to limit royal power and guarantee freedom of conscience. *Areopagitica* appeared in two adaptations opposing renewal of the Licensing Act. Milton's writings were so useful to the Whigs during this period that royalists spread rumors that he had been a crypto-Jesuit and had been blinded by a wrathful deity for his regicide tracts. After the Glorious Revolution, his writings on the right of resistance to tyrants were adapted to support William's accession. *Tenure* appeared in 1689 in a famous adaptation called *Pro Populo Adversus Tyrannos*, which upheld the Revolutionary Settlement. In it, Milton's Presbyterians were metamorphosed into the equally perfidious Jacobites who, after joining with the Whigs in inviting William to England, declared the deposed James II the Lord's annointed and rightful heir. In all of these adaptations, however, Milton's central argument on the accountability of rulers to those they rule was left untouched. A reprint of *Eikonoklastes* that appeared in 1690 argued against the Jacobite cause by recalling the tyranny and lies of Charles I. In 1692 *Pro Populo Anglicano Defensio* appeared in English translation, and in 1693 an adaptation of *Areopagitica* was issued to argue against the renewal of the Licensing Act.[43]

The Whig interests that triumphed in the Glorious Revolution had used Milton in establishing the principle of parliamentary supremacy. However, not all Whigs were satisfied with the Revolutionary Settlement. A minority who desired further political and social reform, together with opposition politicians such as Bolingbroke and Swift, became the self-appointed custodians of the Commonwealth's canon. Caroline Robbins notes that, although these "Real Whigs," or eighteenth-century Commonwealthmen, achieved no significant reforms within England, they formed an important bridge between the English Commonwealth and the American Revolution. They "kept alive political ideas which proved suitable and useful for a great new republic" and which in many cases were institutionalized in the American Constitution and Bill of Rights.[44] The Real Whigs' program included the following aims: restoring balanced government in England, which was then threatened by the emergence of a cabinet system and an overpowerful executive; separation of government functions; enforced rotation of offices to prevent the entrenchment of juntas of willful men; reformation of Parliament through a wider franchise and some redistribution of seats; complete religious freedom, with toleration extended to Catholics as well as to all Protestant denominations; and the extension of secular education.[45] The Real Whigs borrowed directly from Milton's arguments on toleration, education, and the legitimacy of rebellion against tyranny; they went beyond him in wishing to extend toleration to Catholics.

Robert Viscount Molesworth and other Whigs also carried forward the republican concern with the improvement of agriculture as a prerequisite for moral improvement. For example, in a 1723 tract dedicated to the House of Commons of Ireland, Molesworth studied the alternating gluts and dearths that plagued Irish agriculture and undermined the morale of the Irish population, tracing them to poor husbandry and inefficient land tenure practices. He singled out for criticism the subtenanting of oversized farms by land-jobbers, which led to higher rents and the overworking of the land, and called for the establishment of schools of husbandry, laws against land-jobbing and other destructive practices, and relief from overburdensome tithes: a program that harked back to the proposals advanced by the Hartlib circle during the Interregnum.[46]

The Real Whigs made what was perhaps their most important contribution simply in rescuing the prodigious literary output of the Commonwealth from oblivion. Thomas Hollis, an important figure in the transmission of the Commonwealth legacy to the colonies in the middle of the eighteenth century, saw his task as one of preserving the tracts of the Interregnum for the education of future generations in the principles of liberty. Much of the activity of the eighteenth-century Commonwealthmen involved the republication of the literature of the Commonwealth. In 1697 John Toland brought out his first collection of Milton's prose tracts, which he followed the next year with a complete edition of the prose works in Latin and English and an account of Milton's life. To Toland, Milton was

> a man eminent at home and famous abroad for his universal
> learning, sagacity, and solid judgment: but particularly noted
> as well for those excellent volumes he wrote on the behalf of
> civil, religious, and domestic liberty; as for his divine and
> incomparable poems, which, equalling the most beautiful or-
> der and expression of any antient or modern compositions, are
> infinitely above them for sublimity and invention.[47]

When Toland was accused by the high church party of reviving Milton's sentiments—and of thereby reviving the attack on "the sacred majesty of kings, the venerable order of bishops, the best constituted church in the world"—he undertook a spirited defense of his project in *Amyntor* ("father of Phoenix").[48] Indeed, Toland's commentaries on *Eikonoklastes* and on *A Defence*, which he regarded as Milton's masterpiece, did a great deal to spread Milton's ideas.[49] Between 1697 and 1701, the Real Whigs republished works by Milton, Sidney, Ludlow, Neville, and Harrington. Hollis worked with Richard Baron, editor of Milton, Sidney, and Ludlow, in collecting and republishing the writings of the Commonwealthmen in the decade leading up to the Stamp Act (1765). Transmitted to the colonies, these "liberty books" supplied Americans with powerful intellectual ammunition for the building conflict with Britain.

5

Commonwealth Ideas
and the Prelude to Revolution

With the aid of the publishing activities of the English Real Whigs, Milton's writings became well known and generally available in the American colonies by the second quarter of the eighteenth century. It is difficult to gauge his popularity before that period, as records of the ownership and availability of all books in the early years of the century are scanty; however, we know that the libraries of Cotton Mather, the Corporation of the City of New York, and Yale and Harvard universities contained his prose tracts; and this is not the only evidence of American interest in Milton as a controversialist and scholar in the late seventeenth and early eighteenth centuries. Leon Howard suggests that Milton's popularity as a poet during this period may have been greater than a study of scholarly libraries suggests because the New England Puritans did not consider poetry—especially poetry in the vernacular—to be a branch of serious knowledge and therefore would not have included Milton's poetry in such libraries.[1] However, because of the development of colonial journalism in the 1720s, ample evidence of popular tastes exists, and there is no longer any need to speculate about Milton's American reputation: the fairly frequent references to Milton in periodical literature throughout the colonies, in booksellers' newspaper advertisements, and in the catalogues of city libraries all attest to Milton's popularity among the general public in the half-century preceding the Revolution.

Admittedly, the availability of Milton's works is one thing and their political influence is something else. While periodical literature and library catalogues tell us that Milton's ideas were in general circulation in the prerevolutionary decades, their influence is better understood through case studies. We will examine here the manner in which the works of Milton and other Commonwealthmen informed the thinking and sensibilities of two of the colonies' natural political leaders: Jonathan Mayhew and John Adams.

Hollis's "Liberty Books" and the Birth of Resistance

The impact of Commonwealth writings on the American colonists did not escape the notice of their contemporaries. Samuel Johnson, Boswell reports, blamed the American Revolution on the unassuming Thomas Hollis of London because he had rescued so many tracts of the Interregnum and presented these "liberty books" to impressionable Americans.[2] Hollis's chief correspondent in the colonies was Jonathan Mayhew, the illustrious minister of West Church in Boston; the decade-long correspondence between Hollis and Mayhew provides a vivid example of the transmission of the Commonwealth's legacy to America, showing Milton's central place in that legacy and the effect of Commonwealth ideas on colonists' perceptions of the growing conflict with Britain. It also vindicates Hollis's belief that "Nations rise and fall by Individuals not Numbers, as I think all History proveth."[3]

One of the most prominent of the British Nonconformist families, the Hollises maintained ties with New England throughout the eighteenth century. Thomas Hollis's great-uncle, Thomas III (1659–1731), a London merchant, contributed substantial sums to Harvard after his correspondent Increase Mather interested him in the university. His donations founded, among other things, the professorship of Mathematics and Natural Philosophy that was later held by John Winthrop (1714–1779), friend of Mayhew and of future revolutionaries. Hollis's gift to Yale included an edition of Milton. Thomas V, heir to the fortune of his great-uncle, was also a staunch Nonconformist and a self-professed Miltonian. After abandoning the idea of entering Parliament because the rampant corruption there jarred with his political ideals, he evolved a plan that would occupy him for the next fifteen years: to disperse as widely as possible the great books on liberty by ancient Greek and Roman, English, and European writers.

After reading Jonathan Mayhew's *Discourse Concerning Unlimited Submission and Nonresistance to the Higher Powers* (1750), Hollis began sending books to him, including many by Milton, and the two soon began a lively correspondence. Hollis recognized Mayhew as a kindred spirit. A scion of

118

a famous New England family that was active in missionary work among the Indians, Mayhew had attended Harvard in the 1740s along with such future revolutionary leaders as James Otis, Jr., and James Warren. By the time his *Discourse Concerning Unlimited Submission* caught the attention of Hollis and other English Nonconformists, Mayhew was already well known in New England for his outspoken religious and political views. While at Harvard, Mayhew had been caught up briefly in the religious enthusiasm unleashed by "New Light" ministers such as George Whitefield. But Mayhew later denounced the emotionalism of the Great Awakening, concluding that Whitefield was "under the Power of *Satanical Delusions*" and that when under such delusions the preacher became a *"Miserable Enthusiast"* dependent upon "Immediate *Revelations*, rather than on the *Scriptures* to direct him in his Duty."[4]

Controversial in his own day, Mayhew continues to be so in the twentieth century. He has been hailed as a precursor of the patriot cause by commentators from John Adams to Bernard Bailyn. Others disagree; representative of the contrary view is Alan Heimert, who treats Mayhew and the other rationalist ministers of the period not as harbingers of the Revolution but as elitists and conservatives. Heimert concurs with the New Light view that "Arminians" such as Mayhew were more concerned with worldly accomplishments than with true faith and that rationalist, "Old Light" religion was favorable, on the whole, to the "preservation of property rights and political stability." Heimert also argues that the New Light espousal of the doctrine of unconditional election, or predestination, "was not, as [rationalists such as Mayhew] incessantly complained, a hopeless and depressing proposition, but an optimistic and stimulating one" that encouraged the revivalists to view their own efforts as part of a divine plan; they did not oppose the role of human conduct in salvation, Heimert maintains, only the emerging capitalist ethic of self-seeking that was behind many worldly accomplishments.[5]

Mayhew and other rationalist ministers, by contrast, believed that the New Lights had dangerously overemphasized emotion and experimental knowledge to the detriment of scriptural studies and the healthful exercise of reason. Mayhew's own theological views, expounded in his *Seven Sermons* (1749), evolved out of his effort to reconcile faith and reason. He arrived at the position that reason was necessary to determine the validity of apparent revelation and, therefore, that the cultivation of man's divine faculty of reason was necessary for the perception of religious truth.[6] Mayhew also complained that the theology of the Revival implied political passivity. The New Lights, said Mayhew, "look down with contempt upon all *moral duties*, as being below such *spiritual men*." He preached, on the contrary, that *"He that doth righteousness*, and only he, *is righteous."*[7]

Mayhew insisted, moreover, that he was not preaching a religion of works alone, that "real piety" necessarily meant that the inner spirit of the individual believer was affected. However, he continued to emphasize the obligation of every Christian to fulfill his moral obligations, for "Christianity is principally an institution of life and manners; designed to teach us how to be good men, and to show us the necessity of becoming so."[8]

Clearly there were different paths to the Revolution, as the later appearance of both pietists and rationalists in the patriot ranks suggests. Reconciling the views of the twentieth-century advocates of the Old and New Light parties, Patricia Bonomi writes that "an ideology of dissent that linked religious with civil tyranny created a common ground upon which rationalists and evangelicals alike could join to justify their opposition to England."[9] The Miltonic attacks on passive obedience and church establishment that greeted England's efforts to curtail religious and civil liberties in the colonies came mostly from "rational-minded liberals of the educated elite" (who knew the history of their Puritan forebears and of the suppression of liberty in Stuart England and read John Trenchard and Thomas Gordon's *Independent Whig*); but the evangelicals could and did join with their sectarian opponents on the issue of episcopacy.[10]

A leading example of the English libertarian heritage turned against England was Mayhew's *A Discourse Concerning Unlimited Submission*, the sermon that John Adams would later call the opening salvo of the American Revolution. Occasioned by the frenzy of Boston Anglicans in 1750 over the anniversary of Charles I's execution, Mayhew's sermon repeated Milton's arguments that Charles had, in fact, "*unkinged* himself" long before the Great Rebellion by governing "in a perfectly wild and arbitrary manner, paying no regard to the constitution and the laws of the kingdom by which the power of the crown was limited."[11] The sermon drew on the whole Western tradition of political thought; however, it contained clear references to Milton's *Tenure of Kings and Magistrates* and *The Ready and Easy Way* and strongly resembled his *Defence of the People of England*.[12] Mayhew agreed with Milton that resistance to tyrants was not only lawful but obligatory for Christian subjects. It was true, Mayhew said, that St. Paul had commanded, "Let every soul be subject unto the higher powers"; however, when magistrates acted contrary to their offices, they ceased to be the ministers of God. "It is blasphemy to call tyrants and oppressors *God's ministers*," Mayhew argued. "They are more properly *the messengers of Satan to buffet us.*"[13] He concluded that it was the duty of every Christian not only to obey good rulers but to rebel against tyrants.

The response to Mayhew's sermon was highly polarized. Critics charged him with plagiarizing from a sermon by Benjamin Hoadly, a contemporary liberal bishop of the Church of England. Hoadly had hailed

Mayhew as a compatriot in the war against "Enthusiasm & Infidelity" when the Bostonian's *Seven Sermons* were published in London. Mayhew, in turn, was an ardent follower of the influential Whig bishop and had, indeed, closely paraphrased Hoadly's *Measures of Submission to the Civil Magistrate*, an argument for constitutional limitations on royal power. But for a man who declared that the modern teachers of liberty were "Sidney and Milton, Locke and Hoadly," it was no disgrace to be caught borrowing their arguments. As a result of the controversy generated by *A Discourse Concerning Unlimited Submission*, Mayhew became famous in the colonies as a champion of an old cause that was about to take on new urgency: New England's religious independence from the high-church party in England.

Mayhew's intensive reading of the English republican authors and his identification with their struggle against religious tyranny made him sensitive to the slightest infringement of religious and civil liberties in the colonies. His propensity to take alarm at contemporary developments in Anglo-American relations was probably increased by his correspondence with Hollis, which spanned the years from 1759 to 1766, a period of heightened tensions between Britain and the colonies. Two issues dominated the correspondence after 1762: first, the colonists' fear that Britain was secretly trying to establish an American episcopate; and second, the enactment by Parliament in March 1765 of the Stamp Act, which placed duties upon colonial legal documents, newspapers, and other means of information to help finance British military expenditures in North America. Thanks to Hollis's "liberty books" project, Mayhew availed himself of the arguments of Milton and other Commonwealthmen as he addressed what appeared to be a growing conspiracy of ecclesiastical and civil tyranny.

Since around 1756, Hollis had been collecting and republishing tracts of the Commonwealth together with Richard Baron, who had previously published two volumes of Milton's prose and his *Eikonoklastes*, as well as an edition of Sidney and one of Ludlow. Those three writers were Hollis's heroes, and he included some of their works in his first shipment to Mayhew. On August 16, 1759, Mayhew wrote to Hollis thanking him for a shipment of books containing Sidney's *Discourses* and "the admirable Milton's EIKONOKLASTES." Mayhew said he was especially delighted to learn that the gift, which had been sent anonymously, came from Hollis, whose great-uncle had endowed the professorship at Harvard (Mayhew's alma mater) then held by John Winthrop, Mayhew's "particular" friend.[14]

An important part of Hollis's project was the education of youth in the principles of liberty, and included in his shipments to Mayhew were gifts of books for the colonies' universities. Harvard's president, Edward Holyoke, wrote to Hollis in late 1759 thanking him for the volumes of Milton's prose works, "valuable to Us as we have a very high regard for that great man, whom, *his political works* NOT AT ALL WITHSTANDING, we esteem a great honor to the British Name." This comment on Milton's republican politics provoked Hollis to enunciate his own political creed as a Commonwealthman and a Miltonian: "for Algernon Sidney, Milton, and honest Ludlow are my Heroes." Regarding Milton's political views, Hollis observed to Mayhew:

> If I understand Milton's principles they are these. That Government, at least our Government is by compact. That a King becoming a Tyrant, and the compact thereby broken, the Power reverts again to the Constituents, the People, who may punish such Tyrant as they see fit, and constitute such a new form of government as shall then appear to them to be most expedient.[15]

Hollis insisted that it was Charles who had, in effect, forced Milton and his contemporaries to become republicans and that Milton's views were in fact compatible with balanced monarchy:

> It is true indeed that that form of Government which he and many other able honest men inclined to on the death and punishment of the Tyrant Charles was a Commonwealth; which the Army that Hydra-beast prevented; forcing the Nation thereby, against its bent, after numberless vexations, to call back that riot-Prince Charles the second. But Milton nor the warmest Commonwealth's man, never thought of altering the antient form of Government till Charles the first had sinned flagrantly and repeatedly against it, and had destroyed it by his violences. On the contrary there are several and very fine passages in his prose works, where he commends that antient form exceedingly, and with highest justice; and it is undoubted truth, that we owe the most noble and the most happy Revolution [of 1688] to his principles, and to those of his friends; principles that will uphold and cherish every honest virtuous Prince, and check only and confound, which God grant, every bad prince, and every Tyrant. You see, Dear Sir, If I have explained myself clearly, that it is to Milton, the divine Milton, and such as him, in the struggles of the civil wars and the Revolution, that we are beholden for all the

> manifold and unexampled Blessings which we now every
> where enjoy.[16]

Hollis's observation that it was the behavior of "the Tyrant Charles" that drove Milton and his contemporaries to become republicans would apply equally to the case of the American colonies in the 1760s and 1770s, when British policies forced men and women who considered themselves loyal subjects to embrace independence and republicanism. When the Stamp Act was passed, Mayhew warned that such oppressive treatment of the colonies by Britain would effect "an intire Breach between them, which might prove fatal to both!" He asked Hollis to republish an extract from Trenchard and Gordon's classic Whig treatise, *Cato's Letters*, which included a startling image suggesting the inevitability of an American rebellion: "No Creatures suck the Teats of their Dams longer than they can draw milk from thence, or can provide themselves with better Food: Nor will any Country continue their Subjection to another, only because their Great Grandmothers were acquainted."[17]

Mayhew attempted to assure Hollis that President Holyoke's

> political notions, and sentiments concerning Milton, I am
> confident, are not materially different from your own. These
> are indeed the principles which, God be thanked! generally
> prevail in New England, though bigotry in religious matters
> has far too much place amongst us; so much, as almost makes
> me ashamed of my country.[18]

Mayhew wrote further that he had distributed the "duplicates" of the books that Hollis had sent him.

> Particularly, one of the very elegant copies of Milton's *Lives*,
> etc. I gave (as from an unknown person) to Mr. Hutchinson,
> the lieutenant Governor of this province, who is a gentleman
> of capacity and erudition; to whom it was very acceptable.

Milton's liberty books were traveling in important circles.

For Hollis, like many other Commonwealthmen, the cause of liberty was inseparable from that of social and economic progress. In addition to his publishing activities, he was involved in the Society for the Arts, the Royal Society, and the Antiquaries, and he urged Mayhew to start similar societies for the promotion of the arts and sciences in the colonies. In a letter of May 21, 1760, Mayhew congratulated Hollis for his membership in "so many worthy societies . . . instituted for the noble purposes of advancing learning, arts and commerce; for the relief of the distressed, etc."[19] He observed, however, that even the "most learned and public-spirited gentlemen amongst us," with whom he had discussed Hollis's suggestion, felt that the colonies were not ripe for such enterprises. Mayhew later wrote that he had nevertheless communicated the proposal to Winthrop, whose recent lecture on earthquakes he was sending to Hollis, along with James Otis, Jr.'s *The Rudiments of Latin Prosody, etc.* Hollis insisted on the importance of such "noble designs" for promoting learning, explaining to Mayhew

> That neither did we think ourselves ripe enough here in England for such designs, till *so late* as the Year 1660, when the Royal Society was instituted; not by the favor of the many, but by the wisdom and ENERGY *of a few*, the excellent Mr. Hartlib, a foreigner to whom Milton addressed his matchless treatise on education, Mr. Boyle, Dr. Wallis, Dr. Wilkins, Dr. Sprat, and some others.[20]

Hollis shared the common misconception that Hartlib was a founder of the Royal Society; in fact, he was ostracized by the original members, who had made their peace with the restored monarchy. He was too closely associated with the republicanism of the Commonwealth to be considered for membership.[21] It is noteworthy, however, that Hollis associated Hartlib and Milton and that he spoke in the same breath of Milton and of those reformers whose primary concern was to promote scientific innovation and economic progress.

Mayhew's anxiety about a plot by the Church of England to establish an American episcopate first appeared in his letters to Hollis in 1762. Mayhew suspected that the Society for the Propagation of the Gospel in Foreign Parts, an arm of the Church of England founded in 1701 to bring the Gospel to slaves and Indians, was attempting to establish one or more Anglican bishops in the colonies. When in 1759 the Society opened a mission church in Cambridge, on the doorstep of Harvard, under the direction of the ostentatious and bungling East Apthorp, it seemed clear to Mayhew and other Massachusetts Nonconformists that the Society was not confining itself to the conversion of slaves and Indians. Apthorp, residing in his luxurious "Bishop's Palace" (as Mayhew later called it), made no attempt to disguise his view that the English in New England had to be converted and were sorely in need of an Anglican episcopate to "hinder *corruptions* of Christianity from prevailing there," especially as "Many pernicious errors took early root in these provinces."[22] With such provocative references to the Puritan heritage, the battle was joined. Mayhew and others saw the efforts to establish an American bishopric as a continuation of the bloody persecutions that had driven the Puritans to Massachusetts in the 1630s and had led to the English Civil War. If the Church of England were ever established in New England, Mayhew warned, religious oaths would be demanded of the colonists and "all of us [would] be taxed for the support of *bishops* and their *underlings*."[23]

The Society's activities were particularly alarming because they coincided with another momentous development in relations between Britain and the colonies. In 1763 the American colonies had not yet been directly taxed by Parliament. But with the conclusion of the Seven Years' War and Britain's defeat of the French and Spanish in North America, the British government sought to shift to the American colonies some of the burden of administering and defending its burgeoning empire. Chancellor of the Exchequer George Grenville inaugurated this policy with the Sugar Act of 1764, the same year he proposed in Parliament that stamp duties be laid on the colonies to support British outposts. Thus, in the minds of Mayhew and other Nonconforming colonists, as for the seventeenth-century Commonwealthmen, the issues of ecclesiastical and civil oppression, tithes and unlawful taxes, became inextricably entwined. "[I]f bishops were speedily to be sent to America," Mayhew declared,

> it seems not wholly improbable, from what we hear of the *unusual* tenor of some late Parliamentary acts and bills for raising money on the poor colonies *without their consent*, that provisions might be made for the support of these bishops, if not of all the Church clergy also, in the *same way*.[24]

The new breed of aggressive Anglican churchmen in the colonies, together with the swelling number of royal officials, raised the specter of the dark days in England of Archbishop Laud; history seemed to be repeating itself. Mayhew's detractors, in turn, accused him of attempting to set up an inquisition against the "national religion," a scheme they said lacked only Oliver Cromwell and his "Forty Thousand Cut-throats" to be put into action.[25] Staunch Anglicans such as the Reverend Samuel Johnson, who had worked closely with Archbishop of Canterbury Thomas Secker on his plan to establish an American episcopate, remembered that in the English Revolution the cry of "no bishop" had quickly led to that of "no king"—that the cries for religious freedom and political reform had been inseparable.

John Adams, whose "Dissertation on the Canon and the Feudal Law" explained that the settlement of New England had been a decisive blow to the "wicked conspiracy" of ecclesiastical and civil tyranny, summed up the issues of 1763 when he recollected many years later that the Mayhew-Apthorp controversy had

> spread an universal alarm against the authority of Parliament. It excited a general alarm and just apprehension that bishops, and dioceses, and churches, and priests, and tithes, were to be imposed on us by Parliament. It was known that neither King, nor ministry, nor archbishops could appoint bishops in America without an Act of Parliament; and if Parliament could tax us, they could establish the Church of England with all its creeds, articles, tests, ceremonies, and tithes, and prohibit all other churches, as conventicles and schism shops.[26]

In 1762 Mayhew endeavored to enlist the aid of his English correspondent against what in his view was creeping civil and religious tyranny in the colonies. He described "a scheme forming for sending a Bishop into these parts," remarking that "our Governor, Mr. Bernard, a true churchman, is deep in the *plot*," and asked Hollis to use his influence "to prevent this project's taking effect."[27] In response to this request and similar ones related to the Stamp Act crisis, Hollis requested that Mayhew not involve him openly in the Anglo-American dispute. He assured Mayhew that

> You are in no real danger, at present, in respect to the creation of Bishops in America, if I am rightly informed; though a matter extreamly desired by our Clergy and Prelates, and even talked of greatly, at this time, among themselves.[28]

In other letters he quoted Milton—"But evil on itself shall back recoyl"— in writing of Archbishop Secker, who disliked the colonists and "fixed a Spye upon them," in the person of East Apthorp.[29] Hollis directed Mayhew to Milton, along with Marvell, as an authority on the establishment issue.[30]

Despite Hollis's reluctance to become involved directly in the growing conflict, he wrote increasingly about political issues in his letters to Mayhew, beginning in 1765, the year of the Stamp Act. On March 4, he reported a positive reaction among the English Whigs to *The Rights of the British Colonies Asserted and Proved*, by James Otis, Jr. Hollis quoted what a "friend" had written to him about the pamphlet:

126

> All the great and generous Principles of government, that is of
> public good, which ever warmed Milton, Locke, or any patriot
> head, are familiar to the author, and applied to his own
> particular argument in a way they had not thought of, but
> would have honored and approved.[31]

Meanwhile, Hollis had taken up the colonists' cause within Britain,
meeting with that "Chieftan of Liberty" William Pitt and other influential
government figures and making the position of the Americans known
through the publication of such works as Adams's "Dissertation." A year
later Hollis wrote to Mayhew that he had done "all in my little Power" to
effect the repeal of the Stamp Act in 1766.

Mayhew, in response to the repeal of the hated act, preached his
famous sermon *The Snare Broken*. In it, he celebrated the victory of
Liberty, the "celestial maid," but he condemned the lawless rioters who
had indulged their greedy and vindictive natures under the cover of
patriotic zeal.[32] He traced his own commitment to liberty to the early
influence of the classical and modern republican writers:

> Having been initiated, in youth, in the doctrines of civil
> liberty, as they were taught by such men as Plato, Demosthe-
> nes, Cicero and other renowned persons among the ancients;
> and such as Sidney and Milton, Locke and Hoadley, among
> the moderns; I liked them; they seemed rational. Having
> earlier still learnt from the holy scriptures, that wise, brave
> and virtuous men were always friends to liberty; that God gave
> the Israelites a King (or absolute Monarch) in his anger,
> because they had not sense and virtue enough to like a free
> common-wealth, and to have himself for their King; that the
> Son of God came down from heaven, to make us "free in-
> deed."[33]

Mayhew's appreciation of the difference between liberty and license and
his belief that Christian liberty was best realized in a free commonwealth
were part of his debt to Milton.

Milton and the Education of John Adams

For the next generation of American Commonwealthmen, soon to become
leaders of the Revolution, the political tracts of Milton and Sidney served
as handbooks on liberty. But if John Adams is at all typical, it was not

only Milton the polemicist but also Milton the epic poet who left an imprint on that generation. In fact, for Adams it was the poetry that made the earlier impression. Adams read Milton's epic as a young man, at an important juncture in his life—one of those moments when people are especially susceptible to the influence of new ideas. He came away from *Paradise Lost* with a sense of the complexity and lawfulness of the physical universe and of human society that would inform his political outlook throughout life.

In 1756 Adams was twenty-one and a recent graduate of Harvard. Employed as a village schoolmaster, he felt isolated and dissatisfied with his lot ("I have no Books, no Time, no Friends. I must therefore be contented to live and die an ignorant, obscure fellow")[34] and was undecided about the future course of his life:

> I am dull, and inactive, and all my Resolution, all the Spirits I can muster, are insufficient to rouse me from this senseless Torpitude. My Brains seem constantly in as great Confusion, and wild disorder, as Miltons Chaos. They are numb, dead. I have never any bright, refulgent Ideas. Every Thing appears in my mind, dim and obscure like objects seen thro' a dirty glass or roiled water.[35]

Paradise Lost supplied Adams with imagery for describing both his ennui and the state of creative alertness ("bright, refulgent Ideas") that escaped him. Several days later, on April 30, he wrote that Milton's "soul," suffused through the epic, was at once foreign to him, in his present state, and inspirational:

> Reading Milton. That mans Soul, it seems to me, was distended as wide as Creation. His Powr over the human mind was absolute and unlimited. His Genius was great beyond Conception, and his Learning without Bounds. I can only gaze at him with astonishment, without comprehending the vast Compass of his Capacity.[36]

It is interesting to contrast for a moment the young Thomas Jefferson's response to *Paradise Lost*. That Jefferson was also deeply affected by Milton's epic and by *Samson Agonistes* is evident from the sheer number of passages—forty-seven—that he copied into the commonplace book he kept during his student days. (This book contained "the maxims and principles which so impressed his still plastic mind, that by them he was to govern the rest of his life.")[37] But it is also evident, from the selection of passages, that Jefferson's "Milton" was fundamentally different from Adams's, for Jefferson was fascinated primarily with Satan—with his "unconquerable will . . . And Courage never to submit or yield." On Jefferson's selection of excerpts Gilbert Chinard has this to say:

> He read systematically through it, collecting here and there aphorisms and moral developments, . . . Neglecting the purely poetical or theological passages he found in *Paradise Lost* a conception of life with which he was already familiar through his reading of the ancient Sages. It was the same *taedium vitae*, the same grave lamento on the brevity of life, only more solemn. It was, finally, the same lesson of resignation to one's fate and the same aspiration to eternal rest and sleep.[38]

This stoical philosophy was, at least, what Jefferson projected onto *Paradise Lost*. The largest number of quotations he copied on any one topic are those from Satan's defiant early speeches proclaiming his undaunted will and plans for revenge, even in the face of the Deity's omnipotence. "Better to reign in Hell" and "The mind is its own place" are among the passages Jefferson copied out. Anticipating Blake and Shelley, Jefferson apparently saw heroic qualities in Satan's defiance. His Satan is a tragic hero in the classical vein, who refuses to submit to fate and boasts of controlling his own destiny.

To Jefferson, Milton was the champion of individual liberties against oppressive institutions, an eloquent and impassioned spokesman for freedom of religion and of the human spirit. In the contest over church disestablishment in Virginia, one of the most important battles of Jefferson's career, he freely adopted Milton's arguments for the separation of church and state.[39] Milton was, indeed, the champion of liberty that Jefferson imagined him to be. However, Jefferson's fascination with Satan's speeches showed a Romantic bias in his approach to the epic. His "Milton" was more the nineteenth-century individualist and liberal democrat than the seventeenth-century republican.

Adams's response to Milton's epic may be inferred from the comments on Milton in his diary and from the thoughts he recorded there around the time when he was reading *Paradise Lost*. Judging from the entry of April 30 quoted above, Adams seems to have been impressed not by Satan but by Milton himself. In reading *Paradise Lost*, Adams was struck by the vastness of Milton's mind and of the universe, an impression that colored his thinking permanently. On May 1 he commented on the variety and interconnectedness of nature:

> If we consider a little of this our Globe we find an endless
> Variety of Substances, mutually connected with and depend-
> ent on Each other. . . . The Stupendous Plan of operation was
> projected by him who rules the universe, and a part assigned
> to every particle of matter to act, in this great and complicated
> Drama.[40]

This notion of a design in the universe and in human affairs was in keeping with the ideas of contemporary rationalistic thinkers such as Richard Bentley (whom Adams was also reading at the time); however, it was also entirely compatible with the older religious doctrine of design found in Milton. Adams regarded nature's "prodigious variety" of species and the uniformity of distinguishing properties among the individuals of each species as evidence of "the continual and vigilant Providence of God."[41] Thus, for Adams and his contemporaries, increasing knowledge about the highly intricate organization of the natural world provided further evidence of a supreme intelligence ordering the universe—not through miraculous intervention, of course, but through patterns of causality.[42]

Adams's astronomical speculations of the same period (April 25–26) seem also to have been prompted by his reading of the epic. If other globes were inhabited (as astronomers believed at the time), then humanity was "no more in comparison of the whole rational Creation of God, than a point to the Orbit of Saturn," Adams observed. Had the inhabitants of other globes, like man, "committed moral Wickedness"? If so, to which alternative would a Calvinist subscribe: that God assumes the shapes of the various species so as to suffer the penalties of their crimes, or that they are consigned to everlasting perdition?[43] This somewhat fanciful disquisition recalls Adam's conversation with Raphael in Book VIII of *Paradise Lost* ("this Earth a spot, a grain, / An Atom, with the Firmament compar'd / And all her number'd Stars" [17 ff.]; "Dream not of other Worlds, what Creatures there / Live, in what state, condition or degree" [175 f.]; etc.).

The following day Adams corrected his overly hasty assumption that the extraterrestrial beings must be tainted, like human beings, with original sin:

> For 1st. we know not that the Inhabitants of other Globes have
> sinned. Nothing can be argued in this manner, till it is proved
> at least probable that all those Species of rational Beings have
> revolted from their rightful Sovereign.[44]

At the very least we can suppose that Milton's epic triggered these theological speculations; furthermore, Adams appears to have agreed with Milton's rejection of predestination and his insistence on Adam and Eve's responsibility for the Fall. Adams concludes by marvelling at the millions of prospects on the surface of the Earth and of every other celestial body, each prospect filled with infinite variety: "great! and marvellous are thy works!".

During the same period Adams undertook further investigations into the theology of Creation. On May 23, he wrote that he had been reading Duncan Forbes, a contemporary Scottish theologian, and Richard Bentley. He arrived at the following conclusion:

> Thus the Deity produced this vast and beautiful Frame of
> Universe out of Nothing, i.e. He had no preexistent matter to
> work upon or to change from a Chaos into a World. But He
> produced a World into Being by his almighty Fiat, perhaps in
> a manner analogous to the Production of Resolutions in our
> minds.[45]

On this subject, Adams evidently disagreed with Milton, for whom Creation was *ex Deo*.

There is another clear echo of Milton's epic—on the moral level—in Adams's diary entry of April 29, where he writes that the "proper Business" of life is not to accumulate large fortunes or to aspire to high honors or offices, "not to waste our Health and Spirits in Pursuit of the Sciences, but constantly to improve our selves in Habits of Piety and Virtue."[46] (Such ideas bring to mind Raphael's advice to Adam to "be lowly wise: / Think only what concerns thee and thy being" [*PL*, VIII, 173 f.].) Reading Milton seems to have encouraged Adams's speculations about God, Creation, and other theological topics, as well as science and morality.

Reason and Revelation

The vision of a vast and intricate design in the universe, which Adams appears to have derived from Milton and eighteenth-century rationalists alike, was consonant with the providential view of history that he inherited from the seventeenth-century New England Puritans. As the conflict with Britain drew near, Adams (like other Puritan sons) began thinking about America's history and future in millennial terms: the settlement of America, he believed, was the "Opening of a grand scene and Design in

Providence, for the Illumination of the Ignorant and the Emancipation of the slavish Part of Mankind all over the Earth."[47] And although Adams devoted himself to the secular means for realizing John Winthrop's vision of the New World as the "city upon a hill" of Scripture, he shared with the Puritan fathers an intense consciousness of his nation's special calling in the still-unfolding moral and spiritual rebirth of human society that began with the Reformation.

Milton showed a similar sense of millennial optimism and national election in his view of the special role of England in the continuing reformation of the church. The motif of the "chosen nation," which had its roots in the Tudor period, was epitomized in Milton's patriotic declaration that it was God's manner to reveal himself "first to his Englishmen." This had been the case when He chose to begin the Reformation through Wycliffe and in England ("that out of her as out of Sion should be proclaimed and sounded forth the first tidings and trumpet of reformation to all Europe"). In 1644 Milton was convinced by the new stirrings in the "mansion house of liberty" that, once again, God had selected His Englishmen to inaugurate "some new and great period in his Church, even to the reforming of reformation itself."[48]

Milton's conviction about England's national calling in the unfolding history of the true church coexisted with a strong sense of personal vocation. As a young man he aspired to do for his language what Homer, Vergil, Dante, and the ancient Hebrew writers had done for theirs. The historical conjuncture of the 1640s, however, filled him with a sense of obligation to employ his "left hand" in the pamphlet wars postponing the realization of his talents as a poet. In a famous autobiographical passage in his *Second Defence of the English People*, Milton explained retrospectively his decision to delay his poetic calling and enter the conflict in 1641 as a pamphleteer:

> I perceived that men were following the true path to liberty and that from these beginnings, these first steps, they were making the most direct progress toward the liberation of all human life from slavery, provided that the discipline arising from religion should overflow into the morals and institutions of the state.[49]

Thus the Christian notion of time *sub specie aeternitatis*—the intersection of eternity with *chronos*, or ordinary clock time, at certain moments of "fit opportunity"—that Edward Tayler explores in Milton's poetry and in his fulfillment of his poetic calling was also active in Milton's understanding of human history.[50] Milton believed that secular history offered such moments of fit opportunity—England in the 1640s was one—when individuals were called upon to realize God's will. By 1660 the majority of Englishmen had proved unequal to the historical moment; then Milton, like the prophet Ezekiel, addressed himself to the virtuous few, the spiritual remnant, "whom God may raise of these stones to become children of reviving liberty."[51]

John Winthrop had seized on the same image borrowed from the prophet at the close of his famed sermon aboard the *Arbella* in 1630, when he spoke of the city on a hill whose inhabitants had been resurrected, "bone to his bone."[52] The rhetoric of the New England Puritans, like Milton's, was pervaded by such typological habits of thought, through which historical individuals and events were related to the scheme of redemptive history. Thus, Winthrop's biographer Cotton Mather represented the first governor of Massachusetts as a "type" of Nehemiah, the prophet of the return, who led the Israelites back from Babylon to the Promised Land. Winthrop was also linked to Jacob, Moses, Job, John the Baptist, and other biblical figures, all themselves types prefiguring Christ.[53] The typological method was originally a branch of hermeneutics that linked events and persons in the New Testament to their prefigurations in the Old, thereby demonstrating the continuity of God's revelation from one to the other. This method was liberally applied by seventeenth-century Puritans in Britain and America to affirm their own role—through their trials and victories in secular history—in bringing about the final defeat of the Antichrist.

It has been pointed out that typological identifications, like millennialism itself, implied a fundamental optimism, a confidence about the forward progress of history and the ultimate victory of God's chosen, and that this faith helped the New England colonists of the "new Eden" withstand the continual setbacks of famine, disease, Indian attacks, and religious controversy.[54] At the same time, the habit of perceiving experience in terms of figural correspondences—New England as the "New Israel," colonization as the "errand in the wilderness"—conferred on day-to-day existence and the events of secular history a sacred *telos*.[55] The actors in this cosmic drama believed that they were participating in redemptive history through their secular roles. This kind of outlook has been analyzed by Bercovitch, Tayler, and other scholars who stress the difference between allegory and figural exegesis: whereas in allegory the literal represents something of greater importance, in figural exegesis the literal-historical level is all-important. In other words, it was *through their role in history* that Winthrop and other New England "saints" could be said to resemble the succession of Old and New Testament prophets, namely, Moses, Nehemiah, John the Baptist, and Christ.[56] Thus, the typological method itself, in assigning significance to the distinctive human being acting in history, may have fostered a belief in the efficacy and importance of individual initiative and "works."

The continuing hold of the Puritans' "imagistic consciousness based upon typology"[57] is evident in the rhetoric of the American Revolution. For instance, in a letter to Adams in March 1775, Samuel Swift hailed him as a new Moses for his defense of colonial rights in his "Novanglus" letters: "No man is Corn for himself, the publick have a Claim to the Gifts of N. Anglus. . . . as Moses Guided under God the Israelites of Old so let N. Anglus guide direct and Stear this our New English Israel."[58] Swift went on to portray the building conflict between Britain and the colonies as a type of the apocalyptic battle of Revelation. After describing the colonists as "a most Loyal and dutiful people who are ill used and Abused by those who are called but misscall'd the Lords Anointed," he warned that

> There is a party, Devil-drove who now begin to be hagar ey'd and who have Recourse to all that is Hellishly Artful, in order to keep their heads above water and cannot do it neither, for if their infernal Lyes Should Chance to Obtain Credence for 24th hours it is 12 more than Usual. Let Nov Anglus neither eat nor drink til he has slain Paul.[59]

Swift's language, rich in typological identifications, a blend of Milton and the Bible, is representative of the heightened rhetoric that the New England patriots adopted to paint the wiles of their adversary as the Revolution approached.

John Adams's own "Dissertation on the Canon and the Feudal Law" is generally recognized as belonging to the figural genre of literature that began in America at least as early as 1630, the year of Winthrop's "city upon a hill" sermon.[60] In his "Dissertation" Adams depicts the settlement of New England as a decisive episode in Liberty's struggle against the two forms of tyranny, ecclesiastical and civil, and underlines the role that popular education has played in securing freedom in those colonies. The distinctive, millennial character of the work, as Ernest Tuveson argues, arises from Adams's insistence that, historically, the loss of political liberty has stemmed from religious corruption—the perversion of the true church. "This is not a diatribe, of the conventional Enlightenment kind, against religious deceit in general," Tuveson writes. "No disciple of Rousseau or Voltaire would have said 'it was foretold'," as Adams does in writing about mankind's prophesied bondage to the "Romish Clergy."[61]

"A Dissertation" traces the history of the canon and feudal laws and their evolution into an "infernal conspiracy" between temporal and spiritual rulers: the temporal grandees maintained the ascendancy of the priesthood, and the spiritual grandees employed their ascendancy "over the *consciences* of the *people*, in impressing on their minds, a *blind, implicit* obedience to civil magistracy."[62] In a manner reminiscent of Milton's *The Ready and Easy Way*, Adams analyzes the relation between forms of government and the character of the people living under them. He agrees with Milton and other Commonwealthmen that absolute monarchy breeds servility. In the earliest ages of the world, when the people's intelligence was "little higher than the camels and elephants, that carried them and their engines to war," absolute monarchy was the most common form of government. Conversely, "wherever a general knowledge and sensibility have prevail'd among the *people*, arbitrary government, and every kind of oppression, have lessened and disappeared in proportion."[63] Thus, Adams maintains, powerful princes have ever sought to wrest from the people the knowledge of their rights—rights that are antecedent to all earthly government and civil law because derived from the Great Legislator of the universe.

In Adams's history, one dark age succeeds another, and the "wicked confederacy" lasts until God raises up the champions who begin the Reformation. (Thus, Adams repeats the formula of Milton's *Of Reformation* and of countless other Protestant ecclesiastical histories.) From the time of the Reformation to the settlement of America, knowledge increases, especially in England, and, in proportion, ecclesiastical and civil tyranny lose their strength. The people become increasingly sensible of their oppression and determined to rid themselves of it. The struggle against the "wicked confederacy" culminates and becomes bloody under "the *execrable* race of the *Steuarts*."

> It was this great struggle, that peopled America. It was not religion *alone*, as is commonly supposed; but it was a love of *universal Liberty*, and an hatred, a dread, an horror of the infernal conspiracy, before described, that projected, conducted, and accomplished the settlement of America.[64]

Here Adams stresses the twofold concept of liberty that arose in reaction to the ancient collaboration of church and state. However, he also acknowledges and defends the religious nature of the undertaking of those "first Planters," who fled to the wilderness of America hoping to escape the dual tyranny and found a new Eden. He defends them against charges that they were "enthusiastical, superstitious and republican"—a telling combination of offenses. On the contrary, he writes, their religious enthusiasm "was greatly to their honour": no great enterprise was ever achieved "without a large mixture of that noble infirmity." The Puritans' judgment in framing policy, Adams concludes, "was founded in revelation, and in reason too; It was consistent with the principles, of the best, and greatest, and wisest legislators of antiquity."[65]

Adams is insistent on the point that the New England Puritans were not enemies of monarchy or church. They merely recognized that serious abuses resulted when the church acquired temporal powers (as Milton had asserted in *Of Reformation*) and that popular power was needed to balance the powers of both king and priest. The Puritans

> saw clearly, that popular powers must be placed, as a guard, a countroul, a ballance, to the powers of the monarch, and the priest, in every government, or else it would soon become the man of sin, the whore of Babylon, the mystery of iniquity, a great and detestable system of fraud, violence, and usurpation.[66]

The aim of the Puritan fathers who emigrated to America was to establish a church government more consistent with Scripture and a state government more agreeable to the dignity of human nature. Their program, as Adams describes it, resembled Milton's as stated in the anti-episcopal tracts of the early 1640s: removal of feudal inequalities and dependencies in church and state and preservation of a limited monarchy. Thus, the Puritans abolished the system of diocesan episcopacy and established ordination on the basis of the Bible and common sense. This required the clergy to show diligence, learning, and piety and rendered them more independent of the civil powers (as Milton proposed in *The Likeliest Means to Remove Hirelings*).

Linking past tradition with the present, Adams asserts that the Puritan founders transmitted to their posterity "an hereditary ardor for liberty and thirst for knowledge." They also passed on a thoroughgoing contempt for the doctrines of "hereditary indefeasible right" and the "divine miraculous original of government," whereby the priesthood had enveloped the feudal monarchy with an aura of divine sanction. Because the myth of the divine origin of monarchy was the basis for the doctrine of passive obedience and nonresistance to political authority, the Puritans—and Adams—believed that the priesthood represented a threat not just to religious freedom but to civil liberty as well.[67]

Adams's "Dissertation" is cited by J. G. A. Pocock as epitomizing the secularization of thought in eighteenth-century America. It is true that the essay's goal is secular: the "city upon a hill" becomes identified with balanced government in which neither an established clergy nor any other agency of corruption disturbs the virtue and freedom of the people. Yet "A Dissertation" harks back to the millennial thinking of Adams's Puritan forebears, which fitted the battles of secular history to the divine scheme for human redemption. Adams viewed the evolution toward the new secular goal in a way that resembled the older figural outlook: for him, the goal of a balanced republican government gave a shape to history, imposing a *telos* on discrete historical events. Adams would later write that the American Revolution was "an Enterprise that is and will be an Astonishment to vulgar Minds all over the World, in this and in future Generations." The new secular *telos* conferred on the Revolution's participants a decisive role in the great design of world history. On the eve of the Declaration of Independence, Adams remarked that he and his compatriots were living "at a time when the greatest law-givers of antiquity would have wished to have lived."[68]

Civil and Ecclesiastical Tyranny

With Parliament's approval of the Stamp Act in March 1765, Adams's "Dissertation" took on new political urgency, and he devoted its latter sections to an analysis of the Act. He wrote that, in conjunction with the activities of the Society for the Propagation of the Gospel in Foreign Parts, the Act presaged a resurgence of civil and ecclesiastical oppression, a rehabilitation of the feudal and canon laws. "A Dissertation" was well received in Whig circles in England, although it was not at first ascribed to Adams. In 1765 Thomas Hollis had the work republished in the *London Chronicle* as part of his effort to effect the Stamp Act's repeal. He republished it a second time in 1768, in the pamphlet *The True Sentiments of America,* mistakenly ascribing the authorship to Jeremiah Gridley until the Reverend Andrew Eliot advised him that Adams was the real author.

Adams's argument against the Act clearly owed a great deal to Mayhew's political sermons and to the argument of James Otis, Jr., in the famous writs of assistance case of 1761. Otis had argued in that precedent-setting case that Parliament's law empowering royal colonial officials to issue writs (general search warrants) violated the British Constitution's guarantee of property rights. There was a higher law, embodied in the Constitution, to which Parliament had to conform.[69] Such arguments, by now part of a common Whig armamentarium, had been originally formulated by Milton and other Commonwealthmen. Adams's critique of the Stamp Act hinged on two points in particular. First, British liberties were original, inalienable rights antecedent to Parliament, and rulers were merely trustees of the people, who could revoke their authority if it was abused. Second (and this point was interwoven with the first), knowledge was necessary in freeing the people from tyranny. (This principle was particularly Miltonic.) Adams dwelled at length on the early foundation and endowment of colleges in New England and on the region's unique laws directing every town of a certain number of families to maintain a grammar school at the public expense. He attacked the high-church party in Massachusetts for censuring the education of the common people as a needless expense, "an institution productive of idleness and vain speculation among the people, whose time and attention it is said ought to be devoted to labour, and not to public affairs or to examination into the conduct of their superiors." By contrast, Adams pointed out, the early Puritans understood that the chief safeguard against tyranny was "knowledge diffused generally thro' the whole body of people."

> For this purpose they laid, very early the foundations of colleges, and invested them with ample priviledges and emoluments; and it is remarkable, that they have left among their posterity, so universal an affection and veneration for those seminaries, and for liberal education, that the meanest of the people contribute chearfully to the support and maintenance of them every year, and that nothing is more generally popular than projections for the honour, reputation and advantage of those seats of learning. But the wisdom and benevolence of our fathers rested not here. They made an early provision by law, that every town consisting of so many families, should be always furnished with a grammar school. They made it a crime for such a town to be destitute of a grammar school master, for a few months, and subjected it to an heavy penalty. So that the education of all ranks of people was made the care and expence of the public in a manner, that I believe has been unknown to any other people ancient or modern. [70]

Adams regarded the Stamp Act as a design to extinguish this tradition, by imposing duties on books, newspapers, and other means of knowledge and reintroducing the inequalities and dependencies of the feudal system.

In the final installment of "A Dissertation," Adams complained that in recent years and months American colonists had been overly cautious about offending Britain, remaining silent about their grievances. He attacked the view that the colonists owed a filial duty and submission to

Mother Britain: such thoughts were actually rebellious, he argued, in that they presumed that the king and Parliament were imperious, unrelenting tyrants. Adams cited the Magna Carta and the Revolutionary Settlement of 1688 to support his position that British liberties were not grants of princes and parliaments but original rights, coequal with royal prerogative and the institutions of government.

Thus did Adams counter the Tory argument that the patriot Whigs were inciting acts of disobedience against the mother country. The central thrust of "A Dissertation"—its rehabilitation of the Puritan past— served a similar end. Increasingly in the 1760s and early 1770s, Mayhew, Adams, and other Whig leaders in Massachusetts, the vanguard of the movement for independence, called attention to the native source of their principles—those "first Planters," the Puritan founders, whose republicanism and religious ardor Adams extolled. To the Tory charge that they were disobedient children, the patriot Whigs answered, in effect, that they were fulfilling their filial obligations to their true parents, the Puritan founding fathers. Thus, the revived emphasis on the Puritan heritage may have been partly an ideological necessity, a response to the strongly ingrained standards of filial obligation that the Tories invoked.[71] But the ideological motivation of the Whigs does not detract from the truth of the national genealogy they constructed. The patriots of the 1760s and 1770s *were* completing the work of the Puritans who migrated to America and were bringing to fruition the ideas of those Commonwealthmen, such as Milton, who had remained in England. As the conflict with Britain intensified, the patriots drew increasingly on both of these traditions— adapting at will libertarian and millennial ideas and rhetoric—in arguing the justice of their cause.

6

Paradise Lost and the
Language of the Revolution

John Adams, who as a young man reported being captivated by the power of Milton's epic, found in the Satan of *Paradise Lost* an apt figure for depicting the opponents of the American Revolution. It was not only that the British and their supporters in the colonies were the evil adversaries and, hence, devils. From the Whig point of view, there were numerous resemblances between the Tories and Milton's infernal spirits. For one thing, the Tories had overturned the existing political order through "late innovations" such as the tax on tea. This and other attempts to "new-model" the original colonial charters, nullifying their provisions for self-government, made the Tories the diabolical rebels of the conflict, innovators who had necessitated a self-defense movement by the colonies. Furthermore, in their evil, divisive strategies, the Tories exhibited all of the vengeance and cunning of Milton's Satan after his fall from the "Battlements of Heaven."

"The Arch Enemy [General Thomas Gage] is at work again in his infernal Council at Boston," Adams wrote to James Warren in early 1775.[1] Gage, commander in chief of the British army in America, had been appointed governor of Massachusetts in early 1774, succeeding "that damn'd *arch traitor*" Thomas Hutchinson.[2] Gage's instructions from Parliament were to punish the colony for the Boston Tea Party through a series of Coercive Acts, which removed the capital to Salem (away from Samuel Adams and other Sons of Liberty), closed the port of Boston to trade, and quartered British troops in the city. Sam Adams regarded the posting of regiments in Boston as a "Snare" calculated to provoke acts of violence, but he confidently declared, "We shall endeavor by Circum-spection to frustrate the diabolical Designs of our Enemies."[3] Josiah Quincy, Jr., analyzed the act closing the port of Boston in similar terms: as a diabolical attempt to provoke and entrap the colonists. "Shall we impute to those who are dignified as 'the wisest and most august,' the barbarous projection—deliberately to ensnare that they might superla-tively punish?" he asked.[4] Quincy noted that the administration of the Boston Port Bill would pose an enormous temptation for those naval officers and customs officials who were authorized by the bill to order vessels and cargoes to any port in the world: "what scope for malice and ill-will; for pride and haughtiness; for avarice and power to wanton and insult, till one is satiated, and the other wearied! . . . what a cogent temptation is here placed to insnare the most virtuous?"[5] But he, too, was confident that the Massachusetts patriots would triumph over this latest trial, and he registered his optimism by selecting as an epigraph for his pamphlet an excerpt from Michael's lesson to Adam in *Paradise Lost:*

> What MAN can do against them, *not afraid,*
> *Though to* THE DEATH; against such CRUELTIES
> With *inward consolation* recompenc'd:
> And oft supported so, *as shall amaze*
> Their PROUDEST PERSECUTORS. (XII, 493 ff.)

Other Coercive Acts attempted to pack the upper house of the Massa-chusetts legislature with royal appointees; limit town meetings; secure jurors friendly to Britain; remove trials to courts outside the colony, "contrary to the very spirit of magna carta";[6] and inflict further measures that the colonists regarded as flagrant violations of "the immutable laws of nature, the principles of the English constitution, and the several charters or compacts."[7] To the Whigs, Britain's behavior was lawless, a violation of the colonists' natural and constitutional rights: it was *diaboli-cal,* in the manner of Satan's wanton revolt against the lawful hierarchy of Heaven.

Rather than submit to the Coercive Acts, Massachusetts went on the offensive. It initiated the First Continental Congress, elected an indepen-dent provincial assembly that acted as a government in the wings (a model followed by several other colonies), and limited General Gage's arena of political control to Boston.[8] By early 1775 Massachusetts was a tinderbox (The Battle of Lexington came in April); and to Whig leaders such as "the brace of Adamses" and James Warren, the spirit of the growing conflict recalled Milton's depiction of the war in Heaven. Describing the Tory ruling clique in Boston in early 1775, John Adams wrote to Warren:

> I never think of the Junto there, immured as they are, without recollecting, the infernal Spirits in Milton after they had recovered from their first astonishment arising from their fall from the Battlements of Heaven to the Sulphurous Lake—not subdued tho confounded—plotting a fresh assault upon the Skies. "What tho the Field be lost? All is not lost; th'unconquerable Will and Study of Revenge, immortal Hate and Courage never to submit or yield &c. Of this be sure, to do ought good never will be our Task, but ever to do ill our Sole Delight."—&c. Is not this rather too frolick some and triumphant for the Times, which are dull enough—and as bad as they can be. I doubt whether War, Carnage and Havock would make us more unhappy than this cruel state of Suspense we suffer in the Contemplation of them in Prospect.[9]

In Milton's portrait of the fallen rebel angels, plotting new treachery as they lie vanquished on the burning lake, Adams recognized the typical behavior of a defeated political faction regrouping for the next onslaught.

Like Milton's infernal spirits after their fall from Heaven, the Tories had pledged themselves to a vindictive policy, one that Sam Adams described as a "stroke of Vengeance," an "Act of Revenge."[10] However, this strategy, like Satan's, proved self-defeating. Britain and its colonial allies suffered one defeat after another in attempting to establish Parliament's right to tax the colonies without the consent of the provincial legislatures. The Stamp Act, the Townshend duties, and the tax on East India Company tea were impossible to enforce; and Britain's efforts to punish Massachusetts for leading the resistance to these unconstitutional schemes merely catalyzed more opposition. Led by the delegates from Massachusetts and Virginia, the First Continental Congress voted on December 1, 1774, to enact a set of nonimportation and nonconsumption agreements that soon proved remarkably effective.[11] Shortly thereafter, a convention of the Maryland provincial assembly voted to approve the proceedings of the Continental Congress—including a resolution to support Massachusetts or any colony should Parliament attempt to enforce its punitive acts there or forcibly exercise its assumed powers of taxation—and other colonies promised to follow suit. Yet bent on revenge, with the blind pertinacity of Satan and the rebel angels, Britain pursued a provocative policy that the Whig leaders realized was leading headlong to war.

For the moment, the Whigs saw themselves engaged in a battle to win popular support throughout the colonies and to combat the divisive designs of the Tory opposition. In his reply to Adams's letter, Warren remarked that the unity and moral fortitude of the colonies had never been stronger. At the same time, however, he evidently realized that the strategy of the Tories—to sow disunity by seducing colonists to side with the financially and militarily mightier mother country—could not be discounted. Warren found an appropriate image in the cunning of Milton's serpent in the Garden:

> now is the Time, the Exact Crisis to determine the point and
> the sooner the better before the Tories here can Compleat
> their Efforts to disunite and Embarrass. They are more Assid-
> uous than Satan was with our first Parents and equal him in
> deceit and Falshood, and with many find Success, no Stone is
> left Unturned to Effect their purposes. By that means we are
> Continually perplexed, which Added to the Contemplation
> (from one time to Another) of A War at last is (as you say) A
> state as Bad as can be.[12]

Warren went on to report that the Tories had become emboldened of late, "whether from Encouragement taken from the late publications, or A Spirit of delusion diffused Among them by the Infernal Junto at Boston I know not."[13]

Adams and Warren understood that the Tories were pursuing a classically "diabolical" tactic—diabolical like the modus operandi of Milton's Devil, "The Tempter ere th' Accuser of mankind"—in first encouraging Parliament's taxation of America for personal gain and then seeking to corrupt others by appealing to their desires for luxury and social distinction. "These Tories act the Part of the Devil—they tempt Men and Women into sin, and then reproach them for It, and become soon their Tormentors for it," Adams wrote on one occasion, when the Tories had attacked the popular party (the Whigs) for encouraging riotous behavior and general disrespect for law. Adams declared that the real lawlessness in the colonies was the illegal taxation by Parliament. The dissipation of some Bostonians, he explained, was due to the revenue itself, which had created a parasitic class of British pensioners and placemen.[14]

In Britain, some of the more foresighted parliamentary leaders, such as Edmund Burke and William Pitt, regarded ministerial policy toward America as ill-conceived—certain to lose the colonies—and argued for a more conciliatory course. These English Whigs and a small radical party continued to oppose the king and his ministers even after the official decision later in the year to wage war against the colonies to suppress "an open and avowed rebellion."[15] The radicals John Wilkes and David Hartley argued that even if a military victory were achieved it would mean nothing, for the large size and population of the country would make it impossible to keep America in a permanent state of subjugation. Said Hartley, echoing and adapting *Paradise Lost*, "You may bruise its heel, but you cannot crush its head. . . . The new world is before them. . . . When the final period of this once happy country shall overtake ourselves . . . may another Phoenix rise out of our ashes."[16]

The language of Hartley's prophetic warning to the North ministry harked back to the typological tradition of John Winthrop's sermon identifying America as the "city upon a hill" envisioned by the prophet Ezekiel. This tradition, which subsumed the secular event of the colonization of America and later the Revolution under the "grand scene and Design in Providence,"[17] was enriched over the eighteenth century by distinctly Miltonic images. For Hartley and other English Whigs, America in the 1770s called to mind the poet's vision of the grand prospect that lay before Adam and Eve as they ventured forth out of Paradise and into history, charged with forging their own destiny under the guiding hand of providence.

Hartley's remark also bore the imprint of a different, though compatible, tradition of thought: the eighteenth-century theory of the rise and fall of nations. The view that new, virtuous empires arose as older ones decayed and fell was expressed in his image of the phoenix rising from the ashes of "this once happy country" (Britain). The view of history implied in this theory was not merely cyclical, however. According to the Scottish moral philosopher Adam Ferguson, who was widely read in the colonies, "When nations succeed one another . . . the last is always the most knowing."[18] There was progress from cycle to cycle; the empires succeeded each other at higher levels of development, as if along an inclined axis. According to this cyclical-progressive view of history, eighteenth-century America was in the stage of youth, poised to succeed and surpass decadent Britain and become the next great empire. Its future lay before it. As evidence of the decline of Britain and the rise of America—and of the futility of the North ministry's bellicose policy— Wilkes contrasted the population decline in the mother country over the previous century with the burgeoning population of the colonies during the same period.

Whig Satire

The citations of *Paradise Lost* in nonliterary texts of the 1770s—amid more general invocations of the language and principles of the English

Commonwealth—show that Milton's imagery permeated American culture as a whole in this period, not just its literature.[19] For American men of letters of the eighteenth century, Milton was also a preeminent literary mentor, along with Pope and other English Neoclassical writers, and in turning to the political satire of the Revolution we find full-blown allusions to Milton's poetry. The figure of Satan, the guileful archenemy as depicted by Milton; the war in Heaven; the great consult in Pandemonium—these and other images from *Paradise Lost* were taken over by patriot satirists such as Philip Freneau and John Trumbull to portray the diabolical wiles of the colonies' British antagonists.

Freneau's "General Gage's Soliloquy," for example, which appeared at the time of the Massachusetts Coercive Acts, combines Miltonic imagery with Neoclassical prosody and wit. In Freneau's mock-heroic account of the siege of Boston, a blustering Gage imagines himself engaged in a re-enactment of the war in Heaven. Gage, as one would expect, presents the British as the stalwart upholders of God's cause; the revolutionists are lawless and diabolical rebels:

> Let heaven's broad concave to the center ring,
> And blackest night expand her sable wing,
> The infernal powers in dusky combat join,
> Wing the swift ball, or spring the deadly mine;
> (Since 'tis most true, tho' some may think it odd,
> The foes of Britain are the foes of God):
> Let bombs, like comets, kindle all the air,
> Let cruel famine prompt the orphan's prayer,
> And every ill that war or want can bring
> Be shower'd on subjects that renounce their king.[20]

Before long, Gage exposes himself and the ministers who employ him as the real devils in the conflict between Britain and the colonies:

> What is their plea?—our sovereign only meant
> This people should be taxed without consent.
> Ten years the court with secret cunning tried
> To gain this point—the event their hopes belied. (p. 155)

Since guile alone failed, Gage calls on Lord North, George III's prime minister, to back his policy of political bribery with military force and dispatch additional troops "to the states below." Gage prays for the assistance of the archenemy himself:

> That gloomy prince, whom mortals Satan call,
> Must help us quickly, if he help at all—
> You strive in vain by force of bribes to tie;
> They see through all your schemes with half an eye;
> If open force with secret bribes I join,
> The contest sickens—and the day is mine. (p. 156)

The distinction between open force and guile recalls, of course, the council in Hell in Book II of *Paradise Lost*, in which Milton's devils debate which way is best to recover Heaven, "Whether of open War or covert guile." Milton's scene recapitulates a central theme of the classical epics, the question of the relative merits of the methods of Achilles and of Odysseus. And, as the Adams-Warren correspondence suggests, the same debate—whether internal subversion or open confrontation is the more effective method for subduing an enemy—doubtless preoccupied Britain's leaders.

In Freneau's "The Midnight Consultations: or, a Trip to Boston," written shortly afterwards, Gage is revealed in full satanic splendor as "our western potentate" ("western" because he rules the western region of the empire), sitting exalted on "a crimson chair of state." Freneau and other Whig writers fastened on Milton's portrait of Satan as an oriental despot to depict the capriciousness of the apparently law-abiding British. "The Midnight Consultations," satirizing Gage's nocturnal meetings with the other British military leaders—Graves, Burgoyne, Percy, Howe, and Wallace—is directly modeled on the council in Hell:

> These, chief of all the tyrant-serving train,
> Exalted sate—the rest (a pensioned clan),
> A sample of the multitudes that wait,
> Pale sons of famine, at perdition's gate,
> . . . .
> Now Gage upstarting from his cushioned seat
> Swore thrice, and cried—" 'Tis nonsense to be beat!" (pp. 167–68)

Howe and the other exalted generals vent their vexation against North, "the brainless minister that planned / His bootless errand to this hostile land," and engage in mutual recriminations, a touch that is both historically accurate and reminiscent of Milton's quarreling devils. All that the British generals are able to agree on is a raid on some neighboring "rebel" sheep and cattle to secure a hearty roast beef dinner.

Freneau found various other similarities between the British generals and Milton's devils. Satanic pride, for example, is the motive behind his

147

generals' futile endeavor: "Pride sent them here, pride blasted in the bud, / Who, if she can, will build her throne in blood" (p. 178). The generals also execute their cause in a manner reminiscent of their literary originals. In *Paradise Lost* Satan and the apostate angels are ignominiously defeated in the three-day battle in Heaven; coincidentally, the British suffered three successive defeats in attempting to impose the Stamp Act, Townshend duties, and the tax on tea. Freneau seized on this parallel to suggest that Parliament and its minions in the colonies were as arrogant and blind as Milton's devils in continuing to issue proclamations and ultimatums:

> What deep offence has fired a monarch's rage?
> What moon-struck madness seized the brain of Gage?
> Laughs not the soul when an imprisoned crew
> Affect to pardon those they can't subdue,
> Though thrice repulsed, and hemmed up to their stations,
> Yet issue pardons, oaths, and proclamations! (p. 179)

To the relief of the colonists, life seemed to be imitating art.

Trumbull also drew on Milton and the Commonwealth tradition in *M'Fingal*, his mock-epic retrospective on the Revolutionary War, although his more immediate literary model was Samuel Butler's satire *Hudibras*.[21] Not completed until 1782, *M'Fingal* was already germinating during the period of the Boston Tea Party and Port Bill, when Trumbull was an apprentice in the law office of John Adams. The poem reflects Whig sentiments of the time, portraying the Tory forces as rebels against legitimate governments and constitutions. M'Fingal, Trumbull's fictitious Tory leader, is a rebel by birthright, a descendent of a long line of seditious, king-hating Scots who have made their peace with the new king only because of his generous dispersal of pensions. These pensions

> Hush'd down all murmurs of dissensions,
> And with the sound of potent metal,
> Brought all their blust'ring swarms to settle;
> Who rain'd his ministerial mannas,
> Till loud Sedition sung hosannahs;
> The good Lords-Bishops and the Kirk
> United in the public work. (p. 104)

The "public work" in this case is that of overturning the constitutions of the American colonies and enslaving formerly free citizens. Trumbull used to advantage the theological convention, observed by Milton, that placed Satan's rival throne in the northern regions of Heaven. For Trumbull's purposes this convention fortuitously coincided with Scotland's longstanding reputation as a seat of sedition against established government and, during the American Revolution, as a center of support for the extreme Tory position:

> Rebellion from the Northern regions,
> With Bute and Mansfield swore allegiance;
> All combin'd to raze as nuisance,
> Of church and state, the constitutions;
> Pull down the empire, on whose ruins
> They meant to edify their new ones;
> Enslave th'Amer'can wildernesses,
> And tear the provinces in pieces.
> For these our 'Squire among the valiant'st,
> Employ'd his time and tools and talents;
> And in their cause with manly zeal
> Used his first virtue, to rebel;
> And found this new rebellion pleasing
> As his old king-destroying treason. (pp. 104–5)

The opening action of the poem is a debate at a town meeting between M'Fingal and Honorius, leader of the Whig faction. The address by Honorius, couched in language and imagery borrowed from *Paradise Lost*, attributes the conflict between mother country and colonies to the satanic "conceit and pride" of Good Mother Britain. She has passed her "grand Climact'ric," and "Grim death" is on her doorstep.[22] Britain's judgment fails and "Strange whimsies" overtake her brain,

> As Eve when falling was so modest
> To fancy she should grow a goddess;
> As madmen, straw who long have slept on,
> Will stile them, Jupiter or Neptune:
> So Britain 'midst her airs so flighty,
> Now took a whim to be Almighty;
> Urg'd on to desp'rate heights of frenzy,
> Affirm'd her own Omnipotency. (pp. 109–10)

Britain's political behavior is as foolhardly as the delusions of Eve that lead to the Fall. Nevertheless, "For sake of legacies and wages" (the corrupt system of pensions and political bribes) Britain's servants humor her every whim. She has "Struck bargains with the Romish churches"—a

149

reference to the conciliatory Quebec Act of 1774, whereby Britain hoped to win French Catholic allies for a war against the New York and New England patriots. She has "Annull'd our charters of releases" and has torn "our title-deeds in pieces" (violating the self-governing provisions in the colonial charters). Finally, she has instructed "her hangman"—General Gage—to enforce these measures.

But although he is helped by the artful Satan, Gage is too much of a bungler to be a successful devil. Trumbull heaps derision on Gage in a passage brimming with Miltonic allusions:

> And as old heroes gain'd, by shifts,
> From gods, as poets tell, their gifts;
> Our Gen'ral, as his actions show,
> Gain'd like assistance from below,
> By Satan graced with full supplies,
> From all his magazine of lies.
> Yet could his practice ne'er impart
> The wit to tell a lie with art.
> Those lies alone are formidable,
> Where artful truth is mixt with fable;
> But Gage has bungled oft so vilely
> No soul would credit lies so silly,
> Outwent all faith and stretch'd beyond
> Credulity's extremest end.
> Whence plain it seems tho' Satan once
> O'erlook'd with scorn each brainless dunce,
> And blund'ring brutes in Eden shunning,
> Chose out the serpent for his cunning;
> Of late he is not half so nice,
> Nor picks assistants, 'cause they're wise.
> For had he stood upon perfection,
> His present friends had lost th' election,
> And far'd as hard in this proceeding,
> As owls and asses did in Eden. (pp. 112–13)

With the aid of Milton's recoiling-cannon metaphor, Trumbull dismisses Squire M'Fingal's bootless rhetoric:

> But as some musquets so contrive it,
> As oft to miss the mark they drive at,
> And tho' well aim'd at duck or plover,
> Bear wide and kick their owners over:

So far'd our 'Squire, whose reas'ning toil
Would often on himself recoil. (p. 106)

Poetry and Political Culture

Passages such as these suggest the appropriateness and richness of the satanic imagery employed by the popular party on the eve of the American Revolution. In some cases the borrowing from Milton's epic is explicit and acknowledged; in others it is indirect, arising from the body of images, phrases, and concepts that were ultimately derived from Milton's portrait of Satan or from the Bible as interpreted by Milton (that is, with his emphases and elaborations) but that became part of the common idiom of English speakers in eighteenth-century America. Milton's presence is no less palpable in the latter cases than in the former; the indirect borrowing is evidence of *Paradise Lost*'s lasting imprint on the language and habits of thought of Americans.[23]

The preceding chapter considered Milton's importance as a political theorist and pamphleteer in the decades leading up to the Revolution. During this period, Americans' views on natural law, the right of resistance to tyrants, freedom of religion and of the press, church disestablishment, and other leading contemporary issues were informed by their reading of Milton and other seventeenth-century classical republicans. Sometimes American writers closely paraphrased Milton's pamphlets, as Mayhew did in his *Discourse Concerning Unlimited Submission,* which borrowed Milton's arguments opposing capricious, arbitrary government and supporting the notion of a Christian's obligation to resist such government. In 1763 Mayhew cited Milton's arguments for church disestablishment in response to the British attempt to establish an American episcopate. Milton's *Likeliest Means to Remove Hirelings* was reprinted in Philadelphia in 1770 and in New Haven in 1774 (the first two editions of his writings to be published on this side of the Atlantic) when the issues of tithes and a state-supported clergy became urgent.[24] His political writings would play a direct role again in the drafting of new state constitutions; at that time, John Adams acknowledged his debt to Milton among other English political theorists for showing him that a republic was the form of government best calculated to promote the happiness of society.

The imprint of *Paradise Lost* on revolutionary politics was more subtle but no less significant, and that this was so is suggestive of the way literature conditions political culture. It is not known how many copies of *Paradise Lost* circulated in the colonies during the American Revolution;

however, Milton's poetry was popular enough that in 1777 a Philadelphia publisher found it profitable to bring out the first American edition of his poetic works when the outbreak of war disrupted commerce.[25] The epic was popular at this moment of political crisis, I believe, because Milton's rendering of the Fall story addressed a central moral issue that Americans needed to resolve in order to accomplish their political agenda: the issue of immediate self-interest as an obstacle to "consideration of the freedom of posterity."[26] "There must be a positive Passion for the public good, the public Interest, Honour, Power, and Glory, established in the Minds of the People, or there can be no Republican Government, nor any real Liberty," John Adams wrote to a correspondent in 1776.

> And this public Passion must be Superiour to all private Passions. Men must be ready, they must pride themselves, and be happy to sacrifice their private Pleasures, Passions, and Interests, nay their private Friendships and dearest Connections, when they Stand in Competition with the Rights of society.[27]

The conflict between "present appetite" and "foresight for the public"[28] is present in every moment of history, but political events in the colonies pushed it into the foreground of popular consciousness. For although the reasonable course for the colonists was to establish an independent nation, the temptation to put special interests ahead of that national calling had to be overcome repeatedly. The struggle manifested itself in the temptation to break the economic boycotts for private gain during the prerevolutionary period, to succumb on the eve of the War of Independence to fears of an open confrontation with Britain's military and financial might, to profiteer during the war, and to become part of the new aristocracy of money after the Revolution. Like all major political and social transformations, the American Revolution was possible only insofar as people rose above special interests and jointly dedicated themselves to higher tasks.

Thus, when Sam Adams proposed a new, countrywide embargo against British goods in retaliation for the Boston Coercive Acts, he worried that some merchants would put their private economic interests before the "Cause of their Country": "The Trade will forever be divided when a Sacrifice of their Interest is called for," he confided to a correspondent. He hoped, however, that "The virtuous forbearance of the Friends of Liberty may be powerful enough to command Success."[29] Virtuous forbearance versus private passions: the same (Miltonic) conflict between foresight for the interests of posterity and the indulgence of present appetites pervades John Adams's account of the events leading up to the Boston Tea Party.[30] In the minds of Adams and other Whigs, the temptation "to drink tea" came to represent the selfish gratification of all private interests and passions.

Once the War of Independence was under way, broadsides and circular letters regularly called on patriots to put aside private and sectional interests, lest the prejudices and rivalries kindled by the Tories lead to conflicts "detrimental to the People in general." One letter from the Boston Committee of Correspondence implored:

> Gentlemen, At a Time when Degenerate Britons are with brutal rage, and the greatest injustice, using every means in their power [to destroy American liberties] our Country may justly demand not only from those who are immediately concerned in the management of their public affairs, but from every individual his utmost exertions for its defence and security.[31]

The letter asked for the "union and harmony" of all the states in regard to price controls on "the Necessaries of Life" recently enacted in New England to prevent monopoly. The letter acknowledged that these measures had been blatantly defied by some Boston merchants, "Monopolizers and Forestallers, the bane of Town and Country," who put private gain ahead of the public good and exported their goods, leaving their shops bare:

> [B]ut . . . such is the imperfection even of the best laws for preventing monopoly and oppression, that the avaricious and designing often find ways and methods to elude them, and to prevent that full benefit being derived to the People which good Legislators always intend.[32]

In this atmosphere Milton's proud and egocentric Satan came to embody the principle of "doing for self." Satan's seduction of Adam and Eve dramatized on a cosmic scale the temptation felt by many colonists to selfishly pursue private interests—"to drink tea"—rather than serve a higher purpose. Men such as the Adamses, Warren, Freneau and Trumbull, because they were engaged in a political struggle themselves, recognized and exploited the multifaceted political character of Milton's depictions of Satan, of the war in Heaven, and of the temptation of Adam and Eve. The Tories' disrespect for law and constitutions, typified by Trumbull's fictional M'Fingal, made them rebels in the long tradition of

Satan and his cohorts. Their motives—self-aggrandizement, gratification of private interests—were also satanic, as were their methods: corruption of others through the bait of offices, pensions, and luxuries. Even the Tories' political errors, such as their vindictive behavior toward Massachusetts, which catalyzed opposition throughout the colonies, smacked of Satan's stubbornness, his determination "never to submit or yield," which led to his further undoing. Whig propagandists jumped at the opportunity to point out the parallel between Britain and Satan, neither of whom understood that it was the nature of evil to recoil upon itself. In fact, it was the diabolical stubbornness of the North faction in insisting on Parliament's right to raise a revenue in the colonies that eventually led the Whigs to embrace independence, abandoning their earlier, less radical demand for recognition of their rights as Englishmen within the empire.[33]

Thus, the borrowing of Milton's imagery to depict "doing for self" revealed a deeper agreement between Milton and American republicans on political and moral principles. They agreed not only on the nature of tyranny and the lawfulness of just revolution but also on the danger to the public good posed by unbridled private interests and passions, which allowed people to tolerate tyranny. "[L]icense . . . never hath more scope or more indulgence than under tyrants": thus it is that bad people do not hate but welcome tyranny and its many baits.[34] Milton's perception was echoed by the leaders of the popular party on the eve of American independence. In their concern with the socially disruptive nature of private interests, the American leaders were closer to Milton and the classical republican school than to those Enlightenment figures—chiefly Locke—who traditionally have been hailed as the theoreticians of the Revolution. In *The Closing of the American Mind*, Allan Bloom writes that when Locke reconceptualized the reason-passion (mind-body) antinomy of premodern thought as the distinction between society and nature, he transformed a persistent source of conflict into a resolvable problem; for in Locke's system it is in humanity's self-interest (its nature) to form society for protection and profit.[35] But the writers cited above, with their continual warnings over the danger of private passions, belong in the company of Milton and pre-Enlightenment thinkers who were less optimistic than Locke about the possibility of resolving desire and duty, nature and society. A closer examination of the colonists' debt to Milton and, more generally, to the legacy of the English Commonwealth will illuminate the shared cultural sensibility that made these American republicans Milton's "fit audience" and that enabled them to see in his imagery a fitting interpretation of the events of their time.

"Late Innovations"

In their correspondence in early 1775, Adams and Warren treated as satanic the assiduousness with which Gage and the Tories pursued their strategy (a "Study of revenge, immortal Hate and Courage never to submit or yield"). Warren wrote that the Tory ruling clique in Boston showed the cunning of Satan in wooing adherents to its side.[36] Finally, Whigs used the epithet "satanic" to describe the innovative character of British policy toward the colonies over the preceding decade. It was these "late innovations," beginning with the Stamp Act in 1765, that catalyzed broad-based opposition to British rule.

The hated Stamp Act was the first of several attempts by the British to raise a revenue to support royal appointees hitherto financially dependent on the colonial legislatures. Even Thomas Hutchinson, who was later appointed by the king to be governor of Massachusetts, threw his weight against the British measures, as Adams and other Whigs liked to point out in the 1770s. The British commissioners who arrived in 1767 to administer new duties on tea, lead, paper, and painters' colors were denounced not only for their detrimental effect on commerce but also for their partisan involvement in colonial politics—improper behavior that threatened to upset the delicate balance between the provincial legislatures and executives and overturn the principle of mixed and balanced government, to which the colonists subscribed. An agitational pamphlet written in 1770 recalled that the commissioners, "instead of confining themselves to the proper business of their office, . . . became partizans of Governor Bernard in his political schemes."[37] They had "the weakness and temerity" to infringe upon the sacred right of members of the "house of commons" of the colony to vote freely, "not being accountable therefor but to their constituents."[38] Such behavior, in blatant violation of rights guaranteed under the British Constitution, touched off a new round of colonial resistance.

After the failure of the Stamp and Townshend Revenue acts and similarly provocative measures (such as the pouring of British troops into Boston in 1770 to quell the resistance to the Townshend duties), the North ministry evolved the diabolical strategy of creating a class of colonists who would identify with the British and British policies; hence the flow of "places, preferment and pensions" into the colonies rose to unprecedented levels.[39] By the time of the tea tax there was a considerable Tory faction within Boston that stood to benefit from it, as some of the money was certain to find its way into their pockets.

Whigs such as John and Sam Adams and James Warren argued that when Parliament assumed the authority to raise a revenue in the colonies without the consent of the provincial assemblies, it violated the original colonial charters and constitutions. Like the seventeenth-century English revolutionaries, the American Whigs disliked "innovation" and maintained that their own goal was merely to re-establish what Milton called "the known rules of ancient liberty."[40] The Whigs reasoned that the British and their Tory allies were overthrowing the established order; thus they, not the popular party, were the diabolical innovators who had precipitated the growing conflict. At issue was not only the established right of British subjects to consent through their representatives to their own taxation, but also the venerable principle of mixed and balanced government, which had been advocated by English republicans of every stripe, including Milton, Harrington, and Sidney, and both liberal and conservative opponents of Walpole's cabinet government.

Americans regarded their colonial governments as miniature embodiments of England's idealized Constitution, each consisting of three separate "negatives": a governor, who represented the monarchical, or executive, element of the traditional triad; the council, or upper house, representing the aristocratic element; and the lower house, standing for local, popular interests. "These three are distinct and independent of one another," wrote Dr. William Douglas of Boston,

> and the colonies enjoy the conveniences of each of these
> forms of government without their inconveniences, the several
> negatives being checks upon one another. The concurrence of
> these three forms seems to be the highest perfection that
> human civil government can attain to in times of peace . . . if
> it did not sound too profane by making too free with the
> mystical expressions of our religion, I should call it *a trinity in
> unity*.[41]

Douglas's thinking was typical, as Bernard Bailyn points out. The argument for balanced government was practically a political axiom in the colonies, as it had been for seventeenth- and eighteenth-century English republicans.

American patriots, steeped in the classical republican tradition, saw Britain's colonial taxation policy from the 1760s on as an insidious threat to the continuance of balanced government. By freeing provincial judges and other royally appointed officials from their previous financial dependence on the colonial legislatures, the revenue threatened to upset the liberty-preserving balance and remove all obstacles to despotism.[42] Sam Adams wrote that the Tory "Conspirators," once having established a revenue in violation of the Massachusetts charter, endeavored "to appropriate the revenue they had rais'd, to set up an Executive, absolutely independent of the legislative, which is to say the least, the nearest approach to absolute Tyranny." The governor, Thomas Hutchinson, he described contemptuously as the "first American *Pensioner*."[43]

The controversy over these issues intensified after the adoption of a Declaration of Rights by the First Continental Congress. In Massachusetts, the center of the growing confrontation between Britain and the colonists, Daniel Leonard ("Massachusettensis") and John Adams ("Novanglus") carried on their famous newspaper debate. Leonard, a Taunton lawyer who turned against the popular party after the Boston Tea Party, felt that reciprocal relations of protection and subordination between mother country and colonies ought to prevail and argued that the benefits furnished by Britain—protection of American fishing and maritime industries against France and Spain, for example—justified and outweighed the burden of any revenues imposed by Parliament. He minimized Whig grievances by reference to the theories of empire and sovereignty: the colonies, he maintained, were part of the British empire, and as supreme power in any state could only be single, the colonies were properly subject to Parliament's supreme authority.[44]

Adams countered with an intricate and ingenious legal argument, concluding that as Britain was not an empire but a republic (being *"a government of laws, and not of men"*),[45] the American colonies could not be considered part of the realm and were not subject to Parliament's authority. Adams voiced the Whig argument that whereas Americans recognized direct dependence on the king and had in the past consented to the regulation of their trade by Parliament, all matters of internal legislation and taxation were in the hands of their colonial legislatures. To prove his case, Adams cited the protests of Massachusetts and Virginia against the seventeenth-century Navigation Act. They had resisted it "because they were not represented in parliament and were therefore not bound" by the Act until their colonial assemblies approved it.[46] Adams also noted the more recent precedent of colonial resistance to the Stamp Act. In both cases the colonists had claimed that because they were Englishmen, no tax could be imposed upon them without their consent or the consent of their representatives. "It was the principle that united the colonies to oppose it, not the quantum of the tax," Adams explained. Although they had in the past agreed to pay duties for regulating trade because they "thought it just and necessary" that the British "regulate the trade which their power protected," the colonists had vehemently protested against all acts of Parliament that attempted to regulate their internal polity, such as the act to destroy the Land Bank of 1740.[47]

Adams went so far as to charge the Tories with rebellion against His Majesty, with whom the colonies had a direct compact unmediated by Parliament. He maintained that whereas "the minister and all his advocates . . . call resistance, to acts of parliament, by the names of treason and rebellion," the people know that

> parliament has no authority over them, excepting to regulate their trade, and this not by any principle of common law, but merely by the consent of the colonies, founded on the obvious necessity of a case . . . that therefore they have as good a right to charge that minister, Massachusettensis and the whole army to which he has fled for protection, with treason and rebellion.[48]

As Parliament had no legal authority to overturn the colonies' constitutions, Adams argued, anyone who colluded in the violation of these constitutions was "guilty of overt acts of treason and rebellion against his majesty, his royal crown and dignity, as much as if he should take arms against his troops, or attempt his sacred life."[49] It might be argued that Adams employed his own share of guile in insisting that whereas the king's ministers and his American minions were acting treasonously, the colonists were loyal to George III. However, Adams's point—that the capricious violation of natural and constitutional rights, no less than wrongful sedition, constituted a form of rebellion against the principle of law—was a central tenet of Whig political theory. He emphasized the traditional character of the argument by citing—again guilefully—the precedent of Parliament's resistance to the tyrant Charles I:

> That if the American resistance to the act for destroying your charter, and to the Resolves for arresting persons here and sending them to England for tryal, is treason, the lords and commons, and the whole nation, were traitors at the revolution.[50]

The "Infernal Junto"

In the first half of this century, revisionist historians discounted the language of eighteenth-century American revolutionaries as political propaganda—mere rhetoric designed to paint their "adversaries" (a ubiquitous epithet) in the darkest light and to promote their own cause. A deeper understanding and appreciation of this language has emerged, however, following the research of Caroline Robbins and Bernard Bailyn and the scholarship their work has inspired.[51] Previously, there were two dominant interpretations of the origins of the American Revolution. One school of historians identified economic and social conflicts as the paramount causes. A second pointed to the emergence of significant representative assemblies in the colonies—"miniature houses of commons" (the phrase of Charles M. Andrews, a leading exponent of this school)—which found themselves in irreconcilable conflict with Parliament.[52] Bailyn finds the institutional interpretation powerful but limited, "insensitive to what the Revolutionary leaders themselves explained as the background and cause of the events of the 1760's and 1770's and to what they professed to be their own motivations."[53] He points out that modern historians, finding the revolutionaries' accounts of these causes and motivations "extravagant, rhetorical, and apparently far from the realities of the time," have tended to ignore or dismiss them as revolutionary propaganda. "Yet this language, in all its extravagance," Bailyn insists, "is a key not only to the thoughts and motivations of the leaders of the Revolution but to their actions as well."[54]

The revolutionaries spoke passionately of a deliberate "design" afoot, a conspiracy to take away their liberties under the British Constitution. Bailyn's reassessment of their admittedly rhetorical language helps to recover the roots of the revolutionaries' ideas and motives in the political culture of eighteenth-century England, which itself looked back to the period of the English Commonwealth. Writers in this tradition, from Milton and Sidney to Mayhew and John Adams, consistently pursued certain fundamental themes: natural rights, the contractual nature of government and society, and the uniqueness of England's mixed constitution as a bastion against tyranny. These writers also consistently associated free republican government with pervasive moral virtue in a society and perceived a threat to liberty in corruption and moral decay—whether that of a Stuart, a Walpole, or a Hutchinson.

In America these themes were reinforced by the legacy of Puritan millennialism, which accorded the colonization of America a unique place in God's design. Somewhat secularized in the eighteenth century, millennialism assigned a special role to America on the stage of world history, as the inheritor and perfector of human liberty.[55]

As Whigs turned to Milton as a political mentor, they also found—in his Christian epic—images and phrases to express the ideas that motivated them. For Adams, as noted, the Tories called to mind Milton's infernal spirits. In his *Novanglus* letters he portrayed the Tories in diabolical imagery to expose their true character to his compatriots and rouse them to action. *Massachusettensis* was nothing less than a "destroying angel," whose "ambition and avarice," "simulation and dissimulation," "hypocrisy and perfidy" had been revealed to all patriots.[56] He was the "wily Massachusettensis" who engaged in "artful . . . not to say jesuitical" arguments. "My design in pursuing this malicious slanderer, concealed as he is under so soft and oily an appearance, through all the doublings of his tedious course, is to vindicate this Colony from his base aspersions," Adams wrote. As Adams carried out his literary pursuit of the diabolical Massachusettensis "in his own serpentine path," Milton's Satan-in-the-serpent could not have been far from his conscious thoughts.[57]

To Massachusettensis's charge that the press had been taken over by the popular party and had become an engine of oppression and licentiousness, Adams countered that the Tory press was chargeable with slander, that James Otis, Jr., and others of the first generation of patriots "were pelted with the most infernally malicious, false, and atrocious Libels, that ever issued from any press in Boston."[58] Adams's epic intentions were to

> Shew the wicked policy of the Tories—trace their plan from
> its first rude sketches to its present compleat draught. Shew
> that it has been much longer in contemplation, than is gener-
> ally known—who were the first in it—their views, motives and
> secret springs of action—and the means they have employed.[59]

Adams contrasted the ambition of the "encroaching" Tories with the selflessness of the patriots. About the latter, he wrote, they

> are still struggling, at the expence of their ease, health, peace,
> wealth and preferment, against the encroachments of the
> Tories on their country—and . . . are determined to continue
> struggling, at much greater hazards still, and like the Prince of
> Orange resolve never to see its entire subjection to arbitrary
> power, but rather to die fighting against it, in the last ditch.[60]

The reference to the Dutch independence struggle of the late sixteenth century is one of a number made by Adams, reflecting his consciousness of belonging to a continuous republican tradition.

Adams emphasized the contrasting moral character of the Whigs and Tories throughout his Novanglus letters. "That the whigs have ambition, a desire of profit, and other passions like other men, it would be foolish to deny," he conceded. "But this writer cannot name a set of men in the whole British empire, who have sacrificed their private interest to their nations honour, and the public good, in so remarkable a manner, as the leading whigs have done, in the two last administrations."[61] By contrast, he wrote, the Tories were ready to enslave their country to advance their own private interests. Adams traced "all their dark intrigues, and wicked machinations . . . their schemes for enslaving this country" back to "the designs of Andros, Randolph, Dudley, and other champions of their cause towards the close of the last century."[62] Adams described William Shirley, governor from 1741 to 1757, as "a crafty, busy, ambitious, intrigueing, enterprizing man . . . [who] conceived of great designs of aggrandizing himself, his family and his friends." He accused Francis Bernard, who became governor in 1760, of promoting tax increases by Parliament with "artful flattery," "cautious cunning," and "deep dissimulation." An "arch enemy of North-America," Bernard had been selected by the junto to suggest to Grenville a plan for taxing the colonies by an act of Parliament at the close of the war. Adams criticized "The artful flattery with which [Bernard] insinuate[d] these projects into the minds of the ministry, as matters of absolute necessity, which their great penetration could not fail to discover, nor their great regard to the public, omit."[63]

For Adams, the junto's motive, like Satan's in *Paradise Lost*, was the gratification of immediate selfish interests: avarice and political ambition. The junto assured Britain that the revenue was to be applied to national uses in the colonies (e.g., to underwrite the British empire's defense costs). Adams predicted, however, that all the money raised would "be applied not for public purposes, national or provincial, but merely to corrupt the sons of America, and create a faction to destroy its interest and happiness."[64]

Adams saw unfolding a vicious cycle whereby the pensioners and placemen freed from popular accountability promoted submission to future taxes and revenues:

> It was found . . . that the famous triumvirate, Bernard, Hutchinson and Oliver, the ever memorable, secret, confidential letter writers, whom I call the junto, had by degrees, and before people were aware of it, erected a tyranny in the province. Bernard had all the executive, and a negative on the legislative; Hutchinson and Oliver, by their popular arts and secret intrigues, had elevated to the board, such a collection of crown officers, and their own relations, as to have too much influence there: and they had three of a family on the superior bench, which is the supreme tribunal in all causes civil and

criminal, vested with all the powers of the king's bench,
common pleas and exchequer, which gave them power over
every act of this court. This junto therefore had the legislative
and executive in their controul, and more natural influence
over the judicial, than is ever to be trusted in any set of men
in the world. The public accordingly found all these springs
and wheels in the constitution set in motion to promote
submission to the stamp act, and to discountenance resistance
to it.[65]

The passage underscores Adams's belief that a concentration of power
into one center—in this case, the executive—and a lack of balance in
government among executive, legislative, and judicial functions opened
the door for corruption and tyranny. Thus, although the Stamp Act had
been repealed, there was no machinery of government to prevent the
junto from pursuing its diabolical ends by other means. Bernard vetoed
the election to the council of any member of the popular party, "which
was considered as a fresh proof, that the junto still persevered in their
designs of obtaining a revenue, to divide among themselves."[66] Thomas
Hutchinson, after declaring that he agreed with the people that Parliament had no right to tax them, turned around upon becoming lieutenant
governor and argued the case for Parliament's supreme authority.

Corrupted and Corruptors

Thus, Adams blamed the Anglo-American conflict on Governor Hutchinson, Chief Justice Peter Oliver, and their predecessors, who had encouraged Parliament's taxation of America for personal gain and who sought
to corrupt others by encouraging them to make similar pacts with Britain
for political power and lucre. When Adams described their modus operandi as "diabolical," he used the term precisely as Milton had used it in
describing Satan's tactics:

> A Tempter and Tormentor, is the Character of the Devil.—
> Hutchinson, Oliver, and others of their Circle, who for their
> own Ends of Ambition and Avarice, have procured, promoted,
> encouraged, councilled, aided and abetted the Taxation of
> America, have been the real Tempters of their Countrymen
> and Women, into all the Vices, sins, Crimes and follies which
> that Taxation has occasioned: And now by [them]selves and
> their Friends, Dependents, and Votaries, they a[re] reproach-

ing those very Men and Women, with those Vices and follies, Sins and Crimes.[67]

Adams's attack on the Tory junto was part of a broader critique of trends he saw developing as a result of Britain's policies and cultural influence, a critique grounded in the classical republican antithesis of virtue and corruption, which associated unchecked private interests with the moral degeneration of a society. Adams condemned the "universal Spirit of Debauchery, Dissipation, Luxury, Effeminacy and Gaming which the late ministerial Measures are introducing." "How much Profaneness, Leudness, Intemperance, &c. have been introduced by the Army and Navy, and Revenue—how much servility, Venality And Artiface and Hypocricy, have been introduced among the Ambitious and Avaricious by the british Politicks of the last 10 Years?" he asked. The original cause of the vices, he concluded, were "the political Innovations of the last 10 Years."[68]

In denunciations such as this, one hears echoes of seventeenth-century Puritan morality (Milton was similarly revolted by the return of "*Bacchus and his Revellers*" after the English Restoration) fused with eighteenth-century historical theory. Writers in both traditions foretold the moral decline and fall of nations whose citizens had become intoxicated with material prosperity.[69] Adams traced the source of debauchery in the colonies to the mother country, were "luxury, effeminacy and venality" had arrived at "a shocking pitch": "both electors and elected, are become one mass of corruption [and] the nation is oppressed to death with debts and taxes owing to their own extravagance, and want of wisdom."[70] He warned that the revenue was fast replicating this corruption in the colonies:

> Like a cancer, it eats faster and faster every hour. The revenue creates pensioners, and the pensioners urge for more revenue. The people grow less steady, spirited and virtuous, the seekers more numerous and more corrupt, and every day increases the circles of their dependants and expectants, untill virtue, integrity, public spirit, simplicity, frugality, become the objects of ridicule and scorn, and vanity, luxury, foppery, selfishness, meanness, and downright venality, swallow up the whole society.[71]

The conflict between public-spiritedness and venality crystallized over the tea tax. Even after the repeal of the Townshend duties, the North ministry persisted in claiming that Parliament had a right to tax the

163

colonists without their consent; and it sought to establish a precedent by maintaining one of the duties, that on tea. But again British policy recoiled upon itself, precipitating the third crisis in Anglo-American relations since 1765. The colonists (except for a few Boston merchants who were closely connected to Hutchinson) refused to import tea, and the East India Company found itself on the point of bankruptcy. The ministry then removed the tea tax in England, enabling the company to offer its tea at a cut-rate price in America despite the Townshend duty. In this way, the ministry hoped to tempt the colonists to buy the tea and accept the principle of taxation.[72] But Americans realized that

> If the tea should be landed, it would be sold; if sold the duties would amount to a large sum, which would be instantly applied to increase the friends and advocates for more duties, and divide the people; and the company would get such a footing, that no opposition afterwards could ever be effectual.[73]

A petition debated at Faneuil Hall, expressing popular sentiments, urged action against the landing of the tea, warning that "what is much more than any Thing in Life to be dreaded, the Tribute laid upon the Importation of that Article will be fixed and established, and our Liberties, for which we have long struggled, will be lost to them and their Posterity."[74] The patriots saw through the ministry's tactic and regarded the tea as a test of their virtue. The tea had been sent "as a Trial of *American* Virtue and Resolution," a broadside published in Philadelphia stated. The captain of the ship carrying the tea was warned ("You are sent out on a diabolical service") and threatened with tarring and feathering should he attempt to land his baneful cargo.[75] The tea merchants named by the East India Company to receive its shipments resigned everywhere but in the Massachusetts capital, confirming Adams's apprehension that

> Boston is the only place upon the continent, perhaps in the world, which ever breeds a species of misanthropos, who will persist in their schemes for their private interest, with such obstinacy, in opposition to the public good; disoblige all their fellow-citizens for a little pelf, and make themselves odious and infamous, when they must be respected and esteemed.[76]

The Tories argued that the destruction of the tea was not only a reckless breach of law but unnecessary, because the colonists were under no obligation to purchase the tea and pay the duty. But Adams, an astute student of human nature, was too aware of human weakness to believe that the tea, once landed, would sit unbought in warehouses. He reasoned that even if Americans were more virtuous, on the whole, than their degenerate British counterparts, it had been British policy to create a "party" loyal to British interests:

> The British ministry had plundered the people by illegal taxes, and applied the money in salaries and pensions, by which devices, they had insidiously attached to their party, no inconsiderable number of persons, some of whom were of family, fortune and influence, tho' many of them were of desperate fortunes, each of whom, however, had his circle of friends, connections and dependants, who were determined to drink tea, both as evidence of their servility to administration, and their contempt and hatred of the people. These it was impossible to restrain without . . . hazarding more than the tea was worth.[77]

Adams observed that frailty was a fact of human nature since the Fall and that the British, as part of their diabolical strategy, had deliberately fostered a love of luxury throughout the population. "To this tribe of the *wicked*," therefore,

> must be added another more numerous, of the *weak*; who never could be brought to think of the consequences of their actions, but would gratify their appetites, if they could come at the means. What numbers are there in every community, who have no providence, or prudence in their private affairs, but will go on indulging the present appetite, prejudice, or passion, to the ruin of their estates and families, as well as their own health and characters! How much larger is the number of those who have no foresight for the public, or consideration of the freedom of posterity? Such an abstinence from the tea, as would have avoided the establishment of a precedent, depended on the unanimity of the people, a felic- ity that was unattainable. Must the wise, the virtuous and worthy part of the community, who constituted a very great majority, surrender their liberty, and involve their posterity in misery in complaisance to a detestable, tho' small party of knaves, and a despicable, tho' more numerous company of fools?[78]

Better, therefore, to prevent the tea from landing and keep the forbidden fruit out of reach. The view of human nature expressed here was central to Adams's outlook, as it was to that of his predecessors in the classical republican tradition. Its quintessential expression was Eve's susceptibility to Satan's false promises, a momentous instance of the lack of prudence and foresight. But Adams, like Milton and other classical republicans, was also convinced of the virtue of some members of the community (here, happily, a majority), who were justified in acting for the interests of the community as a whole, even in the face of a "backsliding" multitude. For the moment, given the strengthening policy consensus among Whigs, the distinction between the public good and private passions appeared clear-cut. Perhaps this is another reason why Milton's epic, with its sharp distinction between good and evil, was so congenial to the popular party on the eve of the Revolution. The author of "A New Song" expressed the feelings of many others when he depicted the Boston Tea Party as blessed by the Whig heroes:

> O'er their heads aloft in mid-sky
> Three bright angel forms were seen;
> *This* was HAMPDEN, *that* was SIDNEY,
> With fair LIBERTY between.[79]

"Just Rebellion" Against a Tyrannical Parent

In keeping with eighteenth-century political culture, both sides in the growing controversy between colonies and mother country portrayed themselves as defenders of the benevolent traditional political order and their antagonists as rebels against that order. John Adams expressed typical Whig sentiments when he argued in his Novanglus letters that the colonists desired only a restoration of the civil and religious liberties that were their due as loyal British subjects. General Gage's offer of a pardon in June 1775 to all Boston patriots who repented of their resistance (Samuel Adams and John Hancock excepted) provoked a vehement reaction from the Reverend John Cleveland of Ipswich:

> Thou profane, wicked monster of falsehood and perfidy . . .
> your late infamous proclamation is as full of notorious lies, as a
> toad or rattlesnake of deadly poison. . . . Without speedy
> repentence, you will have an aggravated damnation in hell.
> . . . You are not only a robber, a murderer, and usurper, but a
> wicked rebel: a rebel against the authority of truth, law,
> equity, the English constitution of government, these colony
> states, and humanity itself.[80]

A complementary set of rhetorical strategies, to which Jay Fliegelman has recently called attention, arose from the new and competing notions of filial and parental obligation that emerged in the decades preceding the Revolution.[81] The Tories, for their part, used *Paradise Lost*, along with *Clarissa* and other popular novels of parent-child relations, to paint the revolutionists as rebellious, disobedient children, whose rejection of the sacred filial bond would bring them untold woe. Sam Adams, James Otis, Jr., and other instigators of the revolt were portrayed as diabolical Lovelaces, seducers responsible for a hateful, unnatural breach between parent and child. The patriots, on the other hand, used parent-child imagery to make the opposite point. In 1777, the minister Abraham Keteltas aroused his audience with a Fourth of July sermon depicting Britain as an abusive parent, guilty of "ingratitude" for America's military assistance and sacrifices during the late war with France. Britain was waging a most "unnatural war" against "those who were once her most affectionate children, her most faithful and hearty friends, and who still, notwithstanding the unparalleled injuries, suffered from her, earnestly deprecate her ruin, and pray for her peace and prosperity." It was these loving children, Keteltas said, whom Britain now warred against, whose blood she shed, whose houses she burned, whose temples she destroyed, whose lands she desolated, and whose ruin she sought.[82] With such language, Keteltas exemplified a new cultural paradigm of affectional parent-child relations. According to this paradigm, when parents thwarted their children, it behooved the children to declare independence as a matter of self-defense.

Where Tories pictured Britain as the benign parent, patriots invoked a different filial bond. The true fathers, they said, who deserved infinite gratitude, were the Puritan founders, whose "generous Ardor for Civil and Religious Liberty, . . . in the Face of every Danger, and even Death itself, induced our Fathers to foresake the Boston of their Native Country, and begin a Settlement on bare Creation." The broadside just quoted, which was circulated throughout Massachusetts in 1772 to win support for Boston's resistance to the Coercive Acts, expressed confidence that other towns would not stand by "while the Iron Hand of Oppression is [daily] tearing the choicest Fruit from the fair Tree of Liberty, planted by our worthy Predecessors, at the Expence of their Treasure[; and] abundantly water'd with their Blood."[83] Thus, patriot propagandists cultivated and ritually invoked the colonists' sense of obligation to the Puritan fathers, to inspire concerted action against the common danger. Another broadside from 1773, vaunting the destruction of the "accurs'd TEA" in Boston Harbor, called up the specter of what would have been their forefathers' terrifying wrath had the Sons of Freedom shirked their filial obligation:

> Could our Fore-fathers rise from their cold Graves,
> And view their Land, with all their Children SLAVES;
> What would they say! how would their Spirits rend,
> And, thunder-strucken, to their Graves descend.[84]

Such psychologically geared appeals to a strongly ingrained sense of filial duty reinforced the Whigs' more theoretical arguments on the justice of rebellion against tyrants. For example, the 1772 Boston broadside quoted above also warned that the colonists were living in precarious times, in which "revolutions"—used in the Commonwealth-Whig sense to refer to the overthrow of lawful governments and constitutions—could take place at any moment. In such an atmosphere, "it becomes every Well-Wisher to his Country . . . to keep an Eagle Eye upon every Inovation and Stretch of Power, in those that have the Rule over us." The broadside cited the recent example of the prince of Sweden, "once subject to the Laws of the State" but now "able of a sudden to declare himself an absolute monarch." It noted that the Swedes, once free, were now so debased "that they even rejoice at being subject to the Caprice and arbitrary Power of a Tyrant, and kiss their Chains."

In his Novanglus letters, Adams responded to the Tory accusation that the popular party was ready to break the political contract between ruler and ruled at the slightest provocation. He cited the arguments of Sidney, Milton, and other seventeenth-century Englishmen defending rebellion for just causes:

> a manifest design in the Prince, to annul the contract on his
> part, will annul it on the part of the people. A settled plan to
> deprive the people of all the benefits, blessings and ends of
> the contract, to subvert the fundamentals of the constitu-
> tion—to deprive them of all share in making and executing
> laws, will justify a revolution.[85]

With an eye for historical ironies and tactical opportunities, Adams further vindicated the colonies' stance by pointing to Parliament's resistance to Charles I in the preceding century:

> the people of England, and the cause of liberty, truth, virtue
> and humanity, gained infinite advantages by that resistance.

> In all human probability, liberty civil and religious, not only
> in England but in all Europe, would have been lost. . . . It is
> true and to be lamented that Cromwell did not establish a
> government as free, as he might and ought; but his govern-
> ment was infinitely more glorious and happy to the people
> than Charles's.[86]

Using the same satanic terminology as their antagonists, the Tories accused the popular party of inciting an unlawful and unnatural rebellion. From their point of view, it was the Whigs who bore comparison with Milton's apostate angels. Peter Oliver, chief justice of the Massachusetts Superior Court at the time of the Tea Party and the Coercive Acts, depicted the Revolution as ugly, unjustified, and, above all, unnatural. He described James Otis, Jr., whom Massachusetts patriots regarded as one of the fathers of the resistance, in terms that recalled the transformation of Milton's Lucifer and the other apostate angels after their fall from Heaven. To Oliver, Otis was a man of natural talents whose original brightness had faded:

> Mr. *Otis* was designed, by Nature, for a Genius; but it seemed
> as if, by the Impetuosity of his Passions, he had wrested
> himself out of her Hands before she had complemented her
> Work; for his Life seemed to be all Eccentricity. . . . He
> studied Law, under his Preceptor, with great attention; he
> made great Progress in it, & would have been of distinguish-
> ing Figure in it had he not have mistaken a contemptuous
> Pride for a laudable Ambition; given too loose a Rein to the
> Wildness of his Passion. He seemed to have adopted that
> Maxim which *Milton* puts into the Mouth of one of his Devils,
> vizt.
> "Better to reign in Hell than serve in Heaven."
> And his whole Life seemed to be a Comment on his text.[87]

Natural genius gone awry, pride, ambition, wildness of passions—all the elements of Oliver's portrait of Otis seem calculated to evoke Milton's picture of Satan. Perhaps with greater justification, Oliver also described the patriots' practice of tarring and feathering as diabolical: "*Milton* says that Gunpowder & Cannon were first invented at a Pandaemonium of his Devils; but this Art they had not the Sagacity of hinting at, untill it was discovered to them by these modern Disciples."[88] It is noteworthy that Oliver accused Otis of precisely the same vices—pride and ambition— that Adams found in Oliver and the Boston junto. Whig and Tory polemics reflected common moral and political assumptions, although there is little doubt whose reading of his epic Milton would have endorsed.

Another Tory propagandist, Samuel Seabury, also used the same terms as the Whig polemicists to analyze the conflict. He brought to bear the ideas of mixed government, representation, and sovereignty in his attack on the Whig positions. As an epigraph for his pamphlet *A View of the Controversy between Great Britain and her Colonies* . . . , Seabury selected Michael's words to the Arch-foe during the war in Heaven:

> ————————how hast tho instill'd
> Thy *Malice* into *Thousands*, once *upright*
> And *faithful; now* prov'd *false?*[89]

Like Oliver, Seabury emphasized the motif of change: the fall of previously loyal subjects. Seabury's widely read pamphlet, a response to Alexander Hamilton's defense of measures undertaken by the Continental Congress, accused Hamilton of being motivated by party interests, while it portrayed Seabury himself as an "honest supporter of the laws and liberties of our country."[90] The Congress, Seabury maintained, "was founded in sedition," its method of choosing delegates "subversive to all law" because they "were chosen by a party only, and . . . endeavored to tyrannize over the whole people."[91] This argument centered on the same antithesis that the Whigs invoked—that of party and private interests versus the interests of the whole people—but the villains and heroes had changed places. Here, it was the Whigs who were accused of "wantonly . . . fomenting disturbances in the colony, in creating and widening the disunion between the mother country and us."[92] Seabury went to great lengths to show that the Whigs were the innovators:

> The position that we are bound by no laws to which we have
> not consented, either by ourselves, or our representatives, is a
> novel position, unsupported by any authoritative record of the
> British constitution, ancient or modern.[93]

It was a novel position, Seabury claimed, because many of the people in England had no vote in choosing their representatives and were, therefore, governed by laws to which neither they nor their representatives had consented. This was hardly the Tories' most convincing argument.

Jonathan Odell, in his satire *The American Times*, explicitly attacked the notion that the revolutionaries were motivated by reason. He represented Independence as "That brazen serpent, rais'd on Freedom's pole"[94] and depicted the republican leaders as a passion-driven "infernal crew" holding a conclave in Pandemonium. The first devil to appear, one of the Livingston clan, Odell addressed as follows:

> Coward, yet cruel—zealous, yet profane;
> Havoc and spoil, and ruin are thy gain:
> Go, glut like Death thy vast unhide-bound maw,
> Remorseless swallow liberty and law;
> At one enormous stroke a nation slay,
> And thou thyself shall perish with thy prey. (p. 34)

The claim of the patriots that they were acting lawfully on behalf of all, Odell treated as mere pretense. The entire conflict, he maintained, conformed to the war in Heaven as depicted by Milton, with the colonists in the diabolical role:

> O Poet, seated on the lofty throne,
> Forgive the bard who makes thy words his own;
> Surpriz'd I trace thee in prophetic page,
> The crimes, the follies of the present age;
> Thy scenery, sayings, admirable man,
> Pourtrayed our struggle with the dark Divan:
> What Michael to the first arch-rebel said,
> Would well rebuke the rebel army's head;
> What Satan to th' angelic Prince replied,
> Such are the words of Continental pride,
> I swear by him who rules the earth and sky,
> The dread event shall equally apply;
> That Clinton's warfare is the war of God,
> And Washington shall feel the vengeful rod. (p. 42)

Adams answered arguments such as these by drawing on a century of republican political theorizing. He agreed with his Tory adversary Massachusettensis that

> "It is an universal truth, that he that would excite a rebellion, is at heart, as great a tyrant as ever weilded the iron rod of oppression." Be it so: We are not exciting a rebellion. Opposition, nay open, avowed resistance by arms, against usurpation and lawless violence, is not rebellion by the law of God, or the land. Resistance to lawful authority makes rebellion. Hampden, Russell, Sydney, Somers, Holt, Tillotson, Burnet, Hoadley, &c. were no tyrants nor rebels, altho' some of them were

in arms, and the others undoubtedly excited resistance,
against the tories. Don't beg the question, Mr. Massachusettensis, and then give yourself airs of triumph. Remember . . .
"the word rebel is a convertible term."[95]

By the end of February 1775, if not earlier, the popular party had
abandoned hope for reconciliation with Britain, and Adams had begun
citing at length Grotius, Sidney, and other classical republicans on the
lawfulness of rebellion on just occasions: "Be it remembered then, that
there are tumults, seditions, popular commotions, insurrections and civil
wars, upon just occasions, as well as unjust."[96] The Whigs regarded the
seventeenth-century English martyrs to the cause of liberty as their
comrades-in-arms, and when Major-General Joseph Warren was killed in
June by redcoats at the battle of Bunker Hill, a writer for the *New England
Chronicle* pictured him as having joined the Whig pantheon:

> Immortal Hampden leads the awful band,
> And near him Raleigh, Russel, Sidney stand;
> With them each Roman, every Greek whose name
> Glows high recorded in the roll of fame,
> Round *Warren* press, and hail with glad applause,
> This early victim in fair Freedom's cause.[97]

Adams also invoked republican political theory, for example, Puffendorf's
law of nature and nations, in arguing that the resistance to Britain was not
a revolt of lawless masses but a lawful undertaking: "When we speak of a
tyrant that may lawfully be dethroned, we do not mean by the people,
the vile populace or rabble of the country, or the cabal of a small number
of factious persons; but the greater and more judicious part of the subjects
of all ranks."[98]

Where Tory propaganda attempted to portray the revolutionists as
lawless rebels, Adams and other Whigs made a point of emphasizing the
colonists' respect for law and government, as was evident in the lawful
causes for which they rebelled and the lawfulness with which they
prosecuted their revolt. Adams's optimism was at a high point the day
after the Boston Tea Party, which he described as "the grandest, Event,
which has ever yet happened Since, the Controversy, with Britain,
opened!" "The Sublimity of it" charmed him, not only because it hit so
squarely at the heinous principle of parliamentary taxation, but also
because it was carried out with so exquisite a regard for lawfulness and
government. "The Town of Boston," he wrote to James Warren, "was
never more Still and calm of a Saturday night than it was last Night. All

Things were conducted with great order, Decency and *perfect Submission to Government.* No Doubt, we all thought the Administration in better Hands, than it had been."[99] While Tories accused the revolutionists of fomenting mobs and riots, the real lawlessness, Adams wrote to his wife, was the illegal taxation of the colonists—the "Universal Pilfering, Robbery and Picking of Pocketts, which prevails in the Land—as every Mans Pockett upon the Continent is picked every Day, by taking from him Duties without his Consent."[100]

Reason Against Passion

Despite the justice and virtue of the revolutionary cause, the problem of private interests in conflict with public-spiritedness remained a central concern for Adams after Independence was declared as it had been for Milton and other republican thinkers. Adams had portrayed the British as devils, drawing on Milton's elaboration of Satan's character as a tempter, because they had played on the people's desire for luxury and social distinction. Adams, like other Whigs, believed that such corruption was endemic to absolute monarchies, and he cited Sidney's argument that such states had little hope for reform because they so corrupted the people that those who hoped to effect change were driven to use force.[101] However, human corruptibility posed another kind of threat in nascent commercial republics such as the United States, where there was the danger that, once liberated from the bonds of external despotism, individual creative energies might become heteronomous and self-corrupting. For the new nation, Milton's distinction between liberty and license, obedience to reason and thralldom to self, took on heightened meaning. Formerly enslaved to external tyrants, would Americans be successfully tempted by conniving Satans, as Adam and Eve were?[102] This was the question that Adams grappled with, even during his period of greatest optimism.

Adams had always maintained that republicanism depended on the character of the people, "a possitive Passion for the public good, the public Interest, . . . Superiour to all private Passions." Yet even in January 1776 he wrote to Mercy Otis Warren that there was "So much Rascallity, so much Venality and Corruption, so much Avarice and Ambition, such a Rage for Profit and Commerce among all Ranks and Degrees of Men even in America," that republicanism seemed a precarious experiment.[103] During the Revolution itself, Adams was afraid that the revolt might provide scope for the exercise of unbridled passions. He distinguished between "public mobs," whose objective was the defense of essential

173

public liberties, and "private mobs," which cloaked personal aims, ambitions, and vendettas in patriotic garb. Even "legitimate" public violence, Adams felt, encouraged the "excesses of a few, who . . . took advantage of the general enthusiasm, to perpetuate their ill designs."[104]

Adams adhered to the classical republican view that it was the function of reason to overrule the passions and keep them within strict bounds of order and moderation—that the individual should endeavor to balance the affections and appetites under the monarchy of reason. Adams believed that most people often found passion and self-interest irresistible and that some practiced self-delusion to keep from foregoing their "Wishes and Desires." "Their Reason becomes at last an eloquent Advocate on the Side of their Passions, and [they] bring themselves to believe that black is white, that Vice is Virtue, that Folly is Wisdom and Eternity a Moment."[105]

Adams carefully distinguished between liberty and license, as Milton had, and was aware that even in the heady days of the Revolution there were many who confused the two, who championed liberty without understanding it. "[N]othing can Save Us but Government in the State and Discipline in the Army," he wrote to Warren. "There are So many Persons among my worthy Constituents who love Liberty, better than they understand it that I expect to become unpopular by my Preaching."[106] Milton had believed that the inculcation of true virtue was ultimately a spiritual matter, albeit one that could be aided by education and the reform of institutions. Adams's entire corpus is, in a sense, an answer to that position, for he believed that Milton's solutions were necessary but not sufficient—that a mixed and balanced form of government was essential for restricting socially destructive passions and assuring virtuous behavior.[107]

The Superiority of Republican Government

The problem of designing governments that would safeguard the public good against private interests was in the forefront of Adams's thinking when the necessity arose to frame new republican constitutions for the former colonies. In a letter to George Wythe of Virginia in April of 1776, which was subsequently published as *Thoughts on Government*, Adams sketched the form of government he thought best calculated to promote the happiness of society: a republic with a balanced constitution. In the letter Adams acknowledged his debt to "Sidney, Harrington, Locke, Milton, Nedham, Neville, Burnet, and Hoadley," adding, "No small fortitude is necessary to confess that one has read them. The wretched condition of this country, however, for ten or fifteen years past, has frequently reminded me of their principles and reasonings."[108]

Adams wrote *Thoughts on Government* during the Second Continental Congress. The colonies had already been declared to be in a state of rebellion by the British king and Parliament. Prepared for war, the patriots were taking steps to frame new governments. Two delegates from North Carolina, William Hopper and John Penn, separately applied to Adams for a plan of government for their colony. Adams obliged. After seeing *Thoughts on Government*, Wythe of Virginia and Jonathan Dickinson Sergeant of New Jersey put in requests for their own copies. When Richard Henry Lee also asked Adams for a copy of his sketch, the author borrowed Wythe's and Lee had it printed in pamphlet form.[109]

Adams had been thinking about the form the independent governments should take for at least some months. One impetus for making his thoughts public, besides his compatriots' requests for advice, seems to have been the publication of Thomas Paine's *Common Sense*. Because of the pamphlet's strong stance on independence, some readers suspected that Adams was the author. Adams was not flattered. "But altho I could not have written any Thing in so manly and striking a style," he wrote to Abigail, "I flatter myself I should have made a more respectable Figure as an Architect, if I had undertaken such a Work. This Writer seems to have very inadequate Ideas of what is proper and necessary to be done, in order to form Constitutions for single Colonies, as well as a great Model of Union for the whole."[110] The main features of the plan Adams sketched—a two-house legislature, a strong executive, and a distinct judiciary—were direct responses to Paine's call for state governments composed of unicameral legislatures and weak executives.

Paine attacked the traditional notion of mixed and balanced government largely because of its association with "the so much boasted constitution of England." "The more simple anything is," Paine argued, "the less liable it is to be disordered, and the easier repaired when disordered."[111] But Adams believed that the type of government advocated in *Common Sense* would contain no internal checks against capricious swings in popular opinion (the same criticism he later leveled against France's unicameral National Assembly). Adams held that a unicameral assembly returned by the electorate every year or so would be too responsive to the immediate passions of its constituents—passions that might not always be consonant with the public good. A strong executive and a more experienced upper house of legislators, he believed, were necessary to balance the influence of the popular assembly as well as to guard against possible tyranny by its majority faction.[112]

Adams attacked Paine's plan of government as "so democratical, without any restraint or even an attempt at any equilibrium or counterpoise, that it must produce confusion and every evil work."[113] At the same time, because he insisted on democratic principles, Adams found himself also pitted against the proponents of an indigenous monarchy and some form of hereditary aristocratic branch.[114] Frequent elections were essential, Adams asserted, "there not being in the whole circle of the sciences, a maxim more infallible than this, 'Where annual elections end, there slavery begins.'"[115] The sort of republican constitution that Adams was advocating, which sought a middle ground between the two dangers of oligarchy and ochlocracy, inspired enough hostility that he remarked in the draft for Penn that "A Man must be indifferent to Sneer and Ridicule, in Some Companies to mention the Names of Sidney, Harrington, Lock, Milton, Nedham, Neville, Burnet, Hoadley."[116] Adams cited as applicable to his own situation the opening lines of "John Milton on one of his Sonnetts":

> I did but teach the Age, to quit their Cloggs,
> by the plain Rules of ancient Liberty,
> When lo! a barbarous Noise surrounded me
> Of Owls and Cuckoo's, Asses, Apes and Dogs.[117]

In the draft that went to Wythe and was subsequently printed, Adams asked in closing that he remain anonymous. He explained the request by quoting the lines of the "immortal John Milton."

Adams agreed with Milton on a number of related points: the connection between forms of government and the character and happiness of the people living under them, the morally elevating effect of republican constitutions, the importance of participation in local government and grammar schools for instilling and preserving the republican spirit throughout the populace, and the relation between equitable representation and education.[118] Nothing could be more fallacious, said Adams, than Pope's lines,

> For forms of government let fools contest,
> That which is best administered is best.

Adams's entire political philosophy and career were premised on the beliefs that forms of government *were* of the utmost concern and that through the "divine science of politicks" one could discover the form of government "which communicates ease, comfort, security, or in one word happiness to the greatest number of persons, and in the greatest degree."[119]

From the early Commonwealthmen, Adams had learned that "there is no good government but what is Republican." A republic was the best form of government because it was based on the virtue and education of the people and promoted "a conscious dignity of becoming Freemen." Thus, it encouraged good humor, sociability, good manners, and good morals. Citing Sidney, Harrington, and Milton, Adams defined a republic as "an Empire of Laws, not of men," a form of government designed to secure an impartial execution of laws and prevent the capricious exercise of arbitrary personal power.[120] Milton had drawn attention to the distinction in *The Tenure of Kings and Magistrates*, which opposed the Presbyterian ministers and others who held that royal prerogative transcended law. In discussing the origin of kings, Milton characterized them as the people's deputies, entrusted with power to execute justice after the Fall. Their power was derived from the people, and laws and oaths were introduced to restrain its arbitrary exercise because absolute power had proved to be too much of a temptation.

> Then did they who now by trial had found the danger and
> inconveniences of committing arbitrary power to any, invent
> laws, either framed or consented to by all, that should confine
> and limit the authority of whom they chose to govern them:
> that so man, of whose failing they had proof, might no more
> rule over them, but law and reason, abstracted as much might
> be from personal errors and frailities: while, as the magistrate
> was set above the people, so the law was set above the
> magistrate.[121]

Elsewhere, Milton had cited Plato and Aristotle, Cicero and St. Paul against the view of royal prerogative as transcending law. Milton, like Adams, was wary of the two extremes of despotism and ochlocracy, the tyrannies of the one and the many.

In 1776 Adams was optimistic about the character of the American people, which he thought was especially predisposed to the republican form of government. "The Spirit of the People, among whom I had my Birth and Education . . . was always republican," Adams wrote in the first draft of *Thoughts on Government*. He attributed that spirit to the illustrious tradition of the New England town meeting, which encouraged extensive participation in government at the local level, and to the rich infrastructure of schools and colleges:

> It was wholly owing to the Constitution of their Towns, which
> were Small Districts incorporated by an early Law, and vested
> with Powers to assemble frequently, deliberate, debate and
> act, upon many Affairs, together with the Establishment of
> Grammar Schools in every one of those Towns, that Such a
> Spirit was preserved, at all among the People.[122]

This point Adams had treated at greater length in his "Dissertation on the Canon and the Feudal Law." It was no coincidence that Massachusetts—the colony with the pre-eminent educational tradition, with young men schooled in classical political theory from Plato through Milton—was the seedbed of the American Revolution (confirming the fears of Hobbes and others that the study of the classics engendered republican political sentiments).

Given Adams's appreciation of New England's educational and political heritage, it is not surprising that an important theme of *Thoughts on Government* is the necessity of education for securing equitable political representation. In the second draft he wrote: "Two things are indispensably to be attended to—one is some Regulations for securing forever an equitable Choice of Representatives—another is the Education of Youth, both in Literature and Morals." In the third draft he implied that education should be undertaken at the public expense: "LAWS for the liberal education of youth, especially of the lower class of people, are so extremely wise and useful, that to a humane and generous mind, no expence for this purpose would be thought extravagant."[123]

The connection Adams made between education and participation in government was fundamental to his political outlook. Milton would have expressed the connection in somewhat different terms. Education was necessary, he believed, to repair the ruins of the Fall—to inoculate people against the blandishments of deceitful Satans and to make them fit to choose worthy representatives. But Milton's concerns were the same as those of Adams and other more secular republicans. In light of these common concerns, we can understand the powerful fusion that arose in the colonies between the older religious outlook, inculcated through literary texts such as *Paradise Lost* as well as through the Bible and Puritan theology, and classical political theory, with its ideal of liberty-preserving balance. For Adams and others like him, an ingrained Christian consciousness of human fallibility became a powerful impetus to the formation of republican governments with balanced constitutions and with provisions for public education and internal improvements to elevate the people to responsible citizenship. As Adams was to write in 1787, in defense of the mixed and balanced constitutions of the American states, "although reason ought always to govern individuals, it certainly never did since the Fall, and never will till the Millennium and human nature must be taken as it is, as it has been, and will be."[124]

7

Milton Defends the Republic

$\mathbb{P}$*aradise Lost* reached increasingly wider American audiences in the first decades of the Republic, as a revived printing industry turned out an impressive volume of new editions of Milton's poetry. As Leon Howard has written, the reprinting of Milton's poetry was one of the flourishing "infant industries" of the new nation: between 1787 and 1815 his collected poems went through no fewer than twenty-eight American editions, or almost two-thirds as many as appeared in England over the same years.[1]

During this period, Milton was widely cited in American debates on education, particularly in defense of the merits of classical studies in a modern commercial republic such as the United States. In the 1790s, Noah Webster and other advocates of universal public education often echoed Milton in emphasizing the central role of education in a republic, where it was necessary to fortify youth against the temptations of luxury and faction and to prepare them to become politically responsible and productive citizens. American educational reformers hoped that the rapid spread of education would forestall the decline of public virtue that had been the undoing of all previous republics.[2] Some cited *Of Education* and the personal example of Milton in arguing for the utility of classical learning in providing the young with models of behavior.[3] John Quincy Adams, in his famous lectures on oratory and rhetoric at Harvard, pointed to Milton's intimate knowledge of classical languages as a source of his unrivaled capacity for "forceful expression." For Quincy Adams and his contemporaries, who regarded oratorical skill as an essential tool of the good politician (for awakening reason in an audience and for combatting the influence of demagogues), the power of Milton's syntax and imagery had more than academic interest.[4]

However, the most remarkable use of Milton during the 1790s was in the first major political crisis of the Republic, when various factions along the political spectrum—moderates and radicals within both the Federalist and Republican parties—all seized on Milton's satanic imagery to expose the "diabolical" wiles of their antagonists. The crisis of the 1790s was precipitated by the French Revolution, which raised questions about the immediate future of Franco-American relations and about American foreign policy in general. Were the terms of the 1778 treaty between the French monarchy and the United States still binding? Would the United States be drawn into the war between France and Britain on the side of its old ally, or would it adhere to the Washington administration's policy of neutrality?

Moreover, the ideological paradigm of the French Revolution raised serious questions about the future character of the American Republic because it intersected with ongoing domestic conflicts over such issues as the federal government's authority to impose taxes for internal improvements; taxation by the localities for public education; and the relative merits of balanced and pure democracies as represented by the American constitutional government and the French National Assembly under the Jacobins. The entire Commonwealth-Whig tradition, with its dual stress on the strengthening of public virtue (through education and economic improvement) and on the restraint of corruption (through governmental checks and balances), was put to the test. In fact, it was attacked simultaneously by American admirers of the Jacobin model and by an emerging pro-British, high Federalist faction. Ironically, the pro-British faction was well served by its opponents: the rise of francophile democratic societies across the country, with their vocal anti-Federalism and agitation for war against England on the side of France, alarmed much of the American population.

In the war of polemics that accompanied these events, politicians and satirists were drawn to the language and imagery of *Paradise Lost*. Given the epic's broad circulation in the early Republic, audiences could be counted on to recognize Miltonic allusions. Moreover, Milton's depiction of Satan's rebellion once again seemed made-to-order for addressing an immediate political crisis because of the continuing influence in the nascent United States of Commonwealth-Whig principles and rhetoric. In 1796, describing the reaction of pro-French Republicans in the House of Representatives to a political setback, Vice-President John Adams remarked that they "attempted to laugh, but their visages grinned horrible ghastly smiles."[5] Milton's description of Death, who "Grinn'd horrible a ghastly smile," was by now commonly used to insult political opponents, often, as here, to disparage the evil of partisanship (the pursuit of party interests ahead of the common weal). The Miltonic Satan, his council of demagogues, his foul and unnatural offspring Death with its all-devouring maw—these indelible images became favorite metaphors for the evils of faction, warning of its potential to consume and sunder the fragile nation.

Although Milton's infernal imagery was adopted by polemicists of all political persuasions during this period, his rendering of Satan and the council in Pandemonium proved especially suitable for addressing the pitfalls of pure, or unchecked, democracy. The Federalist writer John S. J. Gardiner, for example, incorporated the entire apparatus of the devils' conclave into his satirical portrait of Boston's democratic club,[6] attempting to unmask the club's pro-Jacobin leaders as foreign-supported demagogues whose egalitarian rhetoric cloaked partisan interests. All of the points of contention between the government and its "democratic" opponents—American relations with France and Britain, the mixed and balanced character of the federal Constitution, the government's policy of tax-supported internal improvements and public education, the meaning of popular sovereignty—were treated within the compass of Milton's epic machinery.

In discussing the use of *Paradise Lost* to satirize American Jacobinism, Sensabaugh comments that it was an irony that Milton, "a publicized witness of the revolutionary tradition, was now being invoked to testify in conservative causes."[7] But the logic of such invocations was firmly grounded in the classical republican worldview of Milton himself and of other writers in that tradition, such as Grotius and Vondel. All three used the biblical stories of Satan's rebellion and his seduction of Adam and Eve to express concern about the corruptibility of the uneducated "many." All three recognized that successful manipulation of the people by demagogic Satans had been a frequent cause of the destruction of republican accomplishments. John Adams documented this historical pattern at length in his *Defence of the Constitutions of Government of the United States* (1785–87), fearing, like many others of similar mindset, that the pattern might be repeated in the United States. All of this calls into question Sensabaugh's view, prevalent today, that anti-Jacobinism was necessarily a reactionary cause. In fact, the concern over the "tyranny of the majority" was a continuous feature of the revolutionary tradition that led to 1776. Both the pro-French and the pro-British factions of the 1790s—respectively ultrademocratic and oligarchic—departed from that revolutionary tradition. Thus, the writers who adopted Milton's imagery to expose these more subtle threats to the nascent Republic showed how well they understood both the Commonwealth-Whig political legacy and the republican dimensions of Milton's epic.

The Commonwealth-Whig tradition was still very much alive in the United States in the early decades of the Republic. Although other domestic political tendencies had begun to assert themselves by the late 1780s, in what historians refer to as "the first party system" (the Federalists and the Jeffersonian Republicans), Americans of different party affiliations still shared many of the assumptions that had been widely held during the colonial and revolutionary periods. The classical republican notion of a public good above and distinct from particular interests was still an axiom of political discourse. It followed from this view that parties were "factions," particularities that pursued self-interest to the detriment of the public good; the word "party" was still used in the sense in which Milton had used it in speaking of the Devil's "party."[8] Thus, on the eve of the 1796 national elections, John Quincy Adams spoke not of two parties but of the pro-French "party" and the "friends of the government" and worried that the skillful operations of the former might lead the United States into a new and devastating war with Britain on the side of France.[9] For Quincy Adams, factions and parties were to the body politic as passions were to the individual: unchecked, they usurped the whole and brought about its degeneration.

The search for a mixed and balanced polity, another hallmark of republican political theory from classical times, also continued to preoccupy moderates of both parties, though it was challenged by advocates of pure democracy. The federal Constitution of 1787 built on the older notion of mixed government—which sought to represent and balance the traditional socioconstitutional orders of the one, the few, and the many—adding a system of checks and balances among executive, legislative, and judicial functions. The distinction between the two houses of the legislature was also changed to reflect the dual state-national character of political power in the new Republic. (Nevertheless, the Senate continued to be spoken of as the "aristocratic house" well into the nineteenth century.)

Whereas in the 1770s American Whigs were principally alarmed over the threat to the balance of government from the "one" (the Hutchinsons and Bernards), in the 1790s their concern shifted to the self-interested passions of the "many" and of the "few"—the people and the emerging aristocracy of money. In defending the proposed federal Constitution, Madison had observed that a principal benefit of a geographically extensive republic would be its effectiveness in mitigating the problem of faction—in particular, the tyranny of a majority faction over a minority—to which popular governments were prone. He defined a faction as "a number of citizens, whether amounting to a majority or minority of the whole, who are united and actuated by some common impulse of passion, or of interest, adverse to the rights of other citizens, or to the permanent or aggregate interests of the community."[10] Republics were superior to pure democracies, Madison maintained, in checking the "mischiefs of faction," because the delegation of government to elected officials of superior "wisdom" served to modulate the extremes and vicissitudes of the "public voice." And extensive republics were highly favorable to the election of "proper guardians" owing simply to their large geographical area and diversity of interests, which acted as checks against tyranny by any one faction. The great geographical extent of the American Republic, Madison argued, would also allow for a greater choice of representatives and a higher probability that fit guardians would be found.

To "republican federalists"[11] such as John Adams, the achievements of the American Revolution appeared to be jeopardized by the popular political unrest of the late 1780s and the 1790s. These years saw widespread protests against taxes and complaints of unfair representation, a loss of respect for learning (typified by the refusal to pay taxes to support education), debtors' movements, and demands in some states for the abolition of governors and senates. Historically, Adams argued in his *Defence of the Constitutions*, unbridled democracy had led inevitably to the tyranny of the few—to seizure of power by ambitious aristocratic factions—and he and others feared that the same historical pattern was now unfolding in the United States. Adams has been described disparagingly as "an early convert among Whig liberals to the doctrine of the tyranny of the majority" and criticized for imposing on American political theory the classical and European models of alternating plebian and patrician misrule, transforming "industrious, property-minded American mechanics and farmers into the Athenian mob or the Roman proletariat."[12] However, there is much to be said for the concern Adams and other republican Federalists felt in the wake of popular insurrections such as Shays' and the Whiskey rebellions, given the still-fragile condition of the union. American unity was threatened by the proven capability of foreign powers—both the French and the British—for subversion in the United States; and by the abundance of temptations, in the absence of the restraints of a traditional social structure, for citizens to succumb to ambition, greed, and other passions. Noah Webster noted that in despotic states, children were always expected to take up their parents' occupations. Such a practice, he wrote, "cramps genius, and limits the progress of national improvement" but "is an almost immoveable barrier against the introduction of vice, luxury, faction, and changes in government"—the very problems that the United States was facing.[13] America's unique social fluidity offered individuals greater opportunities for political participation and self-improvement but at the same time provided more scope for the abuse of those opportunities and for the manipulation of weaker citizens by corrupt politicians. America's citizens were freer to achieve but also freer to fall.

In this political climate, Milton's rendering of the council in Hell became a central warning symbol for the pitfalls of commercial republics, one that paralleled on several levels the inner dynamics of both ultrademocratic and oligarchic factions. For example, the devils in Milton's council scene justify their rebellion against God by frequent references to His "tyranny," while their true motives are to satisfy such passions as the desire for social distinction; with similar motives, the American Jacobins of 1790s decried the federal government's violation of their "democratic rights" in imposing taxes upon them. Furthermore, despite Satan's claim that there is no such thing as envy in Hell and therefore no faction, the essential purpose of the devils' bond is mutual advancement of self-interest, a hallmark of all aristocratic factions, including the tory Federalists who clamored for war with France. Also, the rebel angels are a "Party," which for both Milton and the American founding fathers, as we have seen, meant any group pursuing self-interest to the detriment of the public good. Finally, as his faction's leader—and as master demagogue—Satan employs the techniques of the leader of any political clique: he cajoles his followers by heaping flattery upon them and by creating the illusion that the devils are engaging in a democratic debate as his equals.

The Tyranny of the Majority

The Federalist concern over the possibility of tyranny by a democratic majority in the new Republic took on added urgency because of developments in France. Americans at first welcomed the French Revolution and the emergence of a sister republic across the Atlantic; however, as early as August 1790, President Washington warned against the dangers "resulting from too great an eagerness in swallowing something so delightful as liberty."[14] The beheading of Louis XVI and the inauguration of the Jacobin Reign of Terror horrified a considerable portion of the American population, which several years before had enthusiastically greeted the revolution with tricolor cockades and liberty caps. By 1793, while Jeffersonian Republicans generally remained favorable to the French Revolution despite the riots, the executions, and the Terror,[15] many Federalists regarded it as "an outpouring from the depths of society of irreligion, anarchy, and massacre."[16] With the onset of the Terror, John Adams saw in the French Revolution "no tendency to any thing but anarchy, licentiousness and despotism." He was afraid that the social-leveling doctrines of the French Jacobins would spread to the United States, where there was already sympathy for such views: in 1787 he had observed to a correspondent that Daniel Shays was as great a tyrant when he sought to "pluck up law and justice by the roots" as was Thomas Hutchinson when he tried to overrun them partially.[17] The new tyranny of the many, in Adams's view, was as antithetical to liberty as was traditional despotism. In an often-quoted passage, he compared the francophile Republicans to Lovelace (the diabolical villain of *Clarissa*) and their cause to the illusory dream of liberty that Lovelace offers Clarissa:

> The awful spirit of Democracy is in great progress. It is a
> young rake who thinks himself handsome and well-made, and
> who has little faith in virtue. . . . When the people once
> admit his courtship, and permit him the least familiarity they
> soon find themselves in the condition of the poor [seduced
> and pregnant] girl. . . .
> Democracy is Lovelace and the people are Clarissa. The
> artful villain will pursue the innocent lovely girl to her ruin
> and her death. . . . The time would fail me to enumerate all
> the Lovelaces in the United States. It would be an amusing
> romance to compare their actions and character with his.[18]

After the Jacobins had fallen from power in France, John Quincy Adams, then ambassador to The Hague, wrote to his father of the waning of the French democratic societies, which he termed, sardonically, "the most efficacious of all the instruments employed by the tyranny under which France has recently suffered." Borrowing a figure from Milton to drive home his point, he reported that although the societies had been formally abolished by the proposed French Constitution of 1795, they appeared "not less than Archangel ruined, and . . . still extremely formidable."[19] To Quincy Adams, the Société des Jacobins and its offshoots in France and the United States appeared diabolical, in Milton's sense, because they represented the tyranny of self-interested passions in a new guise— the subjection of society to the immediate passions of the people—and because the doctrine of popular sovereignty they espoused held that rebellion against government was legitimate whenever the people so deemed it. While Quincy Adams celebrated the "republican spirit" on the rise throughout Europe—the "aversion to the principle of inheritance"—he was not sanguine about the new style of political fanaticism or the moral condition of Europe's long-oppressed populations. "The myrmidons of Robespierre were as ready to burn libraries as the followers of Omar," he wrote to his father, "and if the principle is finally to prevail, which puts the scepter of sovereignty into the hands of the European Sans Culottes, they will soon reduce everything to the level of their own ignorance."[20]

Quincy Adams had anticipated the instability and the excesses of the Jacobin regime several years earlier in his extended analysis of the defects of France's new unbalanced Constitution. When he began publishing his Publicola letters in the summer of 1791 in response to Thomas Paine's unreserved championing of the new French system, many people attributed the letters to Vice-President John Adams (Lucifer himself, to Dr. Nathaniel Ames and other anti-Federalists). Critics abused the author for advocating aristocracy and monarchy.[21] However, to anyone who actually read the letters, the charge was completely unsupportable, and in the last letter of the series, the young Adams challenged all of his detractors who had "appeared in support of Mr. Paine's infallibility, to produce a single passage to these publications which has the most distant tendency to recommend either a monarchy or an aristocracy to the citizens of these States."[22] What the letters did evidence was the writer's equal hatred of despotism of the Right and of the Left—of "the diadem and scepter" and of "the party-colored garments of democracy."[23] Quincy Adams distinguished sharply between the American and French revolutions and attacked what he considered to be Paine's flippant attitude toward revolutions, cautioning against total dissolution of civil government except after every other avenue for change had been explored. He castigated Paine for his unbounded faith in the power of the "mob," those men who "have nothing to lose by the total dissolution of civil society."[24]

Quincy Adams was particularly anxious to expose the French Constitution's pretensions to being a model of democratic and republican principles. To this end he pointed to the superiority of the *principles* of the British Constitution—stressing their incorporation into the American state and federal constitutions. This contrast between the positive features of the British Constitution and the negative features of the French was apparently the pretext for the calumniation of Publicola as a political heretic, a friend of monarchy and aristocracy. But Publicola was critical not just of the French but also of the English government, whose abuses, he wrote, arose "less from the defects inherent in the Constitution, than from the state of society; the universal venality and corruption" characteristic of "all classes of men in that kingdom, and which a change of government could not reform."[25] He contrasted both the French and the British systems unfavorably with the American. In analyzing the French Constitution, he challenged the principle, upheld by Paine, "that a whole nation" has "a right to do whatever it pleases" and maintained that there were "eternal and immutable laws of justice and of morality" superior to the aggregate desires of the population of a nation at a given time—a Commonwealth principle that the elder Adams had also invoked in his Novanglus letters.[26] Quincy Adams argued that the novel doctrine of popular sovereignty, in confusing the will of the whole nation with that of the majority in the representative assembly at a given moment, actually endangered individual liberty, for if "a majority . . . are bound by no law human or divine, and have no other rule but their sovereign will and pleasure to direct them, what possible security can any citizen of the nation have for the protection of his unalienable rights?"[27] In fact, he concluded, it was not the "rights of men" but the rights of the majority, and only of the majority, that were unalienable in the French system.[28]

The lack of built-in checks and balances led to further problems, Quincy Adams argued. In the hope of avoiding the abuse of power by an all-powerful, single-house legislature, the French Constitution had been made unalterable except by the whole nation in its "original character." This provision, Quincy Adams argued, defeated the very purpose of government, which was to act on behalf of the people. Moreover, the degree of popular representation promised by the new French Constitution was as minimal as that allowed under Britain's corrupt electoral system, owing to restrictive property qualifications and a complicated election process whereby qualified French citizens voted for members of one assembly of electors, who voted for another, and so forth. Quincy Adams pointed out the irony that, contrary to the illusions of Paine and other enthusiasts, the National Assembly of France had not actually ventured to govern the nation under the form of a pure democracy. Finally, he argued, by lodging the power to make war and peace entirely in the legislative branch, the French Constitution had rendered impossible the secrecy and dispatch required to conclude expeditiously treaties between nations, while opening "a thousand avenues for base intrigue, for furious faction, for foreign bribery, and domestic treason."[29]

Regarding the authorship of the letters, Publicola rightly protested that "The Vice-President neither wrote nor corrected them; he did not give his sanction to an individual sentiment contained in them, nor did they 'go to the press under the assumed patronage of his son.' "[30] However, John Quincy's political education had been guided by his father, and as the Publicola letters demonstrated, father and son were of one mind regarding the dangers of France's single-chamber National Assembly. The elder Adams had been the first American to challenge Paine's recommendation that the United States adopt the unicameral system of the Pennsylvania state constitution. Adams had written his *Defence of the Constitu-*

tions, with its unrelenting emphasis on the instability of "governments collected into one [legislative] center," in response to Turgot's advocacy of unmixed government, to combat the growing popularity in the United States, France, and elsewhere of the notion that a governmental framework consisting of a single assembly and a circumscribed executive was superior to the governments of the various states, which (with the exception of Pennsylvania's) had been based on a constitutional foundation of three balanced and separate powers. Adams was equally outspoken regarding the French Constitution of 1789, whose form had been influenced by Paine, Franklin, and other advocates of the Pennsylvania model.

In contrast to most Americans, who were initially enthusiastic about the French Revolution, John Adams believed the new regime would be short-lived because of the flaws in the newly adopted Constitution. From April 1790 through April 1791, he contributed his *Discourses on Davila* to John Fenno's *Gazette of the United States* in order to disabuse the public of its delusion that the American Revolution had been run along lines similar to the French. He took issue with the Enlightenment doctrine of human perfectibility apotheosized by the French Revolution:

> Amidst all their exultations, Americans and Frenchmen should remember that the perfectibility of man is only human and terrestrial perfectibility. Cold will still freeze, and fire will never cease to burn; disease and vice will continue to disorder, and death to terrify mankind. Emulation next to self-preservation will forever be the great spring of human actions, and the balance of a well-ordered government will alone be able to prevent that emulation from degenerating into dangerous ambition, irregular rivalries, destructive factions, wasting seditions, and bloody, civil wars.[31]

Writing to Jefferson late in life, Adams reiterated his differences with the French *philosophes*: "I am a Believer, in the probable improvability and Improvement, the Ameliorabi[li]ty and Amelioration in human Affairs: though I never could understand the doctrine of the Perfectability of the human Mind."[32] He believed that, in disregarding the human "passion for distinction"—which could take the form of ambition, jealousy, envy, or vanity, in addition to the sometimes constructive impulse of emulation—and in failing to establish institutional means for controlling it, the framers of the French Constitution were inviting political instability and new forms of tyranny. On another occasion, Adams pointed out that the passion for distinction was even stronger in republics than in traditional societies because, in the absence of hereditary privilege and inveterate

social classes, individuals felt a greater compulsion to distinguish themselves through money and acquired status. His concerns ran parallel to
those expressed a century earlier by the English Commonwealthmen—
Harrington, Sidney, Milton, and others—who had advocated limitations
on the concentration of power in any center, in order to protect society
against the reign of the passions.

"Jacobins Born in Sin . . ."

When France went to war with Great Britain and dispatched Citizen
Genêt as French minister to the United States, a crisis erupted in
American foreign policy. President Washington decided to honor the
Franco-American treaty of 1778 and receive the new French minister;
however, he simultaneously issued, in the name of the government, a
proclamation of neutrality, which was widely interpreted as prohibiting
individual Americans from aiding or abetting hostilities or otherwise
engaging in acts partial to either France or Britain. Although the Republicans agreed that the United States should remain neutral in the war
between France and Britain, they resented the constraints against their
individual freedom of action, the President's use of the word "impartial,"
and the fact that he had acted without agreement from Congress. On
June 29, 1793, Hamilton, under the pseudonym "Pacificus," published
the first of a series of articles in which he argued that the President was
within his constitutional rights in issuing the proclamation and, moreover,
that war on the side of France would be a disaster for the United States.
But Madison, who in *The Federalist* had advocated a strong executive, now
answered that as Congress controlled foreign policy, neutrality should
have been proclaimed by the legislature; besides, the United States, far
from being "impartial" in the conflict, owed a moral obligation to France
for its support during the Revolutionary War.[33] The nation as a whole was
soon polarized over these issues. Jefferson and other enthusiasts of the
French Revolution saw the nation divided into friends of liberty and
"timid men who prefer the calm of despotism,"[34] an oversimplified view
that grouped all critics of the French Revolution—from moderates like
the Adamses to pro-British Federalists—in the same category. The pro-
French party denounced their opponents as monarchists and aristocrats;
Federalists called the francophiles "Jacobins."

Genêt's conduct in the United States served only to intensify the crisis,
as he acted in blatant defiance of Washington's neutrality proclamation.
He bypassed the President, offering Americans commissions for priva-
teering and even advertising in newspapers for "Friends of France" to

enlist in the French service. When the Washington administration responded in early August of 1793 with the "Rules governing Belligerents," which explicitly prohibited foreign nations from recruiting volunteers and outfitting ships in the United States, Genêt demanded that the President call a special session of Congress to judge between the President and him. By this time Jefferson was disillusioned and shocked by the French minister, describing him as "hot-headed, all imagination, no judgment, passionate, disrespectful & even indecent toward the President."[35] Washington requested Genêt's recall in December, but by that time the Jacobins had taken power in France and Genêt, a Girondist, had been declared a public enemy and removed from office.[36]

In retrospect, John Adams credited his son John Quincy with turning the tide of American sentiment against Genêt and strengthening Washington's position.[37] Writing as "Columbus," Quincy Adams argued that in attempting to bypass the President and negotiate directly with the people, Genêt had insulted not only the government but also the Constitution of the United States.[38] Quincy Adams accused the French minister of spreading faction, of endeavoring

> to support his failing influence by connecting himself and his
> interests with a particular party of American citizens, separate
> from the whole body of the people: a party professing republi-
> can sanctity beyond the rest of their fellow-citizens, and
> scarcely endeavoring to disguise sentiments, hostile to the
> national government of the country.[39]

Another divisive by-product of Genêt's activities, wrote Quincy Adams, was

> a lengthening chain of democratic societies, assuming to
> themselves the exercise of privileges, which belong only to
> the whole people, and under the semblance of a warmer zeal
> for the cause of liberty, than the rest of the people, tacitly
> preparing to control the operations of the government and
> dictate laws to the country.[40]

Genêt himself founded the first of these so-called democratic societies in July 1793 in Philadelphia, center of pro-French enthusiasm. Modeled on the French Société des Jacobins, the American clubs were dedicated to the extirpation of monarchism and aristocracy—under which rubric they included most Federalist policies. They campaigned for candidates whose policies were to their liking, thus anticipating modern political parties (but, in the 1790s, drawing charges of factionalism). They instructed senators and congressmen. And they upheld the cause of France in its war with England, even to the point of responding to requests for men and materiel. As one historian has written:

> All this might seem innocent enough: the Democratic Clubs were simply the Americans for Democratic Action of their generation. But the year was 1794 and the shadow of the French Revolution fell menacingly upon the United States. In the eyes of skittish Federalists, these clubs were the precursors of all the horrors of "Jacobinism." "Beheading Federalists is the present reigning fashion in France," remarked a Federalist newspaper, "and . . . it is too delightful a recreation, not to be universally enjoyed."[41]

The Federalist *Massachusetts Mercury* warned of the Boston club, saying "the business of this Nocturnal Club will be to denounce citizens, pack juries, abuse Government, instruct Congress, and, for aught we know, erect guillotines."[42]

Federalists universally termed the societies "Jacobin clubs." In denouncing the clubs Fisher Ames, an ardent Boston Federalist, spiced his rhetoric with Miltonic imagery: "Jacobins born in sin, impure offspring of Genêt, sons of darkness," and "trumpeters of sedition." The pro-French party was also described in diabolical terms by the author of a widely circulated Federalist pamphlet published in 1795 under the title *The Jacobin Looking Glass, by a Friend to National Liberty*:

> I see all the detestable arts, all the machinations of disappointed demogogues, and all the malice of even Hell itself, employed to deceive the people and destroy our government, . . . The sons of faction leaped like Cerberus in the Styx to quench their thirst with blood and charge their tongues with poison.

Goaded on by Genêt, who was described by the pamphlet as "a member of the Jacobin Club in France, and consequently a connoisseur in the black art,"

> The democratick dens re-echoed with abuse and high-toned anathema against the Supreme Executive. . . . Their object is to overthrow the present Constitution and to establish one upon its ruins more consonant to their depraved appetites.

193

. . . Sowing discontent . . . they effect their diabolical purposes, and could they once attain their object, another ma-
chine would soon be erected, called, in the Jacobin language,
a guillotine or shaving mill, of which every one, not of their
party, would soon feel the effects.[43]

In a more analytical vein, Quincy Adams wrote to his mother from
Europe of his long-standing aversion to popular societies in general. They
were "an efficacious instrument" in destroying an "established power,"
but they were "fit for nothing else," he wrote, pointing to the Jacobin
Terror in France. The overthrow of the Jacobins had created something of
a dilemma for their American supporters, he added:

Our American Jacobins, I imagine, will be puzzled to fix upon
their creed as to French affairs. I question whether they will
give at full length the debates in the Convention of the
present time. If they do, you will perceive that Jacobin Clubs,
Sans Culottism, *Demagogie* (if *we* have no word to express this
idea, it is not for want of the thing,) and all the madness and
all the hypocrisy, which it was so long a fashion to profess and
to admire, are now rated at their true value. There is however
one fundamental political error, from which France has not yet
recovered; it is the unqualified submission, and the unwise
veneration for the *opinion publique*, which is in its nature
inconsistent with any regular permanent system of government or of policy. Until they have the courage to explode this
doctrine, they will not only be without a constitution, but
totally destitute of the means of forming one.[44]

The Infernal Council *Redivivus*

Quincy Adams himself noted that, serious as the American crisis was, a
vast gulf separated political conditions in Europe and the United States,
the agitation of *sans culottes* and that of American Jacobins. Whereas satire
was hardly an appropriate vehicle to address the Reign of Terror in France,
it was a highly fitting one to expose the folly of both extremes of the
American political spectrum: pro-French and pro-British—radical and
aristocratic. And *Paradise Lost* supplied a ready framework to satirists in
this war of polemics. Brockholst Livingston of New York ridiculed members of the state's democratic society—their desire for pelf, their eagerness for war with Britain, and their financial irresponsibility—through
Milton's pictures of Chaos and the council in Hell. Like all true epics,

194

Livingston's *Democracy: An Epic Poem* opens with an invocation to the muse:

> What deeds of glory grace these latter days,
> Of earth the wonder, and of men the praise;
> How, while, around, all single despots die,
> Tumultuous throngs the vacant thrones supply;
> From democratic sway what blessings spring;
> Say, heavenly *Muse*, and aid me while I sing.[45]

The opening theme—the tyranny of the many superseding despotism—was practically a cliché of Whig thought, deriving ultimately from classical republican theory. The putative author of the poem is one Aquiline Nimble-Chops, Democrat. Therefore, the reader is not surprised to learn in the next lines that the poet's muse is neither Homer's nor Milton's but the genius Confusion, who is discovered dwelling in Milton's Chaos:

> Not *thee* I call, by whose diviner aid,
> Malonia's Bard the fate of Troy pourtray'd;
> Nor *thee* upborne by whose adventurous flight,
> Milton essay'd the empyrean light;
> But *thee*, who springing from the central realm,
> Where Chaos rules, rejoicest to o'erwhelm,
> By force supported, and by fraud maintain'd,
> Whate'er of good and fair mankind hath gain'd,
> Thee I invoke, for unto thee belong
> The factious bankrupt, and the noisy throng. (p. 5)

The main action of *Democracy*, a raucous meeting of New York's democratic society and its progress from the Tontine coffee house to City Hall, bears the imprint of Pope's mock-epic *Dunciad* as well as Milton's *Paradise Lost*. Livingston mixes borrowed epic and mock-epic machinery to satirize the democrats' preoccupation with their own private interests and their obliviousness to "The vast, and nobler interest of the whole." What cause, Nimble-Chops wonders, could induce four hundred men, all "Commerce' sons," to leave their shops, pass up their profits, and gather at the Tontine? The suddenly civic-minded democrats have gathered, we learn, because their leader, the might M——k, has uncovered a plot to overthrow the "Wheel of Government":

> That some had swore the wheel should be o'erthrown,
> That Algerines had given it many a hack,

195

And Briton's Sons had made the hub to crack;
Wherefore he begg'd them to convene with speed,
(This day the unspotted patriot had decreed.) (pp. 6–7)

For the radical Republicans, satirized here, Britain's covert support for the Barbary pirates' depredations on American shipping was a *causus belli*.[46] The Federalists, however, accused the Republicans of constantly inventing plots—or at least exaggerating and exploiting Britain's perfidy—to excuse their own anarchistic behavior.

Mighty M——k attempts to impose order and awaken the crowd's civic consciousness—

"Order," and the tumult feebler grows.
"Sure, at this time, the public good requires
Some Chairman fill'd with patriotic fires" (p. 7)

—but he has little success. The noisy crowd eventually adjourns to the more spacious quarters of City Hall—breaking the lock to gain entry—and a debate, a parody of the council in Hell, ensues:

Now much debate, and various sounds, arise,
Several sage speeches, and as sage replies,
And nought was done—'till 'squire Pomposo rose,
. . . .
"Who"—aloud he bawls—
"Hath now conven'd the people in these walls?
The price of Western land is rising, sure—
Who dares to think that we are growing poor?
I've lately speculated there myself,
And hope to gain no little share of pelf;
If not, another bankruptcy will do—
And if for me, why will it not for you?
This to a fortune is the readiest way—" (p. 8)

Pomposo's sentence is for open war against the English:

"The English take your vessels, steal your goods,—
Let's fight them, every man, curse take their bloods!
Wait not for negotiation—that won't do—
But fight 'em, burn 'em—beat 'em, black and blue." (p. 10)

196

He also recommends that the democrats, to demonstrate their opposition to the party of the rich, refuse to pay back any debts. Speakers arise in succession, urging variations on these themes. Finally, one speaker, "a younger leader," simply urges the crowd to seize the reins of government:

> "Then since the CONGRESS are so stupid grown,
> So lost to sense, 'tis time to claim your own;
> And in this period of distress and pain,
> To take yourselves of government the rein." (p. 16)

Hardly immortal poetry, Livingston's *Democracy* does capture the polemical spirit of debate in the country and shows how Milton's imagery was harnessed by moderates to ridicule the folly of pure democracy. That Milton would have been amused to read *Paradise Lost* thus metamorphosed seems likely in view of his own diatribes against the "hucksters" and "inconsiderate multitude" of London, whose agitations against unfair taxes, unequal representation, and the "tyranny" of the central government contributed to the instability of the English Republic.

A more extended and effective adaptation of *Paradise Lost* for the anti-Jacobin cause was John S. J. Gardiner's *Remarks on the Jacobiniad*. The *Jacobiniad* appeared during the period of heightened Federalist-Republican warfare that followed President Washington's signing of Jay's Treaty in late 1794. The administration had come under attack from the Republican opposition in the House of Representatives, led by James Madison and William Giles, and from the rapidly multiplying popular societies, which opposed not just the treaty with Britain but other aspects of Federalist policy as well: federal taxation (for internal improvements and public education) and consolidation of the system of checks and balances (whose principal features were a bicameral legislature, a strong central executive, and an independent judiciary).

The immediate historical background to the *Jacobiniad* was the insurrection in western Pennsylvania in 1794, which arose out of long-standing resistance to the federal tax on distilled whiskey. President Washington regarded the so-called Whiskey Rebellion as the first dangerous fruit of the democratic societies and inserted in his message to Congress in November 1794 a denunciation of the "self-created societies" as the force behind the anti-government insurrection.[47] To Washington, the rebellion was proof that the societies were "the most diabolical attempt to destroy the best fabric of human government and happiness, that has been presented for the acceptance of mankind."[48] The rebellion was exploited by Albert Gallatin (who figures prominently in Gardiner's satire) and

197

other leading Republicans to unsettle the Federalist administration and its neutrality policy. The anti-Federalists in the West regarded all federal taxes as encroachments of tyranny. The whiskey excise was particularly resented because the Westerners drank mostly Monongahela rye and other backyard brews, used whiskey as a medium of exchange in some agricultural regions that lacked hard currency and bank notes, and knew that the excise had been necessitated by the federal government's assumption of state debts after the Revolutionary War. This measure, undertaken to strengthen the nation's credit after the adoption of the federal Constitution, was regarded by many Westerners as a government handout to wealthy Easterners who, indeed, had acquired the lion's share of the state bonds after the Revolutionary War, often at steep discounts from impoverished soldiers and widows. Washington treated the insurrection as a test of the strength of the federal government and, when all other measures failed, instructed the states to call out their militias.

The insurrection was quelled, but the anti-Federalists promptly regrouped in opposition to Jay's Treaty. The Washington administration had undertaken treaty negotiations with Great Britain in March of 1794 in the hope of regularizing relations and reasserting its neutrality vis-à-vis its old antagonist. For some months the British had encouraged attacks by the Barbary corsairs on American trading ships in the Mediterranean. The British were also suspected of intriguing with the Indians against the American armies in the West. The urgency of John Jay's mission to London, beginning in March, was heightened by the Republicans' increasingly strident calls for a second war of independence against Britain (satirized in Livingston's *Democracy*). A month after Jay arrived at the Court of St. James, a Republican-sponsored bill calling for nonintercourse with Great Britain was defeated in the Senate by only the vote of Vice-President Adams. Even the advocates of a negotiated settlement with Britain recognized that the final treaty, signed in London that November, was not without flaws, but they believed it was better than war.

Although the terms were initially kept secret, the mere fact that the United States had signed a treaty of amity and commerce with Britain was sufficient to arouse the anti-British faction. Jay was burned in effigy as a perfidious traitor. Washington, when he signed the treaty, was said to have fallen like Lucifer.[49] The senators who voted to ratify it were denounced as being tainted with aristocratic notions. John Quincy Adams wrote from The Hague that the accounts he had received of popular opposition to the treaty caused him to fear renewed war—"a war in which we should have everything to lose and nothing to gain"—because the United States, polarized as it was in 1794, was in no position to fight Britain. Since the principal *causus belli* was the British-sanctioned pirate attacks, Quincy Adams suspected that the British government was "secretly inclined" to intensify the pro-war frenzy of America's democratic societies:

> An American cannot know, without seeing Europe to witness the fact, with what pleasure and exultation all the partizans of monarchy receive accounts of any popular commotions in America. The insurrection of the last summer [the Whiskey Rebellion] was a delicious feast for them, and they did not fail to make the most liberal use of it; they will undoubtedly do the same upon this occasion. They are inimical to the government of the United States, because it furnishes a constant example to those who maintain the superior excellence of a Republican system. They wish to see some proof of extravagance or folly in America, which they can have the pleasure of attributing to the prevalence of republicanism, as they have done very successfully with respect to the frenzies of France.[50]

The Republican opposition to Jay's Treaty quickly developed into a full-fledged attack designed to clip the wings of the American executive. A radical movement began in the Virginia legislature to effect a constitutional amendment that would give the House of Representatives an equal voice with the Senate in ratifying treaties. The Republican leadership in the House—Madison and his right-hand man, Giles—tried to mediate between the radical faction (including Jefferson), which wished to attack the Constitution itself, and a moderate faction that wished to attack only the wisdom of the treaty.[51] The treaty was further threatened when, in March 1796, Edward Livingston of New York introduced a resolution requesting the president to lay before the legislature the entirety of the secret instructions and correspondence pertaining to Jay's negotiations. The British, meanwhile, were not indifferent to these goings-on and, as Quincy Adams and other Federalists had feared, they began reconsidering their commitment to surrender their posts in the West, a major treaty concession won by Jay. A breach of that commitment would have ended Washington's neutrality policy, for it would have been sufficient pretext for the Republicans to force the nation into a war with Britain.

As Quincy Adams read the dispatches from home with increasing anxiety, he became convinced that the French, the British, and Jefferson's Republicans were all involved in a diabolical conspiracy. He reported to his father that the passage of the Livingston resolution on April 17 was celebrated by America's enemies abroad "as proof of our executive imbecility, or of our legislative perfidy."[52] The Republican maneuver, he wrote, was calculated to provoke the British into noncompliance with the treaty terms, to renew the war with Britain, and to boost the Republicans in the upcoming presidential election.[53]

At this juncture Gardiner, then assistant rector of Trinity Church in Boston, began publishing his *Jacobiniad* in the pages of the *Federal Orrery*. The son of a prominent legal reformer, he was known for championing classical studies as well as the Federalist cause; his successor at Trinity dated the revival of classical studies in Boston from Gardiner's founding of a large school where he taught in addition to performing his parish duties. Later (in 1805), Gardiner became president of the Anthology Society, Boston's Federalist literary club, and he helped to run its *Monthly Anthology and Boston Review*, forerunner of the Whig *North American Review*.[54] (In 1810 he withdrew from the club because of political and literary differences with other Anthologists.) By the first decades of the nineteenth century, his literary and political preferences were decidedly with Johnson and Pope rather than with the republican Milton. For example, in a critical piece entitled "Milton's Moral and Political Conduct," which Gardiner contributed in 1809 to the *Monthly Anthology*, he took issue with "democrats and revolutionists" who had felt impelled to defend Milton "where he is the least defensible, in his moral and political conduct."[55] Nevertheless, simply to label Gardiner a pro-British, high-church hyper-Federalist is to overlook the various currents in Federalism in the 1780s and 1790s and to ignore Gardiner's contribution to political debate and to the development of arts and letters in the early Republic.[56] His *Jacobiniad* is evidence of the intersection of his political outlook in the 1790s with that of republican Federalists such as John and John Quincy Adams.

While the verse form and satiric wit of the *Jacobiniad*, an account of the rise and progress of Jacobinism in Europe and America, owe much to Pope's *Dunciad* and the Augustan Age, the main conceit—a debate among Jacobin devils at the Green Dragon Tavern—is taken from Milton. *Remarks on the Jacobiniad* purports to reproduce extracts from "a rare political satire" published with the editor's accompanying criticism in verse. The action of the putative *Jacobiniad* is a meeting of the Boston Constitutional Club ("alias Jacobin Club") at the Green Dragon in Boston's North End.[57] Formerly a principal gathering place for patriots planning the rebellion against British rule, the tavern also played an important role in the development of Freemasonry in the United States, the Grand Lodge of Massachusetts having been founded there in 1774 with Dr. Joseph Warren as Grand Master. In the 1790s the Freemasons were enthusiastic champions of the French Revolution, hoping to import its radical egalitarianism and to draw America into the war in Europe on the side of France.

The "author" of the poem has represented the fortuitously named Green
Dragon as Milton's Pandemonium:

> At Pandemonium meets the scoundrel throng,
> Hell in their heart, and faction on their tongue.
> Who are the men these caitiff chiefs command?
> A strange, unlettered, multifarious band—
> Some with weak heads, but well-intentioned hearts,
> Are simple dupes to Anti-Federal arts;
> Who, viewing tyrant acts in useful arts,
> Mistake foul Faction's, for fair Freedom's cause.
> The rest are genuine progeny of dirt,
> Who, for a pint of rum, would sell their shirt!
> With heads of adamant, and hearts of steel,
> The worst of passions are the best they feel.
> An envious, restless, swearing, drinking crew,
> Whom sense ne'er guided, virtue never knew;
> Some foreign ruffians, hireling tools no doubt,
> French, Irish, Scotch, complete the "rabble rout."[58]

The "editor" explains that the poet must have written ironically, as "No
one, that has the slightest knowledge of the leading members of the club,
can possibly understand it in the literal sense." His assurance a few lines
later that the members cannot possibly be accused of "acting from
interested motives, when they most generously treat half the rabble in
town with *grog* or *flip;* and receive nought in return, but a few *paltry
votes,*" reveals the principal modus operandi of the diabolical demagogues.

The *Jacobiniad* has been described as "an example of the personal
abuse and political venom of this period."[59] Gardiner, however, has some
astute points to make about America's Jacobin faction. When a Negro
named Prince arrives at the doorway of the tavern seeking admittance to
the club, he finds that the club's egalitarian rhetoric is one thing and its
membership policies are something else. A debate ensues among the club
members over whether to admit anyone with such a name—and of such a
color. In the process, the hypocrisy of the egalitarian Republicans is
revealed; for example, it becomes apparent that their main base of
support, as the editor points out, consists of slave-holding Southerners
and foreigners such as Gallatin "the Genevan," whose interests do not
exactly coincide with those of the newly established United States.

As the gathering of Jacobins opens, the goddess Faction has taken flight
for America and is on her way to Boston. Her westward progress recalls
that of Pope's Dullness, itself a parody of the idea of the *translatio studii,*

the popular eighteenth-century notion that the progress of letters from ancient times to modern was from East to West. Once arrived at the Green Dragon, Faction is happy to find "lank HONESTUS," one of her favorites because of "the unwearied pains he took to excite Shays' rebellion," and she consoles him for having been "worsted by a FEDERALIST" while in her service (I, p. 10). She appoints him president of the club and crowns him with a tiara:

> With silent gravity, unmoved by glee,
> A flight, so strange, no mortal sure, could see;
> From every mouth, loud peels of laughter broke,
> And gloomiest members *chuckled* at the joke.
> In mirthful mood, e'en cold *Honestus* opes
> *His pretty, withered pair of* Chinese *chops;*
> Huge FELLOWS, not unlike a choaking calf,
> Shakes his large sides, and grumbles out a laugh;
> Most horribly grinned VINAL at the whim,
> Famed for his *gorgon* head, strange stoop, and length of limb;
> Nor less was HEWES delighted with the fun,
> The club's wise clerk, and *Shubael's* modest son. (I, p. 19)

The editor points out that

> The *"Chinese chops"* of one gentleman, and the *"horrible grin"* of another, are borrowed from the immortal Milton, and the no less Peter Pindar, although, perhaps, never before so justly applied. Now, the first of these great poets, we are informed, by an eminent critic, used to borrow, not from *poverty*, but *pride;* and we imagine the author of the JACOBINIAD can be influenced only by the same motive. (I, pp. 20–21)

At this point the Negro Prince appears and demands admission, citing the just and noble principle of equality. The ensuing debate over whether to admit Prince despite his color and name (the latter being "of aristocratical, or, what was still worse, of royal origins") is modeled on the infernal council of *Paradise Lost*. The members agree to allow the goddess to decide, like Minerva, after hearing their arguments. That Gardiner could count on his readers to recognize his Miltonic allusions suggests, by itself, the extent and degree of popular familiarity with the epic.

> Thrice, from his seat, his form *Honestus* reared,
> And thrice, in attitude to speak, appeared (I, p. 26)

The character is just like Satan when he first addresses his defeated troops, except that pathetic Honestus cannot get his speech out. "From the lines," the editor remarks with characteristic understatement, "the poet seems to have in his eye that fine passage in *Milton,* where *Satan* is described, previous to his addressing his confederates." The editor proceeds to analyze with mock seriousness the significance of the "obscene use of the *right*" hand, as "a *jacobin* is an enemy to everything *right,* and the use of his left, or sinister, hand." Honestus argues against admitting Prince, saying it would deter others from joining their club, national prejudices being what they are. However, those in favor of admission gain the upper hand. One Adam Colson, who is described as having a great pedigree as a democrat owing to his total lack of "larning," exclaims that it would be an outrage not to admit Prince. Prince, therefore, is admitted to the club with full privileges.

When the action of the poem resumes in the second installment of the satire, one of the club's greatest orators arises, described in language that recalls Milton's fallen archangel:

> —His form had not yet lost
> All her original brightness, nor appeared
> Less than a federalist disgraced. (I, p. 21)

This orator begins by declaring his intention of quitting the society because of the general ignorance of its members: their secretary, the most learned of them, cannot even spell. Worse, they have now admitted a Negro. The orator recapitulates the failure of all of their efforts, among which he includes the Whiskey Rebellion and the opposition to Jay's Treaty, adding that "there remained not the most distant hope of a war." His concluding remarks are a panegyric to the President of the United States—"Most certainly a strong symptom of returning reason," the editor observes—culminating in a celestial figure typical of the Washington-worship of the day:

> Like planets, all the various virtues run,
> Round *Washington,* as round their central sun:
> Of civil light and civil life the source
> Our empire ripening in his daily course. (II, p. 21)

As the dissenter leaves, another member remarks that those remaining should rejoice, because the renegade "thought he had too much knowledge for a good *jacobin*"; all the members are "now nearly *equal* in point of information." In the meantime, they have carried the doctrine of equality to its highest pitch by all becoming equally drunk with "democratic grog"; thus Gardiner parodies the Jacobin doctrine of natural equality. (In response to the claim of the French National Assembly that it had done away with all distinctions among men, John Adams commented, "Impossibilities cannot be performed. Have they levelled all fortunes and equally divided all property? Have they made all men and women equally wise, elegant, and beautiful? Have they annihilated the names of Bourbon and Montmorenci . . . Mirabeau and Bailly?" While insisting that all men are entitled to equal treatment under the law, Adams maintained that "no two men are perfectly equal in person, property, understanding, activity, and virtue," and that to ignore such distinctions is to ensure political instability.)[60]

In the course of the *Jacobiniad*, Gardiner ridicules Republican positions on a number of leading issues of the day. One member of the club arises to argue for the abolition of all federal taxes. Another hopes for the abolition in democratic America of all senates, "which were so aristocratic in their nature as entirely to prevent that happy equalization of property" desired by the Jacobins:

> With senates, brethren, we can well dispense;
> The people's foes, they mar the people's sense,
> By them our favorite questions all are lost,
> Our views discovered and our wishes crost—
> O, for *one* house; where you and I and all,
> In Faction's glorious cause may ever bawl—
> Pass any vote we please at any hour,
> Unchecked, uncurbed by senatorial power!
> Then should the people's *majesty* elate
> Stalk uncontrolled through every *equal* state—
> One despot wealth with grasping hands should seize,
> And level riches as it levels trees—
> Shorn of his head each federalist should fall,
> And *pure* democracy be all in all. (II, p. 34)

In a number of states, including Pennsylvania and Massachusetts, democratic agitators had recently demanded the elimination of the governorship and senate. It is clear from this passage that Gardiner, like Boston Federalists generally, agreed with his city's native son, John Adams, on the factiousness and other dangers of unicameral government. All endorsed the Commonwealth-Whig principle of governmental checks and balances.

The goddess faction—Milton's "illustrious ANARCH"—consoles her followers, noting that the great strength of their party lies in the middle and southern states (those most conspicuously involved in the slave trade, the commentator notes). The American Jacobins have many foreign auxiliaries and can count on the unremitting exertions of Mr. Gallatin, "Geneva's glory," on behalf of their democratic ambition. ("Proceed auspicious! in thy bold design, / And Freedom's valued cause confound with mine.") The goddess then delivers an encomium on the first magistrate of Pennsylvania, home of the Whiskey rebels and traditionally the center of opposition in the United States to mixed and balanced government. (Pennsylvania's unicameral constitution of 1776 had been held up as a model for the French Constitution of 1789 by Paine, Richard Price, and the French liberals Turgot and Condorcet.)[61]

Leading Republicans come in for ridicule in the course of the proceedings. Before his departure, the "great orator" warns that admitting Prince might cause a rupture between Northern and Southern anarchists over the issue of slavery. Among the Southerners are Madison and Giles, who are described as talented men, the "chief pillars of *jacobinism*," although their efforts to involve the country in war with England have been unsuccessful. These Republicans have "uniformly styled the best friends of order and of the federal government, *British faction, old tories*, &c. &c."

The second part of the satire is dedicated and addressed to "the Honorable Thomas J——F——N," who is described as an atheist, as the leader of the seditious elements in the country, and as nakedly pro-French in his sentiments—the standard Federalist jibes against the Republican leader. (Some Federalist satirists went so far as to represent Jefferson as Milton's Satan, the irony of this characterization being that Jefferson himself, in his youthful commonplace book, had expressed admiration for the Devil's magnificent speeches and unrelenting resistance to Divine Omnipotence.) "You have no faith in the existence of a First Cause" but believe in the "infallibility of a French Directory," the anonymous contributor of the dedication remarks. If America were to follow in the footsteps of the French Directory—a course that radical Republicans recommended—

A new order of things would take place. The known integrity
of (R——n——d——lph would insure him command of the
treasury, the rigid chastity of J——f——n P——rk——r
would justly entitle him to the superintendence of morals,
whilst the piety of Thomas Paine would naturally stimulate
him to draw up a religious creed, unless your favorite SYS-
TEM DE LA NATURE should be preferred.

> Under the benign influence of this democratic constellation,
> the tree of liberty would produce the choicest fruit. No jails
> would then disgrace a free country, no penal laws impose
> dangerous restraints on personal freedom. Perfect equality
> would be the result of perfect democracy, and the millennium
> of philosophy would be consummated. (II, pp. x–xi)

Jefferson is also accused of having weak nerves as a military leader, following the epic precedent of Milton's cowardly Satan. Jefferson is nevertheless well suited to act "the part of MACHEATH on the democratic theatre."

The poem ends with the birth of the Federal Genius, whose appearance, like that of the Son in Milton's "Nativity Ode," routs the devils. Invoking the popular idea of the westering progression of virtue and knowledge, the Federal Genius waves Faction and her sons back to the Old World:

> Hence, hence, infernal FURY, dare no more
> With thy fell arts to curse this blissful shore;
> This shore, where *Sense* and *Virtue* ever reign,
> And heaven-born *Freedom* holds her blest domain,
> To *European* climates wing thy way,
> Nor cloud the radiance of *Columbia's* day. (II, p. 51)

The Genius then turns to the "misguided dupes of these mischievous demagogues," purges the mists that cloud their vision (a parody of Michael's enlightenment of Adam), and reveals to them the true character of their leaders:

> He spoke—the club their eyes obedient roll
> And view the depths of every chieftain's soul—
> REBELLION there reclined her horrid head,
> And SLANDER false her treacherous poison spread—
> There dark DISSIMULATION shunned the day,
> And DISAPPOINTMENT leagued with ENVY lay—
> They saw—and turned with loathing from the sight,
> And blest the *genius* as the source of light—

206

Then sought their homes—their various trades pursued,
And left in abler hands their country's good. (II, p. 52)

The Tyranny of the Few

During the same period the pro-British wing of the Federalists was subjected to its own share of satire. The author of *Aristocracy: An Epic Poem* (1795) was one of a number of polemicists who depicted the ambitious advocates of an American aristocracy as agents of Satan, their diabolical nature evident in their pursuit of self-interest and in the conspiratorial methods with which they plotted to deprive the people of their hard-won liberties. The poem is attributed to Richard Alsop, the "Hartford Wit" and moderate Federalist, who several years later turned his satiric talents against the pro-French party, again using Milton's infernal imagery. In *The Political Green-House, for the Year 1798,* Alsop warned of the dangerous manipulation of American policy by the French, who stirred up "Faction" through their undue influence on the press and in Congress and sought new opportunities to ensnare the United States in the war against Britain. In an extended simile Alsop compared the francophile Republican congressmen to "Satan's Deacons."[62]

Whether or not Alsop was the author of both *Aristocracy* and *The Political Green-House,* the two poems conveniently exposed the extremist tendencies, aristocratic and radical democratic, in American politics in the second half of the 1790s. For modern readers they suggest the role that Milton's epic played in countering both extremes. The Adams administration (1796–1800) witnessed escalating pressure from pro-British Federalists for war with France (whose depredations on American commerce were as provocative as those of Britain), as well as continued Republican pressure for war with Britain. By 1800 Adams was convinced that these Tory Federalists constituted an English faction, whose aims were just as detrimental to the nation's interests as those of the French faction. On the eve of the 1800 elections he found himself repudiated by the leadership of both parties and, as a result, suffered defeat at the polls.

Around this time, Adams became increasingly alarmed about the emergence of an American financial and political aristocracy, and he regarded the Society of the Cincinnati as symptomatic of that trend. He was contemptuous of those—including Jefferson and Virginia Republican John Taylor—who thought that laws abolishing feudal vestiges in land tenure and restricting monopoly, incorporation, and the like would effect a decisive blow to the accumulation of land and wealth in the hands of a few. How was a new aristocracy of paper wealth to be prevented, he

207

asked, in a democracy of cupidity, where the "few are craving and the many mad for the same thing"?[63] As a result of his historical research and empirical observation, Adams was especially sensitive to the havoc wreaked on society by unchecked aristocratic factions. In *Discourses on Davila* he treated the bloody struggles in sixteenth-century France between contending aristocratic factions, which neither a strong monarch nor a representative assembly were able to control. In later years Adams wrote to Jefferson, "You are afraid of the one, I, of the few. We agree perfectly that the many should have a full, fair and perfect Representation."[64] The emergence of a new aristocracy—together with the intensification of state and party rivalries—strengthened Adams's belief in the necessity of a well-balanced constitution.

In *Aristocracy*, a warning to the extremists in his own party, Alsop (if the attribution is correct) brought to light the self-interested passions and factiousness of America's would-be aristocrats of the 1790s. The mock epic presents itself as a candid account by an intimate of America's leading oligarch, one Aristus, which fell into the hands of its putative "editor" as he was investigating the spirit of aristocracy on the rise in the nation. In a preface to the reader, the editor attributes the "machinery" of the epic—Milton's council in Hell—to a play of fancy on the part of the poet, "for it could not be meant by him to insinuate that the designs of his friend were infernal." But most infernal they are. The poet addresses his work to

> Illustrious Chiefs! who sought the bliss divine,
> In lordly pomp and titled pride to shine;
> While, bent beneath their oligarchic sway,
> Their native land should tremble and obey;
> . . . .
> While grief and rev'rence all my soul inspire,
> I sing, responsive to the mournful lyre. (I, p. 8)

Now borrowing from Milton's "Lycidas," the poet recalls the days long gone when he and Aristus (presently deceased) were wont to rove and frolic in the countryside, "fill'd with youthful fires, / Ambitious thoughts, gay hopes, and warm desires." The credo of Aristus is unabashed self-aggrandizement:

> 'Tis *Self* alone which charms each mortal's eye.
> By this prest on, we ev'ry danger dare,
> In peace that's hidden, or revealed in war,

> Still then shall men, with pride enormous, boast
> Of souls, to all but public welfare lost? (I, p. 12)

Self-interest versus the public welfare, pride as the chief motive of devils and aristocrats—these are familiar Miltonic motifs. Alsop appears specifically to have had in mind those Revolutionary War heroes who had grand plans to distinguish themselves through new military adventures (perhaps Hamilton and other members of the Society of the Cincinnati), and he offered an important insight about the functioning of aristocratic factions. As Aristus explains,

> For though self-interest all my actions sway,
> Nor other motive these my friends obey,
> Yet mutual interest here with pers'nal blends,
> And mutual aid subserves our private ends.
> Each seeks for power, yet each perceives how vain
> Would be the struggle, place or power to gain,
> Without the aid of others to procure,
> Without the aid of others to insure. (I, p. 13)

This is indeed a new twist on the idea of the public good. Aristus maintains that he and his confederates are joined together by their mutual desire to advance personal ambition (the same kind of "bond" that exists among the apostate angels). Aristus, however, deludes himself about the absence of faction in his clique in the same way as his original, Satan, does. The central action of the poem is Aristus's discovery that his friends have some "new-found motives" contrary to his, and he swears by "ev'ry Power of Hell" to expose their wiles to the people.

Satan responds to his prayers and the scene changes. In Pandemonium the Arch-Enemy, who presides in "awful state" ("High on a throne exalted, SATAN sate"), sees a new opportunity to destroy God's latest creation, the United States:

> Long have I seen, with heart distracting-grief,
> That land to all distress'd extend relief;
> Seen sacred order ev'ry boon bestow,
> And drive far distant every threat'ning foe.
> I fear'd that there, indeed, at length would rise,
> Belov'd of men, and cherish'd by the SKIES,
> A mighty empire, whose resistless force,
> The world involving in its spreading course,
> Beneath one *plan* would ev'ry State combine,

The good of man their great, their soul design;
And hence would flow wealth, liberty, and ease,
And all earth hail the reign of moral peace.
But, lo! to Hell more pleasant prospects shine,
And fair Columbia hastens to be mine. (I, p. 15)

The methods by which Satan hopes to sow disorder are revealed in the second part of the poem: the fomenting of factional disturbances ("By me shall Order's tyrant spells be broke") and of "provincial jealousies, and personal hate," all of which have erupted since the departure of the British, the common foe.

Alsop's analysis of the dangers facing the United States was couched in the Commonwealth-Whig terms that continued to pervade the political discourse of the early Republic. For him, America's unique status as a seat of virtue and prosperity—the latest empire in the *translatio imperii*—was threatened by a noticeable deterioration in the morality of individual citizens. He believed that a high Federalist faction, motivated by consuming self-interest, seriously endangered the public good. The great evil of the day, in his view, was rivalry between factions and states—a rivalry arising from the lust for self-distinction—which made the fragile union easy prey to manipulative foreign powers. In a footnote added in 1813 to *Discourses on Davila*, John Adams suggested that America's budding state and party rivalries were equivalent to the aristocratic factionalism that had wreaked havoc in sixteenth-century France:

> Compare the conduct of our parties for twenty-four years,—
> our federalists and antifederalists; our republicans and federal-
> ists; how easily the federalists united with Clinton and Inger-
> soll in 1812, and the New England republicans with Jefferson
> and Madison in 1800! State rivalries threaten our tranquillity.
> Virginia, Pennsylvania, New York, and Massachusetts may
> keep us in hot water, as Valois, Bourbons, Montmorencis, and
> Guises did France.[65]

The author of *Aristocracy* expressed the same point of view in his warning to the high Federalists who were putting party interests ahead of the common good.

The radical Republican threat of war against Britain and the high Federalist threat of war against France both reached crisis proportions during the volatile years of the Adams administration. On the eve of the crisis, as Alsop reported in his satirical *Political Green-House, for the Year 1798*, the "impartial" press teemed with Republican-inspired stories of

Britain's "deep laid plots, and cunning schemes" for subversion in the United States. But the exposure in the press in April 1798 of the XYZ affair (Talleyrand's agents had demanded a bribe from the American peace commissioners as a prerequisite for their official reception by the Directory) helped to cure the American public of its zeal for France's cause and increased the popularity of the Federalists. The evidence of France's insulting behavior toward the United States immediately turned the tables in Congress and in the nation:

> While joy each Federal feature crown'd,
> And triumph glow'd the Hall around;
> Each Jacobin began to stir,
> And sate, as tho' on chestnut burr.
> Up the long space from chin, to forehead,
> Sate every feature of the horrid;
> Their moon-ey'd leaders stood like beacons,
> Or as a drove of Satan's Deacons,
> When from the burning lake, in ire,
> They sat their feet on solid fire,
> To find if war, or sly pollution,
> Could raise in Heaven a revolution. (p. 6)

The Republicans are "forlorn" because of their failure to incite a war against Britain, a defeat like that of the rebel angels. "Patriotism" spreads like "wild-fire" in response to "The extreme of insult heap'd" on the nation. The narrator, however, cautions against dropping guard against Jacobinism, devils being the persistent creatures they are, and warns Columbia to draw a lesson from the fate of Helvetia:

> For, from Destruction's lurid sky,
> The *Fiend* has mark'd thee with his eye,
> *In hope,* already shakes thy chains,
> And revels o'er thy wasted plains.
> Howe'er his varying features shew,
> If smiles or frowns impress his brow,
> Still fix'd, his views remain the same,
> Nor once he deviates from his aim. (p. 19)

In the meantime, however, another danger intensified—high Federalist pressure for war against France—and it took all of Adams's political wiles to preserve American neutrality. It was this success that cost him the support of the pro-British leadership of his party, contributing to his

211

electoral defeat in 1800. Even Adams's detractors acknowledge his skill in blocking the war policy embraced by many Federalists and in keeping the ill-prepared United States out of a war with France.

To the surviving revolutionaries of 1776, the United States of the first decade of the nineteenth century seemed hopelessly split by party and state rivalries. The machinations of Adams's own party in the 1800 election, and the openly pro-British, secessionist tendencies of the New England high Federalists thereafter, led John Adams, together with John Quincy, to support the Republicans. While criticizing Jefferson's failure to foster internal improvements and to build up the nation's defenses, both Adamses heartily supported other measures of the new administration—the Louisiana purchase and its execution of the War of 1812, for example. This sort of nonpartisan behavior enraged rabid partisans of both parties.

In this context Levi Lincoln, a Massachusetts lawyer and Republican who had argued against the legality of slavery in a famous 1781 case, criticized the "wantonness of faction" during the Jefferson years. He called for a re-examination of "original principles"—a reaffirmation of the ideas of Sidney, Harrington, Milton, and other Commonwealthmen who were the spiritual fathers of the Revolution. Lincoln assailed the "treasonable" behavior of the "tory federalists," those crypto-monarchists who even at the Constitutional Convention had sought to effect a limited monarchy by merging the state governments into a general one. Now they were denouncing President Jefferson and other Republicans as "liars," "disorganizers," "infidels," and "Molochs." More serious even, these tory Federalists were attempting to fracture the union over their dissatisfaction with the Republican administration. "If you are still attached to liberty, to self rule, to an empire of laws of your own forming," Lincoln told his fellow citizens, then "cling to the national constitution; rescue from disgrace, and from a common danger, America's *greatest treasure*, and the world's *best hope*!!"[66]

He advised disgruntled Federalists to put their desires for alterations in the Constitution—for a strengthening of the executive, for example—before the people's representatives and to forswear stealth and faction. Although a Jefferson supporter, Lincoln took the occasion to remind Massachusetts of its debt to John Adams (the "eminent" "republican federalist") "for the most valuable and democratic parts of its constitution,"[67] and he quoted at length from Adams's *Thoughts on Government*. To Lincoln, Adams's 1776 blueprint for several state constitutions represented the highest expression of republican principles: it had been drafted during a period when "Things were viewed with unimpassioned minds. Truth was received as it presented itself, and applied as wisdom and experience directed, for the good of the country."[68] Adams's praise of the Commonwealth tradition, Lincoln added,

> expressed not merely the sentiments of the late president, of "Sydney, Harrington, Locke, Milton, Needham, Neville, Barney, and Hoadley." They were the sentiments of the Adamses, Bowdoin, Hawley, Livingston, Dickinson, Mason, Pendleton, Lee, Randolph, Rutledge, P. Henry, Madison, Jefferson, and Washington, and they were the sentiments of every American. They were the sentiments which you opposed to the claims of tyranny, which carried us through our revolution, gave us our independence, and those republican governments, essential to its support.[69]

Although political times had changed and the nation faced new challenges, one persuasion of Americans continued to see its mission in terms of the tradition represented by Milton and other Commonwealthmen.

Epilogue: Milton,
the Most American of Poets

$\mathbb{A}$ decade ago the British critic An-
drew Milner argued in *John Milton and the English Revolution* that the living
republican tradition in the United States—a tradition that is closer to the
political outlook of Independency that flourished during the English
Commonwealth than is anything in post-1660 Britain—contributed to the
fertility of American Milton criticism in the twentieth century. One of
my hopes in beginning this study was that the reception of Milton in
revolutionary America, when this republican tradition was defining itself,
might provide clues to the political subtext of *Paradise Lost,* suggesting an
alternative to political readings of the epic that reflect the radical-
conservative poles of later, British-dominated criticism.

The eighteenth-century American understanding of Milton's Satan as
an embodiment of the problem of unchecked self-interest provides such
an alternative frame of reference, I believe. Viewing Milton's epic in light
of its American consequents and its seventeenth-century Dutch antecedents points to the political resonances of the Fall story for poets and
audiences of early modern republics in general, in which both human
corruptibility and human ameliorability seemed to acquire greater scope
than before. Such a perspective brings out "latencies" in the text of
Paradise Lost—themes that, in Milton's time, resonated with issues central
to the eighteenth-century commercial republic that had recently emerged
in Milton's England. Further, this perspective highlights issues that
modern democratic republics have yet to resolve, notably the imperfect
association between virtue, on the one hand, and power and wealth, on
the other; to study Milton from this point of view enriches the significance
of the epic for today's audiences. At this writing, Milton's themes are

relevant not only for the industrialized nations but for the newly democratized nations of the East bloc as well.

At the same time, an understanding of Milton's popularity in revolutionary America casts a revealing light on the New World where so many read him and found him a congenial mind. It illuminates the broad consensus that existed in late eighteenth-century American political culture, underlying emerging political differences such as those that divided the nation in the 1790s. Despite these emerging differences, Americans generally agreed on such fundamental ideas as the existence of a public good transcending individual interests; the dangers of faction, parties, and unchecked power; and the power of education and internal improvements to expand the domain of reason in human affairs. They also shared a belief in progress, both providential and secular, and in the importance of the individual acting in history. As recent historical scholarship has shown, these ideas were fed by two strains in colonial culture: the classical republican tradition inherited from the English Commonwealth, via self-described Commonwealthmen of eighteenth-century England, and the typological-millennial heritage of the Puritan founders. Milton's writings resonated with both strains of colonial culture, and his popularity in America reached its peak at the revolutionary moment, when consensus arising from the shared republican and millennial traditions was at its strongest.[1]

Of course, distinctly different, incompatible "Miltons" were already evident, again symptomatic of developments in the political sphere. During the War of Independence, British loyalists such as Peter Oliver and Samuel Seabury identified Milton's God with monarchy (that of George III and his representatives, to be specific) and Satan with American republicanism. This Tory reading of the epic was a direct descendent of post-1660 English royalist interpretations, which opposed Milton's revolutionary politics and claimed him for high church orthodoxy. However, where readers like Dr. Johnson openly expressed their personal distaste for the "surly republican" and attempted to divorce the "bard" from the "rebel," American Tories adapted Milton's epic to their own political agenda: they portrayed James Otis, Jr., Sam Adams, and other revolutionary leaders as proud, ambitious devils who, like Milton's Lucifer, had lost their former promise and brightness. It seems that Milton's republican ideas were too influential in the colonies in the 1770s, too much a part of the common heritage of all American factions, to be simply ignored or dismissed.

Few people today would defend the Tory reading of *Paradise Lost*, which invoked Milton to argue that subjects owe unconditional obedience to their rulers, that rebellion under any circumstances is unwarranted and unnatural—the very claims that the historical Milton combatted in his prose tracts. However, in the same period across the Atlantic another reading of the epic was taking shape, one that despite its quite different inversion of Milton's value system still has widespread currency. This, of course, was the Satanic reading of the epic, which emerged in the 1780s together with the Jacobin fervor sweeping Europe and America. By way of understanding the English Romantics' hostility to Milton's Christian worldview and their admiration for Satan's heroic qualities, one does well to keep in mind a major formative event of their youths: the alliance between the Church and the forces of reaction in the French Revolution. This pattern contrasted with that of the English and American revolutions, in which a significant segment of the clergy was in the vanguard. Perhaps through too easy an analogy between contemporary events and Milton's poem, Satan's revolt against divine Omnipotence became for Blake, Shelley, and other English Romantics an archetype for heroic resistance to despotic regimes in every age and place.

There is no question that the nineteenth-century Romantics and Thomas Jefferson, another admirer of Satan (and, interestingly, an adherent of the French *philosophes* from early manhood), were deeply inspired by Milton's passion for liberty. They certainly grasped his revolutionary spirit better than the Olivers and Seaburies. They showed less perspicacity, however, with regard to another, equally central element of Milton's thought: the distinction he drew between liberty and license, lawful revolution and unlawful rebellion. Blake found Milton's Messiah colorless; his Devil, dynamic. To explain his response Blake hypothesized a conflict within Milton between the true revolutionary poet and Milton's "selfhood," the part of him that was captive to the dogmas of his age. However, the premise of an unconscious and unresolved conflict within Milton, assumed both by Blake and by more recent readers of the epic, ignores the very conscious, deliberate nature of the distinction Milton made between true liberty (which is obedience to God and reason) and its perversion in the self-serving rebellion of Satan. This distinction is not an aberration that first appears after the early books of *Paradise Lost* but is a continuous, intrinsic feature of Milton's thought.

Whereas for Blake and other Romantics, the unfettered nature of the newborn child was the epitome of humanity, for Milton all the Lord's people were not prophets in their "natural," or fallen, state, though they might, "Improv'd by tract of time," ascend to the condition of the angels. In his understanding of the conflict within each individual between reason and passion, social necessity and individual desire, Milton anticipated one of the key issues of the eighteenth-century commercial republic, which Kant addressed on a philosophical plane with his analysis of

217

heteronomy (the subjection of the will to the passions) and with his categorical imperative (an attempt to bring the will into harmony with socially cohesive lawfulness). Hegel, in his critique of Kant, complained that his predecessor's understanding of obedience was cold and lifeless; Hegel counterposed a positive notion of obedience involving the education of desire. Milton was clearly working on some aspect of the same problem when he insisted that obedience must be free—the obedience of the warfaring Christian of *Areopagitica,* who truly prefers the path of virtue, not an obedience dependent on external authority and on a proliferation of laws and rules suitable for children. Milton's Satan is the classic example of the individual who has no internalized sense of virtue: he depends on external rules to keep his passions in check—and then acts out his unrestrained desire when the "great cop" of the universe turns His back.

Despite the obvious problems with both Tory and Jacobin—conservative and radical democratic—readings of *Paradise Lost,* the history of Milton scholarship has been marked by the continual reemergence, in different guises, of these alternatives. In the 1940s, when right-wing critics portrayed Milton as a conservative and even as a monarchist, Arthur Barker pointed out that such interpretations required the suppression of one part of the poet's thinking, as had the efforts of Macaulay and others to reinterpret Milton as a nineteenth-century liberal democrat, albeit to a lesser extent.[2] Nevertheless, both extremes of interpretation have persisted. The reason for this lies not in the realm of literary criticism proper but in the pervasive attenuation over the nineteenth century, in Europe and the United States, of the republican outlook that Milton represented, and its supersession by the growing intellectual hegemony (within Europe, at least) of the two rival schools of *philosophe* rationalism and traditionalism.[3] The rationalist school was marked by an unbounded faith in unfettered human nature and a confidence in the power of the human intellect to remake the world according to the dictates of reason. The traditionalist school had a far more pessimistic view of humanity's natural capacities and put less stock in individual reason than in traditions and institutions that had developed organically over a given nation's history. Both diverged from the "middle ground" occupied by Milton and those American "Miltonists" such as John Adams who attempted to steer a course between radical democracy and conservatism.[4]

It was Tocqueville's insight that although both modern schools claimed to be defenders of liberty, both, when carried to extremes, denied free will. *Philosophe* rationalism did so by locating the springs of human activity not in the decisions of particular individuals but in large, abstract forces such as the evolution of the species and the dialectic of history; traditionalism, by looking to preexisting facts of race, climate, history, and so forth as the prime determinants of individual and social behavior. As political scientist James Ceaser writes,

> Although each school claimed in its own way to support liberty, Tocqueville contended that both ultimately denied that individuals could control their own destiny and therefore eroded a fundamental belief that supported liberty. To maintain liberty, Tocqueville argued, requires more than the acceptance of an idea of rights and certain favorable institutional arrangements, however important each of these may be. Liberty requires a metaphysical foundation in certain views respecting historical causality and free will. It depends on the fact that people can choose and that their choices can make a difference. Without this belief, people lose their "will" to choose and can see no reason to support the idea of rights or legal institutions designed to protect liberty.[5]

In his own project for a new political science, Tocqueville defended the efficacy of philosophical ideas and reason, on the one hand, and the influence of the distinctive, particular characteristics of nations, on the other. He sought to avoid the extremes of both schools and thereby to offer statesmen a guide for preserving liberty in the age of democracy. Tocqueville found inspiration for his project in the example of the United States, where, in contrast to France, he observed a tempered faith in reason combined with a tradition of citizen participation in local government through civic associations, business organizations, political parties, and so forth. Tocqueville believed that this tradition, together with certain conservative features of the American press, legal system, and other institutions, promoted in the population the habits of thought necessary to maintain liberty; together they prevented the excessive fascination with novelty and abstract ideas that makes nations vulnerable to the influence of ideologues, and they inculcated the view that it is within the power of individual citizens to defend their rights.

Milton, in *The Ready and Easy Way to Establish a Free Commonwealth*, had recorded similar insights into the importance of citizen participation in local institutions for preserving liberty.[6] Like Tocqueville, he believed local government could act both as a balance to the concentration of power in central government and as an arena in which individual citizens could exercise their capacity to make choices on matters within their sphere of experience. The synergism Tocqueville observed in early nineteenth-century America between a metaphysical belief in free will and the concrete opportunities for its exercise gave flesh to Milton's notion, central to his epic, that "reason is but choosing."[7] This feature of American political culture helps to explain the continuing affinity between American readers and *Paradise Lost* in the nineteenth century, which inspired the critic R. W. Griswold to observe: "Milton is more emphatically *American* than any author who has lived in the United States.[8]

It is no accident that the most vehement anti-Miltonism in the United States was articulated by early twentieth-century expatriate writers such as Pound and the early Eliot, who shunned America's republican traditions and saw in the country only a vast cultural wasteland. Pound, who flaunted his "personal active dislike" for Milton the individual and for Milton the republican, exemplified the highly political nature of Milton's poetry. "Milton is the most unpleasant of English poets, and he has certain definite and analysable defects," Pound wrote. "His popularity has been largely due to his bigotry, but there is no reason why that popular quality should be for ever a shield against criticism. His real place is nearer to Drummond of Hawthornden than to 'Shakespear and Dante' whereto the stupidity of our forbears tried to exalt him."[9] Thus, Pound attacked both Milton and the tradition in the United States that held Milton in reverence.

Today's New Historicism presents a Leftist critique of the Anglo-American tradition of representative democracy and, with it, a new phase of anti-Miltonism. Milton is cast as a spokesman, an apologist, for bourgeois liberty—an imperfect liberty envisioned exclusively for white, property-holding males. But the very fact that Milton is a focus of such attacks by the New Historicists, who reject the notion that the human essence is the freedom to make choices, attests to his central role in articulating and transmitting to future generations ideas that impelled two major revolutions of the modern world. If these ideas were not perfect, they nevertheless made it thinkable and possible to extend political rights and obligations on a broader scale than before.

Endnotes

Preface

1. Christopher Hill, *Milton and the English Revolution* (London: Faber and Faber, 1977); Andrew Milner, *John Milton and the English Revolution: A Study in the Sociology of Literature* (London: Macmillan, 1981); Christopher Kendrick, *Milton: A Study in Ideology and Form* (New York: Methuen, 1986); Jackie DiSalvo, *War of Titans: Blake's Critique of Milton and the Politics of Religion* (Pittsburgh: University of Pittsburgh Press, 1983). For a sampling of recent essays on the political Milton that focus on questions of gender, class, and race, see *Remembering Milton: Essays on the Texts and Traditions*, ed. Mary Nyquist and Margaret W. Ferguson (New York: Methuen, 1988).

2. *Milton in Early America* (Princeton: Princeton University Press, 1964). Sensabaugh surveys Milton's influence on diverse facets of American culture from colonial days through the first quarter of the nineteenth century, including literature, education, morality, religion, and politics.

When Sensabaugh's study first appeared, it was challenged by Gordon Wood, a historian who has played a major role in demonstrating the American Revolution's debt to English seventeenth- and eighteenth-century republican thought—and a reviewer, therefore, to be taken seriously. Wood found some of Sensabaugh's conclusions about Milton's influence on American political thought "overdrawn" and argued that, even in American poetry, "Milton's imprint was on the language and syntax, not on the content and meaning." The contradictory uses of Milton by early Americans—to defend Toryism as well as Whiggism, Federalism as well as Republicanism—were further proof, wrote Wood, of the eclectic and superficial influence of his writings. Wood agreed that the wealth of allusions amassed by Sensabaugh did show that Milton's imaginative power satisfied the needs of the new republic, but what those needs were, Wood concluded, remained elusive. (In the *New England Quarterly* 37 [1964]: pp. 543–46.)

I agree with Wood that one must be circumspect in ascribing to Milton any direct or specific influence when his voice was, as Wood put it, "only an inextricable part of a diffuse and complete heritage" of libertarian thought. However, as I hope to demonstrate, in significant cases verbal echoes are indicative of a shared sensibility and political agenda; the contradictory uses of Milton's arguments and images by early Americans bespeak not misunderstanding but an underlying consensus, uniting even political antagonists, on such matters as the nature of liberty and the danger of partisanship. Why Milton's writings—*Paradise Lost*, in particular—found such a responsive audience in America at that formative moment in its history is precisely the question I have set out to answer.

3. See especially Caroline Robbins, *The Eighteenth-Century Commonwealthman* (Cambridge: Harvard University Press, 1961); Bernard Bailyn, *The Ideological Origins of the American Revolution* (Cambridge: Harvard University Press, 1967) and *The Origins of American Politics* (New York: Vintage, 1967); Gordon Wood, *The Creation of the American Republic, 1776–1787* (New York: Norton, 1972); and J. G. A. Pocock, *The Machiavellian Moment: Florentine Political Thought and the Atlantic Republican Tradition* (Princeton: Princeton University Press, 1975).

4. See, for example, Patricia U. Bonomi, *Under the Cope of Heaven: Religion, Society, and Politics in Colonial America* (New York: Oxford University Press, 1986); Nathan O. Hatch, *The Sacred Cause of Liberty: Republican Thought and the Millennium in Revolutionary New England* (New Haven: Yale University Press, 1977); Cushing Strout, *The New Heavens and New Earth: Political Religion in America* (New York: Harper & Row, 1974); Sacvan Bercovitch, *The Puritan Origins of the American Self* (New Haven: Yale University Press, 1975); and Alan Heimert, *Religion and the American Mind: From the Great Awakening to the Revolution* (Cambridge: Harvard University Press, 1966).

5. Drawing on the French popular-studies model, David D. Hall's *World of Wonders, Days of Judgment: Popular Belief in Early New England* (New York: Knopf, 1989) explores the "story-framework"—in particular, the framework of religious stories of captivity and deliverance, sin and redemption, defeat and triumph—that the people of the Bay Colony applied in examining and living their lives.

6. Kendrick, *Milton: A Study in Ideology and Form*. For a fuller discussion of Kendrick's view of the Fall story's "neutrality," see the opening of chapter 1 in this book.

7. A notable exception to this trend is Keith W. F. Stavely's *Puritan Legacies: "Paradise Lost" and the New England Tradition, 1630–1890* (Ithaca: Cornell University Press, 1987), which came to my attention after I had completed most of the work on my manuscript. Stavely is concerned with Milton's importance for the American colonies, though he does not discuss the revolutionary period. He argues that *Paradise Lost* anticipated the persistent conflict in New England Puritanism between church authority and the theology of inner conviction and, through the characterization of Satan, foreshadowed the darker side of the capitalist ethic as it manifested itself on these shores. In contrast to those critics who treat Milton as an uncritical legitimizer of the emergent capitalist order, and more in line with my own view, Stavely sees in Milton's depiction of Satan a critique of capitalist covetousness.

8. *John Milton: Language, Gender, Power* (Oxford: Basil Blackwell, 1988, esp. pp. 76–79). Sandra Gilbert's "Patriarchal Poetry and Women Readers: Reflections on Milton's Bogey" (*PMLA* 93 [1978]) is a classic statement of the view of Milton as an inhibiting "masculinist" who engenders anxiety in women writers about their creativity. Nyquist and Ferguson's collection, *Re-membering Milton*, submits to "historical and ideological analysis" such issues as Milton's views on gender relations and his influence on later "marginalized" writers (p. xiv). See especially Mary Nyquist's "The Genesis of Gendered Subjectivity in the Divorce Tracts and in *Paradise Lost*" and Carolivia Herron's "Milton and Afro-American Literature." Herron testifies to the existence of a still-vibrant oral Miltonic tradition in America's black Baptist churches—lacking in their white counterparts—but concludes from her survey of the dialogue between Milton and four Afro-American writers (Phillis Wheatley, John Boyd, Charles W. Chesnutt, and Ishmael Reed) that his influence on the Afro-Americans was mostly inhibiting.

9. "The Politics of Poetry: Feminism and *Paradise Lost*," *Milton Studies* 14 (1980): p. 6. To think of Milton's epic, Webber writes, "as featuring Eve's particular alliance with evil is

surely to distort the myth, and to ignore the historical context (not of misogyny but of revolution) from which the poem came" (p. 5). In "The Genesis of Gendered Subjectivity," Mary Nyquist rebuts "mainstream liberal feminism," proposing to measure Milton's interpretation of Genesis against the more egalitarian interpretations of several of his contemporaries and thereby to demystify his view of companionate marriage and equal rights in general. But the avowed historicism of this critique is deceptive. Were women's rights really a possibility or an immediate item on England's agenda as long as political and ecclesiastical tyranny and economic backwardness enslaved both men and women?

10. As Frederick Crews argued in another context in "Whose American Renaissance?" (*New York Review of Books*, Oct. 27, 1988). His *Skeptical Engagements* (New York: Oxford University Press, 1986) details what has become almost a formula for critical schools on the Left: "In dealing with a given painting, novel, or piece of architecture, especially one dating from the capitalist era, they do not aim primarily to show the work's character or governing idea. The goal is rather to subdue the work through aggressive demystification— for example, by positing its socioeconomic determinants and ideological implications, scanning it for any encouraging signs of subversion, and then judging the result against an ideal of total freedom" (pp. 138–39).

Introduction

1. Charles I's eleven years' personal rule, which began with the dissolution of Parliament in 1629 and included extraconstitutional taxation and persecution of the opposition. See Lawrence Stone, *The Causes of the English Revolution, 1529–1642* (New York: Harper & Row, 1972), pp. 126, 127, 135.

2. This political genealogy, incidentally, more closely tallies with the one set down by an active participant in the events, John Adams, in his *Defence of the Constitutions of Government of the United States*. The contemporary historians responsible for the so-called republican revision in American historiography include Caroline Robbins, Bernard Bailyn, Gordon Wood, and J. G. A. Pocock, whose work is discussed later in this introduction and more thoroughly in chapter 4. Where Locke begins with the individual and the protection of individual rights against interference, the republicans begin with the public good and define individual freedom in terms of participation in civic life. The republican paradigm, in turn, has been subject to revision by those who believe, like Colin Gordon, that in interpreting the Revolution the "neo-Whigs" (Bailyn, Wood, et al.) have placed too much emphasis on conscious thought and common purpose, producing "a received, republican interpretation that obscures social and economic conflict beneath a heavy glaze of ideology" ("Crafting a Usable Past: Consensus, Ideology, and the Historians of the American Revolution," *William and Mary Quarterly* XLVI [Oct. 1989]: p. 674).

3. *PL*, IX, 351–52. This and all subsequent references to *Paradise Lost* are to *John Milton: Complete Poems and Major Prose*, ed. Merritt Y. Hughes (Indianapolis: Odyssey Press, 1957). Hereafter "Hughes."

4. Namely, Grotius's *Adamus Exul* (1601) and Vondel's complementary dramas on Satan's rebellion and Adams's fall, his *Lucifer* (1654) and *Adam in Ballingschap* (1664). See chapter 1.

5. *The Ready and Easy Way to Establish a Free Commonwealth*, Hughes, p. 896.

6. *PL*, III, 96–99.

7. See *PL*, VII, 171–73, where God boasts that His "goodness" is "free / To act or not, Necessity and Chance / Approach not mee, and what I will is Fate." To note the

metaphorical resemblance here between God and humanity is not to take sides in the theological debate over the issue of God's freedom. Arminius and the Cambridge Platonists, Milton's contemporaries, believed that if the universe were governed by a free or capricious God (as Hobbes posited), there could be no possibility of human choice; God, they argued, must therefore be constrained by internal necessity. Regarding Milton's stance on this issue, John Rogers points to evidence in *Paradise Lost* of both the necessitated God of Arminius and the Cambridge Platonists (with their corollary belief in human free will) and the arbitrary God of Hobbes and Descartes. Rogers explains the contradiction as symptomatic of the larger seventeenth-century conflict between the ideas of natural law and divine omnipotence—between the emerging materialist view of the universe as a continuum of matter and the traditional view of a Prime Mover who constantly exerts force ("Milton and the Mysterious Terms of History," *ELH* 57 [Summer 1990]: pp. 281–305). Stephen M. Fallon, on the other hand, believes that Milton consciously rejected the dichotomy in favor of a God ruled by "conditional necessity": Milton's God is "free / To act or not," but once He decides to act, He is moved by an "internal necessity to act well" (" 'To Act or Not': Milton's Conception of Divine Freedom," *Journal of the History of Ideas* 49, no. 3 [1988]: esp. pp. 436–49).

8. Hughes, p. 757.

9. Ibid.

10. Milton's insistence in both theology and politics on rational choice and, where necessary, second, or reconsidered, choice, is anticipated in his views on marriage and divorce: the former being a voluntary contract into which both parties enter freely for their mutual benefit; the latter, an opportunity for "second choys." See Edward W. Tayler, "Milton's Grim Laughter and Second Choices," in *Poetry and Epistemology: Turning Points in the History of Poetic Knowledge*, ed. Roland Hagenbüchle and Laura Skandera (Regensburg, Germany: Verlag Friedrich Pustet, 1986), pp. 76–77. Tayler extends the concept of choice and "second choys" to the very method of *Paradise Lost*, where the reader—like everyone in the postlapsarian world of "moral look-alikes"—is constantly forced to choose in interpreting a word, an image, a character's gesture, and then to choose again; for example, Satan's apparent magnificence in places is, on reconsideration, deflated and exposed as a diabolical parody of classical heroism.

11. Professor Tayler pointed out to me the New Historicism's animus against Milton's concept of human freedom, a discussion of which follows.

12. *Renaissance Self-Fashioning: From More to Shakespeare* (Chicago: University of Chicago Press, 1980), p. 257. Greenblatt writes that his investigations of the impulse of such English Renaissance figures as Wyatt and Marlowe to shape for themselves a distinctive identity led him to conclude that "there may well have been less *autonomy* in self-fashioning in the sixteenth century than before, that family, state, and religious institutions impose a more rigid and far-reaching discipline upon their middle-class and aristocratic subjects" (p. 1).

13. *The Subject of Tragedy: Identity and Difference in Renaissance Drama* (London: Methuen, 1985), p. 5.

14. *Radical Tragedy: Religion, Ideology and Power in the Drama of Shakespeare and His Contemporaries* (Chicago: University of Chicago Press, 1984), p. 258.

15. *The Subject of Tragedy*, pp. 33–34.

16. Ibid., p. 14.

17. Ibid., p. 143. Similarly, Mary Nyquist challenges the prevailing "liberal humanist" view of Milton as "the patron saint of companionate marriage": she holds that Eve's submission to God and Adam, voluntary though it is, served Milton's "deeply masculinist assumptions" and the ideological needs of the emergent capitalist order for an "autonomous" private sphere ("The Genesis of Gendered Subjectivity," in *Re-membering Milton*, ed. Nyquist and Ferguson, pp. 99, 106, 120).

18. Belsey, *The Subject of Tragedy*, p. 8.

19. Dollimore, *Radical Tragedy*, p. 172.

20. Curiously, Belsey cites Satan's boast that "The mind is its own place, and in itself / Can make a Heav'n of Hell, a Hell of Heav'n"—certainly not Milton's view of human freedom—as evidence of liberal humanism's fascination with interiority, its belief in an unchanging human essence identified with the mind (*The Subject of Tragedy*, p. 35). She mistakes the Romantic notion of individualism for Milton's.

21. Ibid., p. 224.

22. In a recent discussion of the Romantic view of Satan, Kenneth Gross complains that "that opposition figure who is commonly called the *Romantic* Satan . . . exists mainly as a straw-man, something of a slander of Milton's stark and foolish angel, as well as a slander of the sophisticated work of many nineteenth-century readers." Gross reminds us that Shelley is ready to condemn Satan's "taints" and argues that both Shelley and Blake ask us not to reverse Milton's polarities of deity and devil, heaven and hell, but to reconceive altogether Milton's dualistic Christian theology: "Shelley and Blake, for all their shrewd emphasis on the place of the devil, rather use Milton's picture of Satan as a way of exposing something crucial about the complex, dynamic system of religious values and images which are taken over and re-imagined in *Paradise Lost* as a whole" ("Satan and the Romantic Satan: a Notebook," in *Re-membering Milton*, ed. Nyquist and Ferguson, p. 320).

It is certainly true that Blake's and Shelley's chief animus is against the traditional religious values embodied in Milton's epic and that their emphasis on Satan's "magnificence" may be, in part, a strategy to undermine those values; yet their admiring portrait of the Devil has stuck, as is evidenced by Satan's appearance as republican hero in the recent work of Christopher Hill, Jackie DiSalvo, Christopher Kendrick, and others (discussed in chapters 1 and 3).

23. John Holly Hanford, "Milton and the Return of Humanism," reprinted in *Milton Criticism: Selections from Four Centuries*, ed. James Thorpe (New York: Collier, 1969).

24. Apposite here is the distinction E. D. Hirsh, Jr., draws between *meaning* (what an author intends by the use of a sign sequence) and *significance* (the relationship of that meaning to the times, to the author, to later readers, and so forth). See *Validity in Interpretation* (New Haven: Yale University Press, 1967), pp. 8, 62–63. It is not surprising that Hirsh enlists the example of *Paradise Lost* in discussing the importance of the distinction between *meaning-in* (meaning) and *meaning-to* (significance): "If Milton really was of the devil's party without knowing it, that would be part of the meaning of *Paradise Lost to* Milton's personality, part of the work's significance, and no doubt such observations do call attention to characteristics of meaning *in Paradise Lost*" (p. 63).

25. Bernard Bailyn, Gordon Wood, and other historians who have studied the English Commonwealth roots of the American Revolution discuss Milton as a "classical republican," borrowing the terminology first used by Zera Fink. In general, I agree with their location of Milton's political thought and sensibility within the Anglo-American political stream known as classical republicanism, whose adherents in the seventeenth and early eighteenth centuries regarded mixed and balanced government as a means of protecting individual liberties and the public good against the encroachments of selfish private interests—whether of arbitrary despots, aristocratic factions, or the uneducated masses. However, more than these historians, I see the classical republican thinkers as having a dynamic attitude toward the third social element in the classical balanced state—the democracy, or the people—an attitude arising from their Puritan heritage; in this book I point to Milton's continual emphasis on education as evidence of his belief in human ameliorability and his rejection of static social categories. As far as I am aware, no one has fully applied to *Paradise Lost* the insights to be gained by an examination of Milton in the context of this seventeenth- and eighteenth-century republican tradition.

26. The views, respectively, of Hill, *Milton and the English Revolution*, and Austin Woolrych, "Political Theory and Political Practice," in *The Age of Milton: Backgrounds to Seventeenth-Century Literature*, ed. C. A. Patrides and R. B. Waddington (Manchester: Manchester University Press, 1980), p. 67.

27. Milton's tractate *Of Education*, wherein he proposes that "The end . . . of learning is to repair the ruins of our first parents by regaining to know God aright" (Hughes, p. 631), has been read as a conservative pedagogical proposal aimed at an elite; however, one school of thought places it in the company of the broad-ranging social and economic proposals of the Comenian reformers (see chapter 2). Milton's continuing support for such proposals, from his earliest to his last pamphlets, negates the view of him as an aristocratic elitist while also underscoring his realistic understanding of the prerequisites for establishing republican self-rule.

The "republican Milton" that I argue for here should not be confused with the centrist one accepted by many critics in the twentieth century. These critics attempt to deal with what they perceive to be contradictions in Milton's prose works—for example, his revolutionary optimism about the English people in *Areopagitica* and his contempt for the "populous rout" in *The Ready and Easy Way*—by arguing either that Milton's political views changed when he became disillusioned about the prospects for reform in England or that elements of both the revolutionary radical and the elitist contended within him.

28. *A Second Defence of the English People* in *Complete Prose Works of John Milton*, ed. Don M. Wolfe et al. (New Haven: Yale University Press, 1953–82), IV, pt. I, p. 671. Hereafter *"YP."*

29. A more detailed discussion of these points, together with relevant citations from Milton's prose tracts, appears in chapters 2 and 3.

30. "Your bodies may at last turn all to spirit, / Improv'd by tract of time, and wing'd ascend / Ethereal, as wee, or may at choice / Here or in Heav'nly Paradises dwell," the angel Raphael instructs Adam (*PL*, V, 497–500). The original significance of the improvement theme in *Paradise Lost* is, of course, ontological and moral; however, the theme has a clear parallel in Milton's prose tracts, where he expresses confidence that England's people, assisted by worthy representatives and an uplifting reform program, will also ascend to the condition of "choice" in matters political.

31. *Captain or Colonel: The Soldier in Milton's Life and Art* (Columbia: University of Missouri Press, 1984).

32. This point is discussed further in chapter 1.

33. *Surprised by Sin: The Reader in "Paradise Lost"* (Berkeley: University of California Press, 1971), pp. 6–7. Fish, of course, subsequently moved away from reader-oriented analyses in which authorial intention embedded within the text was the controlling agent of meaning. He conjectured that it is really the interpretive strategy of the individual reader that "makes" the text; however, when this subjectivist stance threatened to undermine all semblance of a shared and determinate meaning, he advanced the notion of "interpretive communities" as the agency that authorizes meaning: an odyssey that Fish himself recounts in *Is There a Text in This Class?: The Authority of Interpretive Communities* (Cambridge: Harvard University Press, 1980). Interestingly, in a recent discussion of *Areopagitica*, authorial strategy again seems to be in control: Fish argues there that the very method of the tractate—continually to posit an argument and then undermine it—mimics Milton's notion of the pursuit of truth ("Driving from the Letter: Truth and Indeterminacy in Milton's *Areopagitica*," in *Re-membering Milton*, ed. Nyquist and Ferguson).

34. That literature is both "socially constituted" and "socially constituting" is practically a truism today, with the demise of formalism and the rise of the New Historicism, feminism, and other issue-oriented critical schools. The New Criticism, by contrast, sought to sublime poetry to a self-contained, privileged domain apart from history and contingency and,

ironically, in so doing actually denigrated it, as Frank Lentricchia observes in *After the New Criticism* (Chicago: University of Chicago Press, 1980).

35. Jay Fliegelman has called for the broadening of "our understanding of what constitutes a 'political' text." This is necessary, he says, if we are to understand the enormous impact on American revolutionary politics of certain literary texts that have often been ignored by historians. "Only by so revising our frame of reference will we be able to appreciate the larger cultural context of the American Revolution," he writes in *Prodigals and Pilgrims: The American Revolution against Patriarchal Authority, 1750–1800* (Cambridge: Cambridge University Press, 1982), p. 5. Fliegelman, discussed in chapter 6, charts the enormous popularity and broad cultural influence in the colonies of novels such as Richardson's *Clarissa*, which challenged traditional ideas of filial obedience and suggested a new paradigm of affectional parent-child relations.

36. *YP*, I, pp. 815–16.

37. Jefferson compares the powerful moral effect of another poetic masterpiece—*King Lear*—with the effect of prose sermons on the same theme: "a lively and lasting sense of filial duty is more effectively impressed upon the mind of a son or daughter by reading *King Lear*, than by all the dry volumes of ethics and divinity that were ever written." Quoted in Fliegelman, *Prodigals and Pilgrims*, p. 102.

Although the direct influence of Milton's texts on revolutionary Americans cannot be demonstrated, in a strict sense, by frequent citation alone—and is indeed very difficult to prove definitively—the widespread borrowing of Milton's poetic imagery and the frequent invocation of his authority on points of republican political theory clearly establish his central place in late eighteenth-century American culture.

38. *John Milton and the English Revolution*, p. 152. The Independents, the party of Cromwell and Milton, emerged in the mid-1640s as the group within Parliament that wished to reorganize the army along meritocratic lines (the New Model Army) and prosecute a decisive war against royalism and privilege. Among the principles that characterized the Independents' rationalist worldview, Milner includes religious toleration, individualistic interpretation of the Bible, and individual freedom from external and internal restraints—privilege, tradition, and the passions.

39. In *Areopagitica* Milton objects to the high degree of social regulation envisioned in the ideal societies of Plato's *Republic*, Thomas More's *Utopia*, and Francis Bacon's *New Atlantis:* censorship, laws governing marriage and other domestic affairs, proscriptions on the accumulation of wealth, and so forth. Plato, More, and Bacon all sought to control the inner life, particularly the socially destructive passions, through external constraints—an approach exactly opposite to Milton's. See Hughes, pp. 73–74.

Chapter 1

1. Milton's theology of good versus evil, Keats believed, was proof "that a mighty providence subdues the mightiest Minds to the service of the time being, whether it be human Knowledge or Religion." In *Milton Criticism: Selections from Four Centuries*, ed. Thorpe, p. 356. For an example of the reinterpretation of Milton's theology as "phallocratic," see David Riede's "Blake's *Milton:* On Membership in the Church Paul," in *Remembering Milton*, ed. Nyquist and Ferguson. Riede explores Blake's efforts to transcend the "authoritative patriarchal church" of Milton and St. Paul as well as "the language of a Western tradition built on dualisms." He concludes, unhappily, that "Blake cannot tran-

scend Milton's dualism if only because language itself, based on a structure of differences, cannot present 'godmansoul . . .' as a seamless whole" (pp. 273–75).

2. Percy Bysshe Shelley, *A Defence of Poetry*, in *Milton Criticism: Selections from Four Centuries*, ed. Thorpe, pp. 358–59. Shelley, of course, was not indifferent to the "taints of ambition, envy, revenge, and a desire for personal aggrandisement" in Milton's devil, and he condemned the "pernicious casuistry" of those readers who excused Satan's taints on the grounds that his sufferings outweighed his crimes. Kenneth Gross reminds us of this in "Satan and the Romantic Satan" (in *Re-membering Milton*, ed. Nyquist and Ferguson, pp. 320–23). Gross hypothesizes that Shelley condemned even more strongly the pious, moralizing reaction to Satan that itself exemplified the "self-perpetuating system of tyranny, revolution, and revenge . . . built into the morality of both tyrant *and* rebel, both punitive father and violent, devouring child" (ibid., p. 324).

3. *War of Titans*, p. 9.

4. *Milton: A Study in Ideology and Form*, pp. 91–92. According to Kendrick, one of the ways the biblical narrative is reinvested with political energy is by means of covert analogies to historical events.

5. This is not meant to be an exhaustive account of seventeenth- and eighteenth-century interest in the theme of *Paradise Lost*. *La Sepmaine* (1578) and its sequel (1584) by the Huguenot writer Guillaume Du Bartas is another important example of interest in the Fall theme by a reformer. (Given the interest in the theme in states undergoing early capitalist development, it is noteworthy that Du Bartas was a member of the Huguenots, France's commercial class.) Milton knew the French epic of the Creation and the Fall through Joshua Sylvester's popular translation, *Du Bartas His Divine Weekes and Workes* (1608). Sylvester was Groom of the Chamber to "the incomparable Prince Henry," as Donne called him, and one of the circle of courtiers and intellectuals who supported the new science, Puritanism, and the principle of balanced government. See Christopher Hill's *Intellectual Origins of the English Revolution* (Oxford: Oxford University Press, 1965), chap. 4. Masson notes in his biography of Milton that in 1621, when a friend of the Milton family published a new edition of Sylvester's Du Bartas, printed just steps away from their house on Bread Street, the fifteen-year-old Milton's favorite poets were Spenser and Sylvester. Cited in Watson Kirkconnell, *The Celestial Cycle: The Theme of Paradise Lost in World Literature with Translations of the Major Analogues* (Toronto: University of Toronto Press, 1952), p. 587.

6. *PL*, V, 782, 777.

7. For a description of the tradition, see especially Kirkconnell, *The Celestial Cycle*, and J. M. Evans, *"Paradise Lost" and the Genesis Tradition* (Oxford: Clarendon Press, 1968). The quotations that follow from *Adamus Exul*, *Lucifer*, and *Adam in Ballingschap* are Kirkconnell's translations from the Latin and Dutch, respectively. Page references are given in the text.

8. *"Paradise Lost" and the Genesis Tradition*, p. 213.

9. *The Works of John Milton*, ed. Frank Allen Patterson et al. (New York: Columbia University Press, 1931–38), vol. XVIII, p. 260. Milton's nephew Edward Phillips, in his *Life of Milton* (1694), identified "Ten Verses" in Book IV as having been the opening of a tragedy shown to him by his uncle "several years before the Poem was begun."

10. *"Paradise Lost" and the Genesis Tradition*, pp. 212–16. Evans discusses the growing similarity between Milton's successive drafts and the Dutch play, concluding that the convergence between them could not have been coincidental.

11. On the Milton-Vondel relationship, see Edmund Gosse, "Milton and Vondel," in *Studies in the Literature of Northern Europe* (London: N.p., 1879); and George Edmundson, *Milton and Vondel: A Curiosity of Literature* (London: Trubner, 1885).

12. Introduction, *Vondel's "Lucifer,"* trans. Leonard Charles Van Noppen (Greensboro, N.C.; N.p., 1917), p. 108.

13. Fred J. Nichols points out how central to Vondel's characterization of Lucifer is the Devil's deceitful and empty rhetoric. Before the outbreak of the war in Heaven, Lucifer "betrays the fact that he thinks that God is mere language, and could therefore be defeated by a stronger rhetoric"—his own "rhetoric of deceit." In "Vondel's 'Lucifer' and 'Adam in Ballingschap.' " *Review of National Literatures* 8 (1977): p. 47.

14. Introduction, *Vondel's "Lucifer,"* p. 176. Gosse ("Milton and Vondel") discredited a common allegorical reading of the drama in which God was said to represent Philip II of Spain; Lucifer, William the Silent; and the drama as a whole, the Netherlands' uprising against Spain more than seventy years earlier. However, Gosse substituted his own, equally untenable allegorical reading: Lucifer as Cromwell, prince of the English Commonwealth, and God and Michael as Charles I and Laud, respectively. Although Vondel may have decried ambitious politicians and unlawful rebellion, there is no evidence that he supported autocratic tyrants; on the contrary, he was an ally of Grotius and the de Witts, advocates of republican government and Dutch independence from foreign control.

15. In *Adam in Ballingschap* (Adam in banishment), which Vondel said he based on Grotius's drama, this fusion of the two unlike elements is again emphasized: a human being is "composed of flesh and spirit" without inner conflict; "Angelhood and beasthood mingle / In the making of a man" (pp. 448, 449). Immediately after the Fall the union of body and soul is sundered. Adam laments, "The Devil / Grapples and boards me from the fleet of Hell. / A fight already rages in my body: / One thing my soul desires, my flesh another" (p. 473).

16. "Vondel's 'Lucifer' and 'Adam in Ballingschap,' " p. 46.

17. Milton's growing republicanism paralleled that of the Independents in Parliament and the Army. On Dec. 6, 1648, some forty members of Parliament were expelled by the Army in Pride's Purge. On Jan. 4, 1649, the House of Commons declared that the people of England were the source of all power and that the Commons, as their representative, alone exercised power. The execution of the king and the abolition of the House of Lords (Jan. 30 and Feb. 6, 1649) marked the end of the old regime.

18. When Spenser wrote, Arthurian legend was closely associated with the Tudors, who, to substantiate their claims to the throne, had traced their ancestry back to Arthur (and through him back to the Roman Brutus). In this view, Merlin's prophecy concerning the return of Arthur had been realized with the return of Arthur's descendants, the Tudors. See Roberta Florence Brinkley's *Arthurian Legend in the Seventeenth Century* (Baltimore: Johns Hopkins University Press, 1932), chap. 1. Brinkley's monograph is the fullest and most suggestive treatment of the evolution of Milton's thinking on the suitability of the Arthurian legend as epic subject matter. Robert Fallon also treats this issue in *Captain or Colonel*, pp. 91–99. Christopher Hill's *Intellectual Origins of the English Revolution* examines the forward-looking scientific and political thought of the Ralegh circle.

19. *The History of Britain, YP*, V, pt. I, p. 156.

20. Ibid., p. 131.

21. Ibid., p. 451.

22. Brinkley, *Arthurian Legend in the Seventeenth Century*, pp. 140–41.

23. French Fogle, in his introduction to the Digression, argues convincingly for this dating (*YP*, V, pt. I, pp. 427–35). He writes that Milton's pessimistic tone points to this period, when the successes of the first Civil War appeared to be dissipating in the struggle for power among the Presbyterian members of Parliament, the Army (dominated by Independents and Levellers), and the king. Fogle maintains that it was probably Milton himself who excised the Digression when the *History* was eventually published in 1670, perhaps because he felt retrospectively that he had been too censorious of the Interregnum institutions. With the successes of the Independent- and Leveller-dominated Army in the second Civil War, he had soon overcome his deep pessimism.

24. See Milner, *John Milton and the English Revolution*, pp. 102–14.

25. Cited in Fogle's introduction, *YP*, V, pt. I, p. 433.

26. *An Apology Against a Pamphlet* (1642), *YP*, I, p. 891.

27. Robert Fallon argues that Milton's experience during the 1640s convinced him that Arthurian legend presented an entirely unrealistic picture of love and war. Thus, Fallon writes, it would have been "aesthetically indecorous and ideologically contradictory" for Milton to celebrate the Christian virtue epitomized by Cromwell and the New Model Army's "plain russet-coated captain" through the fable of Arthur, "a king, who, in the legend at least, ruled a priest-ridden court that subscribed to an archaic chivalrous code requiring unquestioned loyalty to the monarch and devotion to the church." Fallon sees the contest between Samson and Harapha in *Samson Agonistes* as a clash of the two kinds of soldiers: the Nazarite employs his gift of strength to serve God, while the Philistine giant seeks personal glory. In *Captain or Colonel*, pp. 91–99, 238–49.

28. *YP*, V, pt. I, p. 445.

29. Ibid., p. 443.

30. Ibid., p. 445.

31. Ibid., pp. 449, 447.

32. Hughes, p. 145.

33. *YP*, V, pt. I, p. 449.

34. Ibid.

Chapter 2

1. Richard Weston, *The Compleat Husband-man; or, a discourse of the whole Art of Husbandry both Forraign and Domestick*, 2d ed. (London: Edward Brewster, 1659).

2. See Christopher Hill, *Reformation to Industrial Revolution* (Harmondsworth, England: Penguin, 1969), p. 41. The notion that individualism in its modern, post-Enlightenment sense emerged in this period has been challenged recently by the New Historicism. See below.

3. Stone, *The Causes of the English Revolution*, pp. 65–66.

4. Ibid., p. 72.

5. Hill, *Reformation to Revolution*, pp. 65–66. The general price level is believed to have risen four or five times in the century before 1640 (pp. 15–16).

6. From Hartlib's petition to the House of Commons at the Restoration, quoted in G. H. Turnbull, *Hartlib, Dury and Comenius: Gleanings from Hartlib's Papers* (Liverpool: University Press of Liverpool, 1947), p. 88.

7. In his dedication of Sir Richard Weston's *Discours of Husbandrie used in Brabant and Flanders* . . . (London: William Du-Gard, 1650).

8. H. R. Trevor-Roper, "Three Foreigners and the Philosophy of the English Revolution," in *The Crisis of the Seventeenth Century: Religion, the Reformation, and Social Change* (New York: Harper & Row, 1966), pp. 10, 18.

9. J. Shklar, "Ideology Hunting: the Case of James Harrington," cited in Stone, *The Causes of the English Revolution*, p. 35.

10. Robert Ashton, *The English Civil War: Conservatism and Revolution, 1603–1649* (New York: Norton, 1978), p. 20.

11. Stone, *The Causes of the English Revolution*, p. 71.

12. Stone himself, applying the insights of the multiple dysfunction model of modern sociology, contends that, compared with the orthodox Marxist approach, "A more fruitful

way of linking social and economic change to revolution is through the theory of status inconsistency, which holds that a society with a relatively large proportion of persons undergoing high mobility is likely to be in an unstable condition" (ibid., p. 54). His "multicausal approach" encompasses a host of well-documented disequilibriating factors that arose in England during the century before 1640, including the massive shift of relative wealth and status toward the gentry, jealousies arising from unprecedented social mobility, rising educational and professional opportunities, political frustrations due to the limited access to power, the rise of Puritanism and other new ideas, the breakdown of old feudal ties, and the discrediting of feudal values. Thus, the multiple dysfunction model combines the contradictory theories of Tocqueville (that popular revolutions take place as a result of increasing prosperity) and Marx (that the precondition is increasing misery). Stone writes that "The recipe for revolution is thus the creation of new expectations by economic improvement and some social and political reforms, followed by economic recession, governmental reaction, and aristocratic resurgence, which widen the gap between expectations and reality" (ibid., pp. 14, 17).

13. Ashton, *The English Civil War*, p. 73.

14. See Robert Brenner, "The Civil War Politics of London's Merchant Community," *Past and Present* 58 (1973): pp. 53–107.

15. Christopher Hill, *The Century of Revolution, 1603–1714* (New York: Norton, 1961), pp. 37, 41.

16. In Weston's *A Discours of Husbandrie Used in Brabant and Flanders.*

17. Hughes, p. 898.

18. Ibid., p. 896.

19. *Radical Tragedy*, pt. III, esp. pp. 171–74. Although Hobbes was clearly a materialist in that he grounded human behavior in innate traits rather than in a rational soul, there is little evidence, in fact, that he believed in the social and historical determination of human behavior. On the contrary, Hobbes portrayed "the war of all against all" as the state of nature. Dollimore concedes that Hobbes, while rejecting an essentialist view of man, retains elements of an a priori, unchanging human nature (p. 172).

20. Ibid., p. 172.

21. *Areopagitica*, Hughes, p. 727.

22. Cressy Dymock, *An Invention of Engines of Motion Lately Brought to perfection . . .* (London: R. Woodnoth, 1651). In her seminal study of seventeenth-century English economic thought, Joyce Appleby points to the celebration of human inventiveness in such improvement tracts (along with the emergence in that period of an integrated marketplace of "autonomous negotiators" and the breakdown of a fixed social hierarchy) as a source of natural rights theory, with its belief in the abstract rights of all. "Moralists lamented the materialism and here-nowness of commercial preoccupations, but the economic writers who detailed the orderly round of buying and selling displayed an enthusiasm for these newly discovered attributes of ordinary people" (*Economic Thought and Ideology in Seventeenth-Century England* [Princeton: Princeton University Press, 1978], p. 32 and chap. 2 passim).

23. C. B. Macpherson, *The Political Theory of Possessive Individualism: Hobbes to Locke* (Oxford: Oxford University Press, 1962), p. 3.

24. Ibid.

25. Quoted in ibid., pp. 178, 176.

26. Quoted in ibid., p. 177.

27. Weston, *The Compleat Husband-man*, title page.

28. Weston, *A Discours of Husbandrie Used in Brabant and Flanders*, p. 25.

29. Moses Wall to Milton, May 26, 1659, *YP,* VII, p. 511.

30. In 1947 G. H. Turnbull published excerpts from Hartlib's papers (which were lost in

1667 and not found until 1945), as well as a comprehensive bibliography of all of Hartlib's own writings and others he published, in *Hartlib, Dury and Comenius*. My discussion of Hartlib and the proposals he advanced is based on the original published pamphlets and on the following secondary sources: Turnbull's monograph; Henry Dircks, *A Biographical Memoir of Samuel Hartlib, Milton's Particular Friend* (London: J. R. Smith, 1865); and Trevor-Roper, "Three Foreigners and the Philosophy of the English Revolution." Trevor-Roper was the first to recognize the importance of the three foreigners as "the real philosophers, and the only philosophers, of the English Revolution."

31. Hughes, p. 630. See below for a discussion of Milton's attitude toward the Comenian educational reformers, whose ideas were promoted by Hartlib.

32. In a letter from Hartlib to Joachim Poleman, 1659. Quoted in Turnbull, *Hartlib, Dury and Comenius*, p. 73.

33. In a letter from Hartlib to Dr. John Worthington, June 26, 1661. *The Diary and Correspondence of Dr. John Worthington*, vol. I, ed. James Crossley (Manchester: Chetham Society, 1847), p. 342.

34. This is true, for example, of William Potter's design for a "Bank of the Lands," one of several proposals he made in the 1650s that addressed England's lack of a functioning credit system (and the Protectorate's consequent dependence on tax farming and short-term loans from the City of London, methods that had precipitated the financial crisis of the Stuart regime). The Land Bank envisioned by Potter would issue credit for the improvement of lands (through husbandry, capital improvements, etc.) on the security of the potential wealth embodied therein. The land-backed credit would serve as the basis for an expansion of money to "⅔, ¾, ⅘ or perhaps more of the value of Lands of the Nation" and, thereby, for an "incredible increase of inland commerce, and (consequently) of exportation and foreign trade" (Samuel Hartlib, *An Essay upon Master W. Potters Designe: Concerning a Bank of Lands to be erected throughout this common–wealth* [London: Richard Wodenoth, 1653]). Although Potter's design was never implemented in England, two Americans, John Winthrop, Jr., and John Woodbridge, obtained Potter's writings through Hartlib after 1660, eager to find a means to circumvent the dire shortage of specie in the colonies and to secure economic and financial independence from Britain. Amid great opposition from pro-British interests, a land bank designed according to Potter's specifications was attempted in the Bay Colony in 1671, 1681, and 1686. These attempts served as the basis for the famous Massachusetts Land Bank of 1740, which Elisha Cooke, "Deacon" Samuel Adams (Sam Adams's father), and other political radicals promoted to alleviate the drain of silver specie to England (see E. A. J. Johnson, *American Economic Thought in the Seventeenth Century* [New York: Russell & Russell, 1961], chaps. 5 and 6; and John C. Miller, *Sam Adams: Pioneer in Propaganda* [Stanford: Stanford University Press, 1974; orig. pub. 1936], chaps. 1 and 2).

35. Quoted in Turnbull, *Hartlib, Dury and Comenius*, p. 50.

36. Ibid., p. 49.

37. Ibid., p. 56.

38. Introduction, *YP*, II. My discussion of Comenian educational theory is based largely on Sirluck's summary.

39. Hughes, p. 632.

40. George Snell, *The Right Teaching of Useful Knowledge*, quoted in *YP*, II, p. 190.

41. Disagreeing with Sirluck, Christopher Hill maintains that Milton's educational plans were in broad agreement with those of the Hartlib group. In *Milton and the English Revolution*, p. 146.

42. *Of Education*, Hughes, pp. 638–39.

43. Ibid., p. 633.

44. To the Hartlibean reformers, the wealth of the church offered a way to finance a

national system of education at all levels; however, legislators who had vested interests in the continuation of tithe payments (a significant proportion of tithes were paid to lay "impropriators"—lords and gentry who had acquired church lands since the dissolution of the monasteries) saw no urgency in moving on such reforms.

45. *YP*, IV, pt. I, p. 679.

46. In an often-quoted letter that Wall wrote to Milton in the spring of 1659, he eloquently argued that the persistence of tithes, copyhold tenure, and other remnants of the feudal system stood in the way of both economic prosperity and the moral regeneration of the English people. Milton seems to have been influenced by Wall and others who stressed the economic abuses of the tithe system instead of simply repeating traditional arguments against the principle of mandatory payments in support of a state church. In *The Likeliest Means to Remove Hirelings* Milton denounced tithes as a blatant burden on those who could least afford it, a "seizing of pots and pans from the poor, . . . from some, the very beds." He also presented a sophisticated analysis of the subtle and indirect ways in which an established church can exact its economic burden on a nation, pointing out, for example, that the state endowment of the church that began under Constantine took public lands out of each city, with the result that "the people became liable to be oppressed with other taxes." Turning his attention to the crisis of Richard Cromwell's short-lived government, Milton warned Cromwell against reapplying former church revenues to the support of the ministry, arguing that this civil revenue was "the people's and must save them from other taxes" (Hughes, pp. 866, 872–73).

47. *YP*, VII, pp. 338–39.

48. Hughes, p. 897. According to Milton's plan these local schools would complement an expanded system of local government. Milton's proposal in the same pamphlet for a perpetual senate has been much excoriated; however, in calling at the same time for expanded local schools and academies, local assemblies, and other checks on the power of the perpetual senate, Milton seems to have envisioned a gradual evolution from what was admittedly a political expedient toward the goal of responsible self-government.

49. Ibid.

50. Ibid., p. 891.

51. Ibid., p. 897.

Chapter 3

1. Thus remarked the Hanoverian pastor H. L. Benthem in a 1694 work, after reading the first three books of the epic in the German translation by Milton's friend Theodore Haak. Quoted in Hill, *Milton and the English Revolution*, p. 391. Regarding the epic's political resonances for twentieth-century audiences, Hill notes that according to M. Baring (*What I Saw in Russia*), *Paradise Lost* in Russian translation was one of the most widely read books in the Russian army in 1905 (ibid., p. 230).

2. Terry Eagleton, "The God That Failed," in *Re-membering Milton*, ed. Nyquist and Ferguson, pp. 346–47.

3. In his review of *Milton and the English Revolution*, Blair Worden observed that by drawing too strict an analogy between the English Revolution and Satan's rebellion, Hill overspecifies and parochializes the vision of the poet, "who took all history for his province" ("Milton among the Radicals," *Times Literary Supplement*, Dec. 2, 1977, p. 1394). The problem of inconsistency between Milton's known political and theological views and his poetry is another liability of this approach: if pressed too far, Hill's analogy between the

revolutionaries and Satan "seems to imply that . . . Satan's original act of rebellion must have been similarly justified, and thus that God is evil" (Quentin Skinner, "Milton, Satan, and Subversion," *New York Review of Books*, March 23, 1978, p. 9).

4. Andrew Milner, for example, in *John Milton and the English Revolution*, portrays Milton as a spokesman for philosophical rationalism—the worldview of political Independency—and explores this outlook, with its dual emphasis on individualism and freedom, as it informs both Milton's prose works and his epic.

5. Most modern opinion assigns the composition of *Paradise Lost* to the years 1658 to 1663, following John Aubrey, and assumes a date of 1660 or later for the invocation to Book VII ("On evil days though fall'n," "the barbarous dissonance / Of *Bacchus* and his Revellers," etc.). According to this view, Milton worked on the early books of the epic during the same period in which he completed *Of Civil Power in Ecclesiastical Causes*, *The Likeliest Means to Remove Hirelings*, and *The Ready and Easy Way* and began *The Christian Doctrine*.

6. *A Second Defence of the English People*, YP, IV, pt. I, p. 671; *The Ready and Easy Way*, Hughes, p. 79; and *The Tenure of Kings and Magistrates*, Hughes, pp. 760–73, *passim*. Milton's earliest attack on the problem of private interests was aimed at the luxurious and usurping bishops in the early 1640s. This attack on the bishops, Zera Fink observes in her pioneering study of the English tradition of mixed and balanced government, was in line with the classical republican assumption that mixed states, in which the king, the aristocracy, and the commons all had their due shares of power, were best. The covetous bishops, Milton wrote in *Of Reformation in England*, had corrupted England's traditionally limited monarchy, "divinely and harmoniously tun'd," in seizing secular prerogatives and overconcentrating power in the magistracy. (*The Classical Republicans: An Essay in the Recovery of a Pattern of Thought in Seventeenth-Century England*, 2d ed. [Evanston: Northwestern University Press, 1962; orig. pub. 1945], pp. 95–99). Over the next two decades Milton extended his critique of private interests to the tyrannical king, to the Presbyterians and other backsliders, and finally to the purged Parliament and the English people. The one, the few, and the many of classical political theory, he believed, all had come to be dominated by self-serving passions.

7. The second edition of *The Ready and Easy Way* was published in the spring of 1660 when Charles II's restoration was imminent. *Of True Religion, Heresy, Schism, and Toleration* appeared in 1673. On Milton's post-Restoration mood, Fallon comments: "He was disappointed, certainly, with the course of events in Restoration England; but he apparently remained cheerful, worked hard, and published extensively, even returning to the arena of pamphlet warfare in the final year of life with *Of True Religion*" (*Captain or Colonel*, p. 195).

8. *The Ready and Easy Way*, Hughes, p. 898.

9. Two of the functions of the serious national poet, Milton believed, were "to imbreed and cherish in a great people the seeds of vertu, and publick civility" and, when the public was hardened in vice, to castigate backsliding (*The Reason of Church-Government Urg'd against Prelaty*, YP, I, pp. 816–17). The latter function, the editor points out, was peculiarly Milton's.

10. *War of Titans*, p. 251.

11. (London: Faber and Faber, 1942).

12. *Images of Kingship in "Paradise Lost": Milton's Politics and Christian Liberty* (Columbia: University of Missouri Press, 1983), p. 4. In *Reviving Liberty: Radical Christian Humanism in Milton's Great Poems* (Cambridge: Harvard University Press, 1989), Joan S. Bennett likewise points to "parallels between Milton's prose treatment of Charles and his poetic portrait of Satan" (p. 35): both are usurpers, not representatives, of God's power.

13. *Five Essays on Milton's Epic* (1966). Cited in Hill, *Milton and the English Revolution*, p. 366.

14. *Milton and the English Revolution*, pp. 366–67. Keith Stavely carries this view another step forward, arguing that Satan suggests the fatal shortcomings not only of the mid-century revolutionaries but of the entire emergent capitalist order and that his journey anticipates that of Anglo-American capitalist culture as a whole: "anyone contemplating the broad outlines of Anglo-American development during the past three centuries must see not willful literary manipulation but rather profound historical understanding in the degradation of Satan from a rebel against authoritarianism and an indomitable laborer and builder in the wilderness to an imperialist policy maker and insatiably combative technocrat" (*Puritan Legacies*, pp. 90–91).

15. On Milton's grounding in this political tradition, see Fink, *The Classical Republicans*.

16. Hughes, p. 885.

17. *Milton and the English Revolution*, p. 367.

18. *Milton's Paradise Lost: a new edition with notes of various authors by Thomas Newton* (London: Tonson and Draper, 1749), p. 30.

19. D. P. Harding points out that the line also evokes Achilles' answer to Odysseus in Hades after the latter has hailed him as Lord of the dead—better to be the hireling of a landless man than to rule over all the dead that are departed—but with an important difference: "Hades had humbled the once-proud Achilles almost beyond recognition, but Hell had only served to harden Satan in his ambition" (*The Club of Hercules: Studies in the Classical Background of Paradise Lost* [Urbana: University of Illinois Press, 1962], p. 47). Harding argues that Satan's heroism is not a figment of the Romantic imagination but is part of Milton's conscious plan to show up the inadequacies of the martial heroism of the classical epics. In this way, according to Harding, Milton supported his claim that his Christian epic would surpass the classical. However, as Harding points out, the covert analogies with the classical heroes also function by contrast, revealing Satan's moral inferiority. See chaps. 2 and 3, passim.

20. Satan's loss of reason—and, consequently, of free will—is underscored by the literary devices of travesty and burlesque; he is continually discovered as an unconscious actor in demonic parodies—of Homeric heroics, of the Trinity, even of the Fall. See Tayler, "Milton's Grim Laughter and Second Choices," pp. 82–88.

21. As Winthrop defined "natural liberty" in a speech before the Massachusetts General Court in 1645. From Cotton Mather's *Magnalia Christi Americana*, quoted in Alexis de Tocqueville, *Democracy in America* (New York: Vintage, 1945; orig. pub. 1835 and 1840), vol. I, p. 44.

22. Ibid., pp. 44–45.

23. That passage looks back to the doctrine of Hell found in *Dr. Faustus:* "Hell hath no limits, nor is circumscribed / In one self place. But where we are is hell, / And where hell is there must we ever be," Mephistophilis tells Faustus (Christopher Marlowe, *The Tragical History of Dr. Faustus*, in *The Complete Plays*, ed. J. B. Steane [Harmondsworth, England: Penguin, 1969], p. 283). Having forsaken true science and faith, Faustus seeks knowledge of the black arts to gratify his desire for power and riches. But evil recoils upon itself, as in the case of Milton's Satan, and Faustus's consuming desire for forbidden knowledge becomes a self-imposed hell and the cause of his tragic downfall.

24. Hughes, p. 750.

25. *YP,* IV, pt. I, p. 683.

26. See Davies, *Images of Kingship*. Davies traces several patterns of kingship in the royal imagery that attaches to Satan: lawless kingship like that of Charles I, whom Milton described as satanic in *Eikonoklastes;* Eastern despotism—the great chain of "vitiated" kingship from Moloch to Pharaoh to the Turkish sultan; and finally, Roman imperialism. The last pattern is the most subtle, Davies writes. "The Roman stands for reason in the

service of despotism, the sultan for barbarous savagery; the Romans quelled in order to civilize the barbarians, but the barbarians overwhelmed the empire." Satan is never directly imaged as a Roman emperor, but, as Davies argues, his ascendancy to the throne parallels in many respects "the historical pattern of the Caesars' destruction of the Roman republic": like the Caesars, Satan rises through martial prowess and, to mask his imperial aspirations, makes pseudodemocratic claims and retains the forms of the supplanted government (those of Heaven, in Satan's case) (pp. 6–7).

27. Davies, *Images of Kingship*, p. 55.

28. Ibid., pp. 52–53.

29. James Harrington, *The Oceana and Other Works; with an Account of His Life by John Toland* (Aalen, Germany: Scientia Verlag, 1963; reprint of the 1771 London edition), p. 50. See also pp. 37, 58, 65, 248–50.

30. Davies, *Images of Kingship*, pp. 99, 95, 106, 108.

31. In *Images of Kingship*, Stevie Davies endeavors to explain the apparent paradox by arguing for distinct classes of kingship images that are attached in a consistent way to different major figures in the epic. Thus, whereas Satan is frequently imaged as an oriental despot, God and Christ are associated with monarchy of another type—the fatherly, liberty-guaranteeing kingship of English feudalism. Adam is still another kind of king—a Solomon who falls through concupiscence. But though Satan, God, and Man are clearly associated with different types of monarchy, there is little evidence that Milton admired the lord-vassal relationship of feudalism or that, as Davies contends, Milton's monarchy of Heaven should be regarded in this light.

32. See *A Defence of the People of England* (1651), where Milton argues, countering the royalist polemicist Salmasius, that God gave kings to the Israelites as an ironical punishment for asking for one—a "republican form of government . . . as being better adapted to our human circumstances than monarchy" (*YP*, IV, pt. I, pp. 369, 344).

33. See Fink, *The Classical Republicans*, pp. 95–99.

34. After I had completed this chapter, Mary Ann Radzinowicz's recent discussion of the meritocratic (as opposed to hereditary) nature of the kingship of Heaven came to my attention ("The Politics of *Paradise Lost*," in *Politics of Discourse: The Literature and History of Seventeenth-Century England*, ed. Kevin Sharpe and Steven N. Zwicker [Berkeley: University of California Press, 1987]). The distinctiveness of Milton's heavenly hierarchy, Radzinowicz writes, is its "individualistic, voluntaristic, and meritocratic basis"—which is denied in Satan's "frozen meritocracy or tyranny" (p. 211). Radzinowicz regards the notion of a meritocratic hierarchy as central to the epic's political content. Eschewing two current views of Milton's post-Restoration relationship to politics—"political disengagement and political encryption"—she argues "that in line with Milton's humanistic understanding of the nature and function of heroic poetry, *Paradise Lost* has a public role to play in the poet's own day": it offers "a course in political education" revolving around the interrelated ideas of "freedom, order, and degree" (pp. 205–6).

35. *The Tenure of Kings and Magistrates*, Hughes, p. 754. In his defense of the trial and execution of the king, Milton asserts that self-government is the natural, original condition of mankind, as "all men naturally were born free, being the image and resemblance of God himself . . . born to command, and not to obey" (ibid.).

36. See the invocation to Book IX.

37. Hughes, p. 733.

38. See Tayler, "Milton's Grim Laughter and Second Choices," p. 83.

39. *Areopagitica*, Hughes, p. 728.

40. *The Ready and Easy Way*, Hughes, pp. 897, 885.

41. *PL*, V, 828–31.

42. *The Muse's Method: An Introduction to "Paradise Lost"* (Cambridge: Harvard University Press, 1962), p. 86.

43. Macpherson, *The Political Theory of Possessive Individualism*, p. 3. See chapter 2 of this book.

44. *The Tenure of Kings and Magistrates*, Hughes, p. 766. In this context, Milton defends the establishment of the English Commonwealth as a lawful undertaking but warns the Presbyterian ministers that their backsliding—their sudden abhorrence for the king's execution, their efforts to appropriate the deposed bishops' wealth for themselves, and so forth—reveals their original motives to have been self-serving.

45. *YP,* IV, pt. I, p. 553.

46. *Milton and the English Revolution*, p. 370.

47. *A Second Defence, YP,* IV, pt. I, p. 556.

48. *Captain or Colonel,* chap. 7, esp. pp. 213–14, 217–20.

49. In *A Second Defence* Milton reveals the plan according to which he has addressed "three varieties of liberty without which civilized life is scarcely possible, namely ecclesiastical liberty, domestic or personal liberty, and civil liberty" (*YP,* IV, pt. I, p. 624). Under the second category he includes his divorce pamphlets, *Of Education,* and *Areopagitica.* He writes that he employed himself on the third category only after certain Presbyterian ministers turned against the Independent-dominated Parliament in an effort to reverse the successes of the first Civil War.

50. "On the New Forcers of Conscience under the Long Parliament" (1646?), Hughes, pp. 144–45.

51. *A Second Defence, YP,* IV, pt. I, pp. 650–51.

52. Ibid., pp. 548–49.

53. See especially ibid., pp. 632–35.

54. Walter Raleigh, *Milton* (London: Edward Arnold, 1900), p. 140.

55. F. R. Leavis, *The Common Pursuit* (New York: George W. Stewart, 1952), p. 19.

56. *The Muse's Method,* pp. 43–44.

57. See Davies, *Images of Kingship,* pp. 97–99. Milton's *Defence of the People of England,* Davies notes, attests to his extensive knowledge of Roman history and to "his conviction of its pertinence to the crisis of the English Parliament (figured by the Senate) under Stuart autocracy (imperial Caesar in his many diabolical personifications)" (p. 89).

58. Cited in *Milton's Paradise Lost,* ed. Newton, p. 82.

59. Ibid., p. 87.

60. Ibid., p. 98.

61. Ibid., pp. 98–99.

62. *Milton in Early America,* pp. 195–217.

63. Gilbert, "Patriarchal Poetry and Women Readers," p. 375; Belsey, *John Milton: Language, Gender, Power,* p. 60. Joseph Wittreich, on the other hand, chides feminists for allying themselves with the very "patriarchal criticism" that since the Victorian period has portrayed Milton as a misogynist. The feminists, Wittreich argues, have failed to understand what early female readers of Milton knew: that "the Edenic books of *Paradise Lost* held the poem's political content" and that in those books Milton feminizes his epic prophecy, giving Eve, whose seed shall bruise the head of the serpent, the primary role in humankind's future salvation (*Feminist Milton* [Ithaca: Cornell University Press, 1987], p. 74).

64. As Tayler observes, "two anti-Calvinist principles—the efficacy of reason and the freedom of the will—tend . . . to coalesce [in Milton's thought] into the single principle of reason *as* free will; and Calvin's God of will becomes Milton's rational deity, no longer a determining participant but rather an all-seeing 'guide' who encourages choice and 'second choys' " ("Milton's Grim Laughter and Second Choices," p. 83).

65. The new confession of faith ratified in late 1646 by the Westminster Assembly, a body of divines commissioned by the Long Parliament. Milton expressed his view of the Assembly in his sonnet "On the New Forcers of Conscience."

66. Maurice Kelley, *This Great Argument: A Study of Milton's "De Doctrina Christiana" as a Gloss upon "Paradise Lost"* (London: Oxford University Press, 1941), pp. 15–19.

67. The suggestion that Calvinist predestination represented an aristocratic, politically reactionary doctrine is at odds, of course, with Weber's thesis associating Calvinism with the rise of capitalism in seventeenth-century England and Holland. Andrew Milner reviews some of the evidence supporting a connection between nascent commercial republicanism and Calvinism's theological rival, Arminianism. He points out that the English Revolution "was carried through to its climax, not by Calvinistic Presbyterians, but by their Independent opponents"; it was the *defeat* of Calvinism, not Calvinism itself, that implied the new outlook. In Milton's universe, Milner argues, the elect attain their positions neither by hereditary right nor by predestination (in the orthodox Calvinist sense) but by merit (*John Milton and the English Revolution*, pp. 91–93).

68. *Surprised by Sin*, pp. 38–56.

69. Stavely also finds echoes of Milton's own radical Protestant theology in Eve's speeches (specifically in her answer to Adam in *PL*, V, 322–41) and concludes that her "legitimate urge toward Protestant self-validation has literally become a consuming passion." In contrast to my view, Stavely also finds Adam sententious and domineering. He argues that as Eve's desire for autonomy becomes contentious, Adam's desire for control also hardens, and their disagreement prefigures the ultimate conflict between the two central impulses within Puritanism, the desire for spontaneity and autonomy, on the one hand, and for discipline and control, on the other (*Puritan Legacies*, pp. 56, 51).

70. *The Ready and Easy Way*, Hughes, p. 890.

71. *"Paradise Lost" and the Genesis Tradition*, pp. 92–99.

72. *Genesis Against the Manichees*, vol. II, pp. ix–xi, quoted in ibid., p. 75.

73. *"Paradise Lost" and the Genesis Tradition*, p. 242.

74. *The Christian Doctrine*, Hughes, p. 993.

75. See Howard Schultz, *Milton and Forbidden Knowledge* (New York: Modern Languages Association, 1955), chap. 2.

76. Milton's depiction of the Fall echoes, or at least parallels, both works. Marlowe's Faustus turns to the occult after rejecting the Christian doctrines of grace and free will; he embraces the black arts as an easy means to power and riches. Augustine's Faustus is "a great snare of the Devil . . . and many were entangled by him in that gin of his smooth language." But Augustine claims to have learned to distinguish between the false knowledge of Faustus and truth. Augustine condemns the Manichaeans as astrologers and magicians, who "out of a wicked pride" have turned their backs on God: "they know not that way, (thy Word) by which thou madest these things which themselves can calculate." God creates; they can only calculate (*The Confessions*, trans. William Watts [1631] [Cambridge: Harvard University Press, 1960], vol. I, pp. 211–17). Augustine's story of his encounter with the Manichaean magician anticipates important features of Marlowe's and Milton's works: the smooth language of devils, the distinction between astrology and true knowledge, the danger of curiosity and vain imaginings.

77. Hill comments that Satan's "speech tempting Eve abounds with Ranter echoes. Empson grasped this point, without perhaps fully appreciating it, when he attributed to Eve the Ranter view that she was justified in eating the apple so long as she was firmly convinced that this was what God wanted her to do. Eve's sin was that of the Ranters and of many other radicals recorded by Edwards, 'affecting godhead' " (*Milton and the English Revolution*, p. 397).

78. Sacvan Bercovitch observes that seventeenth-century Protestant spiritual biographies, such as Cotton Mather's *Magnalia Christi Americana*, were careful to invoke the *imitatio* through "types" of Christ (Old Testament figures such as Moses and Nehemiah) rather than Jesus himself, so as to avoid the direct identification with Christ to which the Quakers, the Seekers, and similar groups aspired (*The Puritan Origins of the American Self*, p. 25).

79. *Mysticism and Democracy in the English Commonwealth* (Cambridge: Harvard University Press, 1939), esp. chaps. 2 and 5.

80. The figural-minded Massachusetts Puritans viewed their undertaking in precisely the same terms: "The People in the Fleet that arriv'd at *New-England*, in the Year 1630, left the Fleet almost, as the *Family* of *Noah* did the *Ark*, having a whole World before them to be peopled." In Cotton Mather, *Magnalia Christi Americana*, bks. I and II, ed. Kenneth B. Murdock (Cambridge: Harvard University Press, 1977), bk. I, p. 162.

81. Hughes, p. 750. Milton grasped Plato's insight into the coherence between the outward condition of a state and the inward condition of its people and applied it incisively to show that the ultimate responsibility for the king's tyrannical rule lay with a population dominated by self-interest and custom. But whereas Plato sought to control the inner man though external constraints—censorship, proscriptions against the accumulation of wealth, and other state regulations—Milton took the opposite tack, maintaining that liberty, together with education, was essential for the exercise of right reason and virtue (as in *Areopagitica*, Hughes, pp. 731–33). In *A Second Defence* Milton explains that "laws are made only to curb wickedness, but nothing can so effectively mould and create virtue as liberty" (*YP*, IV, pt. I, p. 679).

82. In *A Treatise of Civil Power in Ecclesiastical Causes* (1659) Milton contrasts the old and new Dispensations thusly: "then was the state of rigor, childhood, bondage and works, to all which force was not unbefitting; now is the state of grace, manhood, freedom and faith; to all which belongs willingness and reason" (*YP*, VII, p. 259).

Chapter 4

1. *The Paper of John Adams*, ed. Robert J. Taylor et al. (Cambridge: Harvard University Press, 1977–79), vol. IV, p. 87 (hereafter cited as *Adams Papers*). The lesser-known figures are Marchamount Needham (1620–1678), Henry Neville (1620–1694), Gilbert Burnet (1643–1715), and Benjamin Hoadly (1676–1761), who are discussed by Caroline Robbins in *The Eighteenth-Century Commonwealthman*.

Adams's inclusion of Locke in his list of republican authorities may puzzle modern readers, as most contemporary historians would place the defender of private rights and private property in opposition to the more communitarian civic humanists. But as Isaac Kramnick has noted, there was a "profusion and confusion of political tongues among the founders," including the languages of republicanism and Lockean liberalism ("The 'Great National Discussion': The Discourse of Politics in 1787," *William and Mary Quarterly* XLV, [Jan. 1988]: p. 4). Lacking the professional historian's concern for fine discriminations, Adams probably marshalled whatever authorities he could to bolster his argument that republics, being empires of laws, not men, were the best form of government to protect individual citizens from the exercise of arbitrary power. On this point Locke and Harrington certainly agreed.

2. Of course, this view of the determinants of the American Revolution is not without its challengers. Alan Heimert, for one, argues that religion, especially Edwardsean Calvinism, played a much more significant role in leading the way to revolution than any political ideas.

Citing Calvinism's challenge to clerical authority and its alternative emphasis on the conversion experience available to all men and women, Heimert maintains that "evangelical religion embodied a radical and even democratic challenge to the standing order of colonial America" and thus served as a rehearsal for the Revolution (*Religion and the American Mind*, p. 12). Bernard Bailyn, on the other hand, argues that political ideas, not religion—and certainly not any particular doctrines—were primary, and that the role of religious discourse was to reinforce essentially political notions ("Religion and Revolution: Three Biographical Studies," *Perspectives in American History* IV [1970]: pp. 85–169). In the text that follows, I mention some of the more recent studies of the American Revolution that seek, in effect, to bring together Heimert and Bailyn—the cases for religious and ideological determinants.

3. "A True *Whig* is not afraid of the name of a *Commonwealthman*, because so many foolish People, who know not what it means, run it down," wrote Robert Molesworth in his famous preface to Francis Hotoman's *Franco-Gallia*. . . . Quoted from *The Principles of a Real Whig; Contained in a Preface to the Famous Hotoman's Franco-Gallia* (London: J. Williams, 1775), pp. 6–7. This version of Molesworth's piece was reprinted by the Whig London Association as part of an effort to remind the British ministry of the principles of the British Constitution and prevent the alienation or total loss of the American colonies. It should be noted that Molesworth was careful to disclaim the *"anarchy* and *confusion"* of the Interregnum; he and other English Real Whigs understood Commonwealth principles to mean mixed and balanced government, in which the king might retain a role as the magisterial power.

4. Tocqueville, *Democracy in America*, vol. I, p. 41. Is it true that Tocqueville "distorted the case Whig style," as Cushing Strout maintains, when he represented the early Puritans as republican forebears? Refining Tocqueville's thesis, Strout argues that, in fact, it was the repressive Andros regime of the late 1680s that first aroused the New England colonists to assert their traditional English liberties, transforming an austere Puritanism into a more republican system that would draw on the Commonwealth political legacy in the 1760s and 1770s (*The New Heavens and New Earth*, pp. 12, 28).

5. Edmund Morgan, *The Puritan Dilemma: The Story of John Winthrop* (Boston: Little, Brown, 1958), p. 92.

6. *Democracy in America*, vol. I, pp. 32–33.

7. Quoted in Sacvan Bercovitch, *The American Jeremiad* (Madison: University of Wisconsin Press, 1978), p. 119, as an example of the effective use of the Puritan jeremiad in mobilizing the country during the Revolution. (The jeremiad was a genre of political sermon that reminded the congregation of its mission in "the New Israel" [America] and castigated backsliders.)

8. Clarendon to Pym, Dec. 1765, *Diary and Autobiography of John Adams*, ed. L. H. Butterfield et al. (Cambridge: Harvard University Press, 1961), vol. I, p. 282.

9. Bonomi, *Under the Cope of Heaven*, p. 190.

10. *God Arising and Pleading* (1777), quoted in Bercovitch, *The American Jeremiad*, p. 110 n.

11. *The Sacred Cause of Liberty*, pp. 3, 12.

12. Ibid., p. 3.

13. *The New Heavens and New Earth*, pp. 9, 12, 50–54.

14. *The Sacred Cause of Liberty*, p. 63.

15. *Under the Cope of Heaven*, p. 9. Bonomi's study marks an important shift in the religion-versus-politics debate. She contests the view that religion was on the decline in the colonies by the eighteenth century but argues that the Great Awakening was a "practice model" for the Revolution because of its anti-institutionalism and its mass character, not because of any particular doctrinal issues. As evidence of the interpenetration of religion and politics in

eighteenth-century America, Bonomi notes that the revivalists drew on *political* arguments (for example, the Magna Carta's defense of the natural rights of Englishmen) to defend religious rights. These arguments reappeared during the political crises of the 1760s and 1770s.

16. In *The Sacred Cause of Liberty*, Hatch describes the convergence of millennial and republican thought in eighteenth-century America alternatively as "civil millennialism" or "Christian republicanism."

17. By way of substantiating this point, Bailyn points out that although the terms "democracy" and "republic" were closely associated in the colonists' minds, they evoked mixed responses: "For if 'republic' conjured up for many the positive features of the Commonwealth era and marked the triumph of virtue and reason, 'democracy'—a word that denoted the lowest order of society as well as the form of government in which the commons ruled—was generally associated with the threat of civil disorder and the early assumption of power by a dictator." Bailyn concludes that the American revolutionaries are best understood as eighteenth-century radicals inasmuch as they were concerned "not with the need to recast the social order nor with the problems of economic inequality and the injustices of stratified societies but with the need to purify a corrupt constitution and fight off the apparent growth of prerogative power" (*The Ideological Origins of the American Revolution*, pp. 282–83). In a similar vein, Gordon Wood writes that American republicanism of 1776 "possessed a decidedly reactionary tone" in its suspicion of parties, factions, and particular interests of all kinds. Although he concedes that the republicans endorsed "equality of opportunity" and believed it would lead to "a rough equality of station," Wood maintains that many Americans harbored ambivalent attitudes toward equality and social status (*The Creation of the American Republic*, pp. 59, 72–75).

18. Harl R. Douglass and Calvin Grieder, *American Public Education: An Introduction* (New York: Ronald Press, 1948), p. 14.

19. See chapter 3 for a fuller discussion of these points.

20. June 14, 1756. *Diary and Autobiography*, vol. I, pp. 33–34.

21. *A Defence of the Constitutions of Government of the United States of America* (London: J. Stockdale, 1794), vol. I, p. 130. If Adams's monarchical metaphor seems strange for a republican leader, one must remember, first, that the image was an eighteenth-century commonplace and, second, that Adams saw no contradiction between constitutional monarchy and republicanism (which he defined as government of laws, not men). In 1775 he argued that the uncorrupted "British constitution is nothing more or less than a republic, in which the king is the first magistrate." Quoted in Wood, *The Creation of the American Republic*, p. 206.

22. Bailyn and Wood treat what they perceive to be a major advance from a classical-republican view of politics toward consensus, or interest-group, theory in the period of federal constitution-writing. Wood argues that this period marked the "end of classical politics." The idea that there was no public good above or apart from the particular interests of individuals had become influential in political theory, he maintains, and with it the idea that political battles would henceforth be fought by competing interest groups (*The Creation of the American Republic*, p. 606–15). Bailyn writes that this new view of politics appeared in the colonies as early as the 1730s and that its advocates, no longer fearful of the destructiveness of "factions," believed that society's competing interest groups could join in conflict within a unicameral legislature and blend themselves into a consensus (*The Origins of American Politics*, pp. 125–28; *The Ideological Origins of the American Revolution*, p. 299).

23. Fink, *The Classical Republicans*, preface to the first edition. The first scholar to identify this tendency in English political thought as classical republicanism, Fink demonstrates that, in the seventeenth century, classical models were as important in politics as in literature and the arts.

24. Hughes, p. 750.
25. Fink, *The Classical Republicans*, p. 151.
26. Ibid., p. 154.
27. Ultimately deriving from Plato, Aristotle, Cicero, and the Greek historian Polybius, who lived in the second century B.C., the theory of mixed and balanced government was passed down to seventeenth-century England via Machiavelli and other Florentine civic humanists of the fifteenth and sixteenth centuries. J. G. A. Pocock argues that the revival of classical political theory in the Renaissance, in a Christian culture that denied the possibility of secular fulfillment, necessarily led to a modification of the classical notion of the republic. The ideal of the perfectly stable republic gave way to the notion of republics as subject to decay and corruption, to the ravages of *fortuna*. One theoretical ramification of this notion was the provision made by Machiavelli, Harrington, and others in their ideal constitutions for a heroic legislator—a Lycurgus or a Solon (or a Cromwell-like figure, in the case of Harrington's *Oceana*)—to step in at the very moment when the republic breaks down to *reform* it. Another was the characteristic vocabulary of republican treatises, with their relentless emphasis on the problem of corruption and self-interest. See Pocock's Introduction to *The Political Works of James Harrington*, ed. J. C. A. Pocock (Cambridge: Cambridge University Press, 1977). Pocock's fullest exposition of his thesis is in *The Machiavellian Moment*.
28. Introduction, *The Political Works of James Harrington*, p. 52.
29. See Austin Woolrych, Introduction, *YP*, VII, p. 215: "Fink . . . drives too far the thesis that the keynote of Milton's politics lies in the concept of the mixed state . . . belief in the mixed state had been a commonplace in English political thought for over a century, and in 1660 the moderate royalists were making far more play with it than any republicans."
30. *YP*, I, p. 599.
31. See Fink, *The Classical Republican*, chap. 4, passim.
32. Ibid., pp. 100–101.
33. *Defence of the Constitutions*, vol. I, pp. 130–31.
34. Ibid., vol. III, p. 363.
35. John Winthrop's definition of "natural" liberty, or license. True liberty he termed "civil or federal." Quoted in Tocqueville, *Democracy in America*, vol. I, pp. 44–45.
36. Quoted in Fliegelman, *Prodigals and Pilgrims*, p. 82.
37. Ibid., chap. 3, passim.
38. *An Old Looking-Glass for the Laity and Clergy, of All Denominations, Who Either Give or Receive Money Under Pretence of the Gospel* . . . (New Haven: Thomas and Samuel Green, 1774; orig. pub. 1770). Included were excerpts from Milton's antiepiscopal tracts, among them *Animadversions upon the Remonstrant's Defence against Smectymnuus*, "containing more Reasons for neither tempting nor permitting the Gospel Clergy to become sacrilegious hirelings," and *Of Reformation*, "wherein he depicts the Bishops in their real Colours both what they originally were, what they are, and what they ought to be."
39. *The Puritan Revolution and Educational Thought: Background to Reform* (New Brunswick: Rutgers University Press, 1969), pp. 40–41.
40. Hughes, pp. 631–32.
41. Even the most advanced position of the Interregnum governments, the Agreement of the Council of Officers (which came out of the Whitehall debates begun on Dec. 14, 1648, by the Council of Officers of the New Model Army), did not break with the principle of state-supported religion, although it upheld liberty of conscience. This and other examples of how Milton's writings were marshalled in the political battles that led to the acceptance of the Glorious Revolution and the Bill of Rights at the end of the century are drawn from George Sensabaugh's *That Grand Whig, Milton* (Stanford: Stanford University Press, 1952). Sensabaugh's study takes off from William Riley Parker's contention in *Milton's Contempo-*

rary Reputation (Columbus: The Ohio State University Press, 1940) that, contrary to the myth of Milton as leading statesman, which Masson invoked, Milton did not exert a powerful influence in politics during the Commonwealth period. Sensabaugh argues that Milton's ideas and writings became influential, but not until later in the seventeenth century.

42. Sensabaugh, *That Grand Whig, Milton*, chap. 2, esp. pp. 30–40.

43. Ibid., chaps. 3 and 4.

44. Robbins, *The Eighteenth-Century Commonwealthman*, p. 386.

45. Robbins argues that the Real Whigs brought together the tendencies of two seventeenth-century political groups: the classical republicans, who were concerned primarily with restoring the balance and stability of England's mixed government; and the Levellers, who sought to broaden political participation and extend civil and religious liberties (ibid., p. 8).

46. *Some Considerations for the Promoting of Agriculture and Employing the Poor* (Dublin: George Grierson, 1723).

47. John Toland, *The Life of John Milton; . . . with Amyntor; or a Defence of Milton's Life* (London: A. Millar, 1761; orig. pub. 1699), p. 1.

48. Ibid., p. 158.

49. Robbins, *The Eighteenth-Century Commonwealthman*, pp. 50–51.

Chapter 5

1. "Early American Copies of Milton," *Huntington Library Bulletin*, no. 7 (April 1935): 173. This paragraph is based on material in Howard's article.

2. *The Life of Samuel Johnson by James Boswell*, cited in Robbins, *The Eighteenth-Century Commonwealthman*, p. 268.

3. Quoted in Charles W. Akers, *Called unto Liberty: A Life of Jonathan Mayhew, 1720–1766* (Cambridge: Harvard University Press, 1964), p. 142.

4. Quoted in Akers, *Called unto Liberty*, p. 35.

5. *Religion and the American Mind*, pp. 93, 77, 55.

6. Akers, *Called unto Liberty*, chap. 5, passim.

7. Quoted in ibid., p. 74.

8. Ibid. The theology of good works and political engagement also went hand in hand for another alleged Arminian, John Milton, as is pointed out in chapter 3 of this study. Although Mayhew's theology was clearly influenced by eighteenth-century rationalism and was heading in a more secular direction, he drew on Milton's tracts to argue, in contradistinction to the Revivalists, that to use reason in the search for religious truth was a universal right and duty. Sensabaugh, who undertakes a passage-by-passage comparison between *Areopagitica* and two of Mayhew's sermons on religious freedom, writes that "Mayhew so felt the impress of Milton's rhetoric that when he preached on the central issues of toleration and freedom of inquiry he perforce recalled large segments of *Areopagitica*, sometimes in loose paraphrase, sometimes with surprising precision" (*Milton in Early America*, p. 59).

9. *Under the Cope of Heaven*, p. 208. Bonomi demonstrates how the tradition of religious dissent that the colonists inherited from Stuart England blended with features of evangelical religion such as the emphasis on individual accountability and the defense of minority rights. She argues that, by 1776, the emotionalism of the Awakening had subsided, modified by rationalist religion (ibid., chap. 7).

10. Ibid., p. 208.

11. In *Pamphlets of the American Revolution*, ed. Bernard Bailyn, vol. I, *1750–1765* (Cambridge: Harvard University Press, 1965), pp. 242, 239.

12. Sensabaugh, *Milton in Early America*, pp. 60–65.

13. *Pamphlets of the American Revolution*, p. 228.

14. "Thomas Hollis and Jonathan Mayhew: Their Correspondence, 1759–1766," ed. Bernhard Knollenberg, Massachusetts Historical Society *Proceedings* 69 (Oct. 1947 to May 1950): pp. 109–10. The following discussion of the Hollis-Mayhew correspondence is based principally on the letters contained in this collection.

15. Aug. 27, 1760. "Hollis-Mayhew Correspondence," p. 116.

16. Ibid., pp. 116-17.

17. Quoted in Akers, *Called unto Liberty*, p. 202.

18. March 19, 1761. "Hollis-Mayhew Correspondence," p. 118.

19. May 21, 1760. Ibid., p. 112.

20. Aug. 27, 1760. Ibid., pp. 114–15.

21. Charles Webster, *The Great Instauration: Science, Medicine and Reform, 1626–1660* (London: Duckworth, 1975), p. 53.

22. Quoted in Akers, *Called unto Liberty*, pp. 181–82.

23. In his *Observations on the Charter and Conduct of the Society for the Propagation of the Gospel* (1763). Quoted in Bailyn, *The Ideological Origins of the American Revolution*, p. 256.

24. Ibid.

25. Quoted in Akers, *Called unto Liberty*, p. 185.

26. Quoted in Bailyn, *The Ideological Origins of the American Revolution*, pp. 256–57.

27. April 6, 1762. "Hollis-Mayhew Correspondence," pp. 128–29.

28. Dec. 6, 1763. Ibid., p. 142.

29. June 24, 1765. Ibid., p. 171.

30. Oct. 10, 1764. Ibid., p. 157.

31. March 4, 1765. Ibid., p. 166.

32. Analyzing both the text and the circumstances of its composition, Bailyn shows that *The Snare Broken* expresses the central problem of eighteenth-century libertarianism—the need to balance individual liberty and social stability—and that Mayhew's approach to the problem is not a sign of the political conservatism attributed to him by Heimert and others. One might add that the need to balance individual liberty and social goals was a primary concern for Milton and for other seventeenth-century republicans as well. In "Religion and Revolution: Three Biographical Sketches," p. 124.

33. Quoted in Akers, *Called unto Liberty*, p. 215.

34. *Diary and Autobiography*, vol. I, p. 22.

35. Ibid., pp. 21–22.

36. Ibid., p. 23.

37. *The Literary Bible of Thomas Jefferson*, ed. Gilbert Chinard (New York: Greenwood Press, 1969; orig. pub. 1928), p. 3. Jefferson's commonplace book contains more extracts from Milton than from any other author.

38. Ibid., p. 21.

39. From *The Reason of Church Government* and *Of Reformation*, Jefferson borrowed arguments on the relation between episcopal government and monarchy and on the popular election of bishops in early Christian times. See "Notes on Episcopacy," in *The Commonplace Book of Thomas Jefferson*, ed. Gilbert Chinard (Baltimore: Johns Hopkins University Press, 1926), p. 384. Again borrowing from Milton, Jefferson argued in his Bill for Religious Freedom that the church did not need the support of temporal authority and, furthermore, that the history of corruption had begun with such support, when Christianity was established as a state religion under Constantine. See Sensabaugh, *Milton in Early America*, pp. 137–46.

40. *Diary and Autobiography*, vol. I, pp. 23–24.

41. Ibid., p. 39.

42. See Stow Persons, *American Minds: A History of Ideas* (New York: Henry Holt, 1958, p. 75), on the compatibility between eighteenth-century and older religious notions of design.

43. *Diary and Autobiography*, vol. I, p. 22.

44. Ibid.

45. Ibid., p. 28.

46. Ibid., p. 23.

47. From Fragmentary Draft of "A Dissertation on the Canon and the Feudal Law" (Feb. 1765), in *Diary and Autobiography*, vol. I, p. 257. Ernest L. Tuveson calls attention to the significance of Adams's choice of the word "scene," which suggests that the event "is part of a drama." Tuveson adds that "it is not unreasonable to assign such an idea to an eschatological source [i.e., Revelation], for no other philosophy of history in the Western World saw the historical process as one dramatic action." In *Redeemer Nation: The Idea of America's Millennial Role* (Chicago: University of Chicago Press, 1968), p. 102.

48. *Areopagitica*, Hughes, p. 743. Bercovitch points out that not all English Puritans subscribed to the idea of national election, and that therein lay an important distinction between English and American Puritanism. The former he divides into two camps: first, the adherents of national election, who believed that England was destined to lead the universal battle against the Antichrist (Rome) and who "concentrated perforce on reforms relevant to the city of man"—Bercovitch places Milton in this camp—and second, the Congregationalists (or Separatists), who denied that the New Jerusalem could be built in England or anywhere else in this polluted world and who therefore emphasized a more personal approach to redemption, beyond secular history. "The Great Migration owes its unique character to its inheritance of both of these strains in its English background," writes Bercovitch. The American Puritans "were children of an improbable mixed marriage—Congregationalists on a historic mission for mankind." See *The American Jeremiad*, chap. 2, esp. pp. 33–39.

49. *YP*, IV, pt. I, p. 622.

50. See *Milton's Poetry: Its Development in Time* (Pittsburgh: Duquesne University Press, 1979).

51. *The Ready and Easy Way*, Hughes, p. 898. Ezekiel's vision of the bones that revive as he speaks to them (Ezek. 37) was frequently mentioned in contemporary Puritan sermons.

52. Andrew Delbanco has recently argued for a revised view of Winthrop's famous sermon. He notes that Perry Miller made the image of the city on a hill into the centerpiece of his theory that the Puritans regarded their undertaking as a beacon of hope for the Old World. But the sermon, Delbanco argues, "is, in fact, considerably more focused on what was being fled than on what was being pursued": it reveals anxieties and even guilt over separation from the Church of England and is more concerned with notoriety than fame (*The Puritan Ordeal* [Cambridge: Harvard University Press, 1989], p. 72).

53. See Bercovitch, *The Puritan Origins of the American Self*, chap. 2, passim.

54. In *American Minds*, pp. 126–28, Stow Persons discusses the idea of progress implicit in American millennialism—postmillennialism, to be exact—which looked forward to the Second Coming at the end of a thousand-year period of gradual spiritual and moral improvement. (By contrast, premillennialism, which anticipated the imminent return of Christ, foresaw the ruin of all earthly kingdoms and other cataclysmic events in the immediate future and encouraged its believers to separate themselves from the hopelessly evil secular world.) Like Persons, Sacvan Bercovitch finds a sense of optimism and a belief in progress in the language of the Puritan sermon, and he contests Perry Miller's portrait of the New England Puritans as predominantly self-deprecating and pessimistic. Bercovitch

writes that although the ubiquitous jeremiads—"state-of-the-convenant" addresses—castigated the congregations for failing to realize their mission in the New Israel, the sermons were essentially optimistic (unlike their European counterparts), affirming "the inviolability of the colonial cause" (*The American Jeremiad*, p. 7).

55. Bercovitch, *The Puritan Origins of the American Self*, p. 52.

56. See, for example, ibid., chap. 2; and Mason I. Lowance, Jr., "Cotton Mather's *Magnalia* and the Metaphors of Biblical History," in *Typology and Early American Literature*, ed. Sacvan Bercovitch (Amherst: University of Massachusetts Press, 1972), pp. 139–60.

57. The suggestive phrase is from Thomas M. Davis, "The Traditions of Puritan Typology," in *Typology and Early American Literature*, ed. Bercovitch, p. 45.

58. March 13, 1775. *Adams Papers*, vol. II, p. 403.

59. Ibid., pp. 403–4.

60. Ibid., vol. I, p. 103 n. Tuveson discusses Adams's *Dissertation* as a case study of the application of millennial theory to the American people (*Redeemer Nation*, pp. 20–25). More recently, Nathan Hatch and Patricia Bonomi have analyzed Adams's work as a prime example of the convergence of religious and political ideas and traditions in the 1760s and 1770s (in *The Sacred Cause of Liberty* and *Under the Cope of Heaven*, respectively).

61. *Redeemer Nation*, p. 22.

62. *Adams Papers*, vol. I, p. 113.

63. Ibid., p. 111.

64. Ibid., pp. 113–14.

65. Ibid., p. 115.

66. Ibid.

67. Ibid., pp. 118, 117.

68. *Thoughts on Government*, in *Adams Papers*, vol. IV, p. 92.

69. Adams, an apprentice in Otis's law practice, had attended the court proceedings and taken thorough notes.

70. *Adams Papers*, vol. I, pp. 118–20. Adams's description of the tradition of local education and government in Massachusetts—a tradition he regarded as the foundation of the republican spirit of 1776—echoes the logic of Milton's proposal on the eve of the Stuart Restoration (in *The Ready and Easy Way*) for the instituting of local assemblies and a nationwide system of local schools to diffuse knowledge to the remotest parts of England. The educational and political infrastructure Adams described, which supported republican government in New England, was a realization of the principles Milton had endorsed.

71. Bercovitch, *The American Jeremiad*, pp. 122–23. See also Fliegelman, *Prodigals and Pilgrims*, for a discussion of the rejection of patriarchal authority as one impulse behind the American Revolution.

Chapter 6

1. Jan. 3, 1775. *Adams Papers*, vol. II, p. 209.

2. As he was called by Samuel Adams and other Whigs. Miller, *Sam Adams*, p. 300.

3. Letter to Charles Thomson, May 30, 1774. *Writings of Samuel Adams*, ed. Harry Alonzo Cushing (New York: Octagon Press, 1968), vol. III, pp. 122–23.

4. Josiah Quincy, Jr., *Observations on the Act of Parliament, commonly called the Boston Port-Bill* . . . (Philadelphia: John Sparhawk, 1774), p. 5.

5. Ibid., pp. 9–10.

6. Boston Committee of Correspondence, *Gentlemen, the Evils which we have long Foreseen*

are now Come . . . (Boston, 1774), p. 1. One act, which allowed cases involving property disputes to be tried outside their countries of origin, called up the specter of an often-cited biblical precedent, Ahab's expropriation of Naboth's property by means of trumped-up charges and false witnesses: "Of what value are our lands or estates to us, if such an odious government should be established among us? Can we look with pleasure on the inheritance left by our ancestors, or on the fields cultivated by *our* industry? When we reflect that all our labours have made them only a more inviting prey to our enemies, will not the vineyard of Naboth be ever in *our* minds?" (ibid.). Another act enabled the governor to send officials or soldiers accused of murder to other colonies or to Britain for trial.

7. From the Declaration of Rights, drawn up by the First Continental Congress in late 1774. This document called for the repeal of any British laws and measures since 1763—from the Stamp Act to the Coercive Acts—that were found to violate the colonists' liberties as the citizens of the British empire. Quoted in John Richard Alden, *The American Revolution, 1775–1783* (New York: Harper & Row, 1954), pp. 15–16.

8. Ibid., pp. 7–8, 12.

9. Jan. 3, 1775. *Adams Papers*, vol. II, p. 209.

10. *Writings of Samuel Adams*, vol. III, pp. 106, 111.

11. The fact that these and other such agreements not to import or consume British goods were referred to as "solemn leagues" or "covenants" underscores the conjunction of political and religious motives in the patriots' behavior.

12. Jan. 15, 1775. *Adams Papers*, vol. II, p. 213.

13. Ibid., p. 214. The "late publications" seems to be a reference to the recent parliamentary elections in Britain, which according to Adams returned most of the "old rotten Rascalls . . . very few new Members" (ibid., p. 209).

14. Letter to Abigail Adams, July 5, 1774. *Adams Family Correspondence*, ed. L. H. Butterfield et al. (Cambridge: Harvard University Press, 1963–73), vol. I, p. 125.

15. The royal proclamation of Aug. 23, 1775. See Alden, *The American Revolution*, p. 62.

16. Quoted in ibid, p. 63. See also pp. 8–10, 16–17, and 62–63 on the opposition to ministerial policy within England.

17. In John Adams's words. *Diary and Autobiography*, vol. I, p. 257.

18. Quoted in John R. Howe, Jr., *The Changing Political Thought of John Adams* (Princeton: Princeton University Press, 1966), p. 39.

19. Admittedly, some of the foregoing references to the Devil do not cite Milton directly; however, they are clearly informed by Milton's portrait of Satan—as self-serving rebel, tempter, and so forth—and therefore evidence either a direct or a mediated experience of *Paradise Lost*.

20. *The Poems of Philip Freneau: Poet of the American Revolution*, ed. Fred Lewis Pattee (Princeton: The University Library, 1902), vol. I, p. 155. Page references are given within the text.

21. In *The Satiric Poems of John Trumbull: The Progress of Dulness and M'Fingal*, ed. Edwin T. Bowden (Austin: University of Texas Press, 1962). Page references are given within the text.

22. The reference to menopausal Mother Britain is a humorous allusion to the popular eighteenth-century theory according to which history consisted of the gradual rise and decline of empires, each beginning virtuously but falling into moral decay with prosperity and luxury. Britain was now said to be in the descendent phase of the inevitable cycle, her leaders and population displaying the immoral behavior characteristic of this phase, whereas America's virtues and fortunes were ascending.

The specter of "grim death," Milton's allegorical figure, pervaded American letters of all types. See Sensabaugh, *Milton in Early America*, p. 125.

23. Sensabaugh writes that "Ministers . . . so absorbed his [Milton's] vast images that their congregations envisioned the Christian story not as depicted in Scripture but as described in *Paradise Lost" (Milton in Early America*, p. 4).

24. See John T. Shawcross, "A Survey of Milton's Prose Works," in *Achievements of the Left Hand*, ed. Michael Lieb and John T. Shawcross (Amherst: University of Massachusetts Press, 1974), p. 334. See also chapter 5 in this book.

25. Howard, "Early American Copies of Milton," p. 176.

26. *Adams Papers*, vol. II, p. 299.

27. To Mercy Otis Warren, April 16, 1776. Ibid., vol. IV, p. 124.

28. Ibid., vol. II, p. 298–99.

29. To Charles Thomson, May 30, 1774. *Writings of Samuel Adams*, vol. III, pp. 123–24.

30. Discussed later in this chapter.

31. *Gentlemen, At a Time when Degenerate Britons* . . . (Boston, 1777), p. 1.

32. Ibid., p. 2.

33. Some historians, such as John C. Miller *(Sam Adams)*, have argued that the latter was never a sincere demand of the more radical Whigs but was merely a rhetorical ploy whereby they pretended to be loyal, sinned-against subjects.

34. *The Tenure of Kings and Magistrates*, Hughes, p. 750.

35. (New York: Simon & Schuster, 1987), pp. 157–72, passim.

36. As in the case of Adams's intimate friend Daniel Leonard (Massachusettensis), whom Adams answered in his Novanglus letters. In old age Adams recalled that Thomas Hutchinson had "Seduced from my Bosom, three of the most intimate friends I ever had in my Life, Jonathan Sewall, Samuel Quincy, and Daniel Leonard" (quoted in *Adams Papers*, vol. II, p. 217 n). Leonard had turned against the patriot cause after the Boston Tea Party, endorsed the policies of the British government, and accepted an appointment from General Gage in August 1774 as one of thirty-six mandamus councilors (under the bill that provided for royal appointment of members of the upper house and eliminated their election by the assembly).

37. *A Short Narrative of the Horrid Massacre in Boston* (Boston: Edes & Gill and Fleets, 1770), p. 6.

38. Ibid., pp. 6–7.

39. *Writings of Samuel Adams*, vol. III, p. 30.

40. As Milton protested in his sonnet "On the Same" ("I did prompt the age"), Hughes, p. 143. See Pauline Maier, *From Resistance to Revolution: Colonial Radicals and the Development of American Opposition to Britain, 1765–1776* (New York: Vintage, 1974), on what she terms the "conservative" impulse of the American founding fathers.

41. *Summary, Historical and Political* . . . *of the British Settlements in North America* (1749–51), quoted in Bailyn, *The Origins of American Politics*, p. 59.

42. See Maier, *From Resistance to Revolution*, p. 113 n.

43. Sam Adams wrote this as "Candidus" in the *Boston Gazette*, April 12, 1773. *Writings of Samuel Adams*, vol. III, p. 29.

44. *Adams Papers*, vol. II, pp. 219–20. Leonard's argument, interestingly, was traditionally cited in defense of royal absolutism and in opposition to mixed government; the argument was derived from Jean Bodin's concept of the indivisibility of sovereignty.

45. Ibid., p. 314. The classic Whig definition of republicanism. See, for example, Milton's *Tenure of Kings and Magistrates*. In discussing the origin and evolution of monarchy, Milton explains that laws and oaths were introduced by the people to forestall the exercise of arbitrary power, "so that man, of whose failing they had proof, might no more rule over them, but law and reason, abstracted as much as might be from personal errors and frailties" (Hughes, p. 755).

46. *Adams Papers*, vol. II, p. 260.

47. Ibid., p. 261. Adams chose his examples carefully. By issuing paper money through the famous Land Bank, Elisha Cooke and "Deacon" Adams, father of Sam Adams, proposed to relieve a depression-causing shortage of currency and give Massachusetts a source of money and credit independent of Britain. The project had clear political overtones: the Massachusetts patriots of the 1760s and 1770s considered themselves heirs of the Land Bank Party of 1740. See Miller, *Sam Adams*, chaps. 1 and 2, passim. The idea for the bank originated with William Potter's 1653 blueprint for an English "Bank of the Lands." See chapter 2 in this book, n. 34.

48. *Adams Papers*, vol. II, p. 246.

49. Ibid., p. 247.

50. Ibid.

51. Namely, Robbins's *Eighteenth-Century Commonwealthman* and Bailyn's *Origins of American Politics* and *Ideological Origins of the American Revolution*.

52. The patriots themselves referred in this way to their assemblies, which were replicas of the British House of Commons.

53. Bailyn, *The Origin of American Politics*, p. 10.

54. Ibid., p. 11.

55. *Diary and Autobiography*, vol. I, p. 282.

56. *Adams Papers*, vol. II, p. 227. Adams assumed, wrongly, that his adversary was Jonathan Sewell, his long-standing sparring partner. Though Adams does not directly cite Milton here, the presence of Milton's Satan is felt nonetheless.

57. Ibid., pp. 263, 272, 243.

58. Ibid., p. 224.

59. Ibid., p. 228.

60. Ibid.

61. Ibid., p. 284.

62. Ibid., p. 233. Edmund Andros, Edward Randolph, and Joseph Dudley, all royally appointed officials of Massachusetts, were especially despised by the colonists for voiding the original charter in 1684.

63. Ibid., pp. 233, 236–37.

64. Ibid., pp. 259–60.

65. Ibid., pp. 273–74.

66. Ibid., p. 274.

67. Letter to Abigail Adams, July 5, 1774. *Adams Family Correspondence*, vol. I, p. 125.

68. Ibid.

69. For example, David Tappan, Hollis professor of divinity at Harvard, explained that in the early historical stages of societies, "their members are usually industrious and frugal, simple in their manners, just and kind in their intercourse, active and hardy, united and brave. . . . But when they have reached a certain point of greatness, their taste and manners begin to be infected. Their prosperity inflates and debauches their minds. It betrays them into pride and avarice, luxury and dissipation, idleness and sensuality, and too often into practical or scornful impiety. These, with other kindred vices, hasten their downfall and ruin" (quoted in Persons, *American Minds*, p. 125). Interestingly, this view of the relationship between prosperity, luxury, and decay resembles in outline the theories of the modern economist Mancur Olson, who sees the economic and political victories of interest groups— trade unions, industry groups, and so on—ultimately becoming an obstacle to national economic growth and a prime source of a society's stagnation. See *The Rise and Decline of Nations* (New Haven: Yale University Press, 1982).

70. *Adams Papers*, vol. II, p. 242.

71. Ibid., p. 255.

72. Alden, *The American Revolution*, pp. 6–7.

73. *Adams Papers*, vol. II, p. 295.

74. Boston Selectmen, *Notification. The Freeholders . . . Tea . . .* (Boston, 1773).

75. *The Tea-Ship being Arrived . . .* (Philadelphia, 1773).

76. *Adams Papers*, vol. II, pp. 295–96.

77. Ibid., p. 298.

78. Ibid., pp. 298–99.

79. Quoted in Kenneth Silverman, *A Cultural History of the American Revolution: Painting, Music, Literature, and the Theatre in the Colonies and the United States from the Treaty of Paris to the Inauguration of George Washington, 1763–1789* (New York: T. Y. Crowell, 1976), p. 249.

80. In an open letter to Gage in the *Essex Gazette*, July 13, 1775. Quoted in Alden, *The American Revolution*, p. 36.

81. *Prodigals and Pilgrims*, chaps. 2 and 3.

82. Abraham Keteltas, *God Arising and Pleading* (Newburyport, Mass., 1777), pp. 21, 29.

83. Boston Town Clerk, *Gentlemen, We the Freeholders . . .* (Boston, 1772).

84. *Tea, Destroyed by Indians. Ye Glorious Sons of Freedom . . .* (Boston, 1773).

85. *Adams Papers*, vol. II, pp. 230–31.

86. Ibid., p. 232.

87. *Peter Oliver's Origin & Progress of the American Rebellion*, ed. Douglass Adair and John A. Schutz (Stanford: Stanford University Press, 1961; orig. pub. 1781), p. 36.

88. Ibid., pp. 93–94.

89. Samuel Seabury, *A View of the Controversy between Great Britain and her Colonies . . .* (New York: James Rivington, 1774).

90. Ibid., p. 5. Seabury was answering Hamilton's *Full Vindication of the Measures of Congress*, which was itself written in answer to Seabury and Wilkins's *Free Thoughts on the Proceedings of the Continental Congress*.

91. Seabury, *A View of the Controversy*, p. 6.

92. Ibid., p. 8.

93. Ibid., p. 10.

94. Jonathan Odell, *The American Times, a satire in three parts. In which are delineated the Characters of the Leaders of the American Rebellion*, in *Cow-chace*, ed. John André (New York: Rivington, 1780), p. 69. Page references are given within the text.

95. *Adams Papers*, vol. II, p. 269.

96. Ibid., pp. 288–89.

97. Quoted in Silverman, *A Cultural History of the American Revolution*, p. 279.

98. *Adams Papers*, vol. II, p. 291. Compare Milton's distinction between the liberty-loving people and the mob in *A Second Defence*.

99. Ibid., pp. 1–2.

100. July 5, 1774. *Adams Family Correspondence*, vol. I, pp. 124–25.

101. *Adams Papers*, vol. II, p. 289.

102. Milton's most sustained and explicit warning about the pitfalls of republics, where so much rests on public virtue, comes at the close of *A Second Defence*. Here he cautions the electorate against handing power to uneducated and ambitious men simply because they promise the most pelf, and he urges legislators to avoid favoritism, embezzlement of public funds, and other abuses of their positions of public trust.

103. *Adams Papers*, vol. IV, p. 124; vol. III, p. 398.

104. As "Clarendon," *Boston Gazette*, Jan. 27, 1776. Quoted in Howe, *The Changing Political Thought of John Adams*, p. 13.

105. Feb. 9, 1772. *Diary and Autobiography*, vol. II, p. 54.

106. Feb. 3, 1777. *Adams Papers*, vol. V, p. 76.

107. In fact, Adams excoriated Milton's proposed perpetual senate of the ablest men as a "wild reverie," an "oligarchy of decemvirs," which would have either ridden roughshod over English liberties or disintegrated into warring factions, setting the stage for the early assumption of power by a single despot (*Defence of the Constitutions*, vol. IV, pp. 465–66).

108. *Adams Papers*, vol. IV, p. 87.

109. April 20, 1776. Ibid., p. 130. See the editorial note to *Thoughts on Government* for a complete account of the various letters and the genesis of the pamphlet (ibid., p. 65).

110. March 19, 1776. *Adams Family Correspondence*, vol. I, p. 363.

111. Quoted in Bailyn, *The Ideological Origins of the American Revolution*, pp. 286–87.

112. One of Adams's criticisms of a single-chamber legislature with no power to offset it was that it would be apt to grow ambitious and make itself perpetual, as did England's Long Parliament and the assembly of Holland. In Britain the upper house was, of course, the bastion of the hereditary aristocracy. How to prescribe the distinction between the popular and upper legislative chambers in America, which lacked the traditional socioeconomic orders of English society, was a principal point of contention among the framers of the Constitution. At times, Adams and others entertained the idea of a more restrictive property classification for the upper house. See Bailyn, *The Ideological Origins of the American Revolution*, pp. 272–301.

113. Quoted in ibid., pp. 288–89.

114. See Howe, *The Changing Political Thought of John Adams*, p. 83.

115. *Adams Papers*, vol. IV, p. 90.

116. Ibid., p. 79.

117. Ibid., p. 80. The opening lines of the sonnet "On the Same" ("I did prompt the age"), which Adams altered slightly in putting down from memory. The sonnet appears to have been a favorite of Adams's. According to a story reported by Catherine Drinker Bowen, he quoted the same lines extempore at a town meeting at Faneuil Hall in 1774 at the time of the Boston Port Bill, when a motion for voluntary contributions to feed Boston's poor drew whistles and catcalls from the assembled merchants and citizens. In *John Adams and the American Revolution* (Boston: Little, Brown, 1950), pp. 443–44, 632. In the original sonnet, written after *Tetrachordon* and *Colasterion* were published, Milton's targets included both the orthodox Presbyterians who had denounced his divorce tracts and the sectaries who had rallied around him, thinking that he advocated divorce at pleasure. "License they mean when they cry liberty," was Milton's answer to the latter.

118. In *The Ready and Easy Way*, Milton wrote that a free commonwealth was the form of government judged by the wisest men of all ages to be "the manliest, the equallest, the justest government, the most agreeable to all due liberty and proportioned equality, both human, civil, and Christian"; and as part of his eleventh-hour effort to forestall the return of monarchy, he advanced a plan for erecting throughout the nation a republican infrastructure of local assemblies and academies for "communicating the natural heat of government and culture more distributively to all extreme parts which now lie numb and neglected" (Hughes, pp. 884, 897).

119. *Adams Papers*, vol. IV, p. 86.

120. Ibid., pp. 87, 92.

121. Hughes, p. 755.

122. *Adams Papers*, vol. IV, p. 74.

123. Ibid., pp. 84, 91. The editor infers that Adams was recommending public support for education.

124. *Defence of the Constitutions*, vol. I, p. 131.

Chapter 7

1. Howard, "Early American Copies of Milton," p. 179.

2. For example, Robert Coram, who endorsed Webster's proposals, believed the two preconditions for successful republican government were an equitable distribution of land and a system of education that gave every citizen an opportunity to rise to a position of public trust. Coram advocated a general tax to fund the schools on the grounds that every citizen would suffer if the education of youth were not publicly supported (*Plan for the General Establishment of Schools Throughout the United States*, 1791). James Sullivan, who had collaborated with John Adams to win support for the Massachusetts state constitution, attributed the popular insurrections after the American Revolution to the public's unreadiness for republican government, and he proposed a national system of schools as a means of rectifying the situation (*Observations upon the Government of the United States of America*, 1791). These and others of the multitude of plans for national educational systems advanced in the 1790s are reviewed in Allen Oscar Hansen's *Liberalism and American Education* (New York: Macmillan, 1926). Hansen examines the plans from a Deweyite perspective, treating them as an outgrowth of the eighteenth-century liberal movement that originated in France.

3. For example, William Wells, whose "Remarks on Classical Learning" won him a Bowdoin Prize. Wells attacked both the modern contempt for the classics and the view according to which "the antients were supposed to have reached the summit of excellence and to have left nothing to future genius, but to admire and imitate them." In *The Literary Miscellany* I (1805): pp. 12–15.

4. *Lectures on Rhetoric and Oratory*, 2 vols. (New York: Russell & Russell, 1962; reproduced from the 1810 ed.).

5. Quoted in John C. Miller, *The Federalist Era, 1789–1801* (New York: Harper & Row, 1963), p. 175. The occasion was the impassioned appeal by Fisher Ames to his fellow representatives in April 1796 to implement the controversial Jay's Treaty, which was intended to regularize diplomatic and trade relations with Britain and to support the Washington administration's neutrality policy. The speech is generally acknowledged as a pinnacle in the career of the "hyper-Federalist" Massachusetts congressman, even by historians more sympathetic to the Jeffersonian Republican tendency. Weak with illness, Ames took the floor of the House and argued that by withholding appropriations for Jay's Treaty, the Republicans were putting partisan politics ahead of the great benefits that would accrue from the treaty to the nation as a whole. Adams remarked that the speech moved everyone present, "except some of the jackasses who had occasioned the necessity of the oratory" (ibid.). Within two days the bill was passed by a narrow margin.

6. *Remarks on the Jacobiniad: Revised and Corrected by the Author; and embellished with Carricatures*, 2 pts. (Boston: E. W. Weld and W. Greenough, 1795–98). Gardiner's satire is discussed further below.

7. Sensabaugh, *Milton in Early America*, p. 263.

8. Gordon Wood, with his "end of classical politics" thesis, maintains that a new conception of interest-group politics, in which the notion of parties and special interests gained legitimacy, emerged during the period when the federal Constitution was written. However, Wood's dating of the shift and his view of it as final and all-pervasive have been convincingly challenged by at least one historian, Daniel Walker Howe. In *The Political Culture of the American Whigs* (Chicago: University of Chicago Press, 1979) Howe shows that the classical-republican (or "country-party") frame of reference was still the norm for the nineteenth-century Whig Party (see pp. 79–81). For example, Whig leaders such as John Quincy Adams and Abraham Lincoln consciously drew on a continuous republican tradition when they denounced a "conspiracy" by slave-holding interests to subvert the national good.

9. *The Writings of John Quincy Adams*, ed. Worthington Chauncey Ford (New York: Greenwood Press, 1968; orig. pub. Macmillan, 1913–17), vol. I, pp. 491–92.

10. Alexander Hamilton et al., *The Federalist Papers*, number 10 (New York: New American Library, 1961), p. 78.

11. The term "republican federalist," as distinguished from "tory federalist," is borrowed from Levi Lincoln, an important figure in Massachusetts politics in the first decades of the nineteenth century. Lincoln's understanding of the central role of the Commonwealth-Whig tendency in the establishment of the American Republic is discussed below.

12. Edward Handler, *America and Europe in the Political Thought of John Adams* (Cambridge: Harvard University Press, 1964), pp. 58, 12.

13. Noah Webster, "On the Education of Youth in America," in *A Collection of Essays and Fugitiv Writings on Moral, Historical, Political and Literary Subjects* (Boston: I. Thomas and E. T. Andrews, 1790), pp. 2–3.

14. Quoted in Miller, *The Federalist Era*, p. 126.

15. Ibid., p. 127. Jefferson, although he deplored the excesses of the Jacobin regime, remained confident that the revolution was salutary and that it would culminate in the triumph of liberty and order.

16. Quoted in ibid., p. 126.

17. Quoted in Howe, *The Changing Political Thought of John Adams*, p. 172.

18. Quoted in Fliegelman, *Prodigals and Pilgrims*, p. 237.

19. *The Writings of John Quincy Adams*, vol. I, p. 403.

20. Ibid., July 27, 1795, pp. 388–89.

21. Ibid., pp. 65–110. The letters, written in response to Paine's *Rights of Man*, were first published in the *Columbian Centinel*.

22. Ibid., p. 108.

23. Ibid., p. 71.

24. Ibid., pp. 82–83.

25. Ibid., p. 81.

26. Ibid., p. 70. See chapter 6 in this book. Moderates such as John and John Quincy Adams and their British predecessors believed that the contractual model of popular consent applied at the moment when a new government was instituted but that the institutions of society would then evolve organically. This view was a kind of fusion of social contract theory and historic conservatism. See Howe, "The Whig Interpretation of History," chap. 4 in *The Political Culture of the American Whigs*.

27. *The Writings of John Quincy Adams*, vol. I, p. 71.

28. Ibid., p. 109.

29. Ibid., pp. 93–107.

30. Ibid., p. 107.

31. *Discourses on Davila*, in *The Works of John Adams*, vol. VI, p. 279.

32. July 16, 1814. Quoted in Howe, *The Changing Political Thought of John Adams*, pp. 39–40.

33. Miller, *The Federalist Era*, pp. 130–31.

34. In 1796 in his famous letter to the Italian liberal Philip Mazzei. Quoted in Charles Warren, *Jacobin and Junto: or Early American Politics as Viewed in the Diary of Dr. Nathaniel Ames, 1758–1822* (New York: Benjamin Blom, 1968; orig. pub. 1931), p. 48.

35. Quoted in Miller, *The Federalist Era*, p. 139.

36. Ibid.

37. John Adams to William Cunningham, Jr., Oct. 13, 1808. *Cunningham Correspondence*, pp. 35–37. Quoted in *The Writings of John Quincy Adams*, vol. I, p. 148 n.

38. *The Writings of John Quincy Adams*, vol. I, pp. 148–76. The letters appeared in the *Columbian Centinel* beginning November 30, 1793.

39. Ibid., p. 155.

40. Ibid.

41. Miller, *The Federalist Era*, p. 160.

42. Nov. 29, 1793. Quoted in Warren, *Jacobin and Junto*, p. 54.

43. Quoted in Warren, *Jacobin and Junto*, p. 52.

44. April 25, 1795. *The Writings of John Quincy Adams*, vol. I, p. 333.

45. *Democracy: An Epic Poem* (New York: N.p., 1794), p. 5. Subsequent page references are given in the text.

46. Marginalia in the American Antiquarian Society copy of *Democracy* identify the mighty M——k as "White Matlack one of the founders of the Democratic Society in New York, and one of its most zealous & active members." Pomposo and the "younger leader," who appear below, are identified, respectively, as James Jarvais, who coined copper for Congress and was the butt of many satires, and Peter R. Livingston, younger brother of the more famous Gov. William Livingston of New Jersey.

47. Compare Satan's boast that he and the other angels were self-created.

48. Quoted in Miller, *The Federalist Era*, p. 161.

49. By Dr. Nathaniel Ames, the brother and bitter anti-Federalist opponent of Fisher Ames. Warren, *Jacobin and Junto*, p. 12.

50. *The Writings of John Quincy Adams*, vol. I, pp. 409–10.

51. Stephen G. Kurtz, *The Presidency of John Adams: The Collapse of Federalism, 1795–1800* (Philadelphia: University of Pennsylvania Press, 1957), pp. 35–36.

52. *The Writings of John Quincy Adams*, vol. I, p. 491.

53. Ibid., pp. 483–84, 491–92.

54. *Dictionary of American Biography* (New York: Charles Scribner's Sons, 1943), vol. IV, p. 137–38; *The Federalist Literary Mind: Selections from the "Monthly Anthology and Boston Review," 1803–1811, Including Documents Relating to the Boston Athenaeum*, ed. Lewis P. Simpson (Baton Rouge: Louisiana State University Press, 1962), pp. 24–26.

55. *Monthly Anthology and Boston Review* VI (Feb. 1809): pp. 87–88. Quoted in Simpson, *The Federalist Literary Mind*, p. 87.

56. Simpson, in his study of the Anthologists and their *Monthly Anthology and Boston Review*, describes Gardiner thus: "Narrow in his learning, believing High Church doctrine, the Federalist creed according to Fisher Ames, and a decadent neoclassic authority to be civilization's unalterable values, he was redeemed from his deadly absolutism by his sociability. But this could not entirely obscure his lack of identity with those Anthologists who were disturbed by strong, if ill-defined, aspirations toward the future" (*The Federalist Literary Mind*, p. 25). Simpson writes that Gardiner's increasing differences with more liberal Anthologists, in both literary and political matters, led him to withdraw from the Society.

57. Satan raises his standard in the north of Heaven, and the Green Dragon Tavern was, in fact, located in Boston's North End: a happy coincidence for the satirist.

58. Gardiner drew broad caricatures of Boston's leading Jacobins, including Benjamin Austin, Jr., their principal writer, known as "Honestus"; Boston justice of the peace Thomas Crafts ("Great Justice Crafts, great Faction's sapient son, / Who holds a sense of gill, of zeal a ton"); and John Vinal, the town writing master, "Who everywhere is seen but in his school, / And passes current for the City fool." In Warren, *Jacobin and Junto*, p. 55. Gardiner's "Prince" may be a reference to the black Bostonian Prince Hall, who founded the African Grand Lodge of Masons in Massachusetts in 1787 when he was denied admission to the white lodge. Subsequent page references to *Remarks on the Jacobiniad*, parts I and II, are given in the text.

59. *Jacobin and Junto*, p. 54.

60. *Discourses on Davila*, pp. 270, 286.

61. In *Discourses on Davila* John Adams wrote that Pennsylvania had chosen a unicameral system in 1776 out of the same concern that had prompted the French liberals to establish the National Assembly—an apprehension that if aristocratic interests (in the case of Pennsylvania, "Proprietary and Quaker interests") were given representation in an upper house, they would prevail over the entire government. Adams felt that this was a dangerous misconception, that the existence of an upper house would in reality contain the influence of the aristocracy and that the two chambers, popular and aristocratic, would check each other's influence (p. 274).

62. Richard Alsop, *The Political Green-House, for the Year 1798, Addressed to the Readers of the Connecticut Courant* (Hartford: Hudson & Goodwin, 1799), p. 6; *Aristocracy: An Epic Poem*, 2 vols. (Philadelphia: N.p., 1795).

63. Quoted in Handler, *America and Europe in the Political Thought of John Adams*, p. 68.

64. Quoted in Gilbert Chinard, *Honest John Adams* (Gloucester, Mass.: Peter Smith, 1976), p. 213.

65. *Discourses on Davila*, p. 289 n.

66. Levi Lincoln, *Letters to the People, By a Farmer* (Salem: William Carlton, 1802), p. 86.

67. Ibid., p. 89.

68. Ibid.

69. Ibid., p. 93.

Epilogue

1. The notion of a consensus based on the colonies' English political and religious heritage, together with the implicit assumption throughout my study that New England played a leading role in the movement for independence, will be considered outmoded by some, I am aware, who look to the contributions to American culture of other geographical regions and other national and ethnic heritages and who emphasize difference and conflict in our early history rather than common purpose. The fact remains, however, that those Americans who drafted the Declaration of Independence and the Constitution were strongly influenced by the Commonwealth tradition to which Milton was a principal contributor.

2. *Milton and the Puritan Dilemma*, p. xiv.

3. James Ceaser analyzes Tocqueville's insights into these two rival schools and argues that Tocqueville conceived of his "new political science" as an alternative ("Alexis de Tocqueville on Political Science, Political Culture, and the Role of the Intellectual," *American Political Science Review* 79 [Sept. 1985], pp. 656–72). The following brief discussion of Tocqueville's ideas is greatly indebted to Ceaser's article.

4. Although some historians have portrayed John Adams as the "American Burke," Edward Handler notes that Adams objected violently to Burke's description of the people as a "swinish multitude" and that he "deviated on major points from both Burke and Paine." Handler also points out that while Adams defended the constitutions of the states as being rooted in "American prejudice," a traditionalist-sounding argument, he added that these prejudices were in accord with reason. "The Whig tradition of liberalism to which Adams belonged represented both defense against radical democracy and challenge to traditionalism and the ramparts of privilege." In *America and Europe in the Political Thought of John Adams*, pp. 158, 159, 48, 191. Adams hated the fanaticism of the French Revolution but was no less alarmed by the restoration of the Bourbons, and in an 1815 letter to Jefferson he spoke of religious revivalism, Mesmerism, the restoration of the Society of Jesus in 1814,

and other symptoms of reaction as a step backward toward "Cruelty Perfidy Despotism Death" Cited in Howe, *The Changing Political Thought of John Adams*, p. 227.

5. "Alexis de Tocqueville on Political Science," p. 660.

6. John Adams also anticipates Tocqueville on this point in "A Dissertation on the Canon and the Feudal Law" and in *Thoughts on Government*.

7. *Areopagitica*, Hughes, p. 733.

8. Cited by Margaret Fuller, *Papers on Literature and Art* (New York: Wiley and Putnam, 1846). Fuller's reference to this statement appears as an epigraph to Keith W. F. Stavely's *Puritan Legacies*.

9. "Notes on Elizabethan Classicists," in *Literary Essays of Ezra Pound*, ed. T. S. Eliot (New York: New Directions, 1968; orig. pub. in *The Egoist* [Sept. 1917]), p. 238.

Bibliography

Primary Sources

Adams, John. *A Defence of the Constitutions of Government of the United States of America, against the Attack of M. Turgot in His Letter to Dr. Price, Dated the Twenty-second Day of March, 1778.* 3 vols. London: J. Stockdale, 1794.

———. *Diary and Autobiography of John Adams.* Edited by L. H. Butterfield et al. 4 vols. Cambridge: Harvard University Press, 1961.

———. *The Papers of John Adams.* Edited by Robert J. Taylor et al. 4 vols. Cambridge: Harvard University Press, 1977–79.

———. *The Works of John Adams.* Edited by Charles Francis Adams. 10 vols. Boston: Little, Brown, 1851–66.

Adams, John Quincy. *Lectures on Rhetoric and Oratory.* 2 vols. New York: Russell & Russell, 1962. (Reproduced from the 1810 edition.)

———. *The Writings of John Quincy Adams.* Edited by Worthington Chauncey Ford. 7 vols. New York: Greenwood Press, 1968. (Originally published by Macmillan, 1913–17).

Adams, Samuel. *Writings of Samuel Adams.* Edited by Harry Alonzo Cushing. 4 vols. New York: Octagon Press, 1968.

Adams Family Correspondence. Edited by L. H. Butterfield et al. 4 vols. Cambridge: Harvard University Press, 1963–73.

[Alsop, Richard?] *Aristocracy: An Epic Poem.* 2 vols. Philadelphia: N.p., 1795.

Alsop, Richard. *The Political Green-House, for the Year 1798, Addressed to the Readers of the Connecticut Courant.* Hartford: Hudson & Goodwin, 1799.

Augustine. *The Confessions.* Translated by William Watts (1631). 2 vols. Cambridge: Harvard University Press, 1960.

Boston Committee of Correspondence. *Gentlemen, At a Time when Degenerate Britons. . . .* Boston, 1777.

———. *Gentlemen, the Evils which we have long Foreseen are now Come. . . .* Boston, 1774.

Boston Selectmen. *Notification. The Freeholders . . . Tea. . . .* Boston, 1773.

Boston Town Clerk. *Gentlemen, We the Freeholders. . . .* Boston, 1772.

Dymock, Cressy. *An Invention of Engines of Motion Lately Brought to perfection. . . .* London: R. Woodnoth, 1651.

Freneau, Philip. *The Poems of Philip Freneau: Poet of the American Revolution.* Edited by Fred Lewis Pattee. 2 vols. Princeton: The University Library, 1902.

Gardiner, John S. J. *Remarks on the Jacobiniad: Revised and Corrected by the Author; and embellished with Carricatures.* 2 pts. Boston: E. W. Weld and W. Greenough, 1795–98.

Hamilton, Alexander, et al. *The Federalist Papers.* New York: New American Library, 1961.

Harrington, James. *The Oceana and Other Works; with an Account of His Life by John Toland.* Aalen, Germany: Scientia Verlag, 1963. (Reprint of the 1771 London edition.)

———. *The Political Works of James Harrington.* Edited by J. G. A. Pocock. Cambridge: Cambridge University Press, 1977.

Hartlib, Samuel. *An Essay upon Master W. Potters Designe: Concerning a Bank of Lands to be erected throughout this common-wealth.* London: Richard Wodenothe, 1653.

Jefferson, Thomas. *The Commonplace Book of Thomas Jefferson.* Edited by Gilbert Chinard. Baltimore: Johns Hopkins University Press, 1926.

———. *The Literary Bible of Thomas Jefferson.* Edited by Gilbert Chinard. New York: Greenwood Press, 1969. (Originally published 1928.)

Keteltas, Abraham. *God Arising and Pleading.* Newburyport, Mass., 1777.

Knollenberg, Bernhard, ed. "Thomas Hollis and Jonathan Mayhew: Their Correspondence, 1759–1766." Massachusetts Historical Society *Proceedings* 69 (Oct. 1947–May 1950): pp. 102–93.

Lincoln, Levi. *Letters to the People, By a Farmer.* Salem: William Carlton, 1802.

Livingston, Brockholst. *Democracy: An Epic Poem.* New York: N.p., 1794.

Marlowe, Christopher. *The Tragical History of Doctor Faustus.* In *The Complete Plays,* edited by J. B. Steane. Harmondsworth, England: Penguin, 1969.

Mather, Cotton. *Magnalia Christi Americana.* Bks. I and II. Edited by Kenneth B. Murdock. Cambridge: Harvard University Press, 1977.

Milton, John. *John Milton: Complete Poems and Major Prose.* Edited by Merritt Y. Hughes. Indianapolis: Odyssey Press, 1957.

———. *Complete Prose Works of John Milton.* Edited by Don M. Wolfe et al. 8 vols. New Haven: Yale University Press, 1953–82.

———. *Milton's Paradise Lost: a new edition with notes of various authors by Thomas Newton.* London: Tonson and Draper, 1749.

———. *An Old Looking-Glass for the Laity and Clergy, of All Denominations, Who Either Give or Receive Money Under Pretence of the Gospel. . . .* New Haven: Thomas and Samuel Green, 1774.

———. *The Works of John Milton.* Edited by Frank Allen Patterson et al. 18 vols. New York: Columbia University Press, 1931–38.

Molesworth, Robert. *The Principles of a Real Whig; Contained in a Preface to the Famous Hotoman's Franco-Gallia.* London: J. Williams, 1775.

———. *Some Considerations for the Promoting of Agriculture and Employing the Poor.* Dublin: George Grierson, 1723.

Odell, Jonathan. *The American Times, a satire in three parts. In which are delineated the Characters of the Leaders of the American Rebellion.* In *Cow-chace,* edited by John André. New York: Rivington, 1780.

Oliver, Peter. *Peter Oliver's Origin & Progress of the American Rebellion.* Edited by Douglass Adair and John A. Schutz. Stanford: Stanford University Press, 1961. (Originally published 1781.)

Quincy, Josiah, Jr. *Observations on the Act of Parliament, commonly called the Boston Port-Bill.* . . . Philadelphia: John Sparhawk, 1774.

Seabury, Samuel. *A View of the Controversy between Great Britain and her Colonies. . . .* New York: James Rivington, 1774.

A Short Narrative of the Horrid Massacre in Boston. Boston: Edes & Gill and Fleets, 1770.

Simpson, Lewis P., ed. *The Federalist Literary Mind: Selections from the "Monthly Anthology and Boston Review," 1803–1811, Including Documents Relating to the Boston Athenaeum.* Baton Rouge: Louisiana State University Press, 1962.

Tea, Destroyed by Indians. Ye Glorious Sons of Freedom. . . . Boston, 1773.

The Tea-Ship being Arrived. . . . Philadelphia, 1773.

Thorpe, James, ed. *Milton Criticism: Selections from Four Centuries.* New York: Collier, 1969.

Tocqueville, Alexis de. *Democracy in America.* 2 vols. New York: Vintage, 1945. (Originally published 1835 and 1840.)

Toland, John. *The Life of John Milton; . . . with Amyntor; or a Defence of Milton's Life.* London: Millar, 1761. (Originally published 1699.)

Trumbull, John. *The Satiric Poems of John Trumbull: The Progress of Dulness and M'Fingal.* Edited by Edwin T. Bowden. Austin: University of Texas Press, 1962.

Vondel, Joost van den. *Vondel's "Lucifer."* Translated by Leonard Charles Van Noppen. Greensboro, N.C., 1917.

Webster, Noah. "On the Education of Youth in America." In *A Collection of Essays and Fugitiv Writings on Moral, Historical, Political and Literary Subjects.* Boston: I. Thomas and E. T. Andrews, 1790.

Wells, William. "Remarks on Classical Learning," *The Literary Miscellany* I (1805): pp. 12–15.

Weston, Richard. *The Compleat Husband-man; or, a discourse of the whole Art of Husbandry both Forraign and Domestick.* 2nd ed. London: Edward Brewster, 1659.

———. *A Discours of Husbandrie used in Brabant and Flanders.* . . . London: William Du-Gard, 1650.

Worthington, John. *The Diary and Correspondence of Dr. John Worthington.* Vol. I. Edited by James Crossley. Manchester: Chetham Society, 1847.

Secondary Sources

Akers, Charles W. *Called unto Liberty: A Life of Jonathan Mayhew, 1720–1766.* Cambridge: Harvard University Press, 1964.

Alden, John Richard. *The American Revolution, 1775–1783.* New York: Harper & Row, 1954.

Appleby, Joyce Oldham. *Economic Thought and Ideology in Seventeenth-Century England.* Princeton: Princeton University Press, 1978.

Ashley, Maurice. *Financial and Commercial Policy under the Cromwellian Protectorate.* London: Oxford University Press, 1934.

Ashton, Robert. *The English Civil War: Conservatism and Revolution, 1603–1649.* New York: Norton, 1978.

Bailyn, Bernard. *The Ideological Origins of the American Revolution.* Cambridge: Harvard University Press, 1967.

———. *The Origins of American Politics.* New York: Vintage, 1967.

———. "Religion and Revolution: Three Biographical Studies." *Perspectives in American History* IV (1970): 85–169.

Bailyn, Bernard, ed. *Pamphlets of the American Revolution, 1750–1765.* Vol. I. Cambridge: Harvard University Press, 1965.

Barker, Arthur. *Milton and the Puritan Dilemma.* Toronto: University of Toronto Press, 1942.

Belsey, Catherine. *John Milton: Language, Gender, Power.* Oxford: Basil Blackwell, 1988.

———. *The Subject of Tragedy: Identity and Difference in Renaissance Drama.* London: Methuen, 1985.

Bennet, Joan S. *Reviving Liberty: Radical Christian Humanism in Milton's Great Poems.* Cambridge: Harvard University Press, 1989.

Bercovitch, Sacvan. *The American Jeremiad.* Madison: University of Wisconsin Press, 1978.

———. *The Puritan Origins of the American Self.* New Haven: Yale University Press, 1975.

Bercovitch, Sacvan, ed. *Typology and Early American Literature.* Amherst: University of Massachusetts Press, 1972.

Bloom, Allan. *The Closing of the American Mind.* New York: Simon & Schuster, 1987.

Bonomi, Patricia U. *Under the Cope of Heaven: Religion, Society, and Politics in Colonial America.* New York: Oxford University Press, 1986.

Bowen, Catherine Drinker. *John Adams and the American Revolution.* Boston: Little, Brown, 1950.

Brenner, Robert. "The Civil War Politics of London's Merchant Community." *Past and Present* 58 (1973): pp. 53–107.

Brinkley, Roberta Florence. *Arthurian Legend in the Seventeenth Century.* Baltimore: Johns Hopkins University Press, 1932.

Ceaser, James. "Alexis de Tocqueville on Political Science, Political Culture, and the Role of the Intellectual." *American Political Science Review* 79 (Sept. 1985): pp. 656–72.

Chinard, Gilbert. *Honest John Adams.* Gloucester, Mass.: Peter Smith, 1976.

Crews, Frederick. *Skeptical Engagements.* New York: Oxford University Press, 1986.

———. "Whose American Renaissance?" *New York Review of Books*, Oct. 27, 1988, pp. 68–81.

Davies, Stevie. *Images of Kingship in "Paradise Lost": Milton's Politics and Christian Liberty.* Columbia: University of Missouri Press, 1983.

Delbanco, Andrew. *The Puritan Ordeal.* Cambridge: Harvard University Press, 1989.

Dictionary of American Biography. Vol. IV. New York: Charles Scribner's Sons, 1943.

Dircks, Henry. *A Biographical Memoir of Samuel Hartlib, Milton's Particular Friend.* London: J. R. Smith, 1865.

DiSalvo, Jackie. *War of Titans: Blake's Critique of Milton and the Politics of Religion.* Pittsburgh: University of Pittsburgh Press, 1983.

Dollimore, Jonathan. *Radical Tragedy: Religion, Ideology and Power in the Drama of Shakespeare and His Contemporaries.* Chicago: University of Chicago Press, 1984.

Edmundson, George. *Milton and Vondel: A Curiosity of Literature.* London: Trubner, 1885.

Evans, J. M. *"Paradise Lost" and the Genesis Tradition.* Oxford: Clarendon Press, 1968.

Fallon, Robert. *Captain or Colonel: The Soldier in Milton's Life and Art.* Columbia: University of Missouri Press, 1984.

Fallon, Stephen M. " 'To Act or Not': Milton's Conception of Divine Freedom." *Journal of the History of Ideas* 49 (1988): 425–49.

Fink, Zera. *The Classical Republicans: An Essay in the Recovery of a Pattern of Thought in Seventeenth-Century England.* 2d ed. Evanston: Northwestern University Press, 1962. (Originally published 1945.)

Fish, Stanley. *Is There a Text in This Class?: The Authority of Interpretive Communities.* Cambridge: Harvard University Press, 1980.

———. *Surprised by Sin: The Reader in "Paradise Lost."* Berkeley: University of California Press, 1971.

Fliegelman, Jay. *Prodigals and Pilgrims: The American Revolution against Patriarchal Authority, 1750–1800.* Cambridge: Cambridge University Press, 1982.

Gilbert, Sandra. "Patriarchal Poetry and Women Readers: Reflections on Milton's Bogey." *PMLA* 93 (1978): 368–82.

Gordon, Colin. "Crafting a Usable Past: Consensus, Ideology, and the Historians of the American Revolution." *William and Mary Quarterly* XLVI (Oct. 1989): pp. 671–95.

Gosse, Edmund. "Milton and Vondel." *Studies in the Literature of Northern Europe*. London: K. Paul, Trench & Co., 1879.

Greaves, Richard L. *The Puritan Revolution and Educational Thought: Background to Reform*. New Brunswick: Rutgers University Press, 1969.

Greenblatt, Stephen. *Renaissance Self-Fashioning: From More to Shakespeare*. Chicago: University of Chicago Press, 1980.

Hall, David D. *World of Wonders, Days of Judgment: Popular Belief in Early New England*. New York: Knopf, 1989.

Handler, Edward. *America and Europe in the Political Thought of John Adams*. Cambridge: Harvard University Press, 1964.

Hansen, Allen Oscar. *Liberalism and American Education*. New York: Macmillan, 1926.

Harding, D. P. *The Club of Hercules: Studies in the Classical Background of Paradise Lost*. Urbana: University of Illinois Press, 1962.

Hatch, Nathan O. *The Sacred Cause of Liberty: Republican Thought and the Millennium in Revolutionary New England*. New Haven: Yale University Press, 1977.

Heimert, Alan. *Religion and the American Mind: From the Great Awakening to the Revolution*. Cambridge: Harvard University Press, 1966.

Hill, Christopher. *The Century of Revolution, 1603–1714*. New York: Norton, 1961.

———. *Intellectual Origins of the English Revolution*. Oxford: Oxford University Press, 1965.

———. *Milton and the English Revolution*. London: Faber and Faber, 1977.

———. *Reformation to Industrial Revolution*. Harmondsworth, England: Penguin, 1969.

Hirsh, E. D., Jr. *Validity in Interpretation*. New Haven: Yale University Press, 1967.

Howard, Leon. "Early American Copies of Milton." *Huntington Library Bulletin* (April 1935): pp. 169–79.

Howe, Daniel Walker. *The Political Culture of the American Whigs*. Chicago: University of Chicago Press, 1979.

Howe, John R., Jr. *The Changing Political Thought of John Adams*. Princeton: Princeton University Press, 1966.

Johnson, E. A. J. *American Economic Thought in the Seventeenth Century*. New York: Russell & Russell, 1961.

Jones, Rufus. *Mysticism and Democracy in the English Commonwealth*. Cambridge: Harvard University Press, 1939.

Kelley, Maurice. *This Great Argument: A Study of Milton's "De Doctrina Christiana" as a Gloss upon "Paradise Lost."* London: Oxford University Press, 1941.

Kendrick, Christopher. *Milton: A Study in Ideology and Form*. New York: Methuen, 1986.

Kirkconnell, Watson. *The Celestial Cycle: The Theme of Paradise Lost in World Literature with Translations of the Major Analogues*. Toronto: University of Toronto Press, 1952.

Knight, G. Wilson. *Chariot of Wrath: The Message of John Milton to Democracy at War*. London: Faber and Faber, 1942.

Kramnick, Isaac. "The 'Great National Discussion': The Discourse of Politics in 1787." *William and Mary Quarterly* XLV (Jan. 1988): pp. 3–32.

Kurtz, Stephen G. *The Presidency of John Adams: The Collapse of Federalism, 1795–1800*. Philadelphia: University of Pennsylvania Press, 1957.

Leavis, F. R. *The Common Pursuit*. New York: George W. Stewart, 1952.

Lentricchia, Frank. *After the New Criticism*. Chicago: University of Chicago Press, 1980.

Macpherson, C. B. *The Political Theory of Possessive Individualism: Hobbes to Locke*. Oxford: Oxford University Press, 1962.

Maier, Pauline. *From Resistance to Revolution: Colonial Radicals and the Development of American Opposition to Britain, 1765–1776*. New York: Vintage, 1974.

Miller, John C. *The Federalist Era, 1789–1801*. New York: Harper & Row, 1963.

——. *Sam Adams: Pioneer in Propaganda*. Stanford: Stanford University Press, 1974. (Originally published 1936.)

Milner, Andrew. *John Milton and the English Revolution: A Study in the Sociology of Literature*. London: Macmillan, 1981.

Morgan, Edmund. *The Puritan Dilemma: The Story of John Winthrop*. Boston: Little, Brown, 1958.

Nichols, Fred J. "Vondel's 'Lucifer' and 'Adam in Ballingschap.'" *Review of National Literatures* 8 (1977): pp. 40–69.

Nyquist, Mary, and Margaret W. Ferguson, eds. *Re-membering Milton: Essays on the Texts and Traditions*. New York: Methuen, 1988.

Olson, Mancur. *The Rise and Decline of Nations*. New Haven: Yale University Press, 1982.

Persons, Stow. *American Minds: A History of Ideas*. New York: Henry Holt, 1958.

Pocock, J. G. A. *The Machiavellian Moment: Florentine Political Thought and the Atlantic Republican Tradition*. Princeton: Princeton University Press, 1975.

Radzinowicz, Mary Ann. "The Politics of *Paradise Lost.*" In *Politics of Discourse: The Literature and History of Seventeenth-Century England*, edited by Kevin Sharpe and Steven N. Zwicker. Berkeley: University of California Press, 1987.

Raleigh, Walter. *Milton*. London: Edward Arnold, 1900.

Robbins, Caroline. *The Eighteenth-Century Commonwealthman*. Cambridge: Harvard University Press, 1961.

Rogers, John. "Milton and the Mysterious Terms of History." *ELH* 57 (Summer 1990): pp. 281–305.

Schultz, Howard. *Milton and Forbidden Knowledge*. New York: Modern Languages Association, 1955.

Sensabaugh, George. *Milton in Early America*. Princeton: Princeton University Press, 1964.

——. *That Grand Whig, Milton*. Stanford: Stanford University Press, 1952.

Shawcross, John T. "A Survey of Milton's Prose Works." In *Achievements of the Left Hand*, edited by Michael Lieb and John T. Shawcross. Amherst: University of Massachusetts Press, 1974.

Silverman, Kenneth. *A Cultural History of the American Revolution: Painting, Music, Literature, and the Theatre in the Colonies and the United States from the Treaty of Paris to the Inauguration of George Washington, 1763–1789*. New York: T. Y. Crowell, 1976.

Skinner, Quentin. "Milton, Satan, and Subversion." *New York Review of Books*, March 23, 1978, pp. 6–9.

Stavely, Keith W. F. *Puritan Legacies: "Paradise Lost" and the New England Tradition, 1630–1890*. Ithaca: Cornell University Press, 1987.

Stone, Lawrence. *The Causes of the English Revolution, 1529–1642*. New York: Harper & Row, 1972.

Strout, Cushing. *The New Heavens and New Earth: Political Religion in America*. New York: Harper & Row, 1974.

Summers, Joseph. *The Muse's Method: An Introduction to "Paradise Lost."* Cambridge: Harvard University Press, 1962.

Tayler, Edward W. "Milton's Grim Laughter and Second Choices." In *Poetry and Epistemology: Turning Points in the History of Poetic Knowledge*, edited by Ronald Hagenbüchle and Laura Skandera. Regensburg, Germany: Verlag Friedrich Pustet, 1986.

——. *Milton's Poetry: Its Development in Time*. Pittsburgh: Duquesne University Press, 1979.

Trevor-Roper, H. R. "Three Foreigners and the Philosophy of the English Revolution." In *The Crisis of the Seventeenth Century: Religion, the Reformation, and Social Change*. New York: Harper & Row, 1966.

Turnbull, G. H. *Hartlib, Dury and Comenius: Gleanings from Hartlib's Papers*. Liverpool: University Press of Liverpool, 1947.

Tuveson, Ernest L. *Redeemer Nation: The Idea of America's Millennial Role*. Chicago: University of Chicago Press, 1968.

Warren, Charles. *Jacobin and Junto: or Early American Politics as Viewed in the Diary of Dr. Nathaniel Ames, 1758–1822*. New York: Benjamin Blom, 1968. (Originally published 1931.)

Webber, Joan. "The Politics of Poetry: Feminism and *Paradise Lost*." *Milton Studies* 14 (1980): pp. 3–24.

Webster, Charles. *The Great Instauration: Science, Medicine and Reform, 1626–1660*. London: Duckworth, 1975.

Williams, E. I. F. *Horace Mann, Educational Statesman*. New York: Macmillan, 1937.

Wittreich, Joseph. *Feminist Milton*. Ithaca: Cornell University Press, 1987.

Wood, Gordon. *The Creation of the American Republic, 1776–1787*. New York and London: Norton, 1972.

———. Review of *Milton in Early America*, by George Sensabaugh. *New England Quarterly* 37 (1964): pp. 543–46.

Woolrych, Austin. "Political Theory and Political Practice." In *The Age of Milton: Backgrounds to Seventeenth-Century Literature*, edited by C. A. Patrides and R. B. Waddington. Manchester: Manchester University Press, 1980.

Worden, Blair. "Milton among the Radicals." *Times Literary Supplement*, Dec. 2, 1977, pp. 1394–95.

Index

Adams, John, 64; administration of, 207–12; American aristocracy and, 207–8, 210, 211; astronomical speculations of, 130–31; authorship of Publicola letters and, 188, 189–90; Boston Tea Party and, 172–73; Commonwealth tradition and, 97; definition of republicanism, 10; doctrine of equality and, 204; education and, 49, 174; factions and, 184–85, 207–8, 210, 211; faculty psychology and, 103; French Revolution and, 186–87, 190; ideal of government, 63; influence of *Paradise Lost* on, 127–28, 129–31; intellectual middle ground and, 218; liberty vs. license and, 173–74; Milton's influence on, 108–9, 127–28, 129–31; Milton's views on government and, 176; private vs. public interest and, 152, 153; providential design and, 99; social reform and, 7, 174; Stamp Act and, 137–39, 157; unicameralism and, 108, 189–90, 204, 251n112; use of Milton's imagery, 159–66, 182; use of Milton's texts, 12, 59, 143. Works: *Defence of the Constitutions of Government of the United States*, 105, 107–9, 183, 185, 189–90, 223n2; *Discourses on Davila*, 208, 210, 255n61; "Dissertation on the Canon and the Feudal Law," 101, 125–26, 134–37; "Novanglus letters," 157–58, 159–62, 166, 168–69, 171–72, 248n36; *Thoughts on Government*, 174–79, 212–13

Adams, John Quincy: American neutrality in French-British War and, 192; democratic societies and, 187, 194; factions and, 184, 252n8; Jay's Treaty and, 198–99; Milton's oratorical skill and, 181–82; Publicola letters, 188–90

Adams, Sam, 141–42, 143, 152, 155, 156–57

Adams, Samuel ("Deacon"), 232n34, 249n47

Addison, Joseph, 78

Agricultural reform, 115

Alsop, Richard: *Aristocracy: An Epic Poem*, 207, 208–10; *The Political Green-House, for the Year 1798*, 207, 210–13

Ameliorability. *See* Corruptibility and ameliorability

America, settlement of, 135–36

American episcopacy, 120, 121, 124–25

American Jacobins, 182, 183, 184, 186, 201–4, 254n58

American republicans, 8–9, 11–12, 14, 241n17. *See also* American Whigs; Federalist-Republican conflict

American Revolution: Adams's "Dissertation" and, 137; Boston junto and, 159–62; Commonwealth tradition and, 97, 114–16, 118–27; English Revolution and, 15; influence of *Paradise Lost* and, 9, 151–54, 227n37; intellectual roots of, 3; interpretations of origins of, 159; private interest vs. public good and, 152–54; rhetoric of, 133–34

American Whigs: British policies and, 155–58; Puritan heritage and, 139; satirical writings of, 145–51; struggle against Tories, 139, 141–45

Ames, Fisher, 193, 252n5, 254n56
Ames, Nathaniel, 188
Anti-Miltonism, 220
Antilia (society), 44–45
Appleby, Joyce, 231n22
Apthorp, East, 124, 126
Aristocracy: An Epic Poem (attributed to Alsop), 207, 208–10
"Arminians," 119, 238n67
Arthurian legend, 12, 27–31, 229n18
Augustine, Saint, 63, 88–89, 90, 238n76
Autonomy, and New Historicism, 5–7

Backsliding, 237n44
Bacon, Francis, 37, 39–40
Bailyn, Bernard, 107, 156, 159, 240n2, 241n17
Barker, Arthur, 218
Baron, Richard, 121
Belsey, Catherine, xii, 6–7
Bennett, Joan S., 234n12
Bentley, Richard, 130, 131
Bercovitch, Sacvan, 100, 239n78, 245n48, 245n54
Bernard, Francis, 161, 162
Bicameralism. See Mixed and balanced government
Blake, William, 17, 172, 225n22
Bloom, Allan, 154
Bolingbroke, Henry St. John, 98
Bonomi, Patricia, 101, 120, 240n15, 243n9
Book licensing, 65
Boston junto, 158–62, 169
Boston Tea Party, 153, 163–66, 172–73
Bowen, Catherine Drinker, 251n117
Brinkley, Roberta Florence, 28–29, 229n18
British Constitution: policies in colonies and, 155, 156, 158, 159; vs. French Constitution, 188–89
Burke, Edmund, 144, 255n4

Calvinism, 22–23, 24, 100–101, 238n67, 239n2
Capitalism, 33–50, 40–41, 79, 235n14, 238n67. See also Individualism
Cato's Letters (Trenchard and Gordon), 123
Ceaser, James, 219
Celestial Cycle (Genesis) tradition, 20
Charles I (king of England), 122–23, 158, 168–69, 223n1, 235n26

Chinard, Gilbert, 129
Choice. See Freedom, individual; Liberty
Church of England, 120, 121, 124–25
Citizen participation, 84, 178, 219–20
Civic responsibility, 110–11
Civil War in England, 72, 73–74
Classical models, 61, 76, 78–79, 92, 235n19, 241n23
Classical republicans, 104–5, 225n25
Clergy: balance in government and, 106; in colonial culture, 101; corruptibility and, 48, 74, 135–36, 234n6; 237n44; Milton's anti-episcopal tracts and, 63, 136; Milton's views on reform and, 48. See also Presbyterian party; Religious liberty
Cleveland, John, 166
Coercive Acts, 141—42, 152, 167
Colonial culture: Commonwealth tradition and, 98, 102, 116, 139; consensus in, 216, 241n22; fusion of politics and religion in, 100–101, 125; "liberty books" and, 116, 118–27; Milton's influence on, 146; popularity of Milton in, 3–4, 99–100, 181, 216; secularization of thought and, 136–37; uses of Milton's imagery in, 4, 12, 14–15, 61. See also United States
Comenius, John Amos, 45, 46–47
Commercial republics, early, 4–5, 19, 186
Commonwealth tradition: Adams and, 174–75, 177; American Revolution and, 154, 159, 168–69; colonial culture and, 3, 15, 137–39, 216, 255n1; early American Republic and, 183–84, 189, 210, 212–13; educational reform and, 112–13; liberty and responsibility and, 110–11; Milton's political thought and, 10–11, 13; republication of literature of, 115; vs. Romantic tradition, 110; Whig satire and, 148. See also "Liberty books"; Republican principles
Commonwealth-Whig tradition. See Commonwealth tradition
Conservative readings of Milton, persistence of, 218
Continental Congresses: First, 142, 143, 157, 247n7; Second, 175
Cooke, Elisha, 232n34, 249n47
Coram, Robert, 252n2
Corruptibility: Adams and, 108–9; British clergy and, 48; British government and, 29–30, 107, 188; consequences of, 59–60; ed-

ucation and, 49; tyrants and, 173; as literary motif, 30; of the many, 183; moral decay of nations and, 162–66
Corruptibility and ameliorability, 101, 109–10; American Republic and, 185–86, 190; Fall story and, 19–20
Council in Hell imagery: in *Aristocracy*, 208, 209; Federalist-Republican conflict and, 194–207; Gardiner's *Jacobiniad* and, 183, 197, 200–207; in *Paradise Lost*, 76–81, 147; Tory use of, 170–71; use in early American Republic, 183, 186
Courage, and defense of truth, 70–71
Creation, theology of, 131
Creativity of God, 67, 70

Davies, Stevie, 53, 60, 61, 235n26, 236n31
De Groot, Huig. *See* Grotius, Hugo
De Witt, Johan, 23–24
Death imagery, 182–83, 247n22
Declaration of Rights, 157, 247n7
Delbanco, Andrew, 245n52
Delegation of power, 106–7
Demagoguery: corruptibility of the many and, 183; Satan and, 21–23, 24, 55, 68–69, 76–81
Democracy, as term, 241n17
Democracy, pure: tyranny of the few and, 185–86, 207, 208–10; tyranny of the many and, 183, 184–91, 197; vs. republican government, 87–88, 184–85. *See also* Popular sovereignty
Democratic societies, 182, 187, 192–94, 195–97, 199
DiSalvo, Jackie, ix, 17–18, 53
Dollimore, Jonathan, 6, 38–39
Douglas, William, 156
Du Bartas, Guillaume, 228n5
Dualism, 89
Dutch antecedents to Milton, 4–5, 18, 20–27, 215

Economic forces, and English Revolution, 36–37, 233n46
Education: Adams's views on, 49, 174; American heritage of, 99, 138, 177–78, 246n70; civic responsibility and, 110–11; corruptibility and, 49; Hartlib's reforms and, 44–46; Hollis's "liberty books" project and, 121–22; Milton's views on, 46–50, 111,

112–13; perversions of knowledge and, 91; regeneration and, 96; republican government and, 49, 252n2; state-supported, 48, 49–50. *See also* Knowledge
Eighteenth-century fiction, 110–11
Engels, Friedrich, 15, 36
English republicans. *See* Commonwealth tradition
English Romantics, 217. *See also* Blake
English Whigs, 144–45
Equality, doctrine of, 204, 241n17
Essentialism. *See* Human nature
Established order: hierarchy in Paradise and, 82–83; Milton's view of change and, 67–68; Vondel's *Lucifer* and, 24–26
Evans, J. M., 20, 88–89
Evil: knowledge and, 89; limitation of scope for, 104–5; as recoiling upon itself, 57, 126, 150, 164. *See also* Reason vs. passion
"Experiential criticism," 12

Factions, 192–94, 201–2, 252n8; aristocratic, 207–8, 210, 211; foreign influence and, 207; John Adams and, 184–85, 210; parties as, 184. *See also* Democratic societies
Faculty psychology, 102–3
Fall story: attraction of Milton to, 4–5, 29–31; Augustine and, 88–89; Dutch antecedents to Milton and, 4–5, 18, 20–27, 215; human corruptibility and ameliorability and, 19–20; political parallels to, 84; Romantic view of Milton and, 17–18. *See also* Council in Hell imagery; *Paradise Lost*; Satan imagery
Fallon, Robert, 12, 72, 230n27
Federal Orrery (Federalist paper), 200
Federalist-Republican conflict: Adamses and, 212; controversy over factions and, 184, 192; council of Hell imagery and, 194–207, 194–213; Gardiner's *Jacobiniad* and, 197, 200–207; war between France and Britain and, 197–200
Federalists: satire of pro-British wing of, 207–13; use of Milton's texts by, 14, 194–207
Feminist criticism, 81–82, 237n63
Ferguson, Adam, 145
Ferguson, Margaret W., 222n8
Figural exegesis, 133–34
Filmer, Robert, 104
Fink, Zera, 104, 106, 109, 234n6
Fish, Stanley, 13, 86

Fliegelman, Jay, 110–11, 167, 227n35
Fogle, French, 229n23
France: American foreign policy and, 182, 191–94, 210–12; Constitution of, 188–89, 190; Reign of Terror in, 186–87, 194; unicameral system in, 187–91; war with Great Britàin, 191–94
Franco-American treaty of 1778, 191
Free will. *See* Freedom, individual; Liberty vs. license
Freedom, individual: American belief in, 219–20; citizen participation and, 219–20; Fall theme and, 5; God and, 223n7; government of Heaven and, 65–66, 67; obedience to higher law and, 7, 57, 69–70, 75, 82–83; obedience to reason and, 3–4, 101; Pelagian sects and, 84; rationalism vs. traditionalism and, 218–19; reason and, 218–19, 235n20, 237n64; responsibility and, 110; virtue and, 65, 110; voluntary servitude and, 7, 57, 69–70, 75, 82–83
Freemasonry, 200
French *philosophes*, 7, 190, 217
French Revolution. *See* France
Freneau, Philip: "General Gage's Soliloquy," 146–47; "The Midnight Consultations," 147–48
Frye, Northrop, 54

Gage, Thomas, 141, 146, 166
Gallatin, Albert, 197, 201, 205
Gardiner, John S. J., 183, 254n56; *Remarks on the Jacobiniad*, 197, 200–207
Gender relations, in Milton's Paradise, 81–82
Genesis (Celestial Cycle) tradition, 20
Genêt, Edmond Charles Édouard, 191–94
Gilbert, Sandra, 222n8, 237n63
Glorious Revolution of 1688, 15, 16
Gnostics, 89
"Good temptation," 86
Gosse, Edmund, 229n14
Governmental checks and balances. *See* Mixed and balanced government
Great Britain: American foreign policy and, 182, 191–94, 197, 198–99; capitalism in, 33–50; English Republic and, 10–11, 52–53, 71; English Revolution and, 15, 18, 35–37; establishment of commonwealth in, 37–38; imagery of, 247n22; policies in colonies, 137–38, 139, 142, 144–45, 155–58

(*see also* Boston Tea Party; Stamp Act of 1765; Taxation, unlawful); rise of landed gentry in, 34–35; threat of U.S. war with, 198–200, 210–11; war with France, 191–94. *See also* British Constitution
Greaves, Richard, 112
Green Dragon Tavern, 200–201
Greenblatt, Stephen, 6, 224n12
Grenville, George, 125
Gridley, Jeremiah, 137
Griswold, R. W., 220
Gross, Kenneth, 225n22, 228n2
Grotius, Hugo, 19, 83, 183; *Adamus Exul*, 20–23

Hamilton, Alexander, 170, 191
Handler, Edward, 255n4
Hanford, J. H., 9
Hansen, Allen Oscar, 252n2
Harding, D. P., 235n19
Harrington, James, 3, 35, 41–42, 77, 99; *Oceana*, 34, 60, 105–6
Hartley, David, 145
Hartlib, Samuel, 33, 37–38, 39, 43–46; Royal Society and, 124; social reform and, 35, 44–46
Hartlib's circle, 43–46, 48. *See also* Weston
Hatch, Nathan O., x, 100
Heaven, government of, 62–72, 236n31, 236n34. *See also* War in Heaven imagery
Hebrews, and rule of law, 95–96
Hegel, Georg Wilhelm Friedrich, 218
Heimert, Alan, 119, 239n2
Herron, Carolivia, 222n8
Hierarchy: fixed by birth, 84; merit-based, 82–83, 85, 88. *See also* Established order
Hill, Christopher, *ix*, 12, 51, 54, 56, 71, 233n3
Hirsh, E. D., Jr., 225n24
Hoadly, Benjamin, 120–21
Hobbes, Thomas, 19, 38–39, 41, 105
Holland. *See* Netherlands, seventeenth century
Hollis, Thomas, 137; "liberty books" project and, 115, 116, 118–27
Hollis family, in Britain, 118
Holyoke, Edward, 122, 123
Hopper, William, 175
Howard, Leon, 117, 181
Howe, General, 147
Human-divine cooperation, 84
Human nature, 5, 6–7, 22. *See also* Reason

Hutchinson, Thomas, 141, 155, 157, 162, 187, 248n36

Improvement tracts, 39–40, 42–43
Independent party (Britain), 29, 46, 72, 73–74, 227n38, 229n17, 234n4
Individualism: perversion of, 85; positive vs. possessive, 38–43; private interest vs. public good and, 19, 40–42, 110–11; societal interests and, 38–40, 84; vs. freedom, 69. See also Possessive individualism
Interest-group politics, 241n22, 249n69, 252n8

"Jacobin clubs." See Democratic societies
The Jacobin Looking Glass (Federalist pamphlet), 193–94
Jacobinism: modern variants of, 8–9, 218; regime in France and, 186–87, 194. See also Romantic tradition
Jay, John, 198
Jay's Treaty, 197, 198–99, 203, 252n5
Jefferson, Thomas, 14, 217, 244n39; Genêt and, 192; influence of Paradise Lost on, 128–29; Satan imagery applied to, 205–6
Jeremiad (sermon genre), 240n7, 246n54
Johnson, Samuel (reverend), 125
Jones, Rufus, 91

Kant, Immanuel, 217–18
Kendrick, Christopher, ix, 18
Keteltas, Abraham, 100, 167
Knight, G. Wilson, 53
Knowledge: Adams's "Dissertation" and, 135; freedom from tyranny and, 138; perversions of, 89–90, 92, 235n23; scientific, 47. See also Education
Kramnick, Isaac, 239n1

Land Bank proposal, 232n34, 249n47
Land ownership, 99, 247n6
"Latencies" in text, 215–16
Leadership: abdication of, 87; elevation of people by, 69; virtue in, 64–65, 75, 83, 94, 106
Leavis, F. R., 51, 76
Lee, Richard Henry, 175
Leftist critics, 53
Leonard, Daniel ("Massachusettensis"), 157–58, 159–62, 248n36

Liberty, varieties of, 237n49. See also Freedom, individual; Religious liberty
"Liberty books," 115, 116, 118–27
Liberty vs. license, 30–31, 217–18; early American Republic and, 173–74; fall of Rome and, 88; Mayhew and, 127; Milton's Satan and, 56–58; seventeenth-century republicans and, 104
Lincoln, Levi, 212–13, 253n11
Literature, and history, 8, 12, 227n35
Livingston, Brockholst, Democracy: An Epic Poem, 194, 195–97, 254n46
Livingston, Edward, 199
Locke, John, 154, 239n1
Love, and rule of law, 96

Macpherson, C. B., 38, 40–41, 69
Madison, James, 88, 191
Manichaean sect, 89
Market society. See Capitalism
Marlowe, Christopher, 90, 235n23, 238n76
Marvell, Andrew, 113
Marxist approach, 36, 230n12
"Massachusettensis." See Leonard
Massachusetts: British-American confrontation and, 157; constitution of, 98–99; education in, 246n70
Massachusetts Mercury (Federalist paper), 193
Mather, Cotton, 133
Mayhew, Jonathan, 100, 118–27, 137, 139; Discourse Concerning Unlimited Submission and Nonresistance to the Higher Powers, 118, 119, 120–21, 151; The Snare Broken sermon, 127
Meaning vs. significance, 225n24
Military leadership, 78
Millennialism, 131–33, 159, 245n54. See also Providential design
Miller, Perry, 245n52, 245n54
Milner, Andrew, ix, 15, 215, 234n4
Milton, John: anti-episcopal tracts, 63, 136; contemporary influence of, 243n41; divorce tracts, 72, 73, 88; historical-political context and, 4–5, 53–54; "misogyny" of, 81–82; nineteenth-century readings of, 220; parliamentary oratory and, 76; persistence of conservative vs. radical democratic readings of, 218; poetic calling of, 132–33; political courage of, 71–72; prose tracts, 44, 52, 69, 70–71, 74, 85, 95, 96, 111–12, 132–33; sonnets, 30, 251n117; topical poems, 72, 73. Works: Areopagitica, 29, 65,

Milton, John (*cont.*)
85, 96, 111, 114, 218, 226*n*33, 243*n*8, 245*n*48; *Defence of the People of England*, 61, 106, 113, 114, 116, 120; *Of Education*, 44, 45, 46–48, 112, 181, 226*n*27; *Eikonoklastes*, 113, 114, 116, 121, 235*n*26; *History of Britain*, 28–31, 58, 229*n*23; *The Likeliest Means to Remove Hirelings*, 48, 136, 151, 233*n*46; *Pro Populo Anglicano Defensio*, 114; *Proposalls of Certaine Expedients*, 48–49; *Ready and Easy Way to Establish a Free Commonwealth*, 10, 38, 49, 55, 71, 106, 107, 113, 135, 251*n*118; *Reason of Church-Government Urg'd against Prelaty*, 14; *Of Reformation in England*, 106, 234*n*6; *Second Defence of the English People*, 52, 58, 71, 132, 250*n*102; *Tenure of Kings and Magistrates*, 5, 30, 58, 95, 104, 106, 114, 120, 177; *Treatise of Civil Power in Ecclesiastical Causes*, 239*n*82
Mixed and balanced government: Adams and, 174–79; American Federalists and, 204–5; American republicans and, 107–9; British republicans and, 105–7; colonial governments and, 156–57; French system and, 189–90; Harrington's model for, 105–6; Milton's views on, 106–7; Paine and, 175–76; problem of passion and, 102–9; tyranny of the many and, 184–85
Molesworth, Robert, 115, 240*n*3
Monarchy: absolute, 135, 177; constitutional, 114–15; in *Paradise Lost*, 60, 62, 63, 236*n*31; republican government and, 96, 106–7, 122–23, 241*n*21; vs. tyranny, 63, 122–23
Monthly Anthology (Federalist journal), 200
More, Thomas, *Utopia*, 41
Morgan, Edmund, 99

National poet, role of, 234*n*9
Natural rights of man, 5, 8, 39, 236*n*35; British policies in colonies and, 137–38, 139, 142. *See also* Freedom, individual
Neo-Marxist criticism, 51–52
Netherlands, seventeenth century, 4–5, 18–19, 21, 31
New Criticism, 9, 226*n*34
New Historicism, 5–7, 8, 38–39, 220, 226*n*34
New Light party, 119–20
Newton, Thomas, 56, 78–79
Nichols, Fred J., 25–26, 229*n*13
Nonconformist (British), 118

North, Lord, 145, 146, 147, 163
"Novanglus." *See under* Adams, John
Nyquist, Mary, 222*n*8, 224*n*17

Obedience: free nature of, 83, 85, 96; subjection and, 92–93; traditional notions of, 111. *See also* Parent-child imagery
Odell, Jonathan, 170–71
"Old Deluder Satan Law," 102
Oldenbarnevelt, Johan, 18, 21
Oliver, Peter, 162, 169
Olson, Mancur, 249*n*69
"Original intent" position, 9–10
Original sin, 130–31
Otis, James, Jr., 124, 126, 137, 160, 169

Paine, Thomas, 188; *Common Sense*, 175–76
Paradise Lost (Milton): Abdiel episode in, 68–72; council scene in, 76–81, 147; depiction of Satan in, 53–62; education in, 110, 111; eighteenth-century readings of, 9–10, 11–13, 14–15, 216–18; Fall of man and, 85–94; government of Heaven and, 62–72; Grotius's drama and, 20–21; inconsistencies in, 51–52, 233*n*3; Milton's political theory and, 11; modern criticism and, 51–52; restoration of man and, 94–96; revolutionary politics and, 9, 151–54; twentieth-century audiences and, 233*n*1; war in Heaven and, 72–76, 142–43. *See also* Council in Hell imagery; Death imagery; Satan imagery; War in Heaven imagery
Parent-child imagery, Tory vs. patriot use of, 166–73
Parker, Samuel, 113
Parliamentary oratory, 76–81, 147
Passion. *See* Corruptibility; Reason vs. passion; Self-interest, unchecked
Peer pressure, problem of, 70–71
Pelagian sects, 84
Penn, John, 175, 176
Pennsylvania, and unicameralism, 205
Persons, Stow, 245*n*54
Phillips, Edward, 228*n*9
Pitt, William, 127, 144
Plato, 239*n*81
Plattes, Gabriel, *Description of the Famous Kingdom of Macaria*, 44
Pocock, J. G. A., 107, 136

Poetry, and political culture, 13–15, 117, 151–54

Political allegory, 12, 53; vs. figural exegesis, 133

Political readings, 51–52, 53–54

Politics and religion, in colonial culture, 100–101, 125, 240n15

Pope, Alexander, 176; *Dunciad*, 195, 200, 201–2

Popular sovereignty, 183, 187–88, 189–90. *See also* Democracy, pure

Possessive individualism: devil's oratory and, 79; Milton's critique of, 7; rise of, 40–41; Satan imagery and, 69

Potter, William, 232n34, 249n47

Pound, Ezra, 220

Predestination, doctrine of, 22–23, 83–84, 119

Presbyterian party (Britain), 28–29, 72, 73–74. *See also* Clergy; New Light party

Press freedom, 65, 111, 112. *See also* Stamp Act of 1765

Pride, sin of, 89–90

Private interest vs. public good: American Revolution and, 152–54; British parliamentarians and, 29, 76–77; early capitalist society and, 41, 42; education and, 49; English Republic and, 75; individualism and, 19; John Adams and, 173; role of government and, 103–4; tea tax and, 162–66; Tory arguments and, 170; tyranny of the few and, 208–10; war in Heaven and, 75–76, 153–54. *See also* Self-interest, unchecked

Protestant Reformation, 132, 135

Providential design, 131–37, 145, 159

Puffendorf, Samuel, 172

Puritan heritage, 131–37, 139, 225n25, 238n69, 245n48, 245n54

Quincy, Josiah, Jr., 142

Radical democratic readings of Milton, persistence of, 218

Radzinowicz, Mary Ann, 236n34

Raleigh, Walter, 53, 76

Ranters (sect), 238n77

Rationalism (philosophical), 218–19, 234n4. *See also* Reason; Reason vs. passion

Reader-response theory, 4, 9

Real Whigs (British party), 98, 107, 114–16. *See also* Hollis

Reason: appeal by Satan to, 21–22; Fall theme and, 5; free will and, 218–19, 235n20, 237n64; human nature and, 5; liberty as obedience to, 101; millenialism and, 131–37; perversion of, 92; religious truth and, 119, 243n8

Reason vs. passion: early American Republic and, 173; education and, 47–48; faculty psychology and, 102–3; gender relations and, 82; liberty and, 3–4, 56–58; Milton's cosmic history and, 59, 94–95; mixed and balanced government and, 102–9; peer pressure and, 70–71; power of passions and, 108–9; temptation of Adam and Eve and, 85–87, 92–93, 108; utopian schemes and, 109

Rebellion. *See* Revolution vs. rebellion

Religious liberty: civil liberty and, 120, 121; as goal in colonies, 101; Jefferson and, 129; Milton's views on, 111–12; political reform and, 125; post-Restoration England and, 113–14; Real Whigs and, 115; republican government and, 38. *See also* Church of England; Presbyterian party

"Republican federalist" vs. "tory federalist," 253n11

Republican government: education and, 49, 252n2; human improvement and, 63, 65–66, 174; monarchy and, 63, 96; proper role of, 103–4; representative government vs. pure democracy and, 87–88; superiority of, 174–79; vulnerability of, 10–11, 19, 250n102. *See also* American republicans; Commonwealth tradition; Mixed and balanced government

Republican principles: American religious tradition and, 100–101; corruptibility and, 30; public good and, 84; Satan's mimicry of, 55

Restoration period, 113–14, 234n7

Revolution vs. rebellion: Mayhew and, 120; notions of freedom in *Paradise Lost* and, 70; Whigs and, 115, 146, 168–69, 172. *See also* War in Heaven

Richardson, Samuel, *Clarissa*, 110–11, 187

Riede, David, 227n1

Robbins, Caroline, 15, 114, 159

"Robinocracy," 98, 107

Rogers, John, 224n7

Romantic tradition: Jefferson and, 129; Milton's Satan and, 13, 17, 56; modern revival of, 17–18; political resonances and, 20
Rome, fall of, 59, 85, 88
Royal Society, 123, 124

Salmasius, Claudius, 61, 62, 71, 106, 113
Satan imagery: Adams and, 159–66; applied to Tories, 159–62, 169–71; British policies and, 162–66; Dutch writers and, 21–23, 66–67; in Federalist writings, 193–94, 205–6; in *Paradise Lost*, 53–62; patterns of kingship and, 235n26; republican view and, 8–9, 13; rhetorical skills and, 21–23, 55, 68, 80–81, 91–92; Romantic reading and, 13, 217; Satan's loss of reason and, 235n20; Tory reading and, 216; tyranny and, 58–61; unchecked self-interest and, 12–13, 56–61, 215–16
Satire: patriot Whigs and, 145–51; of pro-British Federalists, 207–13
Scientific knowledge, 47
Scotland, 148–49
Seabury, Samuel, 170
Secker, Archbishop, 125, 126
Sects, 90–91
Self-interest, unchecked: Boston junto and, 161–62; democratic societies and, 187; moral decay of nations and, 162–66, 239n81; possessive individualism and, 41; Satan imagery and, 12–13, 54, 69–70, 153–54, 215–16; tyranny and, 58. *See also* Private interest vs. public good
Sensabaugh, George, ix–x, 81, 183, 221n2
Sergeant, Jonathan Dickinson, 175
Servitude, voluntary. *See* Freedom, individual
Shays, Daniel, 187
Shelley, Percy Bysshe, 9, 17, 225n22, 228n2
Ship Money, 36–37
Shirley, William, 161
Sidney, Algernon, 3, 104–5, 109, 121; *Discourses Concerning Government*, 104, 121
Simpson, Lewis P., 254n56
Sirluck, Ernest, 46–47
Social contract theory, 253n26
Social reform, 11, 19, 48, 114–15. *See also* Education; Religious liberty
Societal interests. *See* Individualism; Private interest vs. public good
Société des Jacobins, 187, 192

Society for the Propagation of the Gospel in Foreign Parts, 124–25
Sophistry, 78–79
Sovereignty. *See* Monarchy; Popular sovereignty
Spenser, Edmund, 27, 67, 229n18
"Spiritual pilgrimage theme," 110–11
Stamp Act of 1765, 121, 126, 127, 137–39, 143, 155, 157
Stavely, Keith W. F., 222n7, 235n14, 238n69
Stone, Lawrence, 36, 230n12
"Story framework," 222n5
Strout, Cushing, 100, 240n4
Subjectivist criticism, 9
Sullivan, James, 252n2
Summers, Joseph, 67
Swift, Samuel, 133
Sylvester, Joshua, 228n5

Tappan, David, 249n69
Tawney, R. H., 36
Taxation: federal, 183, 197–98, 204; unlawful, 125, 143, 156, 161–62, 173. *See also* Boston Tea Party
Tayler, Edward W., 132, 224n10
Tea tax. *See* Boston Tea Party
Theological controversy, in seventeenth century, 18
Tithes, 48–49, 125, 233nn46
Tocqueville, Alexis de, 98, 100–101, 219–20
Toland, John, 115–16
Tories: argument against patriot Whigs, 139; British policies and, 155; executive abuses and, 98; interpretation of Milton, 216–17, 218; Satan imagery and, 11–12, 141, 153–54; use of Milton's imagery by, 167, 169–71; Whig struggle against, 139, 141–45. *See also* Conservative readings of Milton; Tory junto
Tory junto, 155
Traditionalism, 218, 219
Trevor-Roper, H. R., 36
Trumbull, John, 146; *M'Fingal*, 148–51
Turkish sultan imagery, 60–61, 77
Turnbull, G. H., 45, 231n30
Tuveson, Ernest, 134, 245n47
Typological method, 133–34, 145
Tyranny: bondage to passions and, 94–95; civil vs. religious, 126, 134, 137–39; as

consequence of Fall, 93–95; faculty psychology and, 103; of the few, 185–86, 207–13; of the majority, 175, 183, 184–91, 197; Milton's Satan and, 58–61; unchecked self-interest and, 58

Unicameralism: in France, 187–91; John Adams and, 108, 189–90, 204, 251n112; Paine and, 175–76
United Provinces. *See* Netherlands, seventeenth century
United States: foreign policy of, 182, 191–94, 197, 198–99; popularity of Milton in, 181–82; representative government and, 184–85; uses of Milton's imagery in, 182–84
Utopian schemes, 41, 109, 227n39

Virtue: freedom and, 65; Heavenly republic and, 63–65; leadership and, 64–65, 75, 83, 94, 106; Sidney's definition of, 109; testing of, 87, 163–66
Voluntarism, 100
Vondel, Joost van den, 19, 66–67, 83, 183; *Adam in Ballingschap*, 23, 229n15; *Lucifer*, 23–27, 84

Walpole, Robert, 98, 107
War in Heaven imagery, 72–76, 142–43, 171
Warren, James, 141, 142–43, 144, 155–56, 172
Warren, Joseph, 200
Washington, George, 186, 191–92, 197, 198
Webber, Joan, *xii*
Webster, Noah, 185
Wells, William, 252n3
Westminster Confession, 83, 84
Weston, Richard, 33
Whigs. *See* American Whigs; Commonwealth tradition; English Whigs; Real Whigs (British party)
Whiskey Rebellion, 197–98, 203
Whitefield, George, 119
Wilkes, John, 145
Winthrop, John, 57, 64, 98–99, 118, 121, 124, 132, 133, 232n34; "city upon a hill" sermon, 134, 145
Wittreich, Joseph, 237n63
Wood, Gordon, 221n2, 241n17, 252n8
Woodbridge, John, 232n34
Worden, Blair, 233n3
Wythe, George, 174, 175, 176

XYZ affair, 211